Selected Papers
of
ROBERT C. BINKLEY

LONDON : GEOFFREY CUMBERLEGE
OXFORD UNIVERSITY PRESS

ROBERT CEDRIC BINKLEY

From a photograph by Frances W. Binkley

Selected Papers

of

ROBERT C. BINKLEY

EDITED WITH A BIOGRAPHICAL SKETCH
AND A BIBLIOGRAPHY BY

MAX H. FISCH

Professor of Philosophy
University of Illinois

ॐ

WITH A FOREWORD BY

LUTHER H. EVANS

Librarian of Congress

HARVARD UNIVERSITY PRESS
CAMBRIDGE, MASSACHUSETTS
1948

THE PUBLICATION OF THIS VOLUME HAS BEEN AIDED BY A
GRANT FROM THE HENRY ELDRIDGE BOURNE FUND ESTABLISHED
IN 1936 IN WESTERN RESERVE UNIVERSITY BY THE ALUMNAE
HISTORICAL ASSOCIATION OF FLORA STONE MATHER COLLEGE

PRINTED IN THE UNITED STATES OF AMERICA

To

Frances, Binks, and Tom
to whom Bob would have wished
this volume to be dedicated

Preface

Our younger historians have been coming back from the battle fronts of Europe and the Pacific to write and revise the history of the war in which they have fought. This volume will open to them the experience and work of one who stood high in the generation of American historians who fought in World War I and wrote and revised its history, along with that of the century that preceded and the long armistice that followed.

It will be welcomed also by his friends and colleagues, by admirers among his teachers, by librarians continuing the enterprises he pioneered, by former W.P.A. workers who thanked him for turning their marketless skills to the service of scholarship, and by the students for whom he made the intellectual life excitingly relevant to the world in which they had to find their way. These and many others who knew him at one point or another of his short but many-sided career will be glad to have the whole range of his work and thought laid before them.

Binkley wrote history in a way that commanded the respect of academic historians, because his scholarship met their exacting standards. At the same time he made it interesting to thoughtful laymen by his philosophic grasp and penetration, and by his vigorous and provocative style. Beside his work as a professional historian, he crowded into the fourth decade of his life and of the century a remarkable output in several related fields. He addressed himself to the social, economic, and political problems of his time. He helped bring library and archival policies abreast of the new techniques for organizing and preserving the materials for research. And he enlisted local historians and amateur scholars in tasks once considered eccentric or trivial, but now made fruitful by the new techniques.

The essays here reprinted have been selected and grouped to represent these major phases of Binkley's work. Others of equal interest have been omitted as trenching on ground more definitively covered in his books. With some reluctance, the work of the eight years preceding the last of his "war guilt" essays has been excluded, although, among others, his vivid story of the underground *Libre Belgique* (2) [1] was especially tempting in view of that paper's revival in World War II. Since his book reviews contain some of his best writing, a selection of excerpts from them has been appended.

The editor wishes to thank Floyd W. Miller for placing at his disposal the bibliography on which the one here offered is based; Summerfield Baldwin III and Palmer Throop for counsel in planning the book; Meribeth Cameron, Virginia Corwin, Adeline Barry Davee, Eleanor Ferris, J. Holly Hanford, Robert J. Harris, Winfred G. Leutner, DeForrest Mellon, Elizabeth Richards, G. Carlton Robinson and Eva M. Sanford for helpful material and suggestions; Nelson R. Burr, Luther Evans, Harry M. Lydenberg and Lyon N. Richardson for revising the introduction; Ruth B. Fisch for preparing the index; and Annie S. Cutter and Keyes D. Metcalf for effective help in completing arrangements for publication.

The introduction has been written with such objectivity as could be commanded by one who was Binkley's colleague and friend during his ten years on the faculty of Western Reserve University.

M. H. F.

University of Illinois
May 1, 1948

[1] Numbers in parentheses refer to items in the bibliography.

Contents

Foreword

Robert C. Binkley combined in himself in a most unusual manner many of the culturally creative and enriching traits of the American character and achievement. He was an accomplished historian with a deeply probing curiosity and an insistence on discovering the inner meaning and the general tendency of developments. With the tools available for analysis he speculated creatively and responsibly as to the motives of men and societies. His teaching fired his students with a zeal to do these things also, and he imparted to them a concern to look at history through the most ultimate of the sources left behind by past generations for our use. He was impatient of easy generalization from secondary sources and inherited prejudices, and enjoyed lampooning in private, and to a moderate degree in public, the impostors and the misguided of the historical profession.

Binkley's concern for true and full-bodied history led him far in the promotion of the use of sources. He took up and pushed with great vigor the work of leadership in the Joint Committee on Materials for Research. Microfilm, when he became interested in it, was a means of recording endorsements on checks; when he left it, it was one of the accepted tools of scholarship. He even pursued relentlessly the solution of the problems of microfilm cameras and readers, showing in this an inventive and practical mind. Other methods for the reproduction of the materials of scholarship were studied by him with intense and prolonged concentration, and he became the author of a pioneering book on the subject, one which I believe has not yet been superseded.

Binkley early realized also that the reproduction of source material already known and accessible was only part of the problem. He saw that great bodies of the raw material of fruitful research in many fields of knowledge were lying about unrecognized by scholars who should use them, and uncared for by custodians who should cherish them. The fortuitous availability in the 1930's of a large pool of clerical labor on the relief rolls presented itself to him as a heaven-sent opportunity to do something about the inventory of these resources. He put his vast energy and imagination into the labor of setting up projects, experimenting with techniques and procedures, and developing forms of organization and supervision which could be utilized in making inventories of local archives and other masses of recorded material by the relatively unskilled manpower made available by the Work Projects Administration. In this he was markedly successful and set the pattern for the mass operation of the Historical Records Survey. As the National Director of this project from its beginnings in 1935 to the end of February 1940, six weeks before Binkley's death, I can confidently testify that his imagination and his zealous pioneering in the preceding two years were the firm foundation which made possible such achievements as may be marked down by history to its credit. I had the benefit of his counsel and encouragement in almost every policy or other basic decision which had to be made. I found him wise in the use of the resources of support found in the opinion of groups and the general community, as well as in the use of employees engaged in listing the records of a county judge or editing the abstracts of newspaper stories written by untutored clerks. He taught me to think of inventories of archives, church records, manuscript collections, and so on, plus the depositories containing them, as a sort of second library system. Association with him meant perhaps more to me than it would have meant to many others because of our warm personal friendship which had begun a decade earlier.

In the last months of his life, Binkley threw himself with enthusiasm into the task of exploring the possibility of gearing the efforts of amateurs into the work of historical scholarship. He was perhaps more interested in enriching the lives of the amateurs themselves—and providing a more encouraging intellectual climate for the historical study of community problems—than in using the work of the amateurs as definitive studies. His efforts in this area reflected well his abiding concern for the development by the citizens of a great democracy of an understanding of their own past and an appreciation of the sources of their own great cultural strength.

The enormous range of subjects to which Binkley intensely applied his talents included also the problem of union catalogues of library holdings and the exhibition by various cataloguing, indexing, and abstracting procedures of the fact and idea content of printed matter. Much of his work has borne fruit and still more is to come as his disciples continue the lines of investigation which he laid down.

The disappearance of relief labor with the coming of the war and the appearance of urgencies of war which required men to concentrate upon operating the currently available mechanisms for current tasks, to the detriment of the kind of pioneering work in which Binkley was the great leader, coincided roughly with his death. It is hoped that the almost-stalled engine of exploration in the whole wide area of his library, bibliographical, and archival interests can be accelerated again with competent engineers, so that many of his unfinished tasks can be brought to a successful conclusion. The archives of his creative mind repose on the balcony of my office, and may be used with profit by those who crave the exciting adventure of adding to mankind's tools for knowing and using more effectively the intellectual and cultural heritage of the race.

LUTHER H. EVANS

Library of Congress
April 2, 1948

INTRODUCTION

Robert Cedric Binkley
Historian in the Long Armistice

I. FORMATIVE YEARS

The career of Robert Binkley took its bent from membership in a large but closely knit family with a vigorous life of its own, and from early participation in world-shaping events at the international level, followed immediately by experience in collecting, organizing, preserving, and making accessible to scholars the documentary material upon which the record and interpretation of those events were to be based.

The family into which he was born gave him a vivid and homely sense for the possibilities of life in small units, with local roots, and a bias toward federalism as the principle of organization of larger units. His part in World War I and in collecting and organizing the Hoover War Library sealed his commitment to history as a vocation and made him acutely aware of the rapidity with which the sources for contemporary history are lost by destruction, dispersal, and decay, and of the urgent need for new techniques and a conscious and coördinated strategy on the part of librarians, archivists, and scholars.

He was the second of eleven children. Their father, a poet and essayist, taught English literature until he retired to a California ranch.[1] Of Robert's five younger brothers, two became

[1] Christian Kreider Binkley came of a Mennonite family of small means. Born at Millersville, Pennsylvania, August 6, 1870, and early left an orphan, he was brought up by relatives in Lancaster, and graduated from Millersville State Normal School in 1892. He was married in 1894 to Mary Engle Barr. In the summer of 1898, when Robert was half a year old, the family moved to California, and Mr. Binkley received his A.B.

engineers, one a geologist, one a chemist, and one a contractor. His five sisters married men of like occupations, or ranchmen. Love of nature and a kind of informality and directness in social arrangements, a delight in making things for themselves, a preference for the rough-hewn and substantial as against the refined and delicate, and a tacit agreement never to make a fuss about anything, were family traits accounting for much in Robert Binkley that does not commonly go with scholarship.

The education of so many children on a modest income called for stringent economies and coöperative planning. The family developed and retained an extraordinary solidarity as an economic unit in which the resources of all its members were at the disposal of each. By common consent, intellectual pursuits had first claim, and whatever served only to keep up appearances was sacrificed. There was little room or time for solitude or for personal intimacy. Each member lived in the open community of the family and brought his friends into it.

Robert attended the public schools of Santa Clara County, California. In June, 1917, after two years at Stanford University, he enlisted in the United States Army Ambulance Service

degree in English from Stanford University in the following year. He taught English literature at Cogswell Polytechnic College in San Francisco, and in later years at high schools in San Jose, Palo Alto, and Vallejo. In 1902 he published *Sonnets and Songs for a House of Days* (San Francisco, A. M. Robertson), and in 1903 an essay called *Nature-Lure* (New York, John B. Alden), besides some articles and book reviews later on. For a time he was secretary to Joaquin Miller and accompanied him on his travels, including a bicycle and walking tour of Scotland. Devotion to Emerson led him to Lao-tzu and the Chinese classics, and he set himself to learn Chinese. At various times he used the library facilities of the University of California, the Library of Congress, and Harvard University. Gradually he built up a good working collection of his own for Chinese studies. He made translations of the *Tao Tê Ching* and *Lieh-tzŭ* and of a great many Chinese poems. While teaching English at Vallejo, he had bought a ranch in the mountains of Lake County as a rallying place and refuge for his large family. Later he established a summer camp for boys on the ranch, and finally a year-round school. At the time of his death in 1938 he had ready a volume of verse called "Works and Days of a Homesteader."

and served in France from January, 1918, to the end of the war. His corps was a group of kindred Stanford spirits, idealists conscious of being a part of great events and enjoying the comradeship that comes with seeing action together. He was wounded in action and cited for distinguished and exceptional gallantry at Fléville. He spent the spring of 1919 studying art at the University of Lyons and forming impressions of French middle-class life by living with a *rentier* family.

In June, 1919, Professor and Mrs. E. D. Adams of Stanford arrived in Paris to begin a collection of research materials on the war and the peace conference, for which a fund of $50,000 had been placed at their disposal by Herbert Hoover. In July Binkley was discharged from the army to join Professors Adams and Lutz as assistant and interpreter. He served in this capacity until December of that year.

Their first task was to secure from the delegations to the peace conference their memoranda, propaganda material, and such records as they were willing to surrender. At Binkley's suggestion they began collecting the wartime publications, particularly pamphlets and posters, of patriotic, religious, academic, and trade associations and societies. He himself did most of the work on the French societies; Mrs. Adams and he divided the English societies between them. More than a thousand societies were eventually represented. He also helped secure from the British Foreign Office a large part of the library and the enemy-propaganda collection of the Ministry of Information (179).[2]

These and similar collections from other countries, along with files of army and civilian newspapers and the records of the food administration and relief commissions, formed the nucleus of the War Library endowed by Hoover in 1924 and now housed in a separate building on the Stanford campus as the Hoover Library on War, Revolution, and Peace.

[2] Numbers in parentheses refer to items in the bibliography.

Returning to Stanford in 1920, Binkley registered in the department of history and assisted in organizing the materials in the Hoover collection. In 1920, 1921, and 1922 he contributed to the *Stanford Cardinal* a series of four articles dealing in turn with the Hoover collection (1), the *Libre Belgique* (2), the assassination at Sarajevo (3), and the vicissitudes of Hungarian politics since the war (11). All four were based on materials in the Hoover collection; they reflected Binkley's recent experiences, foreshadowed the direction of his future interests, and gave promise of the skill of his mature writing. For a time he and the novelist-to-be, Archie Binns, edited the *Cardinal* together.

After receiving his bachelor's degree with distinction in 1922, Binkley went on to postgraduate study. From 1923 to 1927 he was Reference Librarian of the Hoover War Library and had the task of classifying the confidential materials in the vault of the library. He began at that time to interest himself in microfilm copy and other techniques for meeting the problems of space and of paper deterioration involved in preserving and making accessible this vast collection of research materials.

At Stanford, as at home, Binkley lived a community life. He was one of a group of close friends who shared each other's rooms and belongings, lent each other money, hatched ingenious practical jokes together, and encouraged each other's idiosyncrasies. The Stanford group merged easily with his family, since so many of them came to his home and since so many of his family—four brothers and a sister besides his father—went to Stanford. Two Stanford women joined the family by marriage. The ambulance corps in France had been Stanford men, and so was the group that gathered and organized the Hoover Library. The continuity was unbroken.

II. War Guilt and Revision

Binkley's postgraduate studies were directed by Ralph H. Lutz, who had been trained by the German historian Hermann

Oncken. Lutz gave him a rigid historical discipline which balanced without diminishing his susceptibility to ideas. To understand the war in which he had taken part, the peace conference, and the treaty of Versailles, Binkley went back to the Congress of Vienna and the events that led up to it. His master's thesis in 1924 was on "The Re-establishment of the Independence of the Hanseatic Cities, 1813–1815" (23). While working on it, he assisted Malbone Graham on *New Governments of Central Europe* (24), published in 1924. In the same year he married Frances Harriet Williams.

His doctor's thesis in 1927 was entitled *The Reaction of European Opinion to the Statesmanship of Woodrow Wilson* (33). The disparity between the promise of the Wilson program and the fulfillment of the peace of Versailles presented a problem, particularly in view of Wilson's own confidence in the efficacy of public opinion in aiding him to realize his program, and in view of the fact that there had appeared to be widespread agreement on Wilson's principles in the period from the armistice to the peace. It was thought by some that if Wilson had appealed more openly to the people for support, they would have rallied to him. Confining himself to Europe, Binkley examined contemporary sources to discover what limits public opinion actually had set to the freedom of decision of the peace conference, and whether there was any evidence of an unexploited reservoir of public opinion favorable to Wilson. He concluded that there was not, and that the consensus on the Wilson program in the autumn of 1918 had been illusory.

In the light of later disclosures and of changes in his own views, this doctoral dissertation soon seemed immature to him, and he published only one chapter, "The Concept of Public Opinion in the Social Sciences" (35). Meanwhile he had been a frequent contributor to Stanford, Palo Alto, Oakland, and San Francisco papers, chiefly on events of the day. His first contribution to a journal of national scope was a short article

in *Current History* for January, 1926, in which he published
in English translation a document which he had found in the
Hoover War Library: the journal of the meeting of the Russian
Council of Ministers on July 24, 1914, containing "the only
diplomatic plan which we know to have been sanctioned by
the full authority of the Russian government." It was pre-
sumptive evidence, he argued, "that the original intent of the
Russian Government (perhaps, by implication, of the French
Government also) was honorable and pacific." This article,
"New light on Russia's war guilt" (28), created something of a
stir in the *New York Times,* the *Nation,* and elsewhere.

Binkley had now hit his stride. In rapid succession came the
articles on the guilt clause in the Versailles treaty which established his reputation as a brilliant young scholar. The first
three of these, written with the collaboration of August C.
Mahr of the German department at Stanford, were published
in 1926 in the *Frankfurter Zeitung* (29), the *San Francisco
Chronicle* (31), and *Current History* (32). These were followed by other articles by Binkley alone in the *Historical
Outlook* (34), the *New Republic* (40), and *Current History*
(44). It was characteristic of his bent of mind that from the
meaning of the terms of Article 231 Binkley went on to explore
the philosophic problems involved in the current notions of
national responsibility and of truth by convention. These problems continued to occupy him to the end of his life.

The thesis of these essays was twofold. (a) Article 231 was
to be construed in a legal, not in a moral or political sense; it
was an assumption of liability to pay damages, not an admission of war guilt. Though the speeches of Allied statesmen
were emphatic in asserting that Germany had criminally premeditated the war, these accusations were not incorporated
in the treaty. (b) The prevailing German opinion to the contrary arose from inaccuracies in the German translation of
Article 231, which had no legal validity. A revision of this
translation, eliminating those moral and political overtones

which went beyond the strict sense of the official French-English text, was therefore in order.

The difference between the juridical and the moral construction of Article 231 was by no means a merely academic question at the time these essays were written. The moral and political interpretation gave "just grounds for a great German national movement for the repudiation of an extorted confession of guilt." On the other hand, a declaration on the part of the Entente governments that the article had only a juristic meaning would "serve a good purpose in quieting title to reparations." [3]

But Article 231 was not thus to be exorcised. The German government's version was, after all, faithful to the intent if not to the language of the official text. The failure of all attempts to deflate it to reasonable proportions was symptomatic of a change in our intellectual climate and culture, which Binkley was to explore in later articles (96, 138). [4]

[3] Pp. 50, 62, of the present volume.
[4] On October 1, 1938, in a letter to a younger historian of the peace conference after reading his manuscript (197), Binkley stated his mature view as follows:

"When you come to the final conclusion of the whole book, you have an opportunity to make a statement which I should like to see put before the world at this time, if it happens that you agree with it. It is this: That in Article 231, within the limits you assign it as a statement of historic fact which derives its sanction not from evidence and research but from contractual agreement, there is established in twentieth-century culture a conception of the nature of truth that involves a complete departure from an intellectual tradition of three centuries.

"One would have to go back to the church councils to find its equivalent. It is the first of a series of efforts to establish more or less formally, and with more or less effective policing, the legal control of historical truth. In terms of the intellectual tradition of science, it is absurd—fantastic—to hold that an historical fact can be verified by procuring a signature to a negotiated instrument or by compelling a formal admission by public authority. And since the 1920's have we not seen the area of human life within which truth seeks this means of establishing itself constantly widening as the zone of free inquiry has been diminishing?

"Even the meeting of French and German historians to negotiate and

In the extensive literature of the late 1920's on revision of the history of World War I, Binkley's article on that theme (34) stands out as centering on problems of archival policy. The argument may be restated as follows:

While a war is in progress, the participants are preoccupied with the consequences they imagine will befall them if they lose but will be averted if they win. In the period immediately after the war, they are preoccupied with the distribution of spoils and penalties. When the air has cleared, it turns out that the penalties which can successfully be exacted are inconsequential in comparison with those effects of the war which befall victors and vanquished alike.

History writing responds to the practical interests of these successive periods. A war in progress is dramatized as a momentous conflict for which all previous history was a rehearsal, and the opposed forces are endowed with opposite moral and spiritual qualities, with a view to evoking maximum effort toward victory. In the postwar settlement, the need on the one side of justifying the penalties, and on the other of weakening

---

reach by mutual consensus a compromise concerning the existence or nonexistence of certain alleged facts of the prewar period is a fantastic perversion of scientific method. If, indeed, that meeting were thought to be merely a convenient assembly in which, as at a meeting of the American Historical Association, scholars who have differed in their interpretation of documents would clarify the extent of their differences, it would have been well within the old tradition; but I am confident that this meeting did not have that character. The French and German historians met as negotiators to compromise in the establishment of a truth.

"There have been critics of historical method who have not hesitated to tell us that history generally is only a lie agreed upon; but even among them there was a feeling that agreement came not by exercising a faculty of compromise, but rather by pursuing a technique of investigation that is imposed on the human mind by the nature of the universe.

"Article 231 has turned out to be more than a treaty article. Like the text of the Holy Alliance, it is a monument in the history of culture, whose significance is derived not from any of the particular obligations to which it gave rise, but rather from the deep implications underlying its very existence."

the will to exact them, induces the historian to sit in judgment and apportion the guilt. But as those consequences of the war which tell on both sides alike come gradually to the fore, the war is envisaged as an episode in a process of general institutional change, the larger outlines of which would have been much the same had the fortunes of war been reversed.

An archival policy that is to meet the needs of future historians must anticipate these shifts of interest, and especially the last, since it approaches most nearly the outlook of that succession of historians in the more distant future who will reëxamine the war for the origins of things as they are at the times when their histories are written.

III. PROFESSIONAL CAREER, 1927–1940

Binkley began his teaching career as instructor in history at Washington Square College of New York University. As his wife and he drove east, they talked about teaching methods. Mrs. Binkley had been stimulated by a course in historical method in her last term in college, and she remarked how much more her history major would have meant if she had had the course in method and theory first instead of last. The conversation ran on to the desirability of imbuing the undergraduate early with the spirit of historical inquiry. Besides those history majors who might reasonably be encouraged to go on to graduate training for history as a profession, many more might be encouraged to look forward to amateur historical scholarship as an avocation.

In many fields, and particularly in local history, there was a great deal of preliminary work that could be done by amateur scholars—work which could not economically be done by professional historians, but whose results would be invaluable to them. The transcontinental highway passed through community after community whose local history was as yet unexplored. Such local studies were indispensable to "the new history," with its emphasis on aspects of culture untouched by the older history; yet the economy of scholarship could not sustain them.

Moreover, besides the potential value in terms of future research, the atmosphere of the classroom would be transformed if a considerable nucleus in each history class had even a transient aspiration to such leisure-time activity. There would be a shift from passive assimilation to active and critical participation, which would spread by a kind of contagion to those students who scarcely aspired even to amateur scholarship. Such an atmosphere would make for the best teaching of which the instructor was capable.

After such reflections, it was natural that one who had himself spent so much time with the sources of history in the formative years of the Hoover War Library should proceed at once to experiment with research methods in undergraduate teaching and should cast about for suitable materials. Binkley found them in the English local history division of the New York Public Library, and sent his large freshman class to comb them for all they could find on the year of the Armada. The librarian, Harry M. Lydenberg, recalls the sequel thus (199):

> The new instructor fired his students with such zeal for contemporary reports on the Spanish armada that our file of Public Record Office publications for the 1588 period was rapidly torn to shreds and tatters. Nothing pleases a librarian more than to see his books used. Few things distress him more than to see books read to pieces when replacement is difficult if not impossible. I asked the new instructor to drop in and talk the problem over. His first words when we met showed intensity, zeal, appreciation of the other man's point of view, willingness to adjust himself to conditions, and at the same time confidence in his cause and insistence on its rightness. That first impression grew more attractive the longer I came to see and talk with the man.

Lydenberg and his associate Keyes Metcalf felt obliged to impose restrictions on the use of their Elizabethan documentary collections by undergraduates. Binkley was thus confronted afresh with the librarian's problem of reconciling maximum use of research materials in the present with their preservation for future generations. At the same time he won the friendship of two of the country's leading librarians, with whom he was to be frequently associated in the years ahead.

Binkley secured striking photographs and other data on the decay of newspapers, magazines, and books in the New York Public Library, and on the measures being taken to arrest the deterioration. On the basis of these data and those he had accumulated from his years in the Hoover War Library, he published in the *Scientific American* for January 1929 an article, "Do the Records of Science Face Ruin?" (39), which was condensed in the *Reader's Digest* (41) and established its author as a forceful leader in the movement to rescue from decay the perishable records of the nineteenth and twentieth centuries and to promote the use of more permanent materials for the records of the future.

In the summer of 1928 the Binkleys took their first, and indeed their only extended, vacation. They bought a canoe, put it into the Hudson at Kingston, and paddled upstream, camping on the small islands at night. They tried a stretch of the Erie Canal, but found it tedious, returned to the Hudson and continued up the river as far as Glens Falls. They camped on an island for several weeks, getting their food from a farmhouse across the river, swimming and fishing in water with a molasses hue and scent from paper mills upstream, and making excursions afoot. They were six weeks on the river and canal, made the acquaintance of barge and lock men, and registered their canoe, the *Minetta*, at the Albany Yacht Club when they stopped overnight to see a movie.

While still at Stanford the Binkleys had begun "an essay on domestic theory," perhaps under the shadow of the death of their first child, Barbara Jean, at the age of eight months in 1926. The drafting was largely done while Binkley was writing his doctor's thesis. It afforded a kind of diversion and a vehicle for making fun of the solemn disciplines the graduate school required him to study. At the same time it served a deeper need, for it was characteristic of the Binkleys that their participation in any enterprise seemed to them blind and inconsiderate until they had thought out a philosophy of it that was not obviously inferior to some other already in the field.

The academically respectable treatises on marriage were for the most part written from the sociological point of view and concerned themselves with the social functions of the family. Under modern conditions those functions were being evaded or usurped, and the learned literature dwelt increasingly on what was wrong with marriage. The social functions of the family were largely foreign to the intentions of the contracting parties, and the assumptions of the social sciences regarding human nature, responsibility, and value were opposites of the assumptions tacitly made by those who married.

What the Binkleys proposed was to view the family not from the standpoint of society or of social science, but from their own as husband and wife. For them there was still much that was right with marriage as a refuge for personality and a school of character; much indeed that was now more than ever needed in a world in which all the varied human relationships except marriage were losing functions they had once fulfilled in the personal life of the individual. To make clear what it was, they developed a conception of the "domestic man" which they put alongside those familiar abstractions, the biological, the economic, the political, the sociological man.

The domestic man, they said, demands, in addition to security and sexual satisfaction, a kind of personal and nontransferable relation characterized by "paramount loyalty" toward another person. Marriage continues to be valued chiefly because it provides the most favorable conditions for the expression of this preponderant interest or paramount loyalty. An individual marriage may be said to have failed, not when it is childless or when one or both of the parties have been sexually unfaithful, but only when one of them is no longer more loyal to the other than to anyone else.

The theory drafted at Stanford was further elaborated during their two years in New York. When Hamilton and McGowan published *What is Wrong with Marriage*, the Binkleys were moved to entitle their book *What is Right with Marriage* (38). It was well received. After nineteen years it continues to be read and to serve for others the need it served for its authors. If it has not yet attained the dignity of a classic, it seems the most likely book in its field to do so; for, as one of the reviewers said,[5]

elaborate and cumbersome as the machinery of this theory seems even when lightened by the humor and intelligence of its propounders, it is only on . . . some such assumption as the one which it makes that the belief in the permanence of the institution of marriage can be based. Economic security, sexual satisfaction, and even parenthood are nowadays to be had by both men and women outside of marriage. . . . Only the *homo domesticus* (if he exists) needs matrimony.

The two years the Binkleys spent in New York at this time (1927–1929) witnessed the heyday of prohibition, home brew, moonshine, bootleggers, hip flasks, and speak-easies. Nullification of the prohibition amendment and the Volstead Act was both an organized industry and a favorite indoor sport on a scale to which they had not been accustomed in wine-drinking California. Binkley explored "the ethics of nullification" in an article in the *New Republic* for May 1, 1929 (45).

Is nullification of a law, he asked, to be regarded, like repeal, as a socially useful part of the total legal process or as mere lawbreaking? He reviewed the history of nullification in England and America as a natural expression of local government in Anglo-Saxon countries. Local discretion in enforcing laws, he concluded, is more clearly a part of our system of self-

[5] Joseph Wood Krutch in the *Nation* 129:386–387, Oct. 9, 1929.

government than the doctrines of sovereignty and of the separation of powers, in whose names it is condemned.

This article is noteworthy as an early and forceful expression of one of Binkley's characteristic biases, that toward a maximum of local autonomy. So able was its legal analysis that it was reprinted in the same month by the *Massachusetts Law Quarterly* (46). In the following year it was incorporated in a book, *Responsible Drinking* (50), which proposed to substitute for prohibition a system of registration for dealers and drinkers, along with other measures to make the liquor industry responsible under the civil damage laws for all the injury it does. The book, like the article, was well received by lawyers but failed to reach as wide a public as its author had hoped for it.

When Sidney B. Fay was called from Smith College to Harvard University, he singled Binkley out as the most promising man in the field of modern European history, chiefly on the strength of his articles on the war guilt controversy, and recommended his appointment to the vacancy at Smith. The Binkleys visited Northampton in the spring of 1929, and he was appointed associate professor. He was flattered by the invitation to succeed so distinguished a scholar; and though he and his wife were reluctant to leave New York, they were expecting a child in the summer and thought Northampton a better place for a growing family.

They spent the summer in Italy, where Binkley represented the Hoover War Library at the First World Congress of Libraries and Bibliography at Rome in June and delivered an address on "The Problem of Perishable Paper" (65). They took courses for foreigners in Italian language and literature, history and archaeology; they went on excursions; they took moonlight walks along the Appian Way; they made the acquaintance of Italian wines and dishes. At the end of the summer their first son, Robert Williams Binkley, was born in Rome.

Binkley worked in the Library of the Chamber of Deputies preparing a bibliography of Italian statesmen, particularly of the *Risorgimento*. He had frequent conversations with A. M. Ghisalberti, who gave the history lectures they were attending and who was becoming the outstanding authority on the *Risorgimento*. These conversations were continued by correspondence after the Binkleys returned to this country.

Among the early fruits of this Italian summer were Binkley's articles, "Free Speech in Fascist Italy" (55) and "Franco-Italian Discord" (60). The full harvest was in the chapter on Italy in his book on European history from 1852 to 1871 (107) in the Harper series, *The Rise of Modern Europe*. That chapter was written *con amore*, and his efforts to reduce it to the scale and style of the remainder of the book were not altogether successful.

The year the Binkleys spent at Smith College is remembered there for the unexpected ease with which he filled the vacancy left by the much-admired Sidney Fay. His wide interests, his enthusiasm, his social gifts, his eagerness to learn from members of other departments besides his own, made up for what he lacked in achievement and maturity. The students took to him quickly. Standing at the top of the steps leading up to Seelye Hall with his hands behind his back and an infectious grin on his face, Binkley liked to watch them throng in and out between classes. His wife and he were not intimidated by the greater reticence and conservatism of their new environment. Their apartment over the plumber's shop not far from the campus (an apartment which one of his colleagues recalls as "like a well-appointed barn" in its simplicity and bareness) became a center of hearty and open-handed entertaining.

In the spring of 1929 Binkley had been invited by the newly founded *Journal of Modern History* to review Winston Churchill's *The Aftermath* and the third and fourth volumes of *The Intimate Papers of Colonel House*. In accepting the invitation, he suggested that he be allowed to include in his review certain other books on the Paris Peace Conference. The editor readily agreed, and the result was "Ten Years of Peace Conference History" (49), published in the December, 1929, issue of the *Journal*.

Several months later the editor said in a private letter to a member of the faculty of Western Reserve University that this article had aroused more comment and evoked more praise than any other contribution to the *Journal* and that at the December meeting of the American Historical Association in Durham Binkley had been a marked man. William Langer of Harvard engaged him to write the volume for the Harper series already referred to (107). Carlton Hayes of Columbia wanted him to write a life of Napoleon III for the series of biographies he was editing for W. W. Norton. The editors of the Berkshire Studies in European History asked him to write the volume on the Russian Revolution. He was engaged to summarize recent revelations on the peace conference for the *Political Science Quarterly* (71), and to write an article on Franco-Italian rivalry in the Mediterranean for *Current History* (60). And he was called back to Stanford University to teach undergraduate and graduate courses in the summer quarter of 1930.

In 1929 Henry E. Bourne, professor of history in Western Reserve University and head of the department in Mather College, took permanent leave to become consultant in history at the Library of Congress and editor of the *American Historical Review*. A thorough canvass of men available to succeed him was made. In November Seymour and Notestein of Yale called the attention of the committee to Binkley. Some members of the faculty were from the first uneasy about the wide range of his interests and the number and variety of his publications, or what one of them called his "unfortunate tendency to tackle any subject or problem regardless of his knowledge or understanding." But this misgiving was overruled by his high reputation as an inspiring teacher, and by the respect of specialists for his more strictly professional articles. He visited Cleveland in March, 1930, and in April was appointed acting professor of history and acting head of the department in Mather College, an appointment which was made permanent two years later.

A glance at the bibliography through the year 1929 will evoke in any sober and right-minded person in academic life a lively sympathy with the faculty in their initial hesitation. The committee persuaded them, however, that the larger salary of Binkley's new position would "ease the pressure for pot-boilers." One can imagine their dismay when, to his previous offenses against professional decorum, he added, about the time of entering upon his new duties in the fall of 1930, the book entitled *Responsible Drinking* (50) which had grown out of his article, "The Ethics of Nullification," and which proposed to treat the liquor problem like the automobile problem.

Among the attractions of his new position in Mather College of Western Reserve University was a tradition of small classes and liberal use of source material. To supplement such obvious source books as Robinson's *Readings* and Commager's *Documents*, members of the department had developed a large collection of mimeographed source materials for use in their various courses. But both source books and mimeographed materials had the disadvantages as well as the advantages of having been selected, lifted out of their contexts, edited, annotated, and of being assigned as containing materials from which the students were to elicit answers to questions formulated by their instructors.

While continuing the use of such time-tested materials during part of the course, Binkley sought to achieve for the freshman student a nearer approach to the experience of the research scholar. This involved confronting the student with an approximately complete collection of the available source materials for a limited area and period, in the form in which the research scholar himself would consult them. Elizabethan England was chosen for this purpose, as being the earliest period in which the language difficulty would not be insuperable.

With the help of funds supplied by a generous donor, the college library acquired the volumes for that period of the Acts of the Privy Council, the Calendars of State Papers, and a score of other archival collections, and rounded out its holdings of contemporary historical narratives, annals, and journals. As Binkley remarked: "The collection is the basic corpus of material acquired by most libraries primarily for graduate research, but purchased in this case especially for freshmen."

These and the necessary research tools were assembled in a section of the reserve room, and later in a separate room of the library. Elizabeth's reign was divided among the various freshman history sections, a block of consecutive months to each section, a single month to each student. The resulting papers dealt with a month in general, with a particular phase of the life of the time, or with a special event. Work on the project began when the classes reached the Elizabethan period, about the beginning of the second semester, and for six weeks or two months about half the preparation time was devoted to this study.

Most of the students enjoyed this handling of sources, and some excellent papers resulted from it. The forty essays selected by the history department, as typical of the best that were written from the initiation of the project in 1931 to 1937, stand on the library shelves in two bound volumes. They were analyzed in the card catalogue, and the students took special pride in being listed as authors. As one of them said, "It is fun for us, after taking in so much material predigested in lectures and textbooks, to turn the tables by going to the sources ourselves and digesting the material for the professor."

Perhaps the chief phase of the research scholar's work not represented in this project was the search for uncollected or unpublished documents. For this purpose, in the senior year the students found open to them courses in local history or business and family history, in which they learned to collect and interpret historically the untouched records that are to be found in almost unlimited quantity in any locality. The rationale of these courses, and of the investigations they were designed to promote, will be found in Binkley's address, "History for a Democracy" (135), which is here reprinted.

During the first five years of his professorship at Western Reserve University, Binkley's leisure was largely devoted to writing his *Realism and Nationalism* (107), covering the years 1852–1871 for the Harper series, *The Rise of Modern Europe*. He was in complete sympathy with the aim of the series to emphasize social, economic, religious, scientific, and artistic developments, and to treat Europe as a whole, avoiding schematization by countries. In his prologue he spoke of the distinctive features of his treatment of the period as "the result of a systematic effort . . . to find the basis of a European history that will not be a sum obtained by adding up the histories of the various states, together with a history of diplomacy."

Two devices have suggested themselves as means of bringing more clearly to the fore those elements of European history that are common to the whole continent and culture. One of them is to begin the story with an account of the non-political side of Europe's development, with the analysis of culture as it was manifested in science, letters, art, religion and business life, where the national units do not press themselves so insistently upon the historian. Then, in the analysis of political history, recourse is made to a concept which has not received the benefit of theoretical exposition in the hands of political theorists, but which seems none the less useful to the historian. This is the concept of "federative policy," applied herein to problems of federalism within a state, confederation among states, and quasi-confederal relations of states generally. *Federative polity*, as the term is used in this narrative, is the polity that emphasizes the political relations of adjustment among equals rather than the political relationships of inferiority and superiority, and of methods of law rather than methods of force.

The conclusion toward which the whole book moved was that "the outstanding fact of European history from 1852 to 1871 was the turning away from federative polity."

It was one of Binkley's favorite paradoxes that every history, however remote the period with which it ostensibly deals, has its real terminus and controlling frame of reference in the time of its composition. *Realism and Nationalism* was published late in 1935, but it had been conceived, outlined, and drafted in considerable part before the triumph of the Nazi party. A second edition was called for in 1939, shortly after the launching of World War II. When Binkley submitted his revisions to Harper & Brothers in January, 1940, he wrote:

> As I look over the text from the standpoint of a new printing it becomes evident to me that the changes necessary to bring the book up to date and make it into the kind of book that might have been written this year would be pretty substantial, because the Hitler policy in Central Europe has changed the terminus *ad quem*.

Since extensive revision was out of the question, he confined himself to repairing a weakness in his account of the turning point of the Crimean War (178).

When Binkley was under consideration for the professorship at Western Reserve University, he had written in reply to inquiries: "The research fields I plan to make my own are the nineteenth century in a broad way, and the period of world reorganization before and after the Armistice of 1918 as a subject of more detailed study." The former field was roughly that of the standard undergraduate course in European history since 1815, for which he was to be responsible; the latter was that of the graduate course he most frequently gave. He was dissatisfied from the beginning with the available textbooks for the undergraduate course, and none that appeared later seemed appreciably better.

As early as 1934 he began to meditate a textbook history that would do for the past century and a quarter what his *Realism and Nationalism* was doing for its short period. There would be the same emphasis on aspects of culture other than the political and military, but the correlation between parallel changes in the various phases of culture would be more systematically worked out. There would be less treatment of events and conditions as important in themselves or as leading to or causing others, and more as "typical illustrations of something to be compared or contrasted with other events or conditions." On the political side, national-state government and legislation would be played down, and local government, administration at all levels, and international politics would be played up, so that the various aspects and levels of political activity would appear as a continuous series. The entire book would be deliberately oriented toward the explanation of matters of urgent public concern in the 1930's. World War I would be treated not as a breach between a prewar and a postwar world, but as an era of accentuated social change in which everything prepared for in prewar Europe was hurried toward its manifestations in the present.

He corresponded with Harper & Brothers about the proposed textbook over a period of two years. In the spring of 1936 he became editor of the Ronald series in European history (149), and it was thought for a time that this commitment might preclude his writing the textbook for Harper & Brothers; but an understanding was reached with both publishers, and a contract for the textbook was signed with Harper & Brothers in July, 1936, calling for two volumes: one of text, the other of documents.

Binkley used his advanced courses, including one in economic history, as proving grounds for ideas to be embodied in the general course and in the textbook. He tried them out on his friends as well, at luncheon, in his home, in discussion groups, and by letter.[6] By the time he came to compose the book in

---

[6] Here are passages from letters to two of his friends.

"This year [1934] I teach a course in economic history—a great morass indeed. One of the ideas I have been playing with is this: that it is just as easy to explain capitalism as a device for quick liquidation of losses as to explain it as an apparatus motivated by the expectation of profit. Corresponding to the great liquidating events of capitalist economy are the periodic general confiscations that have taken place in agrarian society.

1939, it no longer bore the slightest resemblance to the standard history textbook of its period or of any other. It was frankly a study of the recent past, employing such techniques of analysis as seemed likely to be of the greatest value in facing the future, whether for purposes of adaptation or for purposes of control. All pretense of a single continuous narrative was abandoned.

At the time of his death in April, 1940, four chapters and part of the fifth had been drafted; three more were planned but were represented only by notes. These are the chapter headings:

    I. Periods and Distances
    II. Families: Households, Dynasties, Races
    III. Land and Livelihood: Villages
    IV. Cities
    V. States
    VI. The World Net of Power
    VII. The World of Debts and Markets
    VIII. The World of Opinion

Charles Martel—the confiscation of the lands of the Templars—the taking over of church land, or of the right to church appointment, in the sixteenth century—perhaps, in a very different way, the enclosure movement—are successive enterprises of liquidation in which a fixed property system is broken down.

"This line of thought, carried down to the present, would suggest for one thing that losses are the final and absolute certainty in all investment; that an investment will be lost is as certain as death. The entrepreneur plays against this statistical certainty his own chance, thus illustrating the general rule that the essence of individualism lies in the resistance which unique entities or events offer to statistical regularities; and there, at one leap, we are come from economics to metaphysics. I do not know whether this idea is worth playing with, but it has amused me for the last week or two.

"The course on federalism [1938] keeps my mind occupied; it seems to be emerging into a metaphysical course. I have just finished giving the history of three villages from medieval times to the present, taking it in all seriousness—good owners and bad owners, just like good kings and bad kings—and asking why since villages last longer than states they are not more important than states, and since we could get along better without states than without the activities of these villages . . . etc. . . . you see the road leads to Bakunin and Kropotkin."

Addressing himself to the generation that was born and grew to college age during the long armistice of 1918–1939, Binkley invites the individual student to exercise his historical imagination by working out from himself in terms of the various units of geographic and social distance—family, neighborhood, village, township, city, county, district, state, nation, world order —and backward and forward from himself in periods determined by the human life cycle. The primary unit is the generation of approximately twenty years. The larger units are life spans and 500-year ages, the latter divided into early, high, and late periods.

In the subsequent chapters the analysis is applied to typical examples, and we are asked to experience modern European history from the centers—in the second chapter, of the Wedgwood, "Juke" and Coburg families; in the third, of the villages of Crawley, Oberschefflenz and Kock; in the fourth, of the city of Strasbourg; in the fifth, of the power area of Bohemia. After these exercises in perspective, we are prepared to give concrete meaning to the generalizations ventured in the more comprehensive and synoptic chapters on the world territorial-political network, the world of debts and markets, and the world of opinion. Passages in the earlier chapters have already shown how family, village, city, and state are implicated in these world networks; how the city, for example, belongs as a fort to the world of power, as a temple to the world of opinion, as a trading place to the world of debts and markets.

All along, the student has been urged to translate what he reads into terms of his family, his village or neighborhood, his city and state. The typical character of Strasbourg as a city, in spite of its falling alternately into French and German power systems in the modern age, is shown by comparison with Cleveland, Ohio. We follow the gross physical changes at the site of Strasbourg through two thousand years as in a slow-motion picture taken from the air, then descend for angle-shots and close-ups of more recent changes within the city, concluding with its evacuation in 1939. I remember Binkley posing to friends about a luncheon table the question he puts at the beginning and end of this chapter:

What is a city? Here is Strasbourg without people, save as its two symbolic figures—the mayor and the bishop—remain on the ground as a gesture against civic extinction. Houses without people, streets without traffic, a temple without worshipers—are they a city? Does the city of Strasbourg exist in October, 1939? Consider two possible contingencies—that the stones should be leveled by artillery, but the people ultimately return. Or that the stones should be left standing, and the people never return, but a wholly new population settle in the buildings. In either case, I believe we should say that the life of the city had been merely suspended.[7]

If he had lived to finish the book and publish it, it might well have been his most fruitful contribution to historical literature. It might have imposed a new pattern on the teaching of modern European history, and infused new life into the teaching of history generally, in our universities and colleges, and perhaps in our high schools as well, for its pedagogical spirit and design would have made it readily adaptable to any level of instruction. In time it might also have given direction and stimulus to research; for new patterns, new leading ideas not only vitalize teaching, they also evoke fresh research, even in fields that had previously seemed overworked or exhausted.[8]

We have accounted now for all but one of the books which

[7] The prevailing temper and philosophy of the book are well expressed in some jottings in the notebook in which Binkley recorded ideas for it as they came to him:

The rhythm of the book

1. Nominalist always, to protect against ideologies.
2. Extreme federalism to rescue sphere for individual initiative.
3. Purpose attached to individual to foil determinists.
4. Pattern to induce broad view of scene.

[8] The unfinished typescript is the property of Harper & Brothers. It is to be hoped that some young historian of nineteenth- and twentieth-century Europe may yet undertake to revise and complete it for publication.

Binkley published or drafted, and for several of his articles; but we have passed over other articles of equal or greater interest, including the entire series he wrote for his favorite medium, the *Virginia Quarterly Review*. Those which are here reprinted will speak for themselves; for the rest, the reader is referred to the bibliography (70, 96, 101, 114, 123, 138, 155). A word should be said, however, regarding his book reviews. As the excerpts in the appendix show, his reviews have a vigor and incisiveness all too rare in professional journals. They are not chary of praise, and often discern merits to which the authors had laid no claim. But they deal hard-hitting blows, and now and then a rapier thrust. The best of them are contributions in their own right to the literature of the subjects with which they deal. Binkley read widely and rapidly; he came to grips with whatever he read, and he liked to put the result into writing. When he heard of a book he wanted to read with special care, he sometimes asked for the privilege of reviewing it, for he knew and coveted the heightening of critical sense that comes with responsible reading.

The opening sentences of one of his reviews hit off very well his approach to most of the books he read: "In every history textbook there is a philosophy of history, conscious or unconscious, expressed or implied. What is the underlying philosophy of this book?" When he had defined the philosophy he found, he would try the effect of a shift of perspective, a change of postulates, on the probative value of the evidence the author had marshaled, and on the admissibility of evidence he had ruled out or overlooked. He had a sportsman's knack for flushing the game the author had sent to cover. With a bent toward paradox and a suspicion that most settled issues were settled wrongly or not quite rightly, if he could not reopen them directly by a show of fresh evidence he would do it indirectly by opening other issues behind them.

If he was reluctant to permit an author to close an issue, he was equally far from intending that his review should do so.

He wrote not as a judge summing up the evidence or rendering a verdict with its supporting opinion, but as an unpaid advocate seeking a hearing for evidence not yet adduced or principles of interpretation not yet applied. If these considerations had the luck to turn the balance, that would afford him an innocent pleasure; if not, he would cheerfully acquiesce, for the time being, in a verdict which, if rendered before his argument was in, would have offended his sporting instinct.

Though Binkley was among those who think it essential for the historian to be thoroughly grounded in at least one of the social sciences and familiar with the methods and concepts of them all, he valued them only as tools and was not taken captive by the orthodoxies of the moment. One winter, when the historians and the sociologists were both meeting in Washington, Binkley deserted the historians to attend part of one of the sociological sessions, slipping in by a side door after the meeting had begun. During the discussion of one of the papers he made some critical comments leading to an attack on the validity of the method the author had employed. At a certain point in the interchange that followed he mischievously asked, "Are we getting anywhere, or is this just tea-table talk?" Finally someone who had paid the price of admission rose to say, "I don't think this man is a sociologist," but by that time Binkley had disappeared by the side door through which he had come, and was on his way back to the historians. There was an element of banter even in his most serious excursions into economics, political science, and sociology. But younger men in these fields were not offended by his irreverence, and felt that he let fresh air into some of the stuffier corners.

The testimony of his students begins almost uniformly: "He was the most stimulating teacher I ever had." The following may serve as examples of the more specific things they go on to say: "He had a directness of approach to every problem; he did not have to go through the usual academic warming-up exercises." "At the end of a period, he would formulate with dramatic vividness some question for us to take away, as if he were less concerned about our reviewing the things he had said than about our going on for ourselves from the point at which he had left off." "He made us believe that what we found ourselves wanting to do was worth doing and that we could do it; but then he made us see possibilities in it that hadn't occurred to us, so that what we did in the end, if not always recognizable as the thing we had set out to do, seemed always to have grown out of it."

He was able on a moment's notice to drop the matter in hand and shift his whole attention and energy to a fresh problem and, when that was disposed of, to return to the previous task as if there had been no interruption. Thus it was possible for him to do nearly all his work at his office, and yet give himself completely to the students who called upon him at all hours of the day. The door was always open; there were no stated conference hours and no appointment was needed. His hearty laugh and quick friendliness made them immediately welcome. Many a student came in expecting a five-minute impersonal interview on a schedule card and found herself talking for an hour about her hopes and plans for the future. When she left, he would turn to his typewriter and finish the sentence. Again, the dean or a colleague would drop in with a problem and find him directing the work of a secretary and an assistant. It would seem that he could scarcely be giving the matter half his thought, but presently he would dictate a letter or memorandum stating the problem and its solution.

Western Reserve University, caught in a tide of expansion, was harder hit by the depression than most institutions of higher learning. There was a steady decline in its teaching power during the decade Binkley spent on its staff. Many who knew that he might easily have found a place elsewhere wondered why he remained. When he took leave for a year at Harvard (1932–1933) and again when he left for a year at Columbia (1937–1938), they said he would not come back; but he did.

It was no small part of the answer that he was in love with Cleveland. His faith in the university's future was grounded in his faith in the city's.

He had many friends outside academic life and was deeply interested in a wide range of neighborhood, civic, and regional enterprises. He said that Cleveland was big enough to command the resources for large experiments and not too big or too conservative to try them. He made constant use of the Cleveland Public Library's rich collections, and by his counsel helped the history division hold and improve its position as one of the best in the country. "He perhaps did more than anybody else to arouse the city to interest in preserving the perishing records of its early economic, business and cultural life" (189).

At the same time he sank his roots in the neighborhood in which he had bought his home. He liked Dorothy Thompson's reply to the friend who asked what school to send her children to: "The nearest." He found other services by the same rule. He had ready access to the staffs of the Cleveland Clinic and University Hospitals, but preferred the neighborhood doctor.

IV. Joint Committee and W.P.A.

In February, 1930, while he was still at Smith College, Binkley was elected a member of the newly formed Joint Committee on Materials for Research of the Social Science Research Council and the American Council of Learned Societies.[9] In September of that year he became secretary of the committee, and from 1932 until his death he was its chairman. At its first meetings in 1930 the committee set on foot three surveys: first, of the activities of American agencies in relation to materials for research in the social sciences and humanities; second, of the categories of research material which ought to be col-

[9] The story of Binkley's work for the Joint Committee has been genially told by one of its elder statesmen, Harry M. Lydenberg (199). "In some ways I think the man was completely described and summed up when one of his fellow workers said as we heard a door open and a brisk step charge down the hall, 'Here comes Binkley, all five of him.' "

lected and preserved; and third, of the methods for reproducing research materials. The last was entrusted to Binkley and occupied much of his time during his first year at Western Reserve University.

In 1931 he published for the committee a manual, *Methods of Reproducing Research Materials* (64), which he rewrote and expanded for a second edition in 1936 (119). In its revised form, the *Manual* contains descriptions, samples, cost analyses, and evaluations of hectograph, mimeograph, photo-offset, lithoprint, blueprint, Photostat, photoengraving, microfilm, and other reproduction techniques for materials with and without illustrations; of various types of photographic equipment; of binding, vertical filing, and film storage; of readers, projectors, and other devices for reading reduced-scale reproductions; and of sound-recording and -reproducing devices.

All this is set in the framework of a philosophic and strategic reconnaissance of current changes and future possibilities in the division of research labor, in library and archival policy, in conceptions as to what constitutes research and what constitutes publication. We are shown how "collecting and publishing are functionally merged" by the new techniques, which bid fair to emancipate scholars and librarians from their "veneration of book print." Other formulations of this reconnaissance, detached from the technical details of the *Manual*, will be found in the papers printed in Part II of the present volume.

Perhaps, however, the chief concern of the last decade of Binkley's life was neither his writing nor his teaching, nor even the work of the Joint Committee, but a problem and an opportunity arising from the Great Depression.

Not only was there general unemployment on an unprecedented scale, but the proportion of white-collar workers in the total army of the unemployed was so much higher than in previous depressions as to give a new turn to the recurring crisis of capitalist society. Projects were devised readily enough for the employment of writers, artists, musicians, actors, and others in whom that society had made a substantial investment by training them in some of the higher arts.

The best way to preserve the investment was to have the actors act, the musicians play, the artists paint, and the writers write; this part of the program was simple. But it could cover only a trifling fraction of the white collar program. The great bulk of the relief load in the white collar field consists of young people with some high school training; old people who have been thrown out after a lifetime in store or office, and, in general, of clerks (160).

Binkley sought "the most important common denominator of clerical skill" and found it in "the ability to work with records: to make records and to interpret them, to put information on them and to get information from them." He saw at once the potential value of the army of unemployed clerks in preparing for the use of scholars materials hitherto seldom touched because the volume to be unearthed and sifted was out of all proportion to what it would yield for the purposes of any single specialist. He proposed a coördinated set of projects for the inventorying, indexing, and digesting of local public archives and selected newspaper files, including the foreign-language press.

It was largely due to his initiative and perseverance that Cleveland became a national center for this phase of the relief program, at first under the Federal Emergency Relief Administration and later under the Works Progress Administration, and that the *Annals of Cleveland* set the standard for similar enterprises in other centers. When Luther H. Evans received authority in 1935 to set up the Historical Records Survey under the Works Progress Administration, he sought Binkley's aid and counsel, and it was freely given. During the four following years, without salary and without office, Binkley attended numerous conferences with Evans and his chief assistants, helped write manuals of procedure, gave advice on matters of policy and organization, assisted in the selection of personnel, and interpreted the work that was being done to the public it was intended to serve. His greatest contribution was the devising of techniques by which W.P.A. labor could be effectively used on the tasks that needed doing.

It was a problem in human engineering which few would have had the temerity to attempt to solve. Binkley took advantage of the mixed character of the labor supply to divide each task into different levels of skill, with a view to assigning the varying abilities of the available labor to their proper place so that the work might be directed through different levels of intelligence until the final product was complete and ready for publication.

By purposely allowing for a certain amount of repetition in processing, as the work ascended the scale, he was finally enabled, when the system was fully set up and operating, to produce accuracy which was comparable to the research of the best scholars and in numerous instances to surpass their efforts. When a scholar took a note on a document he customarily checked his findings against the original once or twice. In the Historical Records Survey the checking was done a number of times and by different groups so that the final result was likely to be more accurate and comprehensive than the efforts of the individual.

Not only was it necessary to carefully analyze technical procedure, but it was found desirable, in order to obtain uniformity of standards, to compile manuals of instruction for the several projects. These manuals, several of which were masterpieces of simple and explicit direction, enabled field workers, editors, and others, after a period training, to do scholarly work of excellent quality (198).

Not the least value of these projects was the satisfaction it gave the workers to feel that they were contributing to the cultural resources of their country. When there was an exhibit of the white-collar projects of the Cleveland area shortly after his death, these workers paid grateful tribute to "Dr. Binkley" or "Bink" for enabling them to make this contribution and for saving them from being passive recipients of a dole.

In addition to various archival and newspaper projects, a regional union catalogue listing over two million volumes in libraries in Ohio and Michigan was compiled by W.P.A. labor without library training. The work was done and the catalogue is housed, kept up-to-date, and serviced in the library of Western Reserve University. Binkley collaborated with Herbert S. Hirshberg, then University Librarian, in planning and supervising the procedures. Similar union catalogues have been established in other centers to supplement the national union catalogue which is gradually being built up at the Library of Congress.

Among projects of national interest are the inventory of American imprints, the bibliography of American literature, and the bibliography of American history, in various stages of completion.

Related to these W.P.A. projects, there were others which Binkley helped to promote through the medium of the Joint Committee. He had urged for years the rescue, by purchase or microfilming, of unique and important materials in the war danger zones of Asia and Europe. His active interest contributed to the salvaging of a Hong Kong collection of records invaluable for the history of Western business enterprise in China since 1782. A great deal of material in British libraries, selected by the American Council of Learned Societies in coöperation with the Library of Congress, has been reproduced on microfilm and deposited in the Library of Congress, from which copies may be obtained by other libraries on order. Some progress has been made on similar projects in India.

There was, in fact, a larger strategy in which Binkley's work for the Joint Committee and for W.P.A. was brought to a common focus. On the one hand, the materials made available by W.P.A. were widening the range of possibilities for amateur as well as professional scholarship, especially in the field of local history. On the other hand, inexpensive methods of reproduction and distribution were bringing publication within the reach of amateur scholars with limited private means or none. These methods were also opening the way to the large-scale use of amateur scholarship in the work of translation, especially from languages not ordinarily included in the professional scholar's equipment. As a result of Binkley's initiative, W.P.A. workers, in a project sponsored by the Cleveland Public Library, translated documents and treatises from the languages of central and eastern Europe, and Mather College of Western Reserve University became for a time a center of supervised volunteer translation of Latin American literature.

As early as 1934, Binkley had drawn up a memorandum for a project to explore the possibility of extending the range of amateur scholarship, increasing the number of people engaged in it, putting them into communication with each other, and making available to them the guidance of professional scholars in their respective fields. His *Yale Review* article in the following year, "New Tools for Men of Letters" (109), developed some of the ideas in this memorandum and laid them before a wider public. The project was reformulated in several later memorandums. Meanwhile the W.P.A. white-collar projects were demonstrating the ability of the comparatively untrained worker under expert guidance to carry on research at the lower levels. Finally, after his proposals had been discussed and analyzed by many scholars, the Carnegie Corporation made a grant to Western Reserve University in 1940 to establish "The Committee on Private Research." President W. G. Leutner, who had accompanied and supported him in laying the case before the corporation, took the check to show him on his deathbed in Lakeside Hospital. Binkley died on April 11 before the details of the program could be worked out; but the committee was reorganized, was active for two years, and published a useful report (200).

V. Tastes and Traits

Binkley's mind seldom came to rest in art or enjoyment. The arts he practiced were forms of exercise or production: folk dancing, community singing, swimming, canoeing, gardening, wine making, and cooking. What a friend and admirer said of the first of these was more or less true of the others: "He loved to do the intricate steps of the English village dances, and bounded around with a vigor that exceeded the requirements of the English pattern." Even for a game of chess, he would sprawl on the floor in front of his fireplace, and he liked two or three fast games better than one slow one.

He was fond of marching songs, chanteys, drinking songs, barbershop ballads, and spirituals; but the art song was a bit beyond his range. He liked the earthy, the ribald, and the macabre; one of his favorites was "On Ilkley Moor Baht 'At." He had been brought up on poetry; he enjoyed reading it, remembered and recited it with gusto. He liked especially the strong-rhythmed poetry of action—ballad and epic, dirge and ode—and had a flair for nonsense verse and limericks.

He had some feeling, acquired in France just after World War I, for the costume, color, pomp, and strut of opera. He seldom went to the theater on his own initiative, and when he was somehow induced to go he would grow restless toward the middle of the second act and want to leave. In the movies he took only a sociologist's and a parent's interest.[10]

---

[10] Some notes on Binkley as a father:

When his second son was born in 1932, he went about for a day or so asking his friends if they liked their given names. The only one who replied in the affirmative was Thomas G. Bergin, then associate professor of Romance languages in Western Reserve University. Thomas was one of the names the Binkleys had been considering, and Bergin's satisfaction with it sealed their choice. From his hospital bed in the last weeks of his life, Binkley carried on a correspondence with Tommy about his new rifle, how to care for it, and under what circumstances it might be used. Some months later Tommy remarked: "He was a great man. Not many fathers would let a boy of my age have a rifle."

A casual visitor in their home remarked with mild surprise, "You seem to have such a *friendly* relation with the boys." He talked with them easily and naturally about the things he was interested in, with no patronizing assumption that anything was beyond their years. He brought them into conversations, however intellectual, with guests in the home. When he inherited his father's Chinese library and began studying the characters, he had the boys join in the fun. He took them swimming and canoeing. So far as he could, instead of scolding or punishing them for their misdoings, he helped them find a better way

He had, however, a lively interest in painting and made it a point to visit the galleries wherever he traveled. He used examples from the various schools and movements in his teaching and in developing the main theme of his *Realism and Nationalism*. Yet even here his interest was historical rather than aesthetic—an interest in identifying the school and manner, and in determining its relation to the culture of the period. In the same way, he read novels only as expressions or reconstructions of a locale and period he was investigating at the time.

Apart from the techniques of visual reproduction, he was not expert in the practice or criticism of any of the arts, but he knew all the gambits of the philosophy of art; and those to whom the arts themselves were as necessary as their daily bread found no one more stimulating and helpful in exploring their meanings and their social and historical backgrounds.

Though his life with a French family just after the war had been an education in the niceties of cookery and service, his palate was unexacting. He was content with plain fare; indeed, apart from convivial occasions he seemed scarcely to notice what he ate or drank.[11] But he liked company at his rough-

---

to what they wanted. When they dug up the flowers and sold them to buy ice cream cones, he got them a freezer with which to make their own. He had a knack for dramatizing the simplest adventures, such as building a garden pool, dissecting a fish's eye, or preparing and cooking an opossum they had accidentally run down on the road. He engaged in friendly rivalries with his sons, so contrived as to put them on an equality with him. When he was assisting in the unsuccessful campaign to reëlect Senator Bulkley, his elder son Binks was typing pleas for votes for the school levy and passing them out in the neighborhood. After the election Binks taunted his father: "I won my election, but you didn't win yours."

Shortly before his death, he expressed a wish that the boys should be taken to some small western town to grow up. They are now living in Boulder, Colorado, where Mrs. Binkley is Assistant Professor of Library Science and head of the social science division of the University of Colorado Libraries.

[11] When absorbed in his work, he often forgot his meals entirely, including those for which he had engagements. If he remembered later or was reminded, he made contrite apologies, yet assumed that his disappointed hosts would think as little of it as he would have done in their

hewn table; he tossed a good green salad, tried his hand now
and then at French onion soup, and maintained a liberal supply
of homemade *vin ordinaire*. In partnership with several friends,
he had a crusher and press, with fifty-gallon barrels for vats,
and smaller barrels and five-gallon jugs for storage. The eve-
nings they spent in crushing, pressing, racking, sampling, bottle
washing, bottling, corking, and sealing were hilarious. He led
the singing to the rhythm of which the work was done. They
liked to say that the crusher and the fifty-gallon barrels were
temporary expedients until some one of the company should
construct an open vat in which to tread out the grapes.

It was in the nature of things that a man who brought forward so many new ideas should be widely regarded as impractical, that his efforts to give his ideas practical effect should
encounter widespread opposition, and that opposition to the
measures he took should often engender distrust, dislike, and
hostility to the man himself. Bibliophiles were inclined to
deprecate what seemed to them an indiscriminate taste for
microfilm and an indecent haste to disengage the content from
the form of original publication. Scholars who craved the
prestige value of full-dress publication were unwilling to submit their writings to the indignity of the near-print methods
of reproduction. Highly trained specialists, accustomed to
singlehanded research and undivided professional responsibility,
were not easily persuaded that any good thing could come out
of the mass-production techniques of the W.P.A. projects or
the undisciplined enthusiasm of amateurs.

---

place. Other trivia: He was an absent-minded and hair-raising driver,
and gave even less attention to his car's appearance than to his own. He
pretended to think it poor economy to wear an academic gown only on
state occasions, and used his as a smock in his office; but he could never
tell what to do with the long tapes. Once, as he was mounting the platform to deliver a Senior Day address, he dropped the tapes into the
sleeves to get them out of the way. By the middle of the address, they
were dangling from the sleeves with every gesture, and he seemed
puzzled, though not offended, by the smiles and suppressed giggles with
which his most serious passages were received.

Conservative college and university colleagues were suspicious of his pedagogical innovations and proposals; if he were sincere in his appreciation of time-tested educational values, they seemed to say, he should have been a stauncher defender of traditional subjects and methods against the inroads of vocationalism. The unadventurous thought him too ready to sacrifice the advantages of position for the foolhardy sport of carrying the battle into the enemy's camp. Even those who considered themselves liberal and progressive would sometimes say that he was difficult to work with, that he kept changing the plan of campaign without notice and apparently without being aware that he was doing so.

As often as not, the real difficulty was merely that he drew consequences his colleagues failed to draw from the premises they had agreed upon. The impression was not, however, groundless. There was for him no question which might not be reopened at any time, and there were no constants with a clear title to be carried over from problem to problem. It was for thought to determine, in connection with each problem as it arose, what had best be taken as constants for the purpose of solving that problem. With a mind untouched by the academic idolatry which pays to ideas and propositions the reverence that is due only to persons, he brought to every problem an extraordinary fertility of suggestion. But those who felt the need of fixed principles (in others if not in themselves) found it easy to think that he avoided having any in order to give himself the fun of improvising them to suit the occasion.

After his death, it seemed likely that any committee of his peers on the Mather College faculty would draw up a perfunctory memoir at best; they would come to bury Binkley, not to praise him. By a notable departure from precedent, the committee was appointed entirely from the junior ranks. Its members freely confessed their elders' sins in the concluding paragraph of their sketch of his career.

It was with very little encouragement from us that he dreamed his dreams of amateur scholarship, W.P.A. organization of research materials, and a renaissance of local history in the republic of letters. We curled a deprecating smile before the vision of every Mather graduate her own historian. If we find it possible now to take a more generous view of his enterprises, that is in part because the prospect of others still to come has been removed. He had ideas, and nothing is quite safe with a man of ideas about, especially if he will go on having them and neither we nor he can guess what the next will be. Let us confess it humbly, he was a gadfly to our sluggish academic society, and we are as little disposed as ancient Athens to pray that God in his care of us should send us such another.

Even among his admirers, a few of the more sensitive felt that though he was a perfect comrade in arms he left something to be desired as a friend. He had so many ideas, and was so busy thinking them through and enlisting help to put them into operation, that he tended to look on other people as prospective collaborators, or, if not that, to stir them up to develop and apply ideas of their own. Those who sought from friendship only the sharing of experience, the slow perfecting of communication, personal affection, and loyalty, soon divined that he sought both less and more than that. He was no connoisseur of the play of feeling, of the subtler nuances of the emotional life; in other minds, as in his own, he fished for ideas only. Historian though he was, his backward looks were all for the sake of forward looks; he had no wish to live in the past, no flair for reminiscence, no relish for personal anecdote and idiosyncrasy, no desire for exchange of confidences or for personal revelation. He had an essentially public mind, unequipped for intimacy.

This, however, is a minority report. The great majority of those who knew him well, far from acknowledging a defect at this point, would testify to the warm, hearty, and invigorating character of his companionship. As one of them puts it: "When I would fall into sentimental reminiscence he would always pick me up, mentally, and set me down with my thinking turned toward the future."

He seemed to think of his friends—and his family too, for that matter—not as individuals each to be known for his own sake, but as members of an indefinite company of men of good will—the gang, he called it. The original nucleus of the gang—for him—was the family into which he was born. It had expanded to include first the ambulance corps, then the Hoover War Library group and his fellow graduate students at Stanford, and the family he in turn established. Those who later became his friends thereby joined the gang; indeed, he had a way of assuming that they had all met and known each other before and needed no introductions. The groups he worked with on particular projects were but so many committees, as it were, of the gang. The loyalties that moved him most were not to individuals as such but to these groups and to the gang that embraced them all. Yet his generosity was boundless. Old friends spent weeks or months in his home while writing a book or looking for a job. He always lent money to any friend who asked it, and often sent or offered it unasked to one he thought might need it to carry out some cherished plan.

In its informal hospitality the Binkley household was unique. They had bought a plain and inexpensive house in a beach allotment which had a community playground on the shore of Lake Erie. The house became a plaything for the family, and was in a constant state of amateur alteration. In the summer months it was a caravansary for students, friends, and acquaintances from near and far. The Binkleys never knew what hot and thirsty souls would turn up there, to make use of the improvised shower and dressing room in the basement, to draw freely on the wine-cellar stores, to picnic on the beach. If invited guests were already there, the uninvited joined the company without embarrassment. There was no visible effort in this entertaining, though the actual burden of it must have been great enough. The gang came and went, expanded or dissolved at will. They swam, they stretched out in the sun, they talked, they sang. Nowhere else did they find so much good talk, on high and homely themes alike, in so casual and unconfined an atmosphere.

They went away refreshed, and not infrequently they carried with them a basket of food and flowers from the Binkley garden.

The influence of his family and early group life was thus reflected not only in his emphasis on the family in his teaching, in his books on marriage and liquor control, in his unfinished book on nineteenth-century history, and in his strategy for local history and amateur scholarship, but also in his social personality. There was one aspect of the family character, however, which Binkley, though respecting it, did not share; and that was a tendency to find security in withdrawal, in the building of defenses, in keeping open an avenue of retreat. Or perhaps it would be more exact to say that there was a residue of this also in him, but that it was usually overshadowed by the acquired habit of assessing carefully the moving forces of the moment and seeking to direct them toward ends he thought socially desirable. By his actions he seemed to say: there is no force in the world, however weak or spasmodic or barbarous or hostile, which cannot be made to serve the purposes of civilized man, if only he has the wit and will to find a way. Yet one of the most eloquent college addresses I ever heard him give was on the Stoic text: Some things are in our power, others not. That was in the worst year of the depression; and at about the same time, when academic tenure seemed precarious, there was something more than playfulness in the zest with which he, and some of his more congenial colleagues, talked of retiring to a subsistence farm together. They planned to take their families and private libraries and engage in co-operative research, study, and writing (as well as farming) until the storm had blown past. This was over the cups, however; and even then, as we have seen, he was engaged in a campaign to make the depression serve the advancement of learning on a larger scale and in a more positive fashion.

Shortly before the Ohio writer Jake Falstaff died, Binkley met him two or three times and liked him very much. One evening, in a rather large group in which the conversation had been fairly sparkling, one of those present asked a question so far out of key with the rest of the talk as to make the asker seem naïve, even stupid. Falstaff answered not with mere patience or courtesy but with interest and sympathy, in such a way that the awkward question was turned into a positive contribution. That kindness touched and pleased Binkley deeply, and he spoke of it several times. He had a feeling for greatness of spirit, loved it when he found it, reached after and attained it in himself.

Chronology

1897   Born at Mannheim, Pennsylvania, December 10.

1915   Graduated from San Jose High School. Entered Stanford University.

1917   Enlisted in U. S. Army Ambulance Service in June.

1918   Cited for distinguished service, Fléville, France, October 16.

1919   Studied art at University of Lyons. Discharged from Army in July to help gather materials for Hoover War Library.

1920   Returned to Stanford University. Helped organize materials for Hoover War Library.

1922   A.B., Stanford University.

1923–27   Reference Librarian, Hoover War Library.

1924   A.M., Stanford University (23). Married Frances Harriet Williams (A.B., Stanford, 1923), September 13.

1927   Ph.D., Stanford University (33).

1927–29   Instructor in history, Washington Square College, New York University.

1929   Represented Hoover War Library at First World Congress of Libraries and Bibliography at Rome in June (65).

1929–30   Associate professor of history, Smith College.

1930   Acting associate professor of history, Stanford University, summer quarter.

1930–32   Acting professor of history, Western Reserve University.

1930–32   Secretary, Joint Committee on Materials for Research (68, 92).

1931   Member, Beer Prize Committee, American Historical Association.

1932–40   Professor of history, Western Reserve University, and head of the department in Flora Stone Mather College.

1932–40   Chairman, Joint Committee on Materials for Research (102, 126, 139, 156).

1932–33   Visiting lecturer in history, Harvard University.

1933–40   Member, Editorial Board, Records and Documents of the Paris Peace Conference.

1934–36 Member, Editorial Board, *Journal of Modern History.*
1936–40 Editor, Ronald series in European history (149).
1937–38 Visiting professor of history, Columbia University (153).
1937–39 Vice-president, American Documentation Institute.
1938–39 Chairman, Committee on Photographic Reproduction of Library Materials, American Library Association.

Member, National Advisory Committee, Historical Records Survey.

Member, Advisory Committee, Franklin D. Roosevelt Library.

Member, American National Committee on Intellectual Coöperation of the League of Nations (163).

Member, Advisory Board, Cleveland Chapter, American Civil Liberties Union.

Chairman, Committee on Equipment and Mechanical Techniques, American Society of Archivists.

1940 Died of cancer of the lungs at Lakeside Hospital, Cleveland, Ohio, April 11, aged 42 years and four months.

I

The "Guilt" Clause in the Versailles Treaty *

*Article 231: The Allied and Associated Governments affirm
and Germany accepts the responsibility of Germany and her
Allies for causing all the loss and damage to which the Allied
and Associated Governments and their nationals have been
subjected in consequence of the war imposed upon them by
the aggression of Germany and her Allies.*

It has long been recognized that Article 231 of the Versailles
Treaty is ambiguous. It can be read either as a contractual assumption of liability for war damage or as a moral pronounce-
ment relating to the genesis of the war. The ambiguity resides
in two phrases—the first holding Germany and her Allies
responsible for war damage, the second designating the war as
one imposed upon the Allies by the *aggression* of the Central
Powers. Each of the key words bears a double meaning, juridical and ethical. *Responsibility* can mean either legal liability
(German, *Haftbarkeit*) or moral guilt (German, *Schuld*).
The *aggression* alleged to have imposed the war upon the Allies
may be taken to be the merely formal aggression constituted
by prior declaration of war and invasion, or it may be a
morally reprehensible policy and intention from which, according to the now discredited dogma of exclusive German war
guilt, the World War arose.

The difference between these two interpretations is of critical
importance today. If the words are given a moral and political

* Reprinted by permission from *Current History*, May, 1929.

49

interpretation, they are indefensible in the light of contemporary historical knowledge; they falsely impugn German honor, and therefore give just grounds for a great German national movement for the repudiation of an extorted confession of guilt. But if the words have a formal and juristic reading, they relate solely to reparations liabilities. They do not impugn German honor; they are not contradicted by historical research.

Newly revealed documents on the Peace Conference, privately printed by David Hunter Miller, throw light upon the interpretation of the article,[1] for it is a rule of international law that in construing a doubtful text, recourse is to be had to the history of the negotiations.

The negotiations of the reparations section of the Treaty of Versailles passed through four stages—the pre-Armistice negotiations of November, 1918; the debates in the Commission on Reparations in February, 1919; the discussion which engaged the Supreme Council in March and April; the correspondence with the German delegation in May and June. The decisive texts were formulated in the first and third periods of the negotiations; at these times the negotiators were thinking in terms of financial and juristic "responsibility" and formal "aggression." The negotiation of the second and fourth periods, while primarily devoted to the problem of financial and legal liability, introduced a confusing discussion of moral and political guilt.

THE PRE-ARMISTICE NEGOTIATIONS

On November 1, 1918, the Supreme War Council in Paris drew up its demand that Germany, having requested an armistice, agree to make compensation for all damage done to the civilian population of the Allies "du fait de *l'invasion* par l'Allemagne des pays alliés, soit sur terre, soit sur mer, soit en

[1] David Hunter Miller, *My Diary at the Conference of Paris, with Documents,* 20 vols. and maps (privately printed, New York, 1928).

conséquence d'opérations aériennes." [2] This formula was rendered into English in the Lansing note of November 5, thus becoming the contractual basis of a reparations claim: "Compensation will be made by Germany for all damage done to the civilian population of the Allies and their property by the *aggression* of Germany by land, sea and from the air."

The sense of this language is clearly legalistic, not ethical. It has to do with an undertaking to make payments, not a confession of guilt. The word "aggression" refers to the bald, formal fact of invasion, without prejudice to any one or other version of prewar history. The phrase "damage by aggression" was construed by the American peace delegation to mean "physical damage to property resulting from the military operations of the enemy." [3] Other possible meanings of the term "aggression" were discussed. But it did not enter the American view that the word could be construed in a moral and political sense as a reference to German policies.

This formula of the Lansing note was the contractual basis of the Allied claim to reparations. It excluded claims for war costs or indemnities. In later discussions the French and British delegations tried to escape from this limitation, while the American delegation worked to hold the terms of the treaty to conformity with the Lansing note. When in the records of the negotiations there appear drafts of reparations clauses containing the phrase "aggression . . . by land, sea and from the air," the expression signalizes that an effort is being made to keep the language of the treaty as close as possible to the language of the Lansing note. On the basis of evidence now at hand this seems to be the pedigree of the word "aggression" in Article 231.

[2] Mermeix, *pseud.* (Gabriel Terrail), *Les négociations secrètes et les quatre armistices avec pièces justificatives* (Paris, 1919), and Charles Seymour, *The Intimate Papers of Colonel House* (Boston, 1928), vol. IV, give the best accounts of these negotiations.

[3] Memorandum of John Foster Dulles, Feb. 7, 1919, in Miller, *Diary*, V, 204.

THE DEBATES IN THE PEACE CONFERENCE COMMISSION

Despite the fact that Lloyd George had signed away the right
to demand war costs from Germany, he promised the British
people in the general election of December, 1918, that he would
make the Germans pay the entire costs of the war. The French
people were equally expectant that "Germany will pay all."
Thus it came about that the second stage in the drafting of
reparations terms consisted of an attempt by the French and
British delegations to establish that Germany could be held
for war costs because she had started the war.

When the Peace Conference Commission on Reparations
met in February, 1919, it found a French memorandum on
principles of reparations arguing for "integral reparations,"
that is, war costs, on the ground that the ordinary law of
torts makes a wrongdoer liable for all the consequences of his
wrongful act.[4] John Foster Dulles of the American delegation
countered with a memorandum asserting that "reparation would
not be due for all damage caused by the war unless the war
in its totality were an illegal act." [5] But the law of 1914 permitted war-making.

The British delegation opposed the American view in a
memorandum of February 10: "The war itself was an act of
aggression and wrong; it was, therefore, a wrong for which
reparation is due." [6] The Italian memorandum of February 15
made the same claim: "An enemy who is responsible for an
unjust act of aggression owes to [the victims] . . . full reparations for the costs of their defense." [7]

A full dress debate, extending from February 10 to February

[4] French memorandum of Feb. 1, 1919, from Minutes of Reparations
Commission quoted in Miller, *Diary*, XIX, 267. Also in Annex to Klotz:
De la guerre à la paix. (Paris, 1924.)

[5] Dulles memorandum of Feb. 4, in Miller, *Diary*, V, 147–148. (It is not
certain that this memorandum was presented or used; in any case, it ex-
presses the American view.)

[6-7] British and Italian memorandums, from the Minutes of the Commission on Reparations, as cited in Miller, *Diary*, XIX, 268.

19, then took place in the Commission on Reparations. The British led the argument for war costs; Dulles replied that the Allies were bound by the terms of the Lansing note; all the powers save Belgium lined up with the British delegation.[8] The debate ended in a complete deadlock on February 19, when it was voted to refer back to the Supreme Council the question, formulated by the French, "The right to reparations of the Allied and Associated Powers is entire (integral)." The Supreme Council refused to act on this formula when it came before them on March 1, partly because President Wilson was then absent, and partly because interest was shifting from the abstract right to recover reparations to the more practical problem of the total sum that could be recovered. At Lansing's suggestion the commission was instructed to draft alternative reports, covering either the inclusion or rejection of the war costs claim.[9]

While the decision upon the principle of reparations hung fire, Dulles came forward on February 22 with a draft proposal which vaguely anticipated the language of Article 231:

"I. The German Government undertakes to make full and complete reparations, as hereinafter provided, for damage as hereinafter defined, done by the aggression of Germany and/or its allies to the territories and populations of the nations with which the German Government has been at war." [10]

On February 26 this draft took shape as follows:

"I. The German Government recognizes its complete legal and moral responsibility for all damage and loss, of the character set forth in the schedule annexed hereto." [11]

[8] Bernard Baruch, *The Making of the Economic and Reparations Section of the Treaty* (New York, 1920), prints a good account of the debate, with stenographic minutes of some of the speeches. An excellent abstract of the arguments on both sides is printed in Miller, *Diary*.
[9] Minutes of the Council of Ten (B. C., 42), March 1, 1919, printed in full in Miller, *Diary*.
[10] Miller, *Diary*, VI, 21.
[11] Miller, *Diary*, VI, 54.

The explicit linking of the words "legal and moral" in this draft illustrates the degree to which juristic and ethical arguments had been intertwined and entangled in the discussion on principles of reparation. No one had disputed the thesis of German war guilt; the dogma of a war-guilty nation was itself subjected neither to criticism nor discussion. In the drafting of all parts of the treaty this dogma was called upon to justify cruel and unworkable demands—the reparations demands among others. The record of the debates in the commission, in so far as they are accessible, gives no evidence that the delegates of any power strove at this time to make use of the reparations section of the treaty to wring from Germany a confession of war guilt. The dialectic use made of the war-guilt legend in the reparations debate was not unlike the use made of it in the debate on Rhineland occupation or German disarmament. The dogma of German moral and political war responsibility was brought forward to serve as a supplementary basis of reparations liability, different from the contractual basis of liability established in the Lansing note.

PLANS TO INCLUDE A SPECIAL GUILT-ACKNOWLEDGMENT ARTICLE IN THE TREATY

The project to require of Germany a definite acknowledgment of her war guilt was brought forward in the Peace Conference as a matter entirely distinct from the reparations problem. Already, on November 21, 1918, the French Government, in an official plan for the agenda of the Peace Conference, had included:

"VII. Stipulations of a moral order. (Recognition by Germany of the responsibility and premeditation of her directors, which will place in the front rank ideas of justice and responsibility, and will legitimate the measures of penalization and precaution taken against her. . . .)" [12]

[12] Miller, *Diary*, II, 16.

Again, in connection with the drafting of the Covenant, the French delegation tried to insert in the preamble a condemnation of "those who had visited upon the world the war just ended." [13] One of the first acts of the Peace Conference was to set up a Commission on the Responsibility of the Authors of the War and provisions for their punishment. This commission reported on March 29 in language which constitutes an extreme statement of the war-guilt myth: "The war was premeditated by the Central Powers, together with their Allies, Turkey and Bulgaria, and was the result of acts deliberately committed in order to make it unavoidable." [14]

The idea that the treaty should stand as a whole upon the theory of German war guilt is expressed in Lloyd George's famous memorandum of March 25, setting forth his enlightened views on the terms of peace: "The settlement . . . must do justice to the Allies, by taking into account Germany's responsibility for the origin of the war." [15]

The preamble to the Treaty of Versailles is expressive of this same theory, for it designates the war by listing chronologically the Austro-Hungarian and German war declarations and referring to the invasion of Belgium. The final indictment of Germany by the Allies, summed up in Clemenceau's harsh covering letter of June 6, 1919, related not to the particular

[13] Miller, *The Drafting of the Covenant,* 2 vols. (New York, 1928) I, 229–230; II, 299, 476. (Records of the ninth meeting of Commission on League of Nations, Feb. 13, 1919.)

[14] This part of the report of the Commission on Responsibilities is accessible in many editions, notably in English in the *German White Book on the Responsibilities of the Authors of the War,* published by the Carnegie Endowment for International Peace.

[15] "Some considerations for the Peace Conference before they finally draft their terms," *Memorandum circulated by the Prime Minister on March 25, 1919.* Great Britain, *Command Papers,* 1922, Vol. 23, Cmd. 1614, p. 5. Ray Stannard Baker, *Woodrow Wilson and the World Settlement,* 3 vols. (Garden City, N. Y., 1923), II, 495, wrongly attributes this memorandum to General Bliss; in this error he has been followed by von Wegerer in *Widerlegung des Versailler Kriegschuldspruches* (Berlin, 1928).

provisions of the reparations section of the treaty but in general to the treaty as a whole.

There is no disputing the fact that those who drew up the Treaty of Versailles entertained the conviction that Germany was war-guilty and made use of this conviction in justifying the reparations clauses of the treaty among others. But did they choose to write an expression of this belief into the text of Article 231? For an answer to this question we must turn to that period of the negotiations in which the text was formulated.

THE DRAFTING OF ARTICLE 231

As February turned to March and March to April, it became increasingly clear that the size of the sum to be demanded of Germany was a fact of greater moment than the theoretical nature of the German liability. This orientation of interest was already evident in Balfour's remarks in the Council of Ten on March 1, and when, on March 10, reparations were discussed in a special conference by Clemenceau, House and Lloyd George, the problem of the total amount was uppermost. The three decided to set up a small secret committee, consisting of Davis, Montagu and Loucheur, "to discuss the question of reparations. Both Clemenceau and Lloyd George stated that they hoped a large sum would be settled upon, because of the political situation in the Chamber of Deputies and Parliament. They were perfectly willing to have the sum called 'reparations.' " [16] The minutes of this conference indicate an almost cynical indifference to the question of principle that had aroused the commission in the preceding month, and a perfectly frank recognition that it would be distressing to disillusion the French and British people as to the real amount of the prospective reparations revenue.

The moral question slips into the background as the next draft of Article 231 appears. On March 19 the British and

[16] Miller, *Diary*, VI, 316. The report of this committee, dated March 20, 1919, is printed in Baker, *Woodrow Wilson*, III, 376–379.

Americans agreed on the tentative text: "The loss and damage to which the Allied and Associated Governments and their nationals have been subjected as a direct and necessary consequence of the war begun by Germany and her Allies is upward of 40,000,000,000 sterling [$200,000,000,000]." This text was modified next day by substituting for "the war begun by Germany" the phrase, "the war imposed upon them by the enemy States." On March 24 the text was retained, except that the 40,000,000,000 pounds was commuted to 800,000,000,000 marks.[17] The intention of the drafting committee in constructing this formula was expressed by Lamont, the American member, in his covering letter: "The thought was that for political reasons it might be wise to have the Germans admit the enormous financial loss to which the world had been subjected by the war which they had begun." [18]

Thus the wish of Lloyd George and Clemenceau "that the sum might be large" is being complied with, although the secret Committee of Three, appointed on March 10, had reported that the maximum sum collectable from Germany was $30,000,000,000—one-seventh of the amount named in the article. The discrepancy was taken care of by the ensuing article of the draft, prefiguring Article 232 of the treaty, by recognizing that "the financial and economic resources of the enemy States are not unlimited, and that it will therefore be impractical for the enemy States to make complete reparation for the loss and damage above stated, resulting from the aggression of such enemy States."

The language of March 24 is very near to the final language of the treaty. And its intention is legal, formal, financial, not moral. The word "aggression" is used as in the Lansing note, to mean invasion; the phrase relating to the outbreak of the war was originally "war begun by Germany." The sense of the language in this respect is like the language of the preamble to

[17] Baker, *Woodrow Wilson*, III, 387.
[18] Miller, *Diary*, VII, 147.

the treaty. It does not impugn German honor; it leaves open the question of premeditation and political policies generally.

In the subsequent negotiations, of which we can construct a fairly complete record by putting together the evidence offered by Baker, Keynes, House, Baruch, Lamont, Klotz, Tardieu and Miller,[19] it appears that the most important issues were three: (1) The French and British wished to have war pensions included as reparations; (2) Wilson wished to avoid naming a fantastic sum as the total of the German debt; (3) the French wished to exact assurance that Germany would pay "at whatever cost to herself."

The concession relating to war pensions, although the most important at the time, does not bear directly upon the present question. Wilson yielded to the persuasive appeal of the Smuts memorandum of March 31.

Wilson's arguments in the Council of Four on March 30 had a more direct influence upon the drafting of Article 231. The draft of March 24 came before the Council, slightly modified by reducing the sum mentioned from 40,000,000,000 to 30,000,000,000 pounds. But "President Wilson said he did not like the mention of the particular sum stated in the memorandum." He asked, moreover, that the text be brought nearer to the language of the Lansing note.[20] Acting under this instruction, the American experts, on March 31, drafted a text which substituted for the specific sum a general acknowledgment of "responsibility," and elaborated the statement relating to the beginning of the war by adding the word "aggression" —a word which, in the circumstances, must have come from the Lansing note.

[19] In addition to the works already cited (Miller, Klotz, Baruch, House, and Baker), André Tardieu, *La Paix* (Paris, 1920), and the article by Lamont in E. M. House and Charles Seymour, *What Really Happened at Paris* (New York, 1921), as well as John Maynard Keynes, *The Economic Consequences of the Peace* (New York and London, 1920), throw light on this period of the negotiations.

[20] Minutes of the Council of Four (IC 169 C), as abstracted in Miller, *Diary*, XIX, 288–289.

At the meeting of financial experts on March 31 the French withdrew to prepare a proposed amendment, and the British and Americans continued in session.[21] On April 1 the British and Americans came to agreement on the text: "The Allied and Associated Governments affirm the responsibility of the enemy States for all the loss and damage to which the A. and A. Governments and their nationals have been subjected as a direct and necessary consequence of the war imposed upon them by the aggression of the enemy States. . . ." Here the two ambiguous words, "responsibility" and "aggression," appear in a context not much different from that which they were finally given.

Fortunately, we have a memorandum expressing the intent of the experts on April 1, when they drew up the text: "It has been agreed between them that Mr. Lloyd George's plan shall be in substance adopted, that is to say: 1. That Germany shall be compelled to admit her financial liability for all damage done to the civilian population of the Allied and Associated Powers and their property by the aggression of the enemy States by land, by sea and from the air, and, also, for damage resulting from their acts in violation of formal engagements and of the law of nations. . . ." [22] The draft is thus intended as a statement of legal liability, not moral guilt.

Meanwhile Klotz is out preparing the French amendments. Will he seek to introduce the guilt element into the text? Far from it. The French delegation is not trying to substitute a moral declaration on prewar history for a legal recognition of liability. On the contrary, it is trying to make the recognition of liability more decisive. The Klotz draft, as it is put into shape on April 5, after coming before the Council of Four, runs as follows: "The Allied and Associated Powers require and the enemy States accept that the enemy States, at whatever

[21] "Memorandum of progress with the Reparations settlement," in Baker, *Woodrow Wilson,* III, 397.
[22] Baker, *Woodrow Wilson,* III, 397.

cost to themselves, make compensation for all damage done to the civilian population . . . and to their property by the aggression of the enemy States by land, by sea and from the air." [23]

The men who are now whipping the language into shape are not thinking of anything but the amount and degree of financial liability which Germany can be made to assume. The emotional pronouncements on war guilt which had characterized the debates of February are no longer in evidence. The only contribution of the Klotz draft to the permanent language of Article 231 is the phrase, "and the enemy States accept." The Klotz draft of April 5 was referred to a drafting committee consisting of Lamont, Keynes and Loucheur, and reported back to the Council of Four on April 7. The drafting committee had simply gone back to the language of the text of April 1. The phrase from the Klotz draft, "and the enemy States accept," was restored in the meeting of the Council of Four on April 7. It then remained only to substitute "Germany and her Allies" for "the enemy States," and Article 231 emerged in its final form.[24]

At this time the attention of the Council of Four was much more seriously taken up with the language of Article 232. The text of Article 232 was debated and changed on April 7, while Article 231 rode along on the basis of the agreements reached April 1.[25] We have, therefore, the documentary proof of the intention of those who drafted Article 231, namely, the memorandum made at the time of drafting and quoted above. This memorandum established that the negotiators who drew up Article 231 intended the words "responsibility" and "aggression" in the juristic, not the moral-political sense.

With the submission of the treaty to the German delegation there began a debate which has continued to the present day,

[23] Miller, *Diary,* VII, 488–490.
[24] Miller, *Diary,* XIX, 288–289.
[25] Miller, *Diary,* XIX, 291 ff.

linking war guilt and reparations liability. The German delegation interpreted Article 231 in a moral sense. Their translation
leaned to the moral reading of the article.[26] They assumed that
it was based upon the report of the Commission on the Responsibilities of the Authors of the War, and called for the
report of that commission, which Clemenceau refused them. In
point of fact the report of the commission was not embodied
in Article 231, for the article had taken shape by March 24,
whereas the report of the commission was not made until
March 29. In his correspondence with the German delegation
Clemenceau explained that the word "aggression" in Article
231 went back to the use of the same word in the Lansing note.[27]
His explanation happened to be true, although his argument on
it was shifty. When the representatives of the Allied Governments set forth in their final ultimatum their most emphatic
statement of the war-guilt thesis, they were discussing not
Article 231 or the reparations section alone but the whole
treaty, in all its parts.

The idea that Article 231 is a guilt article has grown lustily
since 1919. Entente statesmen have found it convenient to refer
to a German acknowledgment of war guilt, and German patriots
have welcomed a definite text, to the revision of which they
can direct their efforts. On the other hand, in cases involving
legal interpretation, the juristic reading of Article 231 has

[26] Robert C. Binkley and August C. Mahr, *"Eine Studie zur Kriegsschuldfrage,"* in *Frankfurter Zeitung*, Feb. 28, 1926; "A new interpretation
of the Responsibility Clause of the Versailles Treaty," by the same authors, in *Current History*, June, 1926.

[27] Brockdorff-Rantzau's note of May 13 protested against basing reparations claims on the ground that Germany was author (*Urheber*) of
the war; May 20 Clemenceau replied by arguing that the word "aggression" in the Lansing note closed the debate as to the basis of Germany's
liability. May 24 Brockdorff-Rantzau replied that Germany, in accepting
the Lansing note "did not admit Germany's alleged responsibility for the
origin of the war or for the merely incidental fact that the formal declaration of war had emanated from Germany." These texts in many printed
sources, especially Herbert Kraus and Gustav Roediger, *Urkunden zum
Friedensvertrage von Versailles vom 28 Juni 1919* (Berlin, 1920), I.

prevailed. For instance, in the case of Rousseau vs. Germany, argued before the Mixed Arbitral Tribunal of Paris in 1921, it was decided that the German Government had to pay for the equipment of a certain truffle factory on grounds derived from a legal reading of Article 231.[28]

It is time that the ambiguity of this article should be resolved. This could easily be accomplished by a declaration on the part of the Entente Governments, stating that in their view the language of the article has only a juristic, not a moral-political meaning. Such a declaration would put an end to the present uncertainty which permits the article to mean one thing in the chamber of the Mixed Arbitral Tribunal and another thing in the French Chamber of Deputies. The declaration would also serve a good purpose in quieting title to reparations. This latter is at present an important consideration. If our government is anxious that in any project for commercializing the reparations payments, there be no confusion of reparations liability with the question of inter-allied debts, our investors will be equally desirous that there be no confusion of reparations and the war-guilt question. Americans will not wish to have their titles to an investment compromised by the agitation of the *Kriegsschuldfrage;* neither will they wish to have their attitude upon the question of the origins of the war become a matter engaging their economic interests.

[28] *Recueil des décisions des Tribunaux Arbitraux Mixtes,* 1921, p. 379.

II

Ten Years of Peace Conference History *

After witnessing a decade of intensive revising of the history of the origins of the Great War, we have now to look forward to a period no less chaotic in the study of the origin of the peace settlements. The world has come to expect of historians that they will make use of their discipline and their feeling for perspective in the interpretation of events that are still filled with vital meanings. The new cult of indiscretion in the publishing of memoirs has accelerated enormously the speed with which secrets of state are revealed to the public. The fact that the journalist is only too willing to exploit these revelations calls for an effort on the part of the historian to understand and to control them.

Peace Conference studies stand today about where the investigation of the origins of the war stood in 1919–20. The historical problems of the Peace Conference are formulated, like the unrevised problem of the origins of the war, around personalities on the one hand and high-sounding generalities on the other. Just as it once seemed self-evident that every question of importance relating to responsibility for the war came to a focus in the personal equation of William II, so it has been made to appear that the role of Woodrow Wilson or of Georges Clemenceau at Paris includes the whole story of the peace settlement. And just as there were writers who

* Reprinted from *Journal of Modern History*, December, 1929, by permission of The University of Chicago Press.

treated the international situation of 1914 as if it had been the stage of a conflict between such entities as "civilization" and "barbarism," so there have been historians of the Peace Conference who have painted the world-scene of 1919 as if it had been a clearly drawn struggle between such things as Crime and Justice, or New and Old.

The experience of the historical profession in the study of the problem of responsibility for the war should serve at once as a guide and a warning to those who are to develop the investigation of the peace settlements. The study of the war-guilt question was admirable in the persistence with which all possible sources of information were explored, and deplorable in the naïveté with which the issues of the discussion were formulated. A review of the literature upon the Peace Conference indicates that it is tending to develop in a comparable way.

It will be recalled that the earliest official and semiofficial publications—notably Temperley's six-volume *History of the Peace Conference* [1] and the comprehensive publications of the German, Austrian, and Hungarian peace delegations [2]—could pretend to no greater adequacy than had characterized the old red, white, green, and yellow "books" of the 1914 crisis. The defeated powers published exhaustively, having indeed little to relate and nothing to conceal; Temperley's collection of

[1] H. W. V. Temperley, ed., *A History of the Peace Conference of Paris*, published under the auspices of the Institute of International Affairs, 6 vols. (London, 1920–24).

[2] The German documents have been published in several editions, notably the official "white books" entitled *Materialien betreffend die Friedensverhandlungen* (Charlottenburg, 1919–20). A convenient two-volume edition is in the series: *Kommentar zum Friedensvertrage*, edited by Professor Dr. Walter Schuecking, entitled *Urkunden zum Friedensvertrage von Versailles vom 28 Juni 1919*, edited by Herbert Kraus and Gustav Roediger, Parts I–II (Berlin, 1920–21). The Austrian documents are in *Bericht über die Tätigkeit der Deutschösterreichischen Friedensdelegation in St. Germain en Laye*, 2 vols. (Vienna, 1919). The Hungarian documents are in *The Hungarian Peace Negotiations: An Account of the Work of the Hungarian Peace Delegation at Neuilly s/S from January to March, 1920*, 3 vols. and maps (Budapest, 1922).

monographs was voluminous, colorless, and discreet, like any official compilation. Out of the six volumes only a few hundred pages were devoted to an account of the actual progress of negotiations in Paris, the rest being concerned with certain aspects of the history of the war, with the discussion of the historical background of various problems presented to the Peace Conference for solution, and with the story of the carrying out of the provisions of the treaties. Temperley's work came very near to being the official British history of the Conference. A compilation edited by Colonel House and Professor Charles Seymour,[3] as well as a volume by Bernard Baruch [4] and one by Professors Haskins and Lord,[5] had the tone of official American history. And André Tardieu, a man much experienced in writing official histories, published a volume calculated to defend French policy against critics abroad, who thought it too severe toward Germany, and critics at home, who thought it too mild.[6]

But it was not from these writings that the public drew its opinions. The fires of national and factional sentiment required more combustible material. Responsibility for the peace settlement was a domestic political issue in each nation. The internal quarrels and conflicts of policy which had developed in each delegation were exposed. The journalists displayed the greatest zeal in discovering colossal plots and treasons; they used the pattern of their war-time propaganda narratives in constructing their histories of the Peace Conference. Their syntheses, which are today the principal extant theories of the Conference, were used in politics with deadly effect.

[3] E. M. House and Charles Seymour, *What Really Happened at Paris* (New York, 1921).

[4] Bernard Baruch, *The Making of the Reparations and Economic Sections of the Treaty* (New York, 1920).

[5] Charles Homer Haskins and Robert Howard Lord, *Some Problems of the Peace Conference* (Cambridge, Mass., 1920).

[6] André Tardieu, *La Paix* (Paris, 1921); English translation, *The Truth about the Treaty* (Indianapolis, 1921).

The French journalists of the *bloc national* portrayed Clemenceau as a feeble old man who had allowed himself to be deluded into accepting illusory guaranties of national safety, regardless of the warnings of Foch and the sober counsels of Poincaré. The story cost Clemenceau the presidency of the Republic. The German nationalists expounded the theory that the revolutionary government had betrayed the nation by trusting naïvely in the hypocritical Wilson and his Fourteen Points. The story cost Erzberger his life. Italian writers depicted Orlando and Nitti as vain and impractical *renunciatori* yielding the vital interests of their nation to the demands of selfish and ungrateful allies. The story fed the political current which has since swept away democracy in Italy. In England John Maynard Keynes[7] led the chorus of Liberal criticism of the peace settlement in a brilliant polemic which incidentally gave the world a picture it has never forgotten of the sittings of the Council of Four. And nowhere was the effort to discredit the work of the national delegation to the Peace Conference more determined, more intransigeant, or more successful than in the United States, which alone among the participating nations disowned Wilson's work by refusing to ratify the Covenant. The hearings of the Senate Committee on Foreign Relations were patently conducted for the purpose of embarrassing the President rather than for the purpose of enlightening the Senate.[8] Not only in America but in other countries as well, Wilson was the hardest hit of all the leaders. He was held responsible for all disappointments. He was denounced as a man of absurd vanities, ignorant of European affairs, yet refusing to take advice, unskilled in the ways of diplomats, yet insisting on personal participation in the Conference, too stubborn, too

[7] John Maynard Keynes, *The Economic Consequences of the Peace* (New York and London, 1920).

[8] *Treaty of Peace with Germany: Hearings before the Committee on Foreign Relations, Sixty-eighth Congress, First Session, Senate Document 106* (Washington, 1919).

pliant, too hypocritical, too naïvely sincere. His fall left American foreign policy utterly confused, and American liberalism paralyzed for almost a decade.

These controversies quickly broke the seals of secrecy in every country. To defend the German Republic against the charge that it had too quickly disarmed in the expectation of a Wilson peace, the German chancellery published the minutes of the fateful ministerial councils of October, 1918, and the correspondence between the military and civil leaders, establishing in this publication that the responsibility for requesting an armistice lay with the military men.[9] Erzberger had already, in 1919, laid before the Reichstag a fragmentary report of the proceedings of the Armistice Commission relating to the successive renewals of the Armistice.[10]

To defend Clemenceau against his enemies of the *bloc national* Gabriel Terrail, writing under the pseudonym "Mermeix," published ministerial correspondence and excerpts from the minutes of the meetings of the Supreme War Council, the Council of Ten, and the Council of Four, and the Drafting Committee of the Peace Conference.[11] Tardieu also published a few of the papers which had been used by the French delegation, and so did Lucien Klotz, the now discredited finance minister, of whom Clemenceau is said to have remarked, "He is the only Jew I ever knew who understands absolutely nothing of finance." [12] The French ministry of foreign affairs published two Peace Conference memoranda of Marshal Foch relating to the problem of security and arguing in favor of the

[9] *Vorgeschichte des Waffenstillstandes* (Berlin, 1919); English translation by the Carnegie Endowment for International Peace, *Preliminary History of the Armistice* (New York, 1923).

[10] Waffenstillstandskommission, *Drucksache* (Berlin, 1919).

[11] Mermeix, *pseud.* (Gabriel Terrail), *Les négociations secrètes et les quatre armistices avec pièces justificatives* (Paris, 1921); *Le combat des trois* (Paris, 1921).

[12] Louis Lucien Klotz, *De la guerre à la paix, notes et souvenirs* (Paris, 1924).

military frontier of the Rhine.[13] The interview upon the subject given in later years by Marshal Foch to Raymond Recouly, published in the *New York Times* and now available as a chapter in a book of interviews, does not add materially to what was already known of the tension within the French delegation on the problem of security.[14]

In Italy the publication of diplomatic documents began in 1920 with a memorial volume to Count Vincenzo Macchi di Cellere, Italian ambassador at Washington during the war and the period of the Peace Conference, who had died suddenly in September, 1919, while Nitti was trying to make him the scapegoat for the failure of Italy's policy in the Adriatic. The volume of *Memorials and Testimonials*, published by his widow to defend his name, includes his diary during the period of the negotiations of the Adriatic question at the Peace Conference.[15] Francesco Nitti, whose name had come in 1922 to be the symbol in Italy for a policy of renunciation abroad and weakness at home, published in that year his first apologia, and followed it in later years with several others.[16] Nitti made it a point to leave his works undocumented. Although he was premier when the treaty was signed, his knowledge of the making of the Treaty of Versailles was only second-hand, for he had been out of the Italian ministry during the negotiations. To denounce Nitti is now a commonplace of political writing in Italy, but only one work has brought to this campaign any valuable documentary

---

[13] Ministère des Affaires Étrangères, *Documents diplomatiques: Documents relatifs à la sécurité* (Paris, 1922).

[14] *New York Times*, May 12, 1929; Raymond Recouly, *Le Maréchal Foch* (Paris, 1929).

[15] Justus, *V. Macchi di Cellere all'ambasciata di Washington, memorie e testimonianze* (Florence, 1920).

[16] Francesco Nitti, *Europa senza pace* (Florence, 1922). (There are twenty-two translations. The English translations are entitled *Peaceless Europe* [London, 1922] and *The Wreck of Europe* [Indianapolis, 1922].) The second of the series is *La decadenza dell' Europa: Le vie della ricostruzione* (Florence, 1923), English translation, *The Decadence of Europe* (London, 1923). The later volumes of this prolific writer have to do with the enforcement rather than the making of the peace.

material. This is a volume the sources for which were supplied by Vittorio Falorsi, who had been secretary to Count Macchi di Cellere in Washington, and who sought to defend both the memory of his chief and the policies of Sonnino by printing from documents in his possession.[17] The two themes that run through Falorsi's interpretation are, first, that the *renunciatori* (Nitti, Orlando, the *Corriera della Sera*, Salvemini) weakened Italy's hand at the Peace Conference, and, second, that the interest of the United States in the Adriatic settlement was economic not idealistic. Falorsi makes use of excerpts from the embassy's correspondence and the diary of the ambassador.

In 1922 Lloyd George, partly as a gesture of defense against such critics as Keynes, published the "Fontainebleau Memorandum" which he had given to the Peace Conference on March 25, 1919, a document in which it appears that British foreign policy breathes the very spirit of Liberalism.[18] Important among British writings on the Peace Conference is the last part of Wickham Steed's *Through Thirty Years*,[19] written from notes of interviews and from personal records made at the time, and composed without any polemic purpose toward either wing of the British delegation. Steed was the editor of the Paris edition of the *Daily Mail* during the Conference; his specialty was Central Europe, and his sympathy on broad matters of policy was with Wilson.

These random revelations and apologies, French, German, Italian, and British, were still too meager to furnish a basis for the criticism of the official history of the Peace Conference. Such a basis finally came to be supplied by the publication of American documents, printed in connection with the polemics which raged around the head of Woodrow Wilson.

[17] A. A. Bernardy and V. Falorsi, *La questione adriatica vista d'oltre Atlantico (1917–1919), ricordi e documenti* (Bologna, 1923).

[18] *Some Considerations for the Peace Conference before they finally draft their terms* (Cmd. 1614, London, 1922).

[19] Henry Wickham Steed, *Through Thirty Years, 1892–1922: A Personal Narrative* (London, 1924).

The champion who stepped forward to defend Wilson against his detractors was Ray Stannard Baker, who began by answering calumny with calumny and myth with myth. Then the time came when Baker was given access to the complete archives of American policy at the Peace Conference. He used this secret material more lavishly than any of his predecessors, and came thereby to create that theory of the Peace Conference which was at once the most dramatic, the most circumstantial, and the most heavily documented.

Baker is a man of warm human qualities; his contact with Wilson during the Conference was close; his loyalty to his chief was perfect and enduring. No one saw better than he how false were the judgments and stories which were crippling Wilson's work. In America the Senate Committee on Foreign Relations held hearings which were patently conducted for the purpose of discrediting the work of the American delegation. Public opinion was wavering; Wilson collapsed. A few weeks after Wilson's breakdown, in November, 1919, Baker published a small booklet as a campaign document to vindicate the President.[20] *What Wilson Did at Paris* was written from personal recollections, apparently upon a very slight documentary foundation, by the man who had been Wilson's press representative at Paris. It dramatized the story of the peace negotiations around Wilson's personality. It did the thing that Baker had longed to do in the critical months when he had helplessly watched public opinion recede from the Wilsonian cause, knowing that information in his possession might stem the tide if only he were permitted to release it.

The Peace Conference, as dramatized by Baker, was a conflict between the New, whereof the patent symbol was the Covenant of the League of Nations, and the Old, which was ever identified by its attachment to such ikons as "territorial guaranties," "economic concessions," or "strategic frontiers." The tactics

[20] Ray Stannard Baker, *What Wilson Did at Paris* (Garden City, N. Y., 1919).

of the New were tactics of investigation by experts, the tactics of the Old were tactics of barter and bluff. The New was disposed to favor the widest possible publicity; the Old thrived upon secrecy and concealment. And Wilson had gone to Paris as champion of the New, to encounter the enemy in his strongest citadel.

The first encounters had been triumphs for Wilson. He secured the acceptance of the principle that the Covenant must be an integral part of the treaty, and pressed forward the drafting of the Covenant with incredible speed. When attempts were made to divide the spoils of war, Wilson staved off the claims of the greedy ones.

Then the hostile forces gathered strength. There was a "slump in idealism." The enemy worked with diabolical precision for his evil ends. Wilson wished to introduce an atmosphere of security and confidence into the discussion of territorial and reparations questions by imposing upon Germany a definitive disarmament in a preliminary treaty of peace. He secured the acceptance of this principle by the Supreme Council on February 12, just before he sailed for America. As soon as Wilson's back was turned, the representatives of the Old began to undo his work. Balfour and Clemenceau decided to expand the plan for a preliminary peace to include not only the military and naval terms which Wilson had wished to see included, but also the principal territorial and reparations clauses—everything, in fact, except the League of Nations. It was a formidable plot to "sidetrack the League," but Wilson, returning to Paris in March, broke up the evil game with one bold gesture. He announced to the press that the decision to include the Covenant of the League of Nations in the treaty had not been altered. And so the plotters were foiled.

This "February Plot" is the central episode of Baker's 1919 pamphlet. It corresponds in Peace Conference history to the myth of the Potsdam Council in the history of July, 1914. And yet the scene of this episode was laid in exactly that part of the

Peace Conference story about which Baker had least immediate information. He had been in America with Wilson during the period in which the February Plot was alleged to have been concocted and the decisions to which he attributes such diabolical motives were made.

The story then tells how, after foiling the February Plot, Wilson struck another great blow by threatening to return to America early in April, but how the enemies in Washington so weakened him in Paris by demanding amendments to the Covenant that he had to make compromises as to the substance of the settlement in order to save the League. The conclusion to be drawn from this pamphlet was that Wilson was strong enough to defeat his opponents in Paris till the American Senate stabbed him in the back. Responsibility for injustices in the treaty lay with the Republicans.

A year after the publication of Baker's first booklet, Wilson committed his whole personal file of Peace Conference records to Baker's care. In the course of the year 1921, while Baker was studying these records, the controversy over Wilson's role at Paris was sharpened by the appearance of two volumes of reminiscences of Robert Lansing, who had never understood his chief, nor sympathized with his policies, nor forgiven him for incidents of personal friction.[21] Lansing tried to prove that if his advice had been followed Wilson would have kept out of trouble. Did some people object to the precedence Wilson gave to the drafting of the Covenant in the negotiations at Paris? Lansing would have included in the treaty only a resolution on the League of Nations, and left the drafting of the Covenant for a later day. Was the Senate frightened by the seriousness of the commitment implied in Article X? Lansing would not have included in the Covenant any such positive guaranty. The defense of Wilson came thus to involve an

[21] Robert Lansing, *The Peace Negotiations: A Personal Narrative* (Boston, 1921); *The Big Four and Others at the Peace Conference* (Boston, 1921).

attack not only upon the Republican party but also upon the Democratic secretary of state, and finally even upon Wilson's closest collaborator, Colonel House. This new stage of the controversy was reached with the publication of Baker's second work.

In the spring of 1922 Baker began to print in the *New York Times* the chapters of the new book he was compiling from Wilson's papers. The completed volumes appeared a year later as *Woodrow Wilson and the World Settlement.*[22] The new work made a tremendous impression on the world. It was translated and carefully studied in Europe. Edward Beneš said of it that to read it was like reading a Greek drama. It was copiously documented with materials from the minutes of the Council of Ten and the Council of Four. The work was trusted because it was known to be based upon an ample documentary foundation. There was, indeed, much new material in Baker's volumes—material drawn from the Wilson papers. But there was no new synthesis. There was an attempt to fix responsibilities for failure more precisely by developing the theory that Colonel House was too much given to compromise, that he had not fought hard enough for Wilson's principles. There were new and excellent chapters upon particular problems of the peace. But there was no new approach to the story of the Conference as a whole. It was still the gigantic battle of the New and the Old. The three-volume work was essentially an expanded and documented edition of the little booklet of 1919. The story of the February Plot was retained unchanged. Chapter xvii of *Woodrow Wilson and the World Settlement* follows almost word for word the text of chapter v of *What Wilson Did at Paris.* But the old chapter v had been written without documents and covered a period during which Baker had been absent from Paris. The documents were now used to give authenticity to a conclusion which had been reached

[22] Ray Stannard Baker, *Woodrow Wilson and the World Settlement,* 3 vols. (Garden City, N. Y., 1923).

without them. It was Baker's misfortune that this weakest chapter of his work, because of its very dramatic excellence, attracted a disproportionate amount of attention in a history which read like a Greek drama because it had been written like one.

Because of the bristling adequacy of his documentary citations and the lucidity of his exposition, Baker dominated the history of the Peace Conference for four years. But his was the kind of book that calls for a reply. The resentments harbored against Wilson in ex-enemy and ex-allied countries could hardly be dispelled by a drama in which Europe was given the villain's role to play. Even in the American camp Baker had stirred up new resentments by his criticisms of Colonel House. These necessary counterblasts have now appeared, one from Germany,[23] one from England,[24] and one from Colonel House.[25] These three works seem to gather into themselves all of a ten years' harvest of recrimination over responsibilities for the peace settlement. They furnish a starting point from which an irenic revision of the history of this period can proceed. They are themselves rich in important new material, and they happen to appear at a time when other sources of information are being opened with unprecedented abundance.

Nowak's *Versailles* was first published in Germany in 1927. As the title implies, it is not merely an account of the Peace Conference in Paris but also of the peace negotiations of Versailles. It is the first comprehensive story of the peace settlement which has given a due measure of attention to the affairs of the German delegation. To this part of the story Nowak brings a wealth of new and suggestive information gleaned from conversations with its principal members. He

[23] Karl Friedrich Nowak, *Versailles* (New York, 1929).
[24] Winston S. Churchill, *The Aftermath* (London and New York, 1929).
[25] Charles Seymour, *The Intimate Papers of Colonel House* (Boston, 1928), vol. III, "Into the World War"; vol. IV, "The Ending of the War."

describes the cross-currents of opposition within the German government which weakened the hand of the German delegation, even as party politics in America weakened Wilson's hand. Erzberger was the advocate of a policy of humility; he did not wish to raise the question of war-guilt or deny Germany's responsibility for the war lest the only result should be to exasperate the Allies; he proposed that Germany should freely offer to give up her colonies provided their value was counted in as payment on reparations. He had calculated the reparations liability at seven and one-half to nine billions, and the value of the colonies at nine billions. " 'We must give in completely,' he told the cabinet; 'if we give in completely, they will forgive us' " (p. 120). Brockdorff-Rantzau, on the other hand, proposed to stand proudly upon Germany's rights under the pre-Armistice agreement, and to insist that the Wilsonian basis of peace be realized to the letter. He wished, moreover, to raise the war-guilt question in the course of the peace negotiations, in order that his country might repudiate the charge of sole war responsibility. He regarded Erzberger as a "white-feather" politician, while Erzberger regarded him as an *enfant terrible*.

The principal contribution Nowak makes to our knowledge of the facts is in his history of the German delegation. For the rest he has drawn largely upon Baker for details, and upon his imagination for the explanations of motives. The details are not controlled by any close attention to chronology; he uses dates sparingly and often incorrectly, as when he places the Stockholm Conference or Balfour's mission to America in 1918 instead of 1917. But his explanations of motives are always copious. If Baker's work has the literary quality of a Greek drama, Nowak's has the tone of a "modern biography."

In drawing upon Baker for the story of the Paris side of the Conference, Nowak chooses what is already most dramatic in Baker and embroiders upon it. For instance, he increases the element of premeditation in the February Plot by asserting that Balfour on February 12 agreed to the plan for a preliminary military treaty with the mental reservation that everything could be changed as soon as Wilson left Paris (p. 73). He adds the circumstance that Lloyd George, in London, was instructed by his cabinet to carry out the obligations of the secret treaties, and hoped that "there was still time for the matter to be put through before the President's return" (pp. 91–92). It is then made to appear that Balfour's proposal of February 22 that the preliminary military treaty should cover also frontiers of Germany, reparations, war responsibility, and economic settlement was connected in some way with this wish to realize the secret treaties in Wilson's absence (p. 93). Actually, it happens that none of the points which Balfour proposed to include in the preliminaries of peace were covered by secret treaties to which Britain was a party. The consequence of this method of writing is, of course, an increase in the element of fantasy in Peace Conference history.

The book is none the less important because it is a new synthesis. It is written so vivaciously and presents the acts of the German delegation so sympathetically that the version may well become standard in Germany. It is a new scenario, in which some of the elements of Baker's plot are taken over in altered form. The hero of the tragedy is Brockdorff-Rantzau, not Wilson. The malignant atmosphere which poisons the hero's efforts is war-guilt, not the slump in idealism. Baker had described Brockdorff-Rantzau's conduct of the peace negotiations as tactless and incompetent: the Germans "never fully lived up to the opportunity accorded them by laying bare the real defects of the Allies' work of peace." [26] Nowak now returns the charge of incompetence upon Wilson and House. "Professor Wilson" was "a child in all European problems," [27] who "advanced into territory as strange to him as the mountains of

[26] Baker, *Woodrow Wilson and the World Settlement*, II, 505.
[27] Nowak, *Versailles*, p. 153.

the moon." [28] As for Colonel House, he "was a man who seldom grasped or appreciated what was said to him on political topics . . . his second-rate intelligence would never have passed muster in any position in even a minor State in Europe." [29] But the main issue of the conflict is still, in Nowak's account as in Baker's, the "realization" of certain "principles." And the pattern of the melodrama remains.

This withering estimate of Colonel House's character is simply an exaggerated deduction from the hints given in Baker's work. As if in rebuttal there appeared in 1928 the final two volumes of *The Intimate Papers of Colonel House* covering the years 1917–1919. Professor Seymour has not sought to write a history of the peace settlement; his purpose has been frankly biographical; his selection of papers is intended primarily to show the relation of Colonel House to the events rather than the relation of the events to each other. Although the editor has consulted Peace Conference records such as were used by Baker, he has printed only from personal letters and diaries. These personal papers constitute a more complete and authentic record of Wilson's war-time policies than any other account published to date. They are an indispensable documentation on the question of whether American diplomacy prepared adequately during the war for the peace, and whether the American delegation was competent in negotiating it. Some of the important points newly established or verified may here be brought in review.

A complete and circumstantial story of Balfour's mission to the United States in 1917 proves that immediately after America's entry into the war Balfour explained to House and to Wilson the terms of the principal secret treaties. Wilson's statement to the Senate Committee that he had not learned of the secret treaties prior to the Peace Conference is thus known to be inaccurate. Whether Wilson's denial of knowledge came

[28] Nowak, *Versailles*, p. 157.
[29] Nowak, *Versailles*, p. 156.

from an intent to deceive or a confused memory is a question which his biographer must answer.

The influence of America upon interallied policy did not begin with any attempt to modify war aims, but looked rather to the development of more effective agencies of belligerent coöperation. In the autumn of 1917, after the episode of the Pope's peace note, the serious preparation of detailed American war aims began with the setting up of the Inquiry, under the direction of Colonel House. In the winter of 1917, while the Inquiry was at work in America analyzing European problems, House went to Europe to sit in the highest councils of the Allies. Just as his influence in the spring had been thrown in the direction of the coördination of economic and financial agencies, so now he favored the highest degree of military coöperation. At this time, moreover, House raised the question of war aims. The fortunes of the Allies were then at low ebb; Italy had suffered at Caparetto, and Russia, under Soviet leadership, was withdrawing from the war. The slogan, "Peace without annexations or indemnities," was capturing the labor and socialist elements in Europe. A public declaration of definite and liberal war aims, so drawn as to attract wavering loyalties, seemed under the circumstances to be needed as a war measure, but House did not succeed in inducing the Allies to issue such a declaration.

It was because House had failed to secure from the Allies an agreed restatement of their war aims that Wilson issued a statement independently. For, under the pressure of the Russian move for peace, a statement was necessary. Because this statement was made by Wilson in January, 1918, as the speech of the Fourteen Points, and not by the Allies in December as a joint declaration, it became the tactical objective of American diplomacy to bring the Allies to adhere to Wilson's program.

This tactical objective was achieved, by a narrow margin, in the course of the pre-Armistice negotiations. For when House went to Europe in the autumn of 1918 he was in a stronger position than he had occupied a year before. American armed co-operation had been realized upon a colossal scale, and the Germans had already accepted the Fourteen Points as a basis of the Armistice and peace. By threatening that Wilson's moral influence might be turned against them if they held back, and by hinting that there might even be a separate peace with Germany, House brought the Entente statesmen to adopt the Wilson basis of peace, with two reservations, relating to reparations and the freedom of the seas. The papers of Colonel House offer conclusive evidence upon two previously controversial points: that America did not force the Armistice in despite of European military judgment, and that House did force the Entente governments to agree to the Wilsonian basis of peace.

The House Papers raise as many questions as they settle. They prove that American diplomacy was triumphant in November, 1918, but raise the question as to how the fruits of this diplomatic victory were lost. They set forth a full narrative of the diplomatic movements from the Armistice to Wilson's arrival in Paris—the first satisfactory account we have had of this period. They make it appear that House was several times overruled by Wilson in this period of critical decisions. House would have followed up the Armistice with an immediate preliminary peace, but Wilson thought it would be necessary to wait until the situation in Central Europe had cleared. House did not welcome Wilson's decision to attend the Peace Conference or to sit as a delegate, and at first Clemenceau was also embarrassed at this prospect. It was Wilson's decision that fixed upon Paris rather than Geneva as the seat of the Conference.

In the story of the Peace Conference itself the editor of the House Papers takes issue with the custodian of the Wilson papers on the broad question of whether or not it was necessary for the American delegation to make compromises. Baker asserts that House wished "to make peace quickly by giving the greedy ones all they want." Seymour writes that the impossibility of imposing an American peace was revealed after Wilson had left Paris in February.

It was only during the process of intensive study in February and March that the force of European convictions became plain. Then suddenly, and before the President's return, in every technical commission and in the Supreme Council, it was clear that no settlement at all could be reached unless everyone made concessions.[30]

Baker's theory is that House weakened Wilson unnecessarily; Seymour's theory is that Wilson ruined the peace with fruitless intransigeance. This is an issue clearly joined, and well worthy of further study. It can be tested by examining the proceedings of commissions and the records of the political currents of the time. It is to be hoped that the attention of historians will follow such an issue as this, and not pursue further the fate of the melodramatic February Plot.

For the sources now accessible put the story of the February Plot on the level of the Potsdam Council myth not only as regards melodramatic structure but also as regards its fictitiousness. Baker's thesis has been thrice tested by critics no less well equipped than he with secret documentary material, and each time it has been disproved. When Baker's articles first appeared in the *New York Times* in 1922 Lord Balfour asked an official of the British foreign office to check the story in the British archives. The resulting memorandum concludes with the judgment that there "is no trace of that 'intrigue' which Mr. Baker declares one can affirm with certainty to have existed." [31] Mr. David Hunter Miller reached the same conclusion in reviewing the evidence in his possession.[32] Professor Seymour goes even farther, accusing Baker of deliberately mutilating an essential document. "In order to maintain a sem-

[30] Seymour, *Intimate Papers of Colonel House*, IV, 379. (Hereafter cited as *House Papers*.)

[31] Seymour, *House Papers*, IV, 374.

[32] David Hunter Miller, *The Drafting of the Covenant*, 2 vols. (New York, 1928), I, 98.

blance of probability in his charges against the British, Mr. Baker has been forced to omit essential passages from the record." [33] Winston Churchill, writing with all this new evidence before his eyes, picks up the attack upon Baker and carries it on with gusto: "So the man to whom President Wilson entrusted all his most secret papers with leave to publish as he pleased . . . first garbles the record by omitting the vital sentence and then perverts it. . . ." [34] In his reply to Churchill, published in the *New York Times* of March 10, 1929, Baker admits with charming directness that at the time he wrote his book he may have been too close to the events to avoid intense feeling. "If I was, and if I did any injustice to the hard-beset men who played a part in the negotiations, I hope in the biography of Woodrow Wilson . . . to write with greater understanding."

There is danger that the completeness with which criticism has undermined the February Plot may result in an undervaluing of Baker's whole work. The issue at present is not whether the plot against Wilson was as Baker described it, but whether Baker used his materials honestly in trying to prove the existence of the plot. A question involving the scholarly integrity of the custodian of the Wilson papers is worth a thorough probing. And on this question the reviewer sides with Baker.

The case against Baker's honesty narrows down to the use of a single citation. Baker is trying to prove that the decision to make a preliminary *military* peace, which Wilson favored on February 12, was nullified by a resolution which Balfour introduced on February 22 requiring that territorial and economic clauses were also to be prepared for insertion in the peace preliminaries.

In order to test the fairness of Baker's quotation it is necessary to set in its context the passage of Wilson's speech which he is accused of mutilating. In the morning session of Febru-

[33] Seymour, *House Papers*, IV, 376.
[34] Churchill, *Aftermath*, p. 190.

ary 12, Clemenceau had argued against the proposed preliminary military treaty and in favor of including a reparation
clause in the new armistice terms on the ground that French
public opinion required definite settlements on the question of
compensations. "The Supreme War Council would meet again
in a fortnight or three weeks. By that time no one must be able
to say, 'the Associated Governments will not make up their
minds to give us that satisfaction to which we are entitled.' " In
the afternoon session Clemenceau had used a somewhat contra-
dictory argument against the preliminary military peace:
". . . he would not like to discuss a matter of such importance
in the absence of President Wilson." In replying to this last
of Clemenceau's arguments, Wilson said in effect that he would
give carte blanche to his delegates to negotiate the preliminary
military peace, and added that the discussion of boundaries and
reparations would also go on in his absence. Let Baker's excerpt
from Wilson's speech be compared with the authentic text:

BAKER'S VERSION [35]	AUTHENTIC VERSION [36]
Wilson had thus won his contentions. There was to be a preliminary treaty containing the military, naval, and air terms. This was to be worked out by a committee of experts while he was away in America. He said:	He had complete confidence in the views of his military advisers. If the military experts were to certify a certain figure as furnishing a margin of safety, he would not differ from them. The only other question was to decide whether this was the right time to act. On this point he was prepared to say yes. In another month's time, the attitude of Germany might be more uncompromising. If his plan were agreed on in principle, he would be prepared to go away and leave it to his colleagues to
"He had complete confidence in the views of his military advisers. . . .	
"He did not wish his absence to stop so important, essential and urgent a work as the preparation of a preliminary peace [*as to military, naval and air terms*]. He hoped to return by	

[35] Baker, *Woodrow Wilson*, I, 290. (Italics mine.)
[36] Miller, *Drafting of the Covenant*, II, 176. (Italics mine.)

the 13th or 15th of March, allowing himself only a week in America. . . .

"He had asked Colonel House to take his place while he was away."

decide whether the programme drafted by the technical advisers was the right one. He did not wish his absence to stop so important, essential and urgent a work as the preparation of a preliminary peace. He hoped to return by the 13th or 15th of March, allowing himself only a week in America. *But he did not wish that during his unavoidable absence, such questions as the territorial question and questions of compensation should be held up.* He had asked Colonel House to take his place while he was away.

Baker's condensation may be unskillful but is not dishonest. When Wilson said "preliminary peace" he meant "preliminary peace as to military, naval and air terms." Baker's bracketed phrase clarifies this meaning. And the omitted passage relating to "territorial questions and questions of compensation" was not an admission that the preliminary peace might contain other than military terms. On this particular point Seymour's judgment that Baker's addition and omissions "completely alter the sense of the original statement" is much too strong. And Churchill's charge that Baker has garbled and perverted the record is quite unreasonable.

It would hardly be worth while to devote so labored a discussion to the rise and fall of the story of the February Plot were it not that the episode marks a crisis in the study of Peace Conference history, and brings us to a parting of the ways. Are we to devote our energy to establishing or disproving this or that particular anecdote? Are we to follow clues to obscure secrets of motives before we have understood the circumstances of the acts which the motives are supposed to explain? Though Baker's good faith is not compromised, his dramatization is deflated; are we to set up new dramatizations in its place? The two opposed ways of writing about the Conference are exemplified in Miller's *Drafting of the Covenant* and Churchill's *Aftermath*.

Miller in his *Drafting of the Covenant* furnishes an example of the kind of study that will clarify real problems. He does not dramatize his story, nor oversimplify it. He has, indeed, a few scores to pay off. He lashes out at Lansing much as Seymour attacks Baker, and with about the same degree of unfairness in accusing Lansing of misusing documents. But he does not allow his quarrel to distract him from his main purpose. He goes step by step through the events of which he writes, explaining the reasons for each change in the successive drafts of the Covenant, and the circumstances attending each decision. The second volume consists entirely of documents, including the "Minutes of the League of Nations Commission." There is probably no one in the world who knows more of the detailed history of the drafting of the Covenant than Miller himself, and historians are fortunate that he has simply told what he knows without trying to press his facts into a philosophy of history. The League of Nations is for him a problem of finding a consensus of opinion and formulating it in writing. It is not a symbol of the New against the Old.

Whenever there must be a meeting of minds in the preparation of any agreement, there is one apparently universal rule which always has its influence; that rule is this: any definite detailed draft prepared in advance by one of the parties will to some extent appear in the final text, not only in principle but even in language. No matter how many differences of opinion may develop, no matter how much the various papers may be recast or amended, something of the beginning is left at the end. In the drafting of the Covenant of the League of Nations may be found very striking instances of this most interesting result of written words.[37]

[37] Miller, *Drafting of the Covenant*, I, 3.

This passage suggests to the historian that the spade work of the history of the Peace Conference is only beginning to be done. For we have before us the problem not only of the drafting of the Covenant but also of the making of every part of the settlement. How did this particular proposal, by modification and amendment and substitution, become combined with other proposals, and finally reach its place as a definitive decision or an item of the public law of the world? There are other projects and proposals that start on their way and are lost or killed or forgotten; let us also trace their obscure course. This is a task infinitely more difficult than filming the battle of the New against the Old or unraveling plots and conspiracies. But until this task is done, our most impressive interpretations of the Conference will be structures built on sand.

But it is difficult to resist the temptation to dramatize, to pick out the villains and the heroes, to elucidate motives without understanding circumstances, and to color the narrative with ethical judgments. The last man in the world to resist such a temptation would be that gifted *jongleur*, Winston Spencer Churchill.

Having the newly published House Papers and Miller's volumes before him, Winston Churchill concluded his series of memoirs on the world-crisis with a volume devoted to the war's aftermath, written in his usual brilliant style, and combining personal apology and fantasy with informative disclosure. There were three matters whereof Churchill's experience was immediate and of which his knowledge is comprehensive: the Russian entanglement, the Irish settlement, and the tragedy of Greek intervention in Asia Minor which led indirectly to the fall of the Lloyd George coalition. He paradoxically but almost convincingly explains his proposals for intervention in Russia in 1919 as a policy calculated to hasten the end of British commitments in that country and to facilitate demobilization. His interest in the Russian affair derived from his position as minister of war. In telling the story of the Irish settlement, in which his role as a British delegate to the conference with the Irish leaders was of the first importance, he has no apologies to make, and consequently is in a position to give full rein to his narrative powers. In these chapters is included some of Churchill's correspondence with Michael Collins and Sir James Craig, as well as several cabinet papers. The story of the Eastern catastrophe is an attack upon Lord Curzon, whom Churchill blames for failing to act decisively in the Near East. The account of the Armistice and Peace Conference is the part of the book which has excited greatest attention, but is actually the weakest and least important. For Churchill's knowledge of the Conference was not immediate; in preparing these chapters he has depended much upon Baker and House. And that which he presents is rather an expression of an attitude than a disclosure of information.

His attitude is that of an apologist for British policy, which he defends from the khaki election to the signing of the peace. Against Ray Stannard Baker he uses his unparalleled power of invective, and yet he imitates Baker's worst fault—the use of speculative surmises as to motives when he does not fully understand circumstances.

The French plan did not at all commend itself to Mr. Wilson. It thrust on one side all the pictures of the peace conference which his imagination had painted. He did not wish to come to speedy terms with his European allies; he saw himself for a prolonged period at the summit of the world, chastening the Allies, chastising the Germans, and generally giving laws to mankind [p. 112].

With Colonel House Churchill finds that he has much in common. Like House he believes that a peace should have been made quickly, in November, although his reasons for this opinion are different. House was impressed with the fact that American influence in the councils of the Allies stood higher in November than at any later time; Churchill has in mind the rapid loss of influence by statesmen over their own peoples.

All these writers seem to be conscious of some change in the atmosphere: Baker calls it the "slump in idealism"; House thinks of it as a waning of American prestige, and Churchill as the "broken spell of power."

The one constructive contribution to Peace Conference history made by Churchill is his division of the period into "three well-marked phases":

First, the Wilson period, or the period of Commissions and of the Council of Ten, culminating in the drafting of the Covenant of the League of Nations. This lasted for a month, from the first meeting of the Council of Ten on January 14th [*sic*] down to the first return of President Wilson to America on February 16. Secondly, the Balfour period, when President Wilson had returned to Washington and Lloyd George to London, and when M. Clemenceau was prostrated by the bullet of an assassin. In this period Mr. Balfour, in full accord with Mr. Lloyd George, induced the Commissions to abridge and terminate their ever-spreading labours by March 8 and concentrated all attention upon the actual work of making peace. Thirdly, the Triumvirate period, when the main issues were fought out by Lloyd George, Clemenceau and Wilson in the Council of Four and finally alone together. This Triumvirate, after tense daily discussions lasting for more than two months, framed the preliminaries of peace . . . [p. 140].

Churchill's analysis is valuable because it calls attention to the fundamental importance of questions of procedure at the Conference. Was the treaty to be drawn by commissions of experts who would find facts or by the great political magnates who would by mutual concession reach agreement on their divergent interests? Baker would have had the commissions of experts write the treaty; House would have had them prepare questions for decision by the chief delegates; Churchill would have had them wait until the chief delegates had made their decisions, and then give these decisions detailed application. A case in point is the King-Crane Commission on the Near East, to which the British and French refused to appoint representatives. Churchill argues that such a commission at such a time was sure to do more harm than good because it would stir up unrest in the region it was studying; from his point of view a commission of inquiry is a simple household remedy used in postponing decision upon some embarrassing problem of domestic politics, and is not suited to a situation which demands prompt action.

The procedure of the Conference, like the text of the treaty, can be subjected to scholarly study. Churchill's hypothesis that the commissions did not aid materially in drawing up the final instrument can be checked without resort to ethical speculation or *ad hoc* philosophies of history. It would have been quite misleading to begin a scholarly study of the Peace Conference by trying to test the hypotheses of Baker's book, but with Miller and Seymour and Churchill before us, we have something to work upon.

And, fortunately, at this very time there are being opened up new sources of information which will make it possible to pursue the study of the Peace Conference in sound fashion. Among these new sources, first place must be given to the *Diary* privately printed by David Hunter Miller in a limited edition of forty copies, and distributed by the Carnegie Endowment for International Peace to a number of libraries in Europe and America.[38]

The small diary in which Mr. Miller recorded, at the rate of several hundred words a day, his activities and experiences as legal adviser to the American Commission to Negotiate Peace is here supplemented by twenty great volumes of documents, comprising whatever important Peace Conference material happened to remain in Mr. Miller's files after his work in the Conference was completed. Included among these printed documents are the minutes of all but the first seven sessions of the Council of Ten, and complete minutes of five of the Peace Conference commissions (namely, those on the League of Nations, International Régime of Ports, Waterways and Railways, New

[38] David Hunter Miller, *My Diary at the Conference of Paris, with Documents,* 20 vols. and maps (privately printed, 1928). [See note 3, p. 97.]

States, Belgium and Denmark, Ukrainian-Polish Armistice).
More than a thousand miscellaneous letters, memorandums,
and reports of committees or commissions serve to give an in-
sight into the character of the day-to-day work of the American delegates, and to throw new light upon the making of a
number of the important decisions of the Conference. Of espe-
cial interest and value is a volume of *Annotations* upon the
Treaty of Versailles, made in the autumn of 1919 from the
official records of the Conference by some of the American
experts. The *Annotations* give an account of the drafting of
the treaty, article by article, showing by means of excerpts from
the pertinent minutes of councils and commissions the origin
and history of every item. Churchill's guess as to the unim-
portance of the work of the commissions is not sustained by this
document, which traces most of the treaty articles back to a
report from some commission.

The documents have been ably edited, and conveniently indexed. Mr. Miller printed everything in his file which issued
from the Peace Conference, or which constituted a step in the
decision of a claim. The propaganda material distributed by the
delegations of the smaller powers was not reprinted except
in a few cases. A fairly complete collection of the latter type of
material is to be found, however, in the Hoover War Library.
The matters with which Miller was most intimately concerned
were, first, the League of Nations, then the subject of international communications and transit, the economic settlement,
and the minorities treaties. Upon all these matters his files are
copious. The collection of documents on the League of Nations
is much more extensive than the selection which he printed in
the second volume of *The Drafting of the Covenant*.

The Miller Diary is to the history of the Peace Conference
what the so-called "Kautsky Documents" were to the history of
the outbreak of the war; a collection of documents is given to
us just as they happened to come into the hands of one of the
parties to the business. It is raw material which lends itself to

any use, and constitutes therefore not only a great opportunity but also a great temptation.

For if anyone seeks to make use of this material to prove or disprove some Sherlock Holmes theory of the Conference, to eulogize or vilify some statesman, or to construct some new fantasy of Peace Conference history, he will find in the *Diary* and the documents ample material for his purpose. If he is looking for clues to obscure plots and counterplots, there are such items as this:

March 11. . . . Wiseman [a member of the British Delegation] spoke about the Americans who had recently come to Paris and were saying that the Republican Party was the real friend of Europe and that the British and French ought to get together with their leaders and compel the President to do what the British and French wanted.[39]

If he is seeking to sustain the view that the American delegates stood for the new way of doing international business, there is this outburst of Colonel House to Lord Robert Cecil. Cecil was trading British support of the Monroe Doctrine amendment to the Covenant for an assurance that the United States would not outbuild the British navy. He thought that the letter he had received was not strong enough. House then flew at him with this rebuke:

April 10. . . . Colonel House told Cecil that the two questions of the insertion of the Monroe Doctrine clause and the naval program had nothing to do with each other and that he (Colonel House) would take the position that he had taken in everything over here; that the United States was not going to bargain but was going to take the position it believed to be right; these were the instructions he had given whenever the question of bargaining had been brought up; that he did not want the letter on the Naval program back because it represented the policy of the United States; that the American amendment on the Monroe Doctrine would be presented at to-night's session, and the British could oppose it if they saw fit.[40]

[39] Miller, *My Diary at the Conference of Paris*, I, 163.
[40] Miller, *Diary*, I, 235.

Or again, if the reader is seeking for evidence wherewith to rebut the charge that Colonel House was a mild man, forever compromising, here is an entry of April 11:

> Colonel House said that . . . his plan was to ride over them regardless of what they did . . . and during the meeting when I said to Colonel House "I think they will withdraw their objections" he said that they could go to hell seven thousand feet deep, and he was going to put it thru the way it was.[41]

And if one were trying to establish some thesis about American imperialism in the Conference, what more useful document could one ask than this, sent by the state department to the American Commission to Negotiate Peace, May 21, 1919:

> American oil interests are seriously considering examination of Mesopotamia and Palestine with a view of acquiring oil territory. Will such activities meet approval American Government and will conditions of treaty be such as to permit American companies to enter that territory under terms of equality as compared with foreign companies in their relations to their respective governments. . . . People having this matter under consideration are not connected in any way with the Standard Oil Group.[42]

It is to be hoped, however, that Miller's material will be used in another way: that students will seek to unravel in detail the various problems of the settlement, that they will trace the course of some negotiation doggedly from beginning to end, as Miller himself did in his *Drafting of the Covenant*. For such tasks as this the Miller Diary will be of inestimable value— but it will still be insufficient. It multiplies many-fold our stock of published source material on the Peace Conference, and yet it supplies only a tithe of what must be brought to light before our documentation on the war's aftermath approaches the completeness of our documentation on its origin. That the Miller Diary fills twenty volumes, where the "Kautsky Docu-

[41] Miller, *Diary*, I, 242.
[42] Miller, *Diary*, IX, 459.

ments" (in the English edition) filled one, is less than an index
of the greater complexity of the historical problems of the
Peace Conference period. To bring together an adequate political record of the two hundred and twenty-nine days from
the Armistice to the signing of the peace will be more than
twenty times as difficult as to collect the records of the fourteen
days preceding the outbreak of the war.

Fortunately, we have before us the prospect of further addi-
tions to our documentation. The appearance of the Miller Diary
coincides with the release by the Hoover War Library of some
information previously kept secret, and the announcement that
the Yale University Library is soon to render its unpublished
sources accessible to scholars. The Hoover War Library began
to build up its Peace Conference archives even while the Conference was in session.[43] Professor E. D. Adams secured from
each delegation in Paris a file of the propaganda material it was
distributing to the public, together with a set of the memorandums it had presented to the Peace Conference. This valuable collection of authentic delegation propaganda, a catalogue
of which is available,[44] has been supplemented by records of the
proceedings of some of the organs of the Peace Conference.
In the latter class may be mentioned the minutes and records of
the Supreme Economic Council, the minutes of the Peace Conference Commission on the Reparation of War Damage, and
the documents of the Inter-allied Rhineland Commission. Each
year will see the release of additional materials in the Hoover
War Library as the periods of restriction fixed by donors expire.
Then in 1930 or 1931, when the new library building at Yale
is completed, the important collection of unpublished materials
which has been gathered around the nucleus of the House

---

[43] Ephraim Douglass Adams, *The Hoover War Collections at Stanford
University: A Report and an Analysis* (Stanford University, Calif., 1921).
[44] *Hoover War Library Publication*, "Bibliographical Series," No. 1,
*A Catalogue of Paris Peace Conference Delegation Propaganda in the
Hoover War Library* (Stanford University, Calif., 1926).

Papers will be opened for use, although still subject to restriction. Professor Seymour writes of this collection:

Colonel House as well as the others who have given us documents has placed restrictions on the use of such of these papers as have an intimate personal character, and the publication of which might touch the feelings of persons still living. In the case of Colonel House, this is a twenty-five year limit. As regards the use of the mass of the material after 1931, discretionary authority is left to the Curator.

Here and there in other places there will be found stray Peace Conference documents. The New York Public Library possesses photostat copies of the minutes of the Commission on Greek Territorial Claims and the Commission on Yugoslav and Rumanian Territorial Claims. The *Report and Minutes of the Commission on International Labour Legislation* was published *in extenso* in English by the Italian government.[45] The complete minutes of the Commission on the League of Nations are to be found not only in the Miller Diary but also in the second volume of *The Drafting of the Covenant*.

The present situation as regards the accessibility of Peace Conference documents can then be summed up somewhat as follows: Of the two principal councils, the Council of Ten and the Council of Four, we have a nearly complete record of the former and a fragmentary record of the latter, the fragments being scattered through Baker's *Woodrow Wilson and the World Settlement*, Terrail's *Le Combat des Trois*, and the Miller Diary. Of the delegations to the Conference, numbering in the neighborhood of fifty, we have materials from nearly all. Of the commissions and committees of the Conference, of which there were more than fifty, we have the records of about a dozen, without taking into account the collection of material at Yale.

[45] Ufficio di Segretaria per l'Italia della Organizzazione Permanente del Lavoro nella Società delle Nazione. *Lavori e Studi preparatori*, "Serie B," N. 6 bis, *Report and Minutes of the Commission on International Labour Legislation, Peace Conference, Paris, 1919* (Rome, 1921).

The total amount of material is impressive, but there are gaps, even where the documentation could be expected to be most complete. For instance, the Miller Diary includes a dozen documents in amendment and criticism of a certain French plan, January 8, 1919, for the procedure of the Conference. Miller devoted much time to the study of this project. But the original document is missing from his papers, and is nowhere accessible save for a fragment printed by Tardieu. Again, it would be expected that Colonel House's papers would include all the most important material relating to the preparatory negotiations of November, 1918, for House was then Wilson's representative in Europe, and it was at that time, he believed, that he could have brought about a preliminary peace had he been authorized to do so. But it seems that one of the most essential documents of this period is lacking from the House collection, and has come to light in the Miller Diary. This is the French "Project for Peace," given to Colonel House on November 15. Professor Seymour naturally thought that the project of November 15 was the same as the project transmitted to Lansing on November 29, but actually the two drafts differ in a way that is vital in connection with Colonel House's theory that a preliminary peace on American principles could have been negotiated in November.[46]

For the document which Professor Seymour thought was given to House on November 15 accepts the Fourteen Points as the basis of peace, whereas the document actually given to House on that date proposes another basis:

Finally the Congress should adopt a basis of discussion. . . . One single basis seems to exist at the present time; it is the solidary declaration of the Allies upon their war aims, formulated January 10th 1917 in answer to the question of President Wilson, but it is rather a programme than a basis of negotiations.

[46] Seymour, *House Papers*, IV, 234; Baker, *Woodrow Wilson*, III, 56–63; Miller, *Diary*, vol. II, Document 4.

Errors of this kind are of course unavoidable where archives are incomplete. Even the archives of the State Department, the writer has reason to believe, lack complete documentation on the Peace Conference. The only remedy for this situation is to begin early enough such an assiduous search for information as has been carried on by the historians of the *Kriegsschuldfrage*.

If the historians of the Peace Conference profit by the mistakes as well as by the achievements of those who have given their efforts to the study of the outbreak of the war, the question of responsibilities will be kept in the background until the more prosaic study of procedure and drafting has been accomplished, and the environment of the Conference will be thought of in terms of social psychology, not in terms of ethics. Instead of depicting heroes and villains, they will trace projects and amendments; instead of speaking of idealism and justice, they will speak of public opinion. In this way the problem of the Peace Conference can be kept within the reach of sound historical method.

III

New Light on the Paris Peace Conference *

FROM THE ARMISTICE TO THE ORGANIZATION OF THE PEACE CONFERENCE

The statecraft of the authors of the Paris peace settlement is in these days subjected to a double scrutiny. Newly accessible documents are fixing individual and national responsibilities in the making of the treaties, while events are relentlessly exposing the transience or confirming the permanence of the various parts of the treaties themselves. The situation places upon historical scholarship a double responsibility: to make a timely contribution to an understanding of the texts which are today the fundamental public law of the world, and yet to avoid the danger of becoming engulfed in the polemics of treaty revision.

At the root of the question of the stability of the Paris settlement lies the historical problem of the original consensus out of which it arose. What parts of these treaties which are today the juridical basis of international relations represent a fair and free consensus of the parties which signed them? How were the innumerable variant interests brought to agreement upon a common text? What elements of consent, of compromise or coercion entered into the making of each detail of the settlement? By what difficult and treacherous courses did the

* Reprinted by permission from the *Political Science Quarterly*, Academy of Political Science, New York City, Volume 46, No. 3, pp. 335–361, and No. 4, pp. 509–547.

negotiators move from agreement on general principles to the acceptance of concrete propositions?

Historical scholarship is far from being ready to answer these questions. The writing of the history of the Peace Conference is just entering the monographic stage. Only two Sections of the Treaty of Versailles—those relating to Slesvig [1] and to the Covenant [2]—have been favored with adequate monographic studies of their origin and drafting. Professor Shotwell has under way a similar study of the drafting of the Labor Section of the Treaty. Another line of investigation, also undeveloped, is suggested by the work of Professor Bernadotte Schmitt on the origins of the war. Here a great literature of research and controversy had narrowed down the historiographical problem of war origins to a few vital issues, upon which Professor Schmitt was able to take oral testimony from some of the surviving principals of the crisis of 1914. If full use is to be made of the possibility of taking testimony from living witnesses of the Paris Peace Conference, there must first be a combing out of the problem of the Peace Conference as a whole, and a formulating of its most important historiographical issues. It is here that the generosity of Mr. David Hunter Miller,[3] the enterprise of M. de Lapradelle of the Sorbonne,[4]

[1] André Tardieu and F. de Jessen, *Le Slesvig et la paix* (Paris 1928). A Danish edition published by Slesvigsk Forlag (Copenhagen and Flensborg) prints in full some Danish texts of which the French edition prints summaries only.

[2] David Hunter Miller, *The Drafting of the Covenant*, 2 vols. (New York, 1928).

[3] David Hunter Miller, *My Diary at the Conference of Paris, with Documents*, 20 vols. and maps (privately printed, 1928). For a review of the extent of present documentation on the Peace Conference see Robert C. Binkley, "Ten Years of Peace Conference History" in *Journal of Modern History*, I (December, 1929) 607–629. The Miller Diary was printed in an edition of forty copies, and is accessible in the following American institutions: Carnegie Endowment for International Peace, Department of State, Library of Congress, University of California, University of Chicago, Columbia University, Harvard University, University of Michigan, New York Public Library, University of North Carolina,

and the careful stewardship of the Hoover War Library and the Yale University Library have their greatest immediate value. They do not provide at present a documentation adequate for the thorough monographic treatment of the different problems of the Peace Conference, but they do invite the drawing up of tentative conclusions which should lead to the production of more documents and to the taking of more testimony.

If the making of the peace settlement be studied without commitment to any doctrinal system and envisaged without special interest in any cause, the historical problem takes form as a problem of procedure. In what sequence were the questions to be settled, among what parties, and upon what principles? These are the procedural questions of agenda, membership and principles of settlement, and the whole history of the Conference is included in them.

The example of the Armistice negotiations suggested that the approach to permanent peace should be accomplished in four steps. The Armistice conventions had ended the fighting and established general principles; a series of preliminary treaties could then settle concrete essentials, a general peace treaty could make the definitive settlement of details, and then an even more general agreement, including neutrals with the ex-belligerents, could specify the plan of a League of Nations to "organize the peace." This was the agenda which seemed natural in November, but it turned out that there were to be no preliminary peace treaties, no general treaty and no separate conference to organize the peace. Instead of this sequence there

---

Princeton University, Stanford University (Hoover War Library), Yale University. Three additional sets are available as loan copies in the Libraries of the University of California, University of Chicago and Columbia University, to be loaned to other universities.

[4] *Documentation internationale, Paix de Versailles,* 12 vols., of which five have been published, including the stenographic minutes of the Commission on International Ports, Waterways and Railways, and the minutes of the Commission on the Responsibilities of the Authors of the War and Sanctions. [The remaining seven volumes have since been published.]

were five treaties, each definitive, and each including the Covenant of the League.

Among what parties were the negotiations to take place? At what stage were the smaller allies to enter effectively into the discussion of the settlement, and what was to be the form of the discussion with the enemy? The difference between a negotiated peace and a dictated peace was a procedural difference, defined by the amount of elasticity still remaining in the Conference decision at the time the enemy delegates entered the discussion.

Upon what principles was the settlement to be made? The pre-Armistice correspondence had created a contractual basis of peace in the body of Wilsonian texts which required to be elucidated and applied. The fact of the victory had brought into existence other contractual or quasi-contractual principles: the commitments of the Allies to each other through their secret treaties, and the commitments of the Allied statesmen to their peoples through their declarations of war aims. There was the possibility that an appeal might be made to the bare right of conquest. There was also the possibility that the peace terms might be drawn up and justified on the principle that the enemy was responsible for the war and must therefore suffer the consequences. These various principles of peace have been the subject of much polemic writing. It is fortunately unnecessary to discuss their relative ethical standing, for the essential significance of the Fourteen Points as a basis of peace was not their ethical quality but their contractual character. Because these principles had been agreed upon by victor and vanquished, every ostensible departure from them created an element of instability in the final peace. Therefore the historian is well advised to scrutinize the peace negotiations at every point to see how far they were controlled by conscious adherence to Wilsonian principles, and to discover at what points these principles were challenged, ignored or abandoned.

It has been a weakness in interpreting the history of the

Peace Conference to assume that the opposition of one nation
to another in the field of principles was clearly defined. The
more the negotiations are studied in detail, the more it appears
that each of the Great Powers came to Paris with a program
of contradictions. American policy was at once most insistent
upon international organization and most jealous of infringe-
ments on sovereignty; French policy was torn by two contrary
loyalties, on the one hand to the principle of the right of self-
determination, and on the other hand to a Rhineland security
plan in conflict with that right; the British were interested in
creating maximum stability in Europe, but were also committed to a reparations policy which could only mean the
negation of stability; the Italians were involved both in a
pro-Slav Mazzinist policy of national self-determination and
an anti-Slav Treaty of London policy which violated the
principle of nationality; the Japanese opposed in the Commission on International Labor legislation that principle of
equality of treatment which they sponsored so dramatically
in the Commission on the League of Nations.

The period in which the procedure of the Conference was
in its most fluid state was of course the preparatory period,
prior to the formal meetings of the delegates. Almost a
third of the interval between the signing of the Armistice
and the signing of the Peace of Versailles was occupied in
these preparations. And yet the histories of the peace settlement have neglected it because of the lack of definite information. Till 1928 there were only two published documents to
mark the evolution of plans for the Peace Conference during
these ten weeks.[5] Then came the House Papers which served
admirably to expand the history of the first three weeks following the Armistice, but failed in the time of the London Confer-

[5] "French Plan of Procedure" in Baker, *Woodrow Wilson and the
World Settlement*, 3 vols. (Garden City, N. Y., 1923), III, 56–63. Tardieu
published a part of his "Plan des premières conversations" in *La Paix*
(Paris, 1921), pp. 98–100, English edition, *The Truth about the Treaty*
(Indianapolis, 1921), pp. 88–91.

ence (December 2–3, 1918) when the Colonel lost touch with events because of his illness.[6] The Miller Diary now contributes a score of new texts on the evolution of Peace Conference plans. Most of these texts are illustrative of a French initiative, and present a French point of view. If other Powers were equally fertile in their preparatory labors, the documents at present available do not disclose their activities.

With every reservation as to the inadequacy of present documentation, the preparation of the Peace Conference can be described in three stages, each marked by the character of the issue under discussion. In November a series of French drafts were circulated which sought to supplant or supplement the Wilsonian principles of peace with other principles, and to bring all French war aims under a formula which the Conference could be persuaded to accept. It was at this time that the principle of war responsibility entered the dossier of the Peace Conference. In December, after the meeting of the London Conference, attention shifted to the question of the membership in the Peace Conference, and a drift toward the exclusion of the vanquished from effective participation in the settlement made itself felt. After Wilson's arrival in the middle of December the chief issue was the question of agenda, that is to say, the place that the organizing of the League of Nations would have in the sequence of subjects to be considered by the Conference.

THE NOVEMBER PLAN AND THE QUESTION OF THE PRINCIPLES OF THE PEACE

The documentary record of the development of the plans for the Peace Conference begins with a French draft of November 15, 1918, and ends with the Rules adopted by the first Plenary Session of the Conference, January 18, 1919. The Rules were simply an amended fragment of the November

[6] Charles Seymour, *The Intimate Papers of Colonel House*, vol. IV. (Hereafter cited as *House Papers*.)

draft. Three variants of this draft are accessible, the original of November 15, a first revision of November 21, and a version sent to Washington November 29.[7] These drafts necessarily presented a point of view upon agenda and membership as well as upon the principles of the peace, but their most distinctive contribution to the preparation of the Conference was their formulation of principles.

As to the agenda, the November drafts presented the view that was held everywhere at the time. There would be a preliminary peace dictated by the Powers which had just dictated the Armistice. Clemenceau told House that this would take about three weeks' time. After making this preliminary treaty, the Powers would organize a Peace Congress to include all the lesser allies and the enemy states. The Peace Congress would first "settle the war" and then, expanded by the inclusion of neutrals, "organize the peace." Clemenceau thought the sessions of the Congress would last four months.[8] Germans and Allies were both thinking in terms of this procedure for quick preliminary peace. Colonel House thought that it could have been drafted at that time without difficulty.[9] The German Govern-

[7] Draft of November 15 in Miller, *Diary*, vol. II, Document No. 5; revision of November 21, Miller, *Diary*, Document No. 4; revision of November 29, in Baker, *Woodrow Wilson*, III, 56–63.

[8] Summarized from the November draft, Miller, *Diary*, vol. II, Document No. 5. "Provision will have to be made for a first unofficial examination by the Great Powers (Gt. Britain, France, Italy, the United States) of the great questions to be discussed, examination which will lead to the preparation between them of the Preliminaries of Peace and the working mechanism of the Congress of Peace." p. 21. ". . . The Prime Ministers and the Ministers of Foreign Affairs of the Four Great Powers [shall] meet previously at Versailles to settle between them the affairs which the Congress shall have to deal with (that is to say, the Preliminaries of Peace) and the order in which they shall be discussed, as well as the conditions of the sittings of the Congress and its operation." p. 23. Clemenceau's estimates of the time required were made in a conversation with House, November 14, *House Papers*, IV, 213.

[9] A memorandum printed in *House Papers*, IV, 202–203, describes the putative peace terms under this procedure: "As to the armies and navies of the Central Powers, the terms of the Armistice left little to add to the

ment asked five times during the first month of the Armistice that negotiations for the preliminaries be started. Said Erzberger to Foch on December 13, "The only purpose of the armistice is to make a preliminary peace possible." [10] Thereupon Marshal Foch inserted a clause in the renewal convention extending the period of the Armistice "to the conclusion of a preliminary peace, provided the Allied Governments approve." [11] For the Marshal himself, as he has since testified, also favored the speedy conclusion of preliminaries. He thought prompt action necessary for the realization of French war aims on the Rhine. He complained that

Those whose duty it was to draw up the Peace set to work with all imaginable slowness . . . the delay was to cost France dear. The questions of most import to us, reparations and security, became increasingly difficult to settle favorably.[12]

It is curious that each party should look back upon a reputed halcyon period in which the other would have made all the concessions, and that each should regard the failure to negotiate a quick peace as the loss of a golden opportunity. But the theory of an interallied honeymoon in November is not sustained by the records of the peace projects of that date. The French preparatory documents indicate a fundamental opposition to American policies on the one hand, and Italian on the other. The French case was developed in these November drafts chiefly in the discussion of principles.

---

preliminary peace. A fixed sum should have been named for reparations, a just sum and one possible to pay. The boundaries might have been drawn with a broad sweep, with provision for later adjustments. A general but specific commitment regarding an association of nations for the maintenance of peace should then have been made; and then adjournment."

[10] Deutsche Waffenstillstandskommission. *Drucksache*, 1–12, p. 110.

[11] Deutsche Waffenstillstandskommission. *Drucksache*, 1–12, p. 113. (This approval was not given; the clause remained a dead letter till February.)

[12] Raymond Recouly, *Foch. My Conversations with the Marshal* (New York, 1929), p. 161.

The November draft was put together in six sections. The first two, "Precedents" and "Observations," were merely historical. The third, "Draft Rules," was the section which was later adopted, in a modified form, as the "Rules" of the Conference. The fourth section, on representation, made it clear that the enemy powers would come to the general Peace Congress. The fifth section, on "Directing Principles," attacked the Italian claims at the Conference by proposing the denunciation of secret treaties,[13] and recommending that "the right of peoples to decide their own destinies by free and secret vote" be adopted as a basis for territorial settlements. The sixth section, on "Bases of Negotiations," attacked the sufficiency of Wilsonian principles as a guide to the peacemakers, and suggested alternative principles and an alternative order of business. The language in this regard was explicit:

Nor can the fourteen propositions of President Wilson be taken as a point of departure, for they are principles of public law by which the negotiations may be guided, but which have not the concrete character which is essential to attain the settlement of concrete provisions. . . .

The only basis actually existing is the solidary declaration of the Allies upon their war aims, formulated January 10, 1917, in reply to the request of President Wilson, but it is rather a program than a basis of negotiations.[14]

These "directing principles" and "bases of settlement" were not rigorously adhered to throughout the whole draft. Despite the objection to Wilson's principles, the items of business on the proposed agenda were tagged with numbers taken from the

[13] The formula demands "the release from the treaties" by States which "from the fact of their admission to the Congress will renounce their use." As to Italy, "should she not adhere thereto, it is difficult to see how she could be admitted to the discussion; Italy . . . would be allowed to discuss the claims of others only if she should permit the discussion of her own claims." Miller, *Diary*, vol. II, Documents Nos. 4, 5, pp. 14, 22–23.

[14] Miller, *Diary*, vol. II, Documents Nos. 4, 13, 14, pp. 14, 81, 84; also I, 9.

Fourteen Points; despite the attack upon the Treaty of London and the setting up of the principle of nationalities in its stead, there was a reservation that the rights of peoples to decide their own destinies might be modified in favor of "a certain homogeneousness of the states," and the three provinces of the London Treaty bargain, Tyrol, Istria and Dalmatia, were named as illustrations. The documents do not suggest an intent to thwart Italy and America at all costs. The French *arrière pensée* seems rather to have been the wish to shift the Peace Congress to principles which could be used to cover a strong Rhineland policy. France could afford to abandon secret treaties, for the only secret treaty that supported her claims on the Rhine was a dead letter as long as the Soviets ruled Russia; she was committed to opposition to Wilson's Fourteen Points because they halted her at the frontier of 1870.

Colonel House cabled a summary of this draft to Washington, and by a curious oversight omitted the essential paragraph which attacked the foundation of the American case.[15] It is doubtful whether he scrutinized documents or followed events with sufficient thoroughness to give him an understanding of the width of the gulf which separated French from American war aims at that time.

For the war aims of France were reaffirmed in November by bodies representing the overwhelming preponderance of French political power. The position of the military men and the extreme Right was stated by Foch in his memorandum of November 27, which demanded the incorporation of the Rhineland populations in the French military system.[16] The position of the Left, and hence of the whole Chamber, was defined on November 24 in a meeting of the Executive Committee of the Radical Party. The party adopted as its peace program "the

[15] *Ibid.*
[16] *Ministère des Affaires Étrangères. Documents diplomatiques relatifs à la sécurité.* Jacques Bardoux wrote this note under Foch's dictation at Senlis; see Bardoux, *La Bataille diplomatique pour la paix française,* p. 55.

complete repayment of all the costs of the war," the annexation
of the Saar, and the permanent policing of the Rhineland by an
international force.[17] With the Radical Party occupying this
ground, no possible majority of the Chamber could have been
rallied to anything less, a fact attested in the vote of the
Commission on Foreign Affairs on December 2.[18] The views
of the Foreign Office were expressed in a mysterious memorandum of which Paul Cambon claimed authorship, and which
seems to have circulated in London in late November and early
December.[19] This *Projet de préliminaires de Paix* added war
costs to reparations, asked for strategic as well as economic annexations in the Saar region, and demanded "military neutralization, without political intervention" in the Rhineland. The war
aims defined in these documents were those which the French
Foreign Office formulated in the winter of 1916,[20] confirmed
in the agreement with Russia in the spring of 1917, and defended against liberal revision in the dark winter of 1917.[21]
They were the aims for which Clemenceau was to struggle in

[17] *Bulletin du Parti Républicain Radical et Radical Socialiste*, Dec. 14,
1918.
[18] Text of the vote in Louis Barthou, *Le Traité de paix* (Paris, 1919),
p. 142. It calls for "total repayments of the costs of the war and integral
reparation of the damages caused to persons as well as to things," "the
return to France of her frontiers of 1814, including the entire basin of the
Saar" and "a combination of military, political and economic guaranties
on the territories of the Left Bank of the Rhine, such as to protect France
definitely from invasion."
[19] A typewritten copy in the Hoover War Library is dated "November." Another copy, printed in Miller, *Diary*, vol. II, Document No. 48,
was given out by Paul Cambon at the London Embassy on December 7.
Although Cambon declared that it represented only his personal views, it
was certainly approved by the Foreign Office.
[20] Mermeix, *pseud.* (Gabriel Terrail), *Le Combat des trois* (Paris, 1921),
p. 191, for an account of the formulation of French policy under pressure
from Sir Edward Grey. The mission to Russia and the exchange of notes
on the Rhine frontier resulted from a wish to pledge at least one of the
Allies to the French aims before explaining them in London.
[21] *House Papers*, III, 280–281. Permission to publish minutes of the
Inter-Allied Conference on restatement of war aims has been refused
by the French and British governments.

the March and April crises of the Peace Conference. How then could Colonel House have imagined that the French would abandon in the hour of victory what he had not persuaded them to relinquish in the time of defeat?

These were the war aims for which the original November draft made room when it proposed to set up the Allied Declaration of 1917 as a substitute for the Fourteen Points as a basis of negotiations.

In the six days following the first issue of its November draft, the French Foreign Office invented ten modifications which it incorporated in a second draft on November 21. In this draft a cautious "perhaps" was inserted to qualify the suggestion that Tyrol and Dalmatia might be exempted from the purview of the principle of nationalities, and Istria was left out of the list entirely. The "rights of minorities" were mentioned. An extra "directing principle" was suggested: the intangibility of the prewar territories of the victors. On questions of representation there was a softening of opposition to the representation of the British Dominions, and the list of enemy states to be included was qualified by the strange warning that

It would not be permissible for the 25 States of the German Empire to avail themselves of the rupture of the federal bond to pretend to register each one vote in the deliberations and votes.[22]

The novel suggestion was made that Russian interests at the Congress be defended by an Inter-Allied Committee with Russian advisers. The distinction between the "settlement of the war" and the "organization of the peace" was accentuated by the provision that decisions in regard to the latter must be unanimous. Then came the master stroke: two new items were slipped into the agenda list:

VI. Penalties to be visited upon the acts of violence and crime committed during the war, contrary to public law.

VII. Stipulations of a moral nature (acknowledgment by Ger-

[22] Miller, *Diary*, vol. II, Document No. 4.

many of the responsibility and premeditation of her rulers, which would place in the forefront the ideas of justice and of responsibility *and would legitimize the means of punishment and precaution against her,*—a solemn repudiation of the violation of the laws of nations and of the crimes against humanity).[23]

The theory that German war guilt was to be accepted as a ruling principle in determining and justifying the peace settlement first entered the dossier of preparatory Peace Conference documents on November 21, in this seventh item of the agenda. The records of the Conference, so far as they are accessible, indicate that this principle was silently admitted to parity with Wilsonian principles in the preparation of the treaty. The French did not succeed in denouncing the Secret Treaties nor in shelving the Fourteen Points in favor of the Allied Declaration of 1917, but they did succeed in setting up a penal along with a contractual basis of peace. The harsh language of the Peace Conference ultimatum to the Germans in June testifies to the success with which "ideas of justice and responsibility" were "placed in the forefront."

Ten years of wear and tear have proved that those elements of the settlement which were derived from this principle are the rotten wood of Europe's political structure.

On November 19 David Hunter Miller joined Colonel House as legal adviser. He saw at once the significance of the paragraph which attempted to shift the basis of peace from the Fourteen Points to the Allied Declaration of 1917, and met it with crushing firmness in a memorandum which was probably handed to the French:

The statements of the French Note that the fourteen points of the President cannot be taken as a basis of negotiations and that the

---

[23] (Italics mine.) Miller, *Diary*, vol. II, Documents Nos. 4, 13, 14. The cablegram to Washington in describing the innovations of this draft omitted reference to item VI, while citing the full text of item VII. The next revisions, handed to Lansing on November 29, included both items. The omission caused a delay of five days in notifying Washington that the punishment of the war guilty was on the French program.

only bases are contained in the declaration of the Allied Powers of the tenth of January 1917, can in no event be supported. It is hardly necessary to point out that the declaration of January 10th 1917, which is mentioned in the French Note, has never been agreed to by the United States, [whereas the Fourteen Points have been agreed to by all powers, the U. S., the Allies, and Enemy.] [24]

THE SECOND REVISION OF THE NOVEMBER DRAFT

On November 29 a second revision of the November draft was handed to Lansing. In the new text the reservation against Wilson's principles was watered down, and no attempt was made to supplant them with the Allied Declaration of January, 1917.

Neither the four armistices . . . nor the answer of January 10, 1917, nor the President's fourteen propositions, can furnish a concrete basis for the labors of the Congress. That basis can only be a methodical statement of the questions to be taken up.[25]

The "methodical statement" of a proposed agenda, which it was proposed to substitute for all other peace programs, was taken with slight modifications from the earlier November draft. It was neither more concrete in substance nor more methodical in arrangement than the Wilsonian series of points. It was a rough mixture of the Fourteen Points and the 1917 French war aims. Logical arrangement was sacrificed in order to effect this combination, as the following section illustrates:

> 2. *Territorial questions:* restitution of territories. Neutralization for protection purposes.
>   a. Alsace-Lorraine. (8th Wilson proposition)
>   b. Belgium. (7th Wilson proposition)
>   c. Italy. (9th Wilson proposition)
>   d. Boundary lines. (France, Belgium, Serbia, Roumania, etc.)
>   e. International regime of means of transportation, rivers, railways, canals, harbors.[26]

[24] Miller, *Diary*, vol. II, Document No. 7, p. 35, Miller's memorandum of November 22.

[25] Baker, *Woodrow Wilson*, III, 56–63.

[26] Baker, *Woodrow Wilson*, p. 60.

"Neutralization for protection purposes" was not a Wilsonian point; it came straight from the secret French war aims of 1917. The international regime of transportation was not in the pre-Armistice contract with Germany, nor was it even a territorial question. The illogical repetition of the question of Belgian frontiers after the Belgian question has been settled according to the "7th Wilson proposition," and the separation of the question of Alsace-Lorraine from the question of the boundaries of France when Alsace must inevitably be one of the boundaries, were evidently intended, not to make the agenda of the Conference more methodical, but to make it less Wilsonian.

Nine of the Fourteen Points were referred to explicitly in this "methodical statement" (1st, 2d, 3d, 4th, 5th, 7th, 8th, 9th, 12th). Three more were included implicitly. Of the items which lay outside the Wilsonian principles but were none the less introduced in this agenda, the following are the most important: neutralization (of Rhineland), "military guaranties on land and sea," control of raw materials, punishment of the war guilty, and recognition of German war responsibility. On the question of reparations this draft was still pretty close to the terms of the Lansing Note. Although the fatal word "idemnity" was used, the element of war costs seemed to be excluded by the statement that

> Outside of the torpedoing from which the British fleet mainly suffered, Belgium and France alone are entitled to indemnities on account of the systematic devastation suffered by them.[27]

The last section of the "methodical statement" designated the commissions and committees which were to distribute among themselves the work of the Congress. There would be commissions on Polish, Russian, Baltic, Central European, Eastern and Far Eastern affairs, and committees on Jewish affairs, international rivers and railways, international labor, patents and trade marks, punishment for war crimes and "public

[27] Baker, *Woodrow Wilson*, p. 62.

law (free determination of the people combined with the rights of ethnic and religious minorities)." This list of commissions did not agree with the list of agenda subjects. Poland and labor were not mentioned in the agenda, although commissions were to be set up to study them. Subjects combined in the agenda were given to different commissions, and subjects separated in the agenda were assigned to the same commission. The more carefully the draft is scrutinized, the more unworkable it seems.

The anti-Italian tone of the original November draft was accentuated in this second revision. Again it was proposed that the secret treaties be abrogated. Colonies, it was stated, "essentially concern England and France" alone. The settlement of the Italian frontiers was turned over without reservation to Wilson's ninth point and the "right of self-determination of peoples." Italy's interest in reparations was passed over with the remark that only British, French and Belgian claims were to be noted, and that "states which have secured considerable territorial enlargement would have but a slight claim to indemnities." The proposed order of negotiating the treaties was a blow at Italian diplomacy. Italy wished to have the Austrian and German negotiations proceed simultaneously. But the French proposed in this draft that next after the German treaty, the Bulgarian question should be settled "to avoid the dangerous Bulgarian intrigues at home and abroad," and that the Austrian and Turkish treaties (which interested Italy) should be left to the last. There is evidence that the French sent a version of their November draft, containing these anti-Italian points, to the Italian Government. This rumored note on a "method of procedure" was reported to General Bliss through underground channels on December 12, in the following terms:

The principle of reparation and indemnity shall apply to France and Belgium alone. At the Peace Conference Germany shall be first dealt with. After the German question has been disposed of, the problem of the new states to be formed out of Austria Hungary shall be considered. The London Agreement will be denounced by the French Government.

It is believed that the British Government is already in agreement with the French Government with regard to the above points. There is also reason to think that France and Great Britain have reached an agreement regarding the partition of Africa and with reference to all Asiatic questions.

The Italians, I am told, feel that Italy is being excluded from the fulfilment of any colonial aspirations and from the reception of indemnity. The attitude of the Italian Government toward the French proposition is said to be uncompromisingly negative.[28]

Whether or not this report was accurate in its details, it confirms the evidence of other documents in this important respect: the November notes on procedure must be interpreted as serious efforts made by the French Foreign Office to secure the consent of other Powers to the peace program of France.

THE LONDON CONFERENCE AND THE QUESTION OF MEMBERSHIP

We lack the documents which would make possible a study of the state of British and Italian war aims at this time. The New York Public Library possesses a photostat copy of an important British paper on Peace Conference policy, but donor's restrictions forbid its use at present. The Italian Cabinet was evidently divided, until the resignation of Bissolati on December 28, on the question of renouncing the Treaty of London, as the French proposed. The most significant indication of the post-Armistice development of the policies of the Allies, and especially of Britain, is the achievement of the London Conference.

About November 15 Lloyd George had written Clemenceau, "I would suggest to you that we draw up some preparatory memoranda either in London or Paris."[29] By November 25 this suggestion had ripened into an invitation to London to

[28] Miller, *Diary*, vol. II, Documents nos. 60–61, pp. 260–261.
[29] *House Papers*, IV, 206.

attend a Conference which was to be preliminary to the preliminary Conference, preparatory to the preparatory work.[30]
On December 2 and 3 this Conference met. It made only
two decisions touching the content of the future treaty: 1st,
that war costs must be added to the German reparations bill,
and 2d, that the Kaiser must be tried for his crimes. Events
were to show the childish futility of both these solemn resolutions, which were, moreover, completely outside the scope of
the pre-Armistice agreement and the Fourteen Points.[31]

The London Conference marked the beginning of a new
epoch in the preparation of the peace settlement, not because of
the resolutions on indemnities and punishments, but in consequence of a resolution permitting the lesser powers to participate in the preparation of the preliminary peace. The November draft in all its forms had specified that the Great Powers
alone would dictate the preliminary peace. Two forces undermined this proposal: the pressure of the smaller powers, and the
legalistic criticisms of the Americans. David Hunter Miller's
memorandum on the November draft stated:

It is an essential part of the American program that there shall
be open discussion at the Peace Congress between the representatives of the Central Powers and those opposed to them, of the
conditions of peace, and it is an essential prerequisite of that open
discussion that a complete agreement as to peace terms should be
reached among the powers opposed to the Central Powers.[32]

The doors of the preliminary peace conference were thus to
be opened to all the victor states. From the legal standpoint
it was a generous proposal. It seemed to recommend a curbing of the dictatorship of the Great Powers. But from the
practical political standpoint it meant the exclusion of the
defeated powers from effective participation in the settlement.
According to Miller, the Four Powers would still hold their

[30] *House Papers*, IV, 241.
[31] *House Papers*, IV, 247–248.
[32] Miller, *Diary*, vol. II, Document No. 7, p. 32—Finished November 22.

"informal Conference," as indeed they did in January, but instead of emerging from that consultation with a preliminary peace treaty and an invitation to the Germans, they would emerge with nothing more than a preliminary peace conference and an invitation to the lesser allies. While the American representatives were sensitive to the legal aspects of the case, the British Government responded to practical political considerations when, on November 30, it notified the Polish National Committee that "Poland should be represented at the *Conference of the Allied Powers* during discussions relating to Poland.[33] The principle which Miller had expounded, and which had been more concretely illustrated in the British note to the Poles, was formally adopted at the London Conference in the following text:

. . . Before the preliminaries of peace shall be signed an Interallied Conference shall be held in Paris or Versailles, the date thereof to be set after the arrival of the President. France, Great Britain, Italy, Japan and the United States should each be represented by five delegates. British Colonial representatives to attend as additional members when questions directly affecting them are considered. Smaller Allied Powers not to be represented except when questions concerning them are discussed. Nations attaining their independence since the war to be heard by the Interallied Conference.[34]

The decision to include the lesser allies in the Inter-Allied Conference naturally caused attention to shift from the content of the forthcoming peace to the make-up of the forthcoming conference. The Foreign Offices followed up the decision of the London Conference with an attempt to formulate principles of representation. On December 11 the British asked the French for their views, and on December 13 Pichon replied with a very simple scheme. The Great Allies could send five delegates, the

---

[33] Filasiewicz, *La Question polonaise pendant la guerre mondiale* (Paris, 1920), p. 584. (Italics mine.)

[34] *House Papers*, IV, 247–248.

lesser allies three, new states two, the states in formation one, and neutrals one. "Regarding the admission of delegates from the enemy countries . . . this question is not presented." [35]

These categories of states were copied from the November draft, with one modification.[36] They seemed to be clear and simple, but were actually very difficult to apply under the political conditions of December, 1918. To the confusion resulting from the disintegration of states there were added anomalies resulting from the Armistice. With the antipathies created by the war against Germany there were combined hatreds aroused by the crusade against Bolshevism. In Eastern Europe there was fighting everywhere, but juridically no war; along the Rhine and Danube there was a juridical state of war, but actually no fighting. The Austrians and Hungarians claimed that their revolutions had rendered them neutrals and taken them out of the war without a treaty of peace; the Poles and Czechs held that their revolutions had made them belligerents without a declaration of war. The Serbian government denied its own existence and claimed recognition as the government of Yugoslavia, an ally. The Italian government denied the existence of Yugoslavia, and regarded the Yugoslavs as an enemy people. Clemenceau said he did not know whether Luxemburg was a neutral or enemy state, while Miller listed her among the Allies.[37] Foch was at a loss to decide whether the Ukraine was an enemy or an ally, although she was juridically neutral, and actually an enemy at Lemberg, an ally at Odessa.[38]

[35] Miller, *Diary*, vol. II, Document 69, p. 296.

[36] The November draft distinguished between actual and theoretical belligerents in order to cut down the representation of Latin American States. Miller protested against the distinction in his memorandum of November 22 (*Diary*, vol. II, Document No. 7); Pichon omitted it in his note of December, but Tardieu restored the distinction in his draft of January 8.

[37] Minutes of Council of Ten, March 5 (B. C. 44), in Miller, *Diary*, XV, 149; vol. III, Document No. 79, p. 315.

[38] Minutes of Council of Ten, March 19 (B. C. 53), in Miller, *Diary*, XV, 418.

In the final decision thirty-two states or dominions were voted in as members of the Inter-Allied Conference. Of these, only fourteen were of unquestioned status as Allies.[39] The eligibility of eighteen of them had been challenged in one way or another during the preparatory negotiations,[40] and eleven states which in the end were left out of the Conference had been nominated at one time or another for admission.[41] The cases of doubtful status in Allied circles outnumbered the cases of certain status by more than two to one.

The settlement of these knotty problems of Conference membership prejudged many points in the treaty itself. The decision of the colonial question was anticipated when the British Dominions[42] and the Hedjaz[43] were admitted to the Conference membership, and Japan included with the Great

[39] These were United States, Great Britain, France, Italy, Japan, Belgium, Brazil, Greece, China, Portugal, Liberia, Poland, Czechoslovakia.

[40] The status of the following states was challenged: Serbia (should be merged in Yugoslavia, Miller, *Diary*, vol. II, Document No. 79); Hedjaz (opposed by France, Leon Krajewski: "La création du Royaume du Hedjaz" in *Revue Politique et Parlementaire*, 127, 1926, pp. 441–459); Siam (omitted by French in November draft); Bolivia, Ecuador, Peru, Uruguay (states which had broken relations with Germany, but were regarded as neutrals in November draft); Cuba, Panama, Guatemala, Nicaragua, Haiti, Honduras (November draft suggests that the United States represent these "to avoid crowding"); Canada, Australia, New Zealand, South Africa, India (admission opposed in November draft "for why should not a similar claim be presented by each of the different States composing the Federation of the United States").

[41] The following were proposed for admission, but not admitted: Costa Rica (a belligerent, included in Tardieu draft, left out because the United States had not recognized its Government: Miller, *Diary*, vol. III, Document No. 159); Montenegro (November draft); Santo Domingo, Salvador, Yugoslavia, Egypt, Luxemburg, Persia, Finland (*ibid.*, vol. II, Document No. 79, Miller's comment on Pichon note of December 13th); Albania (*ibid.*, vol. III, Document No. 106); Russia (*ibid.*, vol. II, Document No. 4, first revision of November draft).

[42] Conceded January 13, Minutes of Council of Ten in Hoover War Library.

[43] Allowed January 17, when Balfour observed, semi-ironically, that the name had been omitted by oversight.

Powers.[44] The Eastern question, from Constantinople to Finland, revolved around the representation of Russia,[45] as the Adriatic question turned on the recognition of Yugoslavia and Montenegro.[46] The whole tone of the final treaty was necessarily dependent upon the degree of collaboration with the enemy powers which the Conference organization would permit.

THE AGENDA: LEAGUE AND TREATY

When Wilson arrived in the middle of December the discussion of principles of settlement had subsided and the question of membership in the Conference was uppermost. He at once raised a new issue: the agenda. The November draft

[44] Japan was not represented at the first meeting of the Supreme Council, January 12; when her delegates appeared on January 13 they brought the number of members up to ten.

[45] Two rival plans for dealing with Russia defined themselves early in December. The British wanted a round table conference in Paris—a scheme not unlike the plan of the November draft for representation by an Inter-Allied Committee with Russian counsellors. (A. L. P. Dennis, *The Foreign Policies of Soviet Russia*, pp. 69–70, dates the British suggestion and its rejection in early December.) On December 13 Clemenceau telegraphed that the "Inter-allied plan of action" was to "interdict to the Bolsheviks access to the Ukraine regions, the Caucasus and Western Siberia." (Pichon's statement in Chamber of Deputies, Dec. 29, 1918, in C. K. Cumming and Walter W. Pettit, *Russian American Relations*, p. 273.) On December 21 Clemenceau confirmed his definition of the *cordon sanitaire*. This issue was decided January 21 in favor of conference with the Russians. (Minutes of the Council of Ten in U. S. Senate Document 106, 1919. *Treaty of Peace with Germany. Hearings*, pp. 1240–1244.)

[46] On December 7 Orlando "with tears in his eyes" pledged Clemenceau to refuse recognition to Yugoslavia. (Henry Wickham Steed, *Through Thirty Years, 1892–1922: A Personal Narrative*, II, 262–263.) Yugoslavia, therefore, was not put among the Allies in the Tardieu Draft which was the basis of discussion by the Council of Ten. The Montenegrin question was still open when the first plenary session met; on January 21 the Council of Ten authorized the King of Montenegro to telegraph his people that they would be given an opportunity to choose their form of Government. (Minutes of Council of Ten in Hoover War Library.)

in all its forms had taken for granted the division of the agenda
into two principal parts: first, the settlement of the war and
second, the organization of the peace. Manley O. Hudson, who
was on Miller's staff, pressed the criticism that

> . . . a separate and consecutive consideration of what the French
> have called (a) The Settlement of the War, and (b) The Elabora-
> tion of the League of Nations would unduly segregate the tasks
> of the Congress.[47]

But Miller did not incorporate this criticism in his final memorandum of November 22. It does not appear that House objected to the plan of postponing the consideration of the League
till after the peace settlement had been made, although he
discussed with Wickham Steed a scheme for giving the League
early consideration.[48] It was not apparent, for the moment,
that an attempt to telescope the League of Nations with the
preliminary peace would be likely to eliminate the preliminary
peace entirely.

When Wilson appeared on the scene he told House, in their
first interview, that he intended "making the League of Nations the center of the whole program and letting everything
revolve around that." [49] The logic of the position was that if
the League should be evolved first, not only would its acceptance be assured, but it would strike the keynote of the whole
conference and affect the decision of all other points in the
treaty. Its protection could be offered as a substitute for
strategic frontiers.

Clemenceau and Lodge were both opposed to this inversion
of the agenda as it had been envisaged in November. On
December 21st Senator Lodge insisted in a speech to the Senate
that the League must come after the treaty, and that the first

[47] Miller, *Diary*, vol. II, Document No. 6, p. 26. Hudson's preliminary
memorandum on the French plan, November 21.

[48] Henry Wickham Steed, *Through Thirty Years*, II, 264.

[49] *House Papers*, IV, 251–252. The conversation took place December
14.

thing must be "physical guaranties" to "hem in Germany," and climaxed his argument with a denunciation of any "attempt to attach the provisions of an effective League of Nations to the Treaty of Peace." Clemenceau explained his thought to the Chamber on December 29, asserting that he adhered to the "old system" by which countries "saw that they had good frontiers." Henry White replied to Lodge immediately in a private letter: "Unless whatever League of Nations is to be formed should be one of the first subjects considered at the Peace Conference, it will never be founded at all." [50] Wilson answered Clemenceau publicly within twenty-four hours in his Manchester speech, in which he gave warning that the price of American coöperation in peace was a general League of Nations. On January 8 André Tardieu, in the final draft of the French proposal for procedure, placed the territorial settlement with Germany first on the agenda, and stole Wilson's argument by claiming that "this is the essential problem dominating all others, and its solution will react upon the entire rulings of the treaty." [51] Thus the great question of principle emerged again in January in the guise of a problem of agenda.

The Tardieu draft of January 8, entitled *Plan des Premiers Conversations*, was the last of the long line of French preparatory documents, and the first paper to be set before the Peace Conference. That part of it which related to the rules of the Conference was copied from the November draft, and those provisions which had to do with representation followed the principles laid down on December 13 in Pichon's note. The agenda list was the vehicle of its special political purpose. Its

[50] Allan Nevins, *Henry White. Thirty Years of American Diplomacy*, (New York and London, 1930), p. 362.

[51] André Tardieu, *La Paix* (Paris, 1921). This document is not accessible in complete form, but must be reconstructed from the fragment published by Tardieu and the criticisms upon the whole draft in Miller, *Diary*, vol. III, Document No. 159 *et seq.*, as well as from the minutes of the first meetings of the Council of Ten which are in the Hoover War Library.

author had evidently studied the November drafts and the criticisms that had been made of them, and had taken into account the demand made by Wilson for early consideration of the League of Nations, and had then come forward with proposals to meet the American and Italian positions halfway.

The Tardieu draft dropped the proposal to abrogate the Treaty of London, but retained the principle of the "right of nations to self-determination." It dropped the suggestion that the Austrian treaty should wait till after peace was made with Bulgaria, but did not concede that it could be drafted simultaneously with the German. It gave up the attempt to prove that the Fourteen Points were unsuited to serve as a basis of the settlement, but still introduced certain non-Wilsonian principles on a parity with the Fourteen Points. To the "Statutes of the League of Nations" it allowed a certain precedence, but only as a "directing principle," along with nine other directing principles, some of which were non-Wilsonian. Following the adoption of these principles, there would ensue the detailed territorial and economic settlement, beginning with the frontiers of Germany. Finally, the war being ended and the "principal foundations" of the League of Nations having been laid,

it will remain to
   a. Provide for the League's maintenance.
   b. Codify such measures resulting from the guiding principles stated in the first paragraph, which may not have been covered in the treaty clauses.

Under the Tardieu plan, the drafting of the Covenant would still have been postponed to the last. The concessions to Wilson's demands were more apparent than real.

The key to the Tardieu draft is the list of guiding principles. The list starts out boldly with the first four of the Fourteen Points in their Wilsonian order:

   1. Open diplomacy.
   2. Freedom of the seas.

3. International economic relations.
4. Guaranties against the return of militarism and limitation of armament.

Tardieu's fourth principle included more than Wilson's fourth point. Wilson had spoken of "guarantees given and taken that national armaments will be reduced to the lowest point consistent with domestic safety." Tardieu stretched this till it called up the picture of an interallied army on the Rhine. The next five principles were taken intact from various parts of the earlier French drafts.

5. Responsibility of the authors of the war.
6. Restitutions and reparations.
7. Solemn repudiation of all violations of international law and the principles of humanity.
8. Right of peoples to self-determination, combined with the right of minorities.
9. International arbitral organization.

Then follows the fourteenth Wilson point:

10. Statutes of a League of Nations.

And then a final word from the Quai d'Orsay:

11. Guaranties and sanctions.[52]

Of the eleven guiding principles, only five came from the Fourteen Points.

Tardieu complains in his book that the Council failed to adopt his agenda because of the "instinctive repugnance of the Anglo-Saxons for the systematized constructions of the Latin mind." [53] Actually his plan was neither comprehensive nor clear. He omitted colonial and labor questions entirely, did not mention Belgium, put Yugoslavia under rubric 2-b and left Serbia to be considered under rubric 4, listed military

[52] This eleventh directing principle is omitted in the English edition of Tardieu (p. 88) but published in the French edition (p. 98).

[53] Tardieu, *The Truth about the Treaty* (English edition), p. 91.

clauses in several places by implication, but nowhere directly, and deliberately obscured the question then at issue of the relation of the League to the Treaty. Half of his space was devoted to the listing of categories of principles, although, according to the American view, the principles were already defined and only their application was at stake. Under "territorial problems" he included as a fourth item this conglomeration of subjects, which he ingeniously concluded with an "etcetera."

> d. The right to guaranties against an offensive return of militarism, adjustment of frontiers, military neutralization of certain zones, internationalization of certain means of communication, liberty of the seas, etc. . . .

Tardieu's draft agenda was "systematic" only as an attempt to bring the French claims under principles which the Conference would accept.

On January 12 the Tardieu draft was presented to the meeting of the delegates of the Great Powers which later became the Council of Ten. From that day to January 18, when the Conference was organized, the part of the draft which related to agenda came twice under discussion.

On January 13 Pichon "explained that the messages and notes of President Wilson had been taken as the basis for the order of debates in Section II "[54] (evidently the section on principles in the Tardieu draft). But President Wilson brushed aside the appeal and introduced his own agenda list: (1) League of Nations, (2) reparations, (3) new states, (4) territorial boundaries, (5) colonial possessions.

After having offered this formal substitute for the order of business of the Tardieu draft, Wilson added that he hoped that those present would not agree upon any fixed order of discussion. For instance, he believed it more important at the moment that those present should consider the whole question

[54] Minutes of the Council of Ten, January 13 (B. C. 1), in the Hoover War Library, and Tardieu, *The Truth about the Treaty.*

of the treatment of Russia rather than the publicity of treaties. It was a point well scored against Tardieu's agenda, which had placed "open diplomacy" first, in superficial deference to the order of the Fourteen Points, and left the Russians to the very last.

On January 17 the question of agenda came up again, this time in connection with the program for the first Plenary Session. Pichon started off with Wilson's list of topics, and then read the last part of the Tardieu draft. The discussion showed that the Council was no longer interested in the agenda solely as a matter governing the principles and content of the peace treaty; it was concerned also with satisfying public opinion and keeping control of the Conference organization.[55] Lloyd George then happily hit upon three innocuous topics which would please the public without causing contention among the Allies:—the punishment of the war guilty, the responsibility of the authors of the war, and international labor legislation. As the discussion ended, "M. Clemenceau explained that he would invite all the delegations to submit views on all the questions mentioned in section III of the French plan of procedure, and they would then be passed on by the Secretariat for the information of the Great Powers."[56] Thus, contrary to Tardieu's assertion,[57] his agenda was adopted, but under conditions of Conference organization that deprived it of importance.

[55] Minutes of the Council of Ten, January 17 (B. C. 4). When Pichon read Wilson's list of five topics, proposed them "as the basis for the program of the work of the Conference," and declared he would "ask each delegation to submit their recommendations" regarding these subjects, Wilson objected that he had intended his list for the Council rather than the whole Conference. "Mr. Balfour thought that if this list were submitted to the full conference, many a burning question would immediately arise." Then, after a discussion of the use of committees in the Conference, Lloyd George made his suggestions and Pichon read from the Tardieu draft.

[56] Minutes of the Council of Ten, January 17 (B. C. 4).

[57] Tardieu, *The Truth about the Treaty*.

In the first Plenary Session of the Conference on January 18 the delegates were asked to prepare memorandums on war responsibility, and were informed that the question of the League of Nations was to be first on the agenda of the next meeting. Thus it appeared that the French had made good their innovation of November 21, and Wilson had secured the adoption of the principle he confided to House on December 14. In the meantime what had become of that fundamental order of business upon which there was such pleasant unanimity in November—the idea of the preliminary peace? The first article of the Rules adopted by the Conference indicated that the unanimity still prevailed:

The Conference, summoned with a view to lay down the conditions of Peace, in the first place by peace preliminaries, and later by a definitive treaty of peace, shall include the representatives of the Allied and Associated Powers.[58]

But when the League of Nations question was presented, as had been promised, to the second Plenary Session on January 25 the Conference voted that "The League should be created as an integral part of the General Treaty of Peace." [59] No one noticed that whereas the Rules of the Conference stated that there would be two treaties, the vote on the League of Nations implied that there would be only one.

What progress had been made toward a peace treaty in the ten weeks elapsed since the Armistice? The broad lines of the territorial settlement of Central Europe had been laid down, not by any decision taken in Paris, but by the action of peoples and armies over which Paris could exercise only the most remote and tenuous control. The German Government had clarified its foreign policy: it would stand squarely on the contractual basis of the Fourteen Points. The French attempt overtly to sidetrack this basis of peace had been given up.

[58] Miller, *Diary*, vol. III, Document No. 199, p. 410.
[59] Miller, *Drafting of the Covenant*, I, 230.

But two movements hostile to the carrying out of the contractual terms had defined themselves: the French suggestion that war responsibility be examined as a principle of the peace settlement had been adopted by the Conference, and the British general election, by its character and result, had committed the British delegation to two policies which could not be reconciled with the contractual basis of peace—the punishment of the war guilty and the levying of a war indemnity on Germany. Wilson had made himself the sponsor of a special order of business which was only indirectly related to the contractual basis of peace, and upon this issue—the combination of League and Treaty—the American opposition to Wilson had defined its stand. Upon this point the decisions of the Peace Conference included contrary theses in a self-contradictory formula of agreement. At this moment the problems of principles, membership and order of business ceased to be the vehicle of peace conference politics, and attention turned to the setting up of the conference organization.

THE ORGANIZATION OF THE CONFERENCE

COUNCIL AND CONFERENCE

In November, 1918, peace negotiations were devoted to clarifying the principles of the settlement, and in December to determining conference membership and order of business. In the middle of January the problem of organization tended to absorb those issues which had previously appeared in isolation as questions of principle, membership and agenda. The representation of the lesser allies had been admitted in December, but it remained to determine how far the Conference organization would permit them to exercise effective influence on the settlement. Agenda topics had previously presented themselves in the abstract as items on a list but now they came up concretely as proposals to create and instruct commissions and committees. The old issue of precedence between the "settlement of the war" and the "organization of the regime of peace" took on a new form when, in the flux of relationships, two opposed jurisdictions came to define themselves, a Council which regarded itself as Supreme and a Conference which referred to itself as Plenary. In the contest for power, which received no formal adjudication, and in the distribution of functions, which appears to have occurred without plan, it came about that the Council made good its supremacy in the settlement of the war, while the Conference exercised its plenary authority in the organization of the peace.

In the fall of 1917 the Supreme War Council had been created by France, Britain, Italy and the United States, as their paramount political organ. When it assumed the conduct of the Armistice negotiations, representatives of Belgium, Greece, Serbia, and possibly Japan were invited to attend its sessions. The heir of this Council was the Council of Ten, with its descendants, the Council of Five and the Council of Four. The French plans of November had assumed that this body would make the preliminary peace as it had made the Armistice, coöpting into its sessions the delegates of the smaller allies when questions especially concerning them were under consideration. David Hunter Miller had criticized this plan in a mild way, proposing that

instead of a preliminary discussion among only four Great Powers with other powers admitted when and as the case might require, there would be a discussion of each particular question among all the powers directly interested, which would always include the Great Powers.[60]

This issue was left in abeyance while it was decided that the small powers would attend the Conference, and while the number of delegates to be allotted them was canvassed. In January the two opposed conceptions of the role of the small powers,

[60] Miller's draft cablegram of November 25, in *Diary*, vol. II, Document No. 10, p. 53.

and hence of the very nature of the Conference organization, came into conflict.

Wilson had undoubtedly pictured himself as able to "lead the weaker powers" against the French and British.[61] This no doubt led him to look with suspicion upon that clause of the Tardieu draft of January 8 which provided that whereas the representatives of the five Great Powers should "take part in all sittings and Commissions," those of the other powers should "take part in the sittings at which questions concerning them are discussed." [62] The discussion of this clause raised the question whether the authority of the Peace Conference was to be vested in a continuation of the Supreme War Council which would give informal hearings to the representatives of lesser states, or in a new organization, in which the great states would set themselves up as an informal steering committee. The meaning of the sharp passage of arms between Wilson and Clemenceau on January 12 is obscured by an imperfection in the minutes, but the general course of the argument can still be followed.

The Supreme War Council had just finished discussing the Armistice renewal terms, dismissed the military experts, and picked up the Tardieu draft. Wilson asked Pichon "whether this subject was not for the more general conference." Pichon replied correctly that it was first necessary to set up the more general conference. In that moment the actual organizing of the conference began. There took place an inconclusive discussion of the representation of Montenegro and Russia. Then the trouble started.

[61] Wilson to House, about November 15, *House Papers*, IV, 213; also his plan of April 6 to threaten the Council of Four that if they did not keep to the Fourteen Points he would appeal to Plenary Sessions. *Ibid.*, pp. 401–402.

[62] Miller, *Diary*, vol. III, Document No. 170, p. 274. (It is not certain that this is the exact language of the Tardieu draft; the minutes of the Council do not indicate any amendment, although they record a warm discussion, as is noted below.)

M. Pichon stated that they would then have to consider the representation of the Great Powers. It was understood that the enemy powers should not be represented until the Allied Powers had reached an [*end of page 14 of mimeographed set of minutes in the Hoover War Library. Page 15 then begins with a parenthesis, as follows*] (A remark by the President). Mr. Lloyd George stated that at the Supreme War Council the smaller nations were only consulted when their intentions were involved. The President said he did not like the appearance of [*not?*] consulting nations that we are protecting unless they were interested. Mr. Lansing remarked that if they followed that procedure they would be imitating the Council of Vienna. The President was in favor of holding informal conversations among the Great Powers, but believed that they must have an organization of all the nations, otherwise they would run the risk of having a small number of nations regulate the affairs of the world, and the other nations might not be satisfied.

Mr. Balfour proposed that they have private talks to reach formal conclusions, and then put these conclusions before the smaller nations for their examination and admit them to the conference to hear their observations.

M. Clemenceau then spoke at some length. . . .[63]

In the course of his long speech Clemenceau protested that Honduras and Cuba could not be allowed the right to give an opinion on all questions of the world settlement, and that "the five great powers should reach their decision upon important questions before entering the halls of the Congress to negotiate peace." He demanded that "meetings be held in which the representatives of the five countries mentioned shall participate, to reach decisions upon the important questions, and that the study of secondary questions be turned over to the commissions and the committees before the reunion of the Conference."

Since there are defects and uncertainties both in the available text of the Tardieu draft and in the minutes of the debate, the issue between the two champions is not as clearly defined as it should be. It seems certain, however, that Baker is wrong

[63] Minutes of the Council of Ten, January 12, 1919 (B. C. A-1), in the Hoover War Library. Clemenceau's speech is printed in Baker, *Woodrow Wilson*, I, 179–180.

when he asserts that Clemenceau was unwilling "even to consider consultation with the smaller nations." [64] The only practical problem at stake was the formal relation of Council to Conference and the representation of the lesser powers on the commissions.

The questions debated with such heat on January 12 were left undecided by the statesmen, but events made the decision. The body which Wilson called "informal," which Balfour legitimized as "private" and which Clemenceau wished to make sovereign, met thereafter regularly. By coöpting two Japanese delegates it became, in the language of the newspaper men, the Council of Ten.

When the Plenary Conference met on January 18 it appointed the five great Powers as its Bureau. The Americans thenceforth designated the Council of Ten as the "Bureau of the Conference," heading their copies of the minutes with the letters "B. C." as if the Council were the creation of the Conference with its authority derived at second hand. But the Conference Secretariat took a different view. In the official schedule of membership and organization [65] it asserted that the Bureau of the Conference was one thing and the "Supreme Council of the Allies" another. The British did not seem to commit themselves, but listed all meetings of all Councils and Conferences under the letters "I. C." (Inter-Allied Conference).

The distinction between the authority of the Conference and that of the Council was also important in connection with the work of the five commissions, on League of Nations, War Responsibility, Reparations, Labor Legislation and International Transit, set up by the Plenary Conference on January 25. Although the resolutions creating these commissions had been

[64] Baker, *Woodrow Wilson*, I, 179.
[65] *Conférence des préliminaires de la paix. Composition et fonctionnement.* In Hoover War Library; reprinted in Miller, *Diary*, I, 378-499, and in *Documentation internationale. Paix de Versailles*, I, 199-311. The minutes of the Council of Ten will hereinafter be cited as "B. C."

adopted in the Council of Ten on January 21 and 23, and the action of the Conference did not come till January 25, these commissions were regarded by the Secretariat as creations of the latter date. The American members of these commissions several times made use of the fact that the parent body was the Conference rather than the Council. On February 13 Wilson told the Council that he wished to present the report of the League of Nations Commission to a plenary session of the Conference without even showing it to the smaller group of the Great Powers. When Clemenceau objected, Wilson replied:

That the League of Nations Commission was not a Commission of the Conference of the Great Powers but of the Plenary Conference. Consequently the first report ought, as a matter of fact, to go to the Plenary Conference.[66]

Lansing used a similar argument in the Commission on Responsibilities in order to block a resolution calling upon the Supreme War Council to insert in the terms of renewal of the Armistice a clause calling for the arrest of suspects and the seizure of documents. Lansing declared that "the present Commission was not appointed by the Supreme War Council but by the Peace Conference; it is therefore before the Peace Conference that the resolution must be presented." [67] The Commissions on League of Nations and International Labor Legislation made their reports punctiliously to the Plenary Conference, taking care that the most trivial amendments were duly laid before the parent body and adopted. Each of these commissions appeared twice before the plenum. The Commission on Responsibilities saw its report adopted in the sixth plenary session on May 6.[68]

[66] B. C. 31, February 13, 1919, in Miller, *Diary*, XIV, 418.
[67] *Documentation internationale. Paix de Versailles*, III, 28. (Minutes of the 2d session of the Commission, February 7.)
[68] Minutes of the 6th Plenary Session, May 6, 1919, in Miller, *Diary*, XX, 149.

Two of the Conference commissions failed to report back to the parent body. The Commission on Ports, Waterways and Railways began like the commissions on Labor and League of Nations to prepare general international conventions for adoption at plenary sessions, but this activity was suspended early in March to make way for the hurried drafting of treaty clauses with Germany.[69] The Commission on Reparations, assigned to report on a subject which was strictly a question of war settlement rather than permanent international organization, proved unable to carry out its task. Thus these commissions, insofar as they came to concern themselves with the treatment of the vanquished by the victors, lost their close connection with the jurisdiction of Plenary Conference and tended to assimilate their role to that of the committees appointed by the Council.

The Conference, for its part, had very little to do with the treaty terms. It heard a brief oral résumé of them at its plenary session of May 6, the day before the text was handed to the Germans. The agenda carefully described this presentation, not as a report to the Conference, but as a "declaration relative to the terms of peace." [70] When Tardieu had finished the declaration, Clemenceau as Chairman made the situation brutally clear by saying:

Gentlemen, this is merely a simple communication to begin with. Nevertheless, it is my duty to ask whether there are explanations.

The same procedure was attempted in the case of the Austrian Treaty on May 29,[71] but the small powers revolted and in-

---

[69] Minutes of this commission in Miller, *Diary*, vols. XI and XII; a different text, covering nearly half the sessions, in *Documentation internationale. Paix de Versailles*, vol. VI.

[70] Minutes of the 6th Plenary Session, May 6, 1919, in Miller, *Diary*, XX, 149–181.

[71] Minutes of the 7th Plenary Session, May 29, Miller, *Diary*, XX, 188–189; the minutes of the 8th session, May 31, are accessible in the Hoover War Library.

sisted on a fuller hearing on May 31. Thus only two sections of
the Treaty, the Covenant and the Labor Section, were ever
adopted by the Paris Peace Conference. The other sections, including the territorial clauses, were presented to the enemy, not
only without receiving the formal approbation of the Conference, but even without giving any of the lesser allies (except
Belgium) more than a day's notice of the frontiers that were
being submitted to the enemy on their behalf.[72]

Thus the original French plan for peace terms dictated by
the Great Powers and a new international order established by
a general conference was substantially realized except for the
circumstance that the two conferences were simultaneous rather
than consecutive.

THE GREAT AND SMALL POWERS

The Plenary Conference was not only the agency used to
legislate upon the future international order, but also the forum
in which the smaller states sought to turn to account their
theoretical equality with the Great Powers. There were twenty-
two of these "Powers with Special Interests." Together they
held thirty-six seats to the Great Powers' twenty-four. The
personnel of their staffs totaled about five hundred, only one
hundred less than the number accredited to the Conference
organization by the Great Powers.[73] In the week of idleness
between January 18 when the Conference was organized and
January 25 when the second plenary meeting was held, these
delegates became restive. When they got their opportunity in

[72] Note Pichon's statement in Council of Five, F. M., 24, June 12, 1919,
Miller, *Diary*, XVI, 386.

[73] The size of the various delegations including experts, etc.:

British Empire ..	184	Serbia	104	China	62
France	136	Belgium	71	Czechoslovakia ...	46
Italy	120	Japan	64	Rumania	37
United States	108	Poland	64	Greece	32

These states sent 90% of the Conference personnel.

the second meeting, eleven of the plenipotentiaries made speeches of protest. Said the Brazilian representative:

It is with some surprise that I constantly hear it said: "This has been decided, that has been decided." Who has taken this decision? We are a sovereign assembly, a sovereign court. It seems to me that the proper body to take a decision is the Conference itself.[74]

Clemenceau replied with complete frankness:

. . . I will remind you that it was we who decided that there should be a Conference at Paris, and that the representatives of the countries interested should be summoned to attend it . . . if we had not kept before us the great question of the League of Nations we might perhaps have been selfish enough to consult only each other.

Although in certain parts of his speech Clemenceau seemed to admit the theory that the authority of the Great Powers over the Conference proceedings was in their capacity as an officially designated Bureau, he clearly indicated that he regarded the participation of the small powers as a concession to the need of founding a new international order.

This principle was consistently applied in the appointment of commissions. The small states were not admitted to commissions concerned with territorial or military problems. They were appointed to the five commissions created on January 25, for these were Conference commissions from which it would have been impossible to exclude them. They demanded and received increased representation beyond the five places which the Great Powers offered them in three of these commissions (League of Nations, Transit, Reparations).[75] But thenceforth they were given seats in only four of the many organs which the Council brought into being. Each of these later commissions which had small-state members was concerned in one way or another with the general problem of a permanent inter-

[74] Protocol of the second plenary session of the Conference in Miller, *Diary*, vol. IV, Document No. 230, pp. 68, 77.

[75] Minutes of the meeting of the Powers with Special Interests, January 27, Miller, *Diary*, vol. IV, Document No. 231, pp. 142–153.

national regime: economic, financial, aeronautic or Moroccan. No Belgian sat on the Belgian Commission, no Pole on any of the three Polish Commissions, and when it was necessary to draft conventions to apply to the New States, no representative of any of the New States had a place on the commission. With respect to their particular interests the Conference membership of the lesser powers gave them no privileged standing, for the Syrians and Armenians who were not Conference members were allowed to appear before the Council to present their special claims. Thus it came about that the "Powers with Special Interests" had nothing but general interests confided to them.

Japan, though ranked as a "Power with General Interests," and given a right to sit on all commissions, tended to restrict her role to the defense of her special interests alone. She had representatives on only three of the six territorial commissions, and on only three of the five commissions concerned with Armistice renewal. The Morocco Committee had a Belgian and Portuguese member, but no Japanese. There was no Japanese member of the Supreme Economic Council. When the Council of Four became the paramount authority over the drafting of peace terms, Japan's place as a Principal Allied Power remained only nominal. Any one of the smaller European powers probably had more influence than Japan over the general character of the settlement.

The small powers varied greatly among themselves in influence upon the negotiations. Eleven of them took all the places on the commissions, leaving eleven with nothing to do but make speeches in the plenary sessions.[76] The neglected states, most of them the small Latin-American countries, tried

[76] The importance of the smaller powers, as indexed by the number of commissions on which each was represented, was:

Belgium 9	Greece 6	Brazil 2
Serbia 7	Portugal 6	Cuba 2
Poland 7	Czechoslovakia 4	Uruguay 2
Rumania 7	China 3	

(Only nine commissions had small-state members.)

unsuccessfully to revolt against their more favored colleagues in early March. The occasion was the invitation to appoint five delegates of the "Powers with Special Interests" to the Economic and Financial Commissions. The meeting voted to demand that the number be increased to ten upon each commission, and refused to select five members.[77] Jules Cambon, who was presiding, persuaded them to be more conciliatory; they accordingly offered two lists of ten each, arranged in alphabetical order, and including Hejaz, Peru, Ecuador and Bolivia. The Council of Ten sent back the lists and asked the small powers to name their five representatives, and add four supplementary names to be used as a panel. But the South American States formed a combination and packed the five places in the Financial Commission with four of their own number. The Council of Ten simply upset the result of the election and named the small European states and Brazil to the places. Thus the third-rate states failed to advance themselves to equality with second-rate countries. The maneuver resulted in a further loss of influence, for in fixing the membership of the Aeronautic Commission—the last Commission which was to include small-state delegates—the Council quietly designated the states which were to be represented, not permitting any election "lest the incident relating to the election of the delegates to the Financial and Economic Commissions be repeated." [78]

THE COMMISSIONS AND COMMITTEES

The commissions of the Peace Conference, whether they emanated from the Conference or the Council, whether they

[77] B. C. 42, March 1, 1919, in Miller, *Diary*, XIV, 132; B. C. 44, March 5, pp. 150–151; B. C. 47, March 8, pp. 254–258; B. C. 48, March 10, p. 287. (Chile is a misprint for China.) Minutes of Conference of Powers with Special Interests, Miller, *Diary*, XX, 209–244.

[78] B. C. 31, March 15, in Miller, *Diary*, XV, 366. This commission further reduced the influence of the small states by leaving them off its subcommissions.

concerned themselves with the settlements of the war, the setting up of the new international order, or both, and whether
they were staffed by the Great Powers alone or by great
and small powers together, were the principal agencies by
which the central authority took action on its long agenda list.
The Franco-German frontier, the Italian frontier and the question of guaranties were the only important subjects in the
treaty which were deliberately withheld from consideration by
commissions. The treaty, in the large, was written in texts proposed by the commissions and committees. Therefore the problem of the relation of the commissions to the central authority
and to each other was no less significant than the problem of
the relation of Council to Conference and great to small
powers.

How many commissions, committees and subcommittees
were set up in the course of the negotiations? Tardieu thought
that there were about fifty-eight, a number which has since
been much quoted, and which may perhaps be based upon
the list printed in April by the Secretariat, which does in fact
list fifty-eight bodies (including certain subcommittees not
actually appointed).[79] Temperley, in a list which takes into
account developments of later months, brings the number up
to sixty-six, but a casual examination shows that there are
many omissions from this longer list. Three committees of
which we possess complete minutes in the Miller Diary are
ignored in the Temperley list: namely the Subcommittee on
Kiel which held four meetings from March 11 to April 24,[80] and
the Commission on a Polish-Ukrainian Armistice together with
its subcommission, which between them held eleven meetings
from April 26 to May 15.[81] These happen to be instances in
which the complete minutes have come to hand. The cases in

[79] Miller, *Diary*, I, 447–499; Tardieu, *La Paix*, p. 102 (English edition,
p. 93); Temperley, ed., *A History of the Peace Conference of Paris*
(London, 1920–24), 497–504.
[80] Miller, *Diary*, XII, 412–436.
[81] Miller, *Diary*, X, 318–488.

which our knowledge of the existence of committees other than those named in Temperley's or the Secretariat's list is based upon more fragmentary material are numerous indeed. The commissions and subcommissions frequently appointed small drafting committees which took the heaviest load of work, but left no formal record of their deliberations. For instance, the first part of the report of the Commission on Responsibilities was drafted in that way. This document is the only part of the work of this commission which has had a lasting influence in European politics. As the statement of the Allied thesis upon German war guilt it has become a political symbol of first importance, and has continued to attract a literature of criticism after the other parts of the work of the commission, relating to the trial of the Kaiser and the punishment of war atrocities, have been forgotten. The minutes of the Commission on Responsibilities show that this vital chapter was not debated in any formal session, but was written by a drafting committee of which even the membership is uncertain. Lieutenant Colonel Biggar of the Canadian Army, Premier Massey of New Zealand, Captain Masson of the French Army, and M. Politis, the Greek statesman, were probably the authors of this document, but there is no record of its drafting.[82] No sharp line of demarcation distinguished the procedure of such small special subcommittees or drafting committees from mere informal meetings, nor the informal meetings from dinner or telephone conversations. Sometimes a subcommission was appointed by the authority of the Council, without the intermediate action of the Commission. This was the case in the appointment of a Kiel Canal subcommission of the Commission on Ports, Waterways and Railways. The same action was taken when preparations were being made to negotiate with the Germans, and the Peace Conference Secretariat appointed subcommissions by

---

[82] Minutes of the February 24 and March 5 meetings of the first subcommittee of the Commission on Responsibilities, in *Documentation internationale. Paix de Versailles*, III, 254–259.

telephone,[83] this method being used in this case to keep the small powers off the subcommissions. The documents now accessible do not make it possible to draw up an exhaustive list of the organs of the Peace Conference, but they are sufficient to throw light upon the way the system worked.

THE COMMISSIONS AND THE CONFERENCE AGENDA

The Foreign Offices had understood from the first that much of the labor of the Peace Conference would have to be delegated to commissions. The first November draft had recognized this principle, the third November draft had set up a list of proposed commissions and committees, and this list, or a modification of it, probably formed a part of the Tardieu draft of January 8.[84] The need for commissions in Conference organization was never at issue, but there was a question how they would be used. Was their work to precede or follow the work of the Council? Were they to prepare questions for decision or carry out in detail decisions already made? How much of the work of the Conference was to be farmed out to them? These were vital questions because they affected the efficiency of the whole peace-making system.

Those who have written upon the Conference do not agree as to which of the ways of using commissions would have contributed most to efficiency. Wickham Steed and Colonel House thought that circumstances demanded the immediate appointment of committees to study and report upon all subjects, before they had been considered by any supreme authority.[85]

[83] Minutes of the 30th meeting, June 7, of Commission on Ports, Waterways and Railways, in *Documentation internationale. Paix de Versailles*, VI, 442–452. The sharp protest of the small-state members against this procedure, and the explanation of what had been done, are omitted in the official version of the minutes as printed in Miller, *Diary*, vol. XII.

[84] Miller, *Diary*, vol. III, Document No. 159, p. 245.

[85] Steed has described the plan worked out with House while Wilson was on the water (early December): "it was, broadly speaking, that oratory should be barred from the outset by a self-denying ordinance;

Winston Churchill on the contrary writes scornfully of commissions of inquiry as "the usual household remedy" in domestic politics.[86] From his standpoint "all depended upon a serious discussion from the outset between Gt. Britain, France, Italy, Japan and the United States, at which the main principles could be settled" and not upon the speed and thoroughness with which the problems were farmed out to commissions for analysis and report.[87] Ray Stannard Baker regarded the problem of the use of commissions as a moral issue, the issue between the New and the Old.

The old way was for a group of diplomats, each representing a set of selfish interests, to hold secret meetings, and by jockeying, trading, forming private rings and combinations with one another, come at last to a settlement . . . the new way so boldly launched at Paris . . . was first to start with certain general principles of justice, and then have those principles applied . . . by dispassionate scientists—geographers, ethnologists, economists,—who had made studies of the problems involved.[88]

Baker's distinction is not fully applicable to the concrete situations that arose during the Conference; his interest is in the ethical plane of the negotiation, but there is no evidence that this was higher in the commissions than in the Council. In fact, the most downright, obstinate, and narrow declarations of national policy are more likely to be found in the minutes of the commissions than in the records of the meetings of the Council.

---

that assent to the establishment of a League of Nations should be the first point on the agenda of the Conference . . . the plan provided also for the immediate appointment of expert committees upon the principal questions of the Peace Settlement, these committees being instructed to report by definite dates to the heads of the Allied and Associated Governments, and to cast the gist of their reports into the form of articles of a Peace Treaty." Steed, *Through Thirty Years*, II, 264.

[86] Winston S. Churchill, *The Aftermath* (London and New York, 1929), p. 384.

[87] Churchill, *Aftermath*, p. 114.

[88] Baker, *Woodrow Wilson*, I, 112.

The first definite proposal for making use of commissions came before the Council of Ten on January 17. President Wilson made the suggestion, which was exactly in line with the plan that House and Steed had discussed in December,

that the presiding officer of the Conference should appoint committees on different subjects, and then have the delegations submit their reports on the different subjects to these committees.[89]

Had Wilson's suggestion been adopted, the whole agenda would have been farmed out among commissions on the same day upon which the Plenary Conference was organized. This was the plan for using uninstructed committees of inquiry, in all its simplicity.

But Lloyd George objected. He feared that

If the committees were set up a machinery might be created which it would be impossible to control. He thought it necessary to confine the action to reports on matters which concerned the delegates individually. These reports would go to the Secretariat, and be submitted to the Great Powers for their information.

This suggestion to delay the farming-out of the territorial questions until the Council of Ten was in possession of written statements of claims seems to have been inspired more by a fear of the exigent small states than by a lack of confidence in the experts, but it implied that the procedure would be to set up committees only after the Council itself had studied questions, and given instructions. The routing of a territorial question would run from the delegation to the Secretariat, from the Secretariat to the Council, from the Council to a Committee.

Clemenceau loyally explained this decision to the plenary session on the following day. He asked the representatives of the powers which had special interests

to deliver to the Secretariat General memoranda on questions of every kind—territorial, financial or economic—which particularly interest them. This method is somewhat new, but it has not seemed right to impose upon the Conference a particular order of work.

[89] B. C. 4, January 17, 1919, in the Hoover War Library.

To gain time, Powers are invited first to make known their claims. All the people represented at the Conference can put forward, not only demands which concern themselves, but also demands of a more general character. The delegations are begged to present these memoranda as soon as possible.

On these memoranda a comprehensive work will be compiled for submission to the Conference . . . at the head of the order of the day for the next session stands the League of Nations.[90]

The three meetings of the Council of Ten which immediately followed the first Plenary Conference were taken up with the Russian and Polish problems. The Conference had been organized without Russia, but a Russian policy was necessary. The decision to call a Russian conference at Prinkipo was taken on January 21. Then Paderewski's request for military assistance took up half of the following day. Wilson fended off the suggestion that Poland's frontiers should be hurriedly agreed upon in connection with the problem of military aid. And then, on the afternoon of January 21, the Council came back to the main task of making the Treaty. In accordance with Wilson's proposed agenda, already announced to the plenary session, the first item of treaty-making was the League of Nations.

The Chairman thought it very desirable that the different delegations be put to work as soon as possible. He understood that President Wilson would submit the question of a League of Nations at the next meeting. If so, he suggested that it would be well to proceed to consider the question of reparation of damages.

Mr. Lloyd George stated that he agreed to this, and suggested that the question of the League of Nations be taken up at the next meeting, and that those present lay down the general principles and then appoint an international committee to work on the constitution of the League.[91]

On the following day, January 22, the resolution was adopted which disposed of the question of the League of

[90] Preliminary Peace Conference, Protocol No. 1, January 18, 1919, in Miller, *Diary*, vol. III, Document No. 199, pp. 407–408.

[91] B. C. 6, January 21, 1919, in Hoover War Library. The second paragraph quoted above is also printed in Baker, *Woodrow Wilson*, I, 237.

Nations not only by creating a commission but also by settling in advance the question whether the League should be "created as an integral part of the general treaty of peace," whether it should be open to all, what its object should be, and what should be the outlines of its organization.[92] When Baron Makino sought to withhold Japan's consent to such a detailed commitment, Wilson pinned him down to the pre-Armistice contract:

President Wilson pointed out that Mr. Lloyd George's proposal included nothing that was not contemplated when the Peace Conference was called, and that the principles of the League of Nations had been accepted at the time of the Armistice. He therefore asked whether Baron Makino wished it to be understood that the Japanese government reserved its decision with regard to bases which other powers had already accepted? [93]

The Commission on the League of Nations was the most adequately instructed of the great commissions. The Commissions on Labor Questions and on Ports, Waterways, and Railways received no instructions at all, but were never deadlocked for the lack of them. The setting up of the Commission on Responsibility of the Authors of the War gave rise to no debate, but was accomplished in a resolution sufficiently definite to guide the commission debates and to constitute a step in recognizing the non-contractual and punitive principle in the peace settlement. The Economic and Financial Drafting Committees, which were set up on January 23 and 27 in order to "classify and frame in suitable language all questions coming under these categories" [94] were examples of the type of commission which House had described in December—they were expected to prepare subjects for another authority to decide rather than carry out decisions already made.

[92] Miller, *Drafting of the Covenant*, I, 76. According to Miller, the word "created" was altered to "treated" by a misprint in the minutes.

[93] B. C. 7, January 22, 1919, in the Hoover War Library.

[94] Clemenceau, B. C. 10, January 24, 1919, in Miller, *Diary*, XIV, 21. On March 1 these committees were reconstituted as full commissions with authority to work out solutions of the problems they had listed.

The Council of Ten covered most of its agenda list except territorial questions in the commissions set up during the last days of January. There were two subjects, however, which did not yield successfully to commission treatment. These were reparations and disarmament. A Reparations Commission was set up without adequate instructions and came to grief in consequence; the project for the creation of a Disarmament Commission was rejected on the ground that it would be necessary first to prepare adequate instructions. It is noteworthy that these two subjects, which have had such a poisonous history in post-Versailles Europe, showed themselves intractable in the earliest stage of the Conference. Both procedural methods were applied—the system of giving the commission a free hand, and the procedure of waiting until the Council could prepare adequate instructions, and both methods failed.

It is worth following in more detail the history of these attempts to arrange the discussion of two of the items on the agenda list. On January 21, as has been noted, Lloyd George referred to the question of "reparation of damages," on the following day he made a proposal to appoint a "commission to consider the question of reparation and indemnity. President Wilson suggested that it might be well to omit the word 'indemnity.' " [95] In this mild way, Wilson indicated his opposition to the inclusion of war costs in the reparations bill. But he did not pin Lloyd George to the terms of the Lansing Note as he had pinned Makino to the principles of the League of Nations. The Lansing Note of November 5 limited the Allies' claims to the reparation of damages suffered by the civilian population. The commission was put to work without instructions on the critical point whether the Allies would hold to their pre-Armistice contract or go beyond it by demanding war costs. After a month of futile wrangling the commission reported its deadlock back to the Council of Ten, and asked for a decision. By this time (March 1st), Wilson was absent,

[95] B. C. 7, January 22, 1919, in the Hoover War Library.

and the Council refused to accept responsibility for making the decision. When Wilson returned, the serious study of the problem was taken out of the hands of the commission by experts who reported directly to the Heads of States, and who regarded the commission organization as an obstacle which should "make its report and get out of the way." [96]

The suggestion to set up a Commission on Disarmament was made by Balfour on January 21, at the same session which saw the first steps toward instructing the League of Nations Commission, and the mention of the need for a Commission on Reparations. The three topics came up simultaneously, but each received a different kind of treatment. Wilson at this time agreed that the question of disarmament was closely related to the question of strategic frontiers, but he thought it would be better for "those present to compare their views before referring it to a committee." [97]

Although there was no such comparison of views as Wilson had proposed, Lloyd George brought in a draft resolution to set up a Disarmament Commission on January 23. This was the meeting at which the resolutions setting up Commissions on Labor, Reparations, Responsibilities and Transit were adopted, but the parallel resolution on Disarmament was not accepted. The instructions as Lloyd George had drafted them called upon the commission

1. To advise on an immediate and drastic reduction of the armed forces of the enemy.

2. To prepare a plan in connection with the League of Nations for permanent reduction in the burden of military, naval and aerial forces and armament.[98]

Lloyd George was interested in facilitating rapid demobilization of British troops by reducing the German army "to the minimum necessary for the maintenance of internal safety." (This

[96] Norman Davis to President Wilson, March 25, 1919, in Baker, *Woodrow Wilson*, III, 384.

[97] B. C. 6, January 21, 1919, in the Hoover War Library.

[98] B. C. 8, January 23, 1919, in Miller, *Diary*, XIV, 3.

was in fact the very formula of Wilson's fourth point.) But here the consequence of excluding the Germans from the Preliminary Peace Conference appeared, for, as Wilson remarked, it would be necessary to consult the Germans, so as to give the Germans a chance to state the numbers they actually needed, and the means of consulting them would be the Armistice Commission. Orlando followed out the logic of this position by suggesting that

. . . we could obtain prompt demobilization of the German armies more effectively by dealing with it as a condition of the renewal of the armistice through the agency of Marshal Foch and the Allied Military Advisers than by treating it as a question for the Peace Conference.[99]

Out of the discussion there emerged, therefore, not a commission of the Peace Conference to draft articles of a treaty but a committee of military advisers to concoct conditions for the renewal of the Armistice. In February, when it came time to consider the actual presentation of these terms to Germany, this decision was reversed, and the subject was moved back from the category of Armistice to the category of Peace by the impracticable suggestion that the military clauses should be the basis of the Preliminary Peace with Germany.[100]

By January 24 most of the proposed agenda which had been listed with such "system" in the November draft and the Tardieu draft had received some kind of attention in the Council of Ten. Aside from territorial questions only the following subjects had been entirely neglected:

"Stipulations of private law; settlement of credits; liquidation of sequestrations" (November draft)
"Reëstablishment of the conventional regime upset by the war" (November draft)

[99] Miller, *Diary*, XIV, 5.
[100] See minutes of Supreme War Council, February 12, 1919, in Miller, *Drafting of the Covenant*, II, 165 *et seq.* This is the starting point of the episode which Baker dramatized as a plot to leave the Covenant out of the Treaty.

"The freedom of the seas" (November draft and Tardieu draft)
"Publicity of Treaties" (November draft and Tardieu draft)
"International Organization for Arbitration" (November draft and Tardieu draft)
"Guarantees and Sanctions" (November draft and Tardieu draft)

The apparent neglect of certain of these items must have been noticed by Clemenceau, for he introduced a resolution on January 27 calling for the appointment of a commission to consider three of them among a very curious list of subjects.

Reëstablishment of the conventional regime of treaties.
Settlement of private claims.
Enemy ships seized at the beginning of the war in allied ports (Hague Convention of 1907).
Goods on enemy ships that have taken shelter and remained in neutral ports.
Restoration of illegal prizes.
Goods which have been stopped without being captured. (O. C. March 11, 1915.) [101]

The agenda of Clemenceau's proposed commission was something of a catchall for neglected subjects, but it was also a disguised way of bringing up the question of the Freedom of the Seas. The Council voted against setting up Clemenceau's commission, after a brief but pungent debate:

Mr. Lloyd George was of the opinion that a very big issue was raised by this proposal, but he did not think that all these questions could be settled in the Peace Treaty with the enemy. The whole subject appeared to him to be more suitable for the League of Nations. These matters, moreover, could be discussed in a more favorable atmosphere in the League of Nations than in a debate with Germany. It would be far more difficult for himself to make concessions in dealing with the enemy than in dealing with the League of Nations.

Evidently the canny Welshman understood that this was to become the Commission on the Freedom of the Seas. Sonnino then proposed a compromise: "four fifths of these subjects would be better dealt with by the League of Nations," but

[101] B. C. 11, January 27, 1919, in the Hoover War Library.

some of them, such as the disposal of enemy ships, "were strictly for inclusion in the Peace Treaty." Clemenceau agreed with Sonnino, Wilson gave his approval, and it was voted that the special cases concerning shipping should be referred to the Commission on Reparations, and questions of general principles reserved for the League of Nations.

Critics and apologists of the Paris Peace Conference have continued to point to this January period as an era of mistakes. "The great fault of the political leaders," writes Professor Seymour, "was their failure to draft a plan of procedure . . . the heads of Government did not approve, or at least did not set in motion, any systematic approach to the problems of the Conference." [102] Tardieu ascribed this indifference to the "instinctive repugnance of the Anglo-Saxons to the systematized constructions of the Latin mind." Wickham Steed thought it was a consequence of the illness of Colonel House during the critical period in January, by which the Conference was deprived of "his guiding influence" when it was most sorely needed. "Before he could resume his activities things had gone too far to mend." These criticisms call for certain modifying comments. About half the Treaty was written by commissions appointed between January 21 and January 27. Before the end of January all the significant items in the agenda lists had been laid before the Council and farmed out to commissions for study except four:

> Territorial questions
> Freedom of the Seas
> General disarmament
> Guaranties

Freedom of the Seas and general disarmament had been considered in the Council and postponed; territorial questions had been consigned to a procedure which left it to the claimant

[102] *House Papers*, IV, 271–273; the citations from Tardieu and Steed are given in these pages.

powers to deposit their demands with the Secretariat. The critics underestimate the grasp of the peace problem as a whole which the Conference showed in its first days.

TERRITORIAL QUESTIONS

The Conference made two mistakes in procedure in connection with territorial questions. The first was in trusting the small powers to deposit their claims with the Secretariat, the second was in yielding to the desire of the small powers to be heard by the Council.

It has been noted that on January 18 a regular procedure had been ordained for the presentation of memorandums on all subjects through the Secretariat; on January 23 this procedure was reaffirmed as a special method for treating territorial questions. The Council of Ten had just finished setting up its five principal commissions, when Clemenceau turned to the next items on the program.

M. Clemenceau said that a number of territorial and colonial questions remained to be discussed. Of these the territorial were the most delicate problems.

Doubtless each power would feel inclined to put off their discussion, but it must be undertaken. Before discussion these questions required classification. He would therefore beg the Governments to think of this, and at a later meeting to bring with them a classification.

M. Sonnino asked whether the most practical means would not be to fix a time by which each Delegation should present their wishes. The meeting would then have a notion of the ground to be covered. This applied to the Great Powers and to the smaller countries alike. A complete picture of the whole problem would then be available.[103]

At this point Lloyd George proposed that first consideration be given to oriental and colonial questions; he met Wilson's

---

[103] B. C. 8, January 23, in Miller, *Diary*, XIV, 10–12. Cf. Baker, *Woodrow Wilson*, I, 253, where some of this material is quoted. The minutes do not confirm Baker's assertion that Wilson secured a postponement of the consideration of colonial questions.

objections by explaining that "he only suggested dealing with the East and with the Colonies in order to save time while the various delegations were preparing their case."

M. Clemenceau suggested that a date be fixed by which all Delegations should be requested to state their cases in writing. (It was then decided that the Secretary General should ask all Delegations representing Powers with Territorial Claims to send to the Secretariat their written statements within ten days.) [The ten days would expire on February 1st.]

In the whole month of January the principal preoccupations of the Council, apart from the organizing of the Conference and commissions, were four questions: the renewal of the Armistice with Germany, the establishment of a Russian policy, the provisional protection of undefined Polish frontiers against Germans, Russians, and Czechs, and finally the disposition of the German colonies. Two of these questions—the Polish and the colonial—were essentially territorial questions, but they were not treated as such. The Polish frontiers were not defined, the colonies were not assigned, even as mandates. The object of the Council was to keep peace in Poland and to decide upon a general regime for colonies. In both of these matters it was Wilson's policy that prevailed. Foch wanted the Polish frontier fixed so that the Germans could be ordered to respect it.[104] Dmowski presented Poland's territorial claims in full on January 29, but the Council postponed action.[105] The policy of the Council in territorial matters was evinced in the "solemn warning" issued to the belligerents on January 24 that the use of armed force in securing possession of territories to which they laid claim would prejudice their claims and "put a cloud upon every evidence of title . . . and indicate their distrust of the Conference itself." [106] The Council did not at this time envisage its territorial problems in terms of particular boundary

[104] B. C. 7, January 22, 1919, in Hoover War Library.
[105] B. C. 15, January 29, 1919, in Miller, *Diary*, XIV, 62–70.
[106] B. C. 9, January 24, 1919, Miller, *Diary*, XIV, 17.

lines, but rather as a general necessity for maintaining the authority of the Conference, holding down the lid on explosions of violence, and postponing the consideration of questions which would threaten the harmony then prevailing.

The Polish question, like the armaments question, was presented to the Council as a problem to be settled definitely for the Treaty, but was acted upon only in its transitory aspect, as a matter of Armistice administration. The colonial question was treated differently from the Polish to the extent that in this case the principles of a new international order—the text of an article in the Covenant—were agreed upon, but the cases were treated alike in that the only immediate action taken lay in the field of Armistice administration. An interallied commission was sent to Warsaw to try to keep the peace, and a military committee was instructed to report upon a method for sharing the costs of occupying the colonial areas, especially Asiatic Turkey. There was no action upon Polish frontiers and none upon the distribution of colonies, although the claims were presented in each case. The Council would not even draw provisional frontiers, or assign provisional mandates. When the Belgians came in at the close of the long colonial debate to ask for a piece of East Africa, Lloyd George closed off the discussion by saying:

Belgium asked for something that they had not yet started to discuss, namely, who should be the mandatory. They were making out a case that they should be a mandatory in respect to those territories, a question which had not yet been reached.[107]

Thus it came about that January ended with no steps taken toward allotting territories or assigning boundaries.

In the two meetings of the Council on January 29 the Poles had presented their full territorial claims, and the Czechs had presented their claims to Teschen. The result of the debate

[107] B. C. 18, January 30, 1919, in Miller, *Diary*, XIV, 120. The discussion of the colonial question began January 24 and ended January 30.

was the decision to send a mission to keep peace in Teschen between the two new States. The next meeting of the kind was staged on January 31, to give the Rumanians and Serbs an opportunity to argue about their claims to the Banat— an argument which was bitter but wholly indecisive. These meetings were not intended to contribute toward making peace with the enemy, but only to help in keeping peace among the Allies. In that respect they were an application of the policy enunciated in the "warning to belligerents" of January 24.

The long hearing given to the Poles and Czechs had shown how wasteful of time it was to present to the Council matters which were not prepared for decision. When Clemenceau wanted to pass on from the Polish-Czech dispute to the Serbo-Rumanian quarrel Lloyd George objected.

> . . . some sort of an Agenda should be formulated. . . . He inquired whether the Conference now intended to discuss European territorial questions. He thought the discussion of Poland and Czecho-Slovakia the other day had been a mistake; a report should have been submitted before the matter had been broached in the Conference.[108]

There ensued an argument as to whether or not time had been wasted, and Clemenceau went on to rationalize the conduct of the Council:

> President Wilson had proposed that they should begin to deal with territorial questions. They began with the Pacific, then passed to Africa. Now they had come to Europe, beginning with Poland, because there was a pressing necessity and fighting was taking place there. If it were not decided to hear the Rumanian case the following day, well, let it be so; but they must have courage to begin with those questions one day or other.

Lloyd George protested that he had no objection to hearing the Rumanian case, provided it was a "serious discussion" of the territorial question. At this point Wilson reverted to the

---

[108] B. C. 18, January 30, in Miller, *Diary*, XIV, 121 *et seq.* The further quotations are from same source.

plan which he had first proposed on January 17, and which Lloyd George had then killed lest it should create commissions which the Council could not control.

His suggestion was that the British students of the subject, and the Americans, French, Italians and Japanese if they had a body of students conversant with those things, should take up any one of those questions and find out how near they were in agreement upon it, and then submit to the conference for discussion their conclusions as to what, for example, the territory of Rumania should be. They then should submit their conclusions to the Rumanians for their opinion. By this means they would eliminate from the discussion everything in which they were not in agreement.

The proposal as Wilson now formulated it was less respectful of the *amour propre* of the smaller powers than any of the earlier proposals. The experts were not to begin with a study of claims made by the interested power, but were to work out tentative conclusions independently. This method seemed all the more necessary because the delegations had not filed their claims with the Secretariat. But it was not a procedure which the small powers could be expected to accept without a murmur. Balfour was thinking of this aspect of the matter when he objected:

He was not sure that it would not be wise to allow those people to have their day to explain their case. He thought they would be much happier, though he admitted it took up a great deal of time. He thought it would make a great difference to them if they came there and said that they would put their whole case before the conference.

Balfour's point of view prevailed. Efficiency was sacrificed to courtesy. The principle was adopted that the starting point of a discussion of boundaries would be an oral statement by a claimant. This was a departure from the earlier procedure, which had required the presentation of claims to the Secretariat. The old procedure was formally abandoned on February 1, when "Orlando invited attention to the fact that the period granted for the submission of documents relating to territorial claims would expire on that date, and . . . no documents had been received by the Secretariat General except a part of the Greek case and a report by the Czecho-Slovak delegation." [109] It remained then to try the new procedure, and to work out a way in which the plenipotentiaries would use their experts and the Council its committees. This problem came up on the same day, immediately after the Rumanians had stated their case.

As the Rumanian delegates left the Council chamber, Lloyd George proposed the creation of a commission of experts to "clear the ground." If the experts disagreed

> The representatives of the Great Powers would be compelled to argue out the case there in that Council Chamber. But there were many questions regarding which the Great Powers were perfectly impartial. . . . He fully admitted that this procedure could not be introduced as a permanent arrangement, or be accepted as a precedent for universal application; but in the particular case of the Rumanian claims he hoped the experts would be allowed to examine the ground in the first instance, and the representatives of the Powers would eventually decide the question.

This was exactly the treatment which Wilson had proposed giving to the questions prior to their presentation to the Council. The commission would not apply instructions to facts but merely organize material regarding which the Council had made no decision and hence issued no instruction. As if to emphasize that this was the character of the work to be allotted to the commissions, Wilson added that "only those aspects of the question which did not touch the purely political side of the problem should be examined by the experts." He wished to reserve the protection of minorities to the Council of Ten. Orlando opposed the use of commissions. "He failed to see how such procedure would expedite matters." Baker has quoted his

[109] B. C. 20, February 1, 1919, in Miller, *Diary*, XIV, 161 *et seq*. Further quotations from same source.

speech in full as an illustration of the difficulties with which Wilson had to contend when he tried "to use the weapons of the new diplomacy against the old." [110] But as Baker's own text admits, it was not Wilson but Orlando who was left isolated, fighting a lone hand, in the matter of the appointment of the commission.

Despite Lloyd George's assurance that the procedure adopted for the study of the Rumanian claims would not be a precedent, it became the standard procedure. The formula of instruction (except in the case of the Belgian committee) was very broad: "to reduce the question for decision within the narrowest possible limits, and to make recommendations for a just settlement."

Throughout the month of February the Council was setting up territorial commissions and farming out territorial questions. Six commissions were set up, and eight territorial questions distributed among them. [111] All the territorial problems were thus distributed except those directly affecting the Great Powers. On February 18 when the Yugoslav claims had been heard Sonnino and Clemenceau agreed that neither Italian nor French territorial claims could be submitted to a committee. [112]

These territorial committees (except the committee on Belgium) received no special instructions. A debate on questions of principle took place in the Council just before the appointment of the Rumanian Committee, but did not result in an instruction. The question was raised whether the secret treaty of 1916 was still valid even though Rumania had broken

[110] Baker, *Woodrow Wilson*, I, 185–186.

[111] February 1, Rumanian Commission; February 4, Greek Commission; February 5, Czechoslovak Commission; February 12, Belgian Commission; February 18, Jugoslav frontiers assigned to Rumanian Commission; February 21, Danish frontier assigned to Belgian Commission; February 24, Albanian frontier assigned to Greek Commission; February 26, Commission on Polish frontiers; February 27, Central Territorial Commission.

[112] B. C. 35, February 18, 1919, in Miller, *Diary*, XIV, 501.

it in making peace with Germany. Orlando took the pro-Rumanian view, while Clemenceau declared that the Council had already ruled against the validity of the secret treaty when it agreed to admit that country to the Peace Conference.[113] The Council came to no agreement, and left it to the committee to recur to the same debate. At the first meeting of the committee (on February 8) the Italian delegates tried to introduce the treaty "as a basis for the labors of the committee," the British and American members objected, and the question was left "in suspense." [114]

The question of principle which arose in Belgium's case was taken more seriously because it involved a neutral power. Belgium wanted Dutch territory in Limburg and Flemish Zeeland, but had difficulty in bringing such a territorial claim under the jurisdiction of an Inter-Allied Conference. The Belgian program called for compensations to Holland at the expense of Germany. Wilson and Balfour both saw the difficulty when Hymans was presenting the Belgian claims, and they took care to avoid entanglement by limiting the mandate of the committee to the investigation of the transfer of Malmédy and Moresnet to Belgium and "the possible rectification of the German-Dutch frontier on the lower Ems as compensation to Holland for meeting Belgian claims." [115]

The committee found these instructions unworkable and asked to have them changed. The French expert observed at the first meeting: "it does not seem possible to study the com-

---

[113] B. C. 20, February 1, in Miller, *Diary*, XIV, 178–179. The minutes of the meeting to which Clemenceau alluded are in the Hoover War Library, B. C. A-1, January 12: "Mr. Balfour did not mind Rumania's being treated as an ally for purposes of representation but he did not want to put Rumania in the same position in which she would have been if she had fought successfully to the end. 'I think Rumania ought to get a part of Russia.'"

[114] Minutes of the Committee on Rumanian territorial claims, photostat copy in New York Public Library, 1st meeting, February 8.

[115] B. C. 28, February 11, in Miller, *Diary*, XIV, 322–324; text of instruction, B. C. 29, February 12, p. 381.

pensation to be offered to Holland without considering at least in a general way the concessions which would be demanded on the Scheldt and in Limburg";[116] but the Council on February 26 persisted in its refusal to authorize the committee to discuss the territorial claims of Belgium against the Netherlands.[117] The committee confined itself to its instructions to the extent of making no comments on Limburg and Zeeland, but nevertheless it exceeded its mandate in another direction. It had been instructed to report on the cession of German territory "on the lower Ems" but it actually reported in favor of the cession of territory in the Rhine Valley, much richer, much more populous, and over a hundred miles from the lower Ems.[118]

The instruction given on February 12 to the Belgian Commission is interesting from another point of view. It was the first decision of the Council which had a formal bearing upon the question of the German frontier. In that it approved in principle the cession of German territory to Belgium and the Netherlands it went clearly beyond the contractual basis of peace with Germany. The Fourteen Points provided for Belgian restoration but not for Belgian aggrandizement. Wilson and Lansing did not advert to this aspect of Belgium's claim in the Council, and Haskins made only the mild gesture of asking:

Whether it is possible or just to demand of Germany concessions on her Dutch frontier? In this connection there is a question which ought to be considered before proceeding further. In approaching this question of compensation, the Commission should be guided by the general principles of the Fourteen Points of President Wilson.[119]

[116] Minutes of the Belgian Committee, February 25, in Miller, *Diary*, X, 8.

[117] B. C. 40, February 26, Miller, *Diary*, XV, 81.

[118] Report of the Belgian Committee, Miller, *Diary*, X, 127.

[119] Minutes of the Belgian Committee, February 25, Miller, *Diary*, X, 9–10.

From the legal as well as the ethnic standpoint the satisfaction of Belgian claims on Germany's west frontier demanded departures from the Fourteen Points at least as great as would have been required to carry out all the demands of France in the Saar. The Belgian Committee, with the American expert concurring, reported in favor of asking Germany to surrender the industrial region of the lower Rhine. If the same committee of experts had been given a free hand to decide the Saar question, it probably would have given the valley outright to France.[120]

This history of the Belgian Committee, like that of the Polish Committee, proves that the "experts" were more hostile to Germany or more easily persuaded by interested parties than the statesmen who sat in the Supreme Council. This is exactly the reverse of the picture presented by Baker. The Council disagreed with both these committees, in each case modifying in the interest of Germany the unanimous reports of their subordinates. Ten years of experience in the working of the Treaty has taught us that the Council was right in these cases and the territorial committees were wrong, and that the Treaty would have been better if the Council had gone further than it did in upsetting the decisions of the experts.

Nowhere did the Council squander more time to less advantage than in the hearings given to the small powers. The debate on colonial claims which, as Baker has rightly observed, might well have been postponed till the more pressing European problems were solved, fills ninety-six pages of the minutes, while the territorial hearings to which the Council committed itself fill one hundred and seventy-four. The debate on colonies resulted in an important decision of principle, but the territorial hearings were staged merely to soothe the feelings of the claimant delegates, and except in the Belgian case,

[120] The American territorial experts had recommended this solution—see their report of January 21, in Miller, *Diary*, vol. IV, Document No. 246, p. 212; compare with the more reserved attitude in February, *ibid.*, vol. VI, Document No. 441, pp. 43–52.

led to no decisions whatsoever. After Wilson left Paris the proposal which he had originally made for preliminary examination by committees was revived by Sir Robert Borden. On February 18, after a session had been wasted in hearing the Yugoslavs, Sir Robert said:

It had occurred to him that possibly time might be saved if the Council made up its mind what questions could suitably be sent to the committees in anticipation of hearing statements. A list of such questions might be established beforehand, and thereby in each instance a meeting of the Council might be saved.

Mr. Lansing observed that this had been discussed before the departure of President Wilson. It had been thought that many delegations anxious to make statements would be dissatisfied if referred direct to committees.[121]

The Council took no action upon the hearings given to the Syrians, Libanese, Armenians and Zionists, being as unwilling to assign to a committee the question of the carving up of the Ottoman Empire as to delegate its authority over the Rhine and Italian frontiers. This was in line with the policy used from the start in setting up the territorial committees, that they were to keep their hands off the big political questions. When the territorial committee system was crowned on February 27 by the appointment of a Central Territorial Commission to correlate the work of the various committees and to "make recommendations as to any part of the frontiers of the enemy states which are not included in the scope of any commissions," a special exception was made of "such frontier questions as any of the Powers concerned may reserve for discussion in the first instance at the Quai d'Orsay." [122]

[121] B. C. 35, February 18, in Miller, *Diary*, XIV, 503.
[122] B. C. 41, February 27, Miller, *Diary*, XV, 102. The French did not actually keep the Rhine and Saar questions out of the hands of committees. On March 10 at an informal meeting of House, Clemenceau and Lloyd George a committee was appointed to study the Rhineland problem—an uninstructed committee to study and report differences; on April 1 a Committee on the Saar was appointed to carry out definite instructions.

The question naturally arises, why was not this system of territorial committees, as completed on February 27, set up at the time the other elements of the commission system were established? The answer is not to be found, as Baker implies, in the Council's suspicion of the experts, for the February system of territorial committees still left the big political questions in the hands of the Council. Neither is the delay explained as Tardieu declares by Anglo-Saxon antipathy toward systematic procedures, for all the sections of the agenda except the territorial were systematically farmed out, and it was the Anglo-Saxon Wilson who twice proposed the preliminary farming out of the territorial questions. The reason for the delay was twofold, first: preoccupation with problems of future international organization, and second: the fear of trouble with the smaller powers. On January 17 there seemed to be danger that the delegates of the lesser states would be too influential, and on January 30 that they might become too resentful to permit the smooth working of the peace-making machinery. The two territorial procedures, making use of the Secretariat in January, and of the Council in February, were designed first to muzzle and then to placate the lesser Allied States. The real work of drawing the frontiers began in the committees.

THE PRELIMINARY PEACE

Although Article I of the Rules of the Conference stated that it was the first object of that body to make a preliminary peace, the principal decisions made in the first month of its sessions, while Wilson was present, had to do either with the Armistice or with the Covenant. The day-to-day administration of European affairs in enemy and allied countries, and the working out of plans for a new international order, so far occupied the attention of the negotiators that the idea of a preliminary peace had to be born again, and to assume its first clear and practical form as an extension in their minds of the idea of the

Armistice. The Armistice problem had made such encroach-
ments upon the time of the Council that the transition seemed
to be a natural one. The increase, at the expense of the Peace
Treaty, of Armistice and related business can be calculated
from the space given to each in the minutes of the Council.
In the seventeen sessions from January 12 to 27, while the
Conference and the great commissions were being set up, the
Armistice took up only fifteen per cent of the time; in the
twenty-one sessions from that day to February 14th, when
Wilson left Paris, it took thirty-six per cent, and if the time
consumed in the hearings given to the smaller powers be regarded as a concession to the need of maintaining order from
day to day (which it was) and not as a contribution toward
agreement on territorial questions (which it was not), the proportion of time given to the study of the emergencies of the
hour, as against the permanencies of the treaty, rises to seventy-
two per cent.[123]

This increased proportion of time devoted to Armistice
affairs was the revenge which Europe exacted of the Conference for the delay in making peace. The French November
plan had segregated four stages in the settlement: the Armistice was to run till the Preliminary Peace was made: the Preliminary Peace was to lead the way to a General Peace or

---

[123] The following computations are based upon number of topics discussed and number of words in the official minutes. They can have only
approximate accuracy:

The Distribution of Working Time in the Council of Ten

	17 Sessions Jan. 12–27	21 Sessions Jan. 28–Feb. 13
Setting up the Conference. (Representation; Press; Language, procedure, etc.)	60%	
Farming out work to committees	13%	5%
The debate on the colonies (acceptance of mandatory principle)	12%	23%
Hearings to small powers on territorial questions		36%
Armistice administration	15%	36%

settlement of the war, which in turn was to make possible the Organization of the Peace or the League of Nations. The London Conference telescoped the membership, and Wilson telescoped the agenda, of these various peace conferences. But the problem which a preliminary peace was intended to solve remained, and pressed upon the Conference so persistently that the subject matter of a preliminary peace was constantly detaching itself from the procedure for formulating a general peace, and entering the agenda of the Armistice negotiations. The problem of German disarmament was transferred in this way on January 23, because the Armistice Commission was the only allied organ in contact with the enemy.[124] The resulting confusion between Armistice and Peace was evidenced on February 1, when the Admirals were asked to report on "Naval clauses to be introduced into the Peace Treaty," whereas the military men had been instructed to prepare clauses for the Armistice.[125] Still other subjects appeared on the borderland of Armistice and Peace. The opening of hostilities between Germans and Poles made the Polish frontier appear to be an Armistice question; the advance of winter and the march of hunger through Central Europe called for elaborate Armistice negotiations over the import of food and raw materials into Germany. German disarmament was found to call for the establishment of some control over her metallurgical industries. The Armistice Commission was becoming the agent in such highly complex negotiations covering so many fields that it was logical to consider giving to it a less exclusively military character. Accordingly Wilson and Lloyd George proposed on February 7 that further negotiations with the Germans should be entrusted to a civilian commission.[126] On February 10 Klotz proposed certain financial clauses for the Armistice renewal which Wilson thought should be

[124] B. C. 8, January 23, Miller, *Diary*, XIV, 5.
[125] B. C. 20, February 1, Miller, *Diary*, XIV, 182.
[126] B. C. 25, February 25, Miller, *Diary*, XIV, 242.

left to the Economic Commission of the Peace Conference and the final Treaty.[127] The Commission on the Responsibilities of the Authors of the War discussed on February 3, and voted on February 7, a demand that the enemy should be required to surrender documents and suspected individuals as a condition of Armistice renewal.[128] Balfour mentioned this demand to the Council of Ten on February 7, but did not press it.[129] On February 12 Clemenceau presented a memorandum asking that "in the next agreement concerning the renewal of the Armistice" the Germans should be required to hand over 5,200 horses, 204,000 cattle, and comparable quantities of her livestock and seed. This was a matter properly falling within the domain of the reparations settlement. Thus there was a tendency in the first part of February to pour the pressing problems into the Armistice negotiations, because the Armistice Commission alone was in contact with the enemy, and the Peace Conference was not. If the Peace Conference was using its time to keep order among the Allies, must the Armistice Commission thus undertake to impose the elements of a peace settlement upon the enemy?

In the morning session of February 12 Balfour analyzed with his usual clarity the tendency to confuse Peace terms and Armistice terms, and proposed

that only inevitable small changes, or no changes whatever, should be made in the Armistice until the Allies were prepared to say to Germany: "these are the final naval and military terms of peace, which you must accept in order to enable Europe to demobilize and so to resume its life on a peace footing and reëstablish its industries."

President Wilson said that Mr. Balfour's proposal seemed to suggest to him a satisfactory solution. . . .[130]

[127] B. C. 27, February 10, Miller, *Diary*, XIV, 302.
[128] Minutes of the Commission in *Documentation internationale. Paix de Versailles*, III, 25.
[129] B. C. 27, February 10, in Miller, *Diary*, XIV, 310.
[130] B. C. 29, February 12, Miller, *Diary*, XIV, 335–336.

It was just three weeks since the vote of the Council of Ten had shifted this subject of German disarmament from the agenda of the Peace Conference to the Armistice, and now it was shifted back again. The Council voted to force Germany to accept "detailed and final military, naval and air terms," and after the "signature of these preliminaries of peace" to permit food and raw material to go through to her.

With this proposal, which Baker erroneously ascribed to Wilson, the Conference turned full circle and came back to the idea of a preliminary peace.[181] It must be noted, however, that the February plan for a preliminary peace bore no procedural relation to the November plan, which had by this time been forgotten. The November plan had been inspired by a feeling that the political terms must be dictated to the enemy; the February plan owed its origin to the thought that the military terms be discussed with him. The November plan had provided for the admission of the Germans to the Peace Conference after the signing of the preliminaries; the February plan envisaged no such consequences, but provided rather that the result of the signing of a preliminary peace would be an easing of the blockade.

The flow of subject matter from the Peace Treaty to the Armistice renewal terms had caused the latter to be rechristened a preliminary military treaty. The same process continued after Wilson left. On February 22 the settlement of frontiers, reparations, economic clauses and war responsibility was given precedence along with the military terms. This was exactly the content of the preliminary peace as planned in November. But then the American delegates, by using the phrase *inter alia*, left the way open for the inclusion of the Covenant in the preliminary treaty,[132] and when Wilson returned to Paris

---

[181] Baker, *Woodrow Wilson*, I, 290.

[132] B. C. 37, February 22, in Miller, *Diary*, XV, 19; *House Papers*, IV, 340. Colonel House noted in his diary his intention to block any future attempt to exclude the League of Nations from a preliminary peace.

he clinched the point on March 15 by reminding the public and the Conference that the decision to include the League as an "integral part of the general treaty of peace" had not been abandoned. Thus once again, in February and March as in December and January, the preliminary peace was telescoped with the general peace by expanding its agenda.

When this second cycle was completed with Wilson's announcement of March 15, the situation differed from that of January in the all-important respect that the Covenant was already drafted, and the statesmen were finally immersed in the occupation of assigning territories and specific advantages to the Allied countries at the expense of the enemy. It now appeared that the supremacy of the Plenary Conference, the participation of the small powers in the settlement and the preoccupation with the general international aspect of problems constituted an inseparable triad. When the agenda shifted from the "organization of the Peace" to the "settlement of the war," the Plenary Conference was finally and conclusively superseded by the Council.

The work of the Plenary Conference, the great task of defining the outlines of a new international order, had been carried as far as it was destined to be carried by the end of February. The draft of the Covenant had been presented to the Plenary Conference, and the Labor Section of the treaty had passed its second reading. The Transit Commission was still working on general conventions of freedom of transit. The ground that had not been won for international institutions by the 28th of February was not destined to be won at all. Thenceforth there was recession, not only in general spirit but in numerous points of detail.

At this moment the drafting of the specific peace settlement with the enemy was just getting under way. The creative effort of the Plenary Conference was ending, and the arduous task of the Supreme Council was beginning. It was the natural consequence of this change that the Supreme Council should undergo further development to equip it for its greater responsibilities. Between March 7 and March 24 an informal meeting of Clemenceau, Lloyd George and House developed into the Council of Four, a new form of the Supreme Council, which made no pretense of recognizing the formal legal consequences of the membership of the lesser states in the Conference. When membership, organization and agenda were different, is it strange that the spirit of the Conference should be different too? Observers detected a "slump in idealism," a "revival of imperialism," an increase in the tension of rivalries all along the line.

A historical judgment on the organization of the Peace Conference depends largely upon an evaluation of this changed atmosphere. Did it arise because the most contentious questions were then brought forward or because they had not been brought forward earlier? Was it a merit of the Conference to postpone contention and preserve a semblance of harmony until the principles of the new international order were established, or was it a fault in the Conference to permit widespread unrest and uncertainty to strain the patience of the people to the point where their clamor made wise solutions difficult? If, for instance, Fiume had been discussed in February, and the League postponed to April, would Italian opinion have been more conciliatory on Fiume or less coöperative in the question of the League? Would it have been possible for the Conference at any time and by means of any possible organization to have established stability without destroying hope and illusion? At this point the historical problem of Peace Conference organization merges with the broader problem of public opinion upon the terms of peace.

Part II

THE ECONOMY OF SCHOLARSHIP

IV

The Problem of Perishable Paper *

The invention of writing provided mankind at one stroke
with two new instruments: a means of communication and a
new device for remembering. This double function of writing
is reflected in the double purpose which libraries are expected
to fulfill. Our civilization expects our libraries to be at once
institutions for the diffusion of contemporary ideas, and depositories of the records of the race.

The policies of libraries, both in acquisition and in administration, inevitably compromise between these two purposes.
The current files of periodicals or even of newspapers are kept
up and made available to those who would use them. The new
books are acquired as they are announced in the publishers'
trade lists. This service of libraries to contemporary culture is
indispensable. Our whole organization of intellectual life takes
it for granted. The librarian is justly proud of his competence
in maintaining this service. But his real heart is elsewhere. That
part of his work which he cherishes most deeply is his duty
as the custodian of ancient records for the man of today, and
the transmitting of contemporary records to the generations
of the future. This high responsibility infuses with its dignity
the most humble tasks of librarianship.

Now it has come about, almost in our own time, that the
two duties of librarians diverge from each other, so that they

* Read at First World Congress of Libraries and Bibliography, Rome,
June, 1929.

can no longer be combined in a simple and automatic policy. It used to be possible to receive the important records of the moment, use them so far as contemporary need required and then preserve these same documents as a legacy to the future. This was the practice of the archivist priests of Egypt and Mesopotamia, of the librarians of the Roman world, of China, and of Europe down almost to the present time. The practice did not arise, necessarily, in any consciousness of a duty to history. It was rather an automatic result of the fact that the writing materials, were they clay, wood, papyrus, parchment, or paper, were *durable*. They outlasted the libraries in which they were stored, the cities which had built the libraries, even the civilizations which had created the cities.

The nineteenth century made us more conscious of our duty to history. It instructed us in what we call the scientific attitude toward history; it taught us the value of preserving records for "the historian of the future." It gave us to understand that an accurate knowledge of all aspects of our past was essential to clear thinking upon the present. And having thus taught us the value and sanctity of all records, it began to print its records upon highly perishable paper!

The change from hand-made paper of the early nineteenth century to the machine-made product of the latter half, and from paper of which the predominant ingredient was cotton or linen to one which was predominantly grass or wood, was a change as significant in the history of civilization as the change from papyrus to parchment in the ninth century, and from parchment to paper in the fifteenth. The importance of the change from the old paper to the new is first of all that the new paper is very cheap, and second that it is very perishable.

The cheapness and abundance of the new paper have contributed heavily to the development of the culture of the last fifty years. Democracy on the one hand and specialization of intellectual interests on the other have taken this medium of communication for granted. The revolution in the publishing trades which gave us our enormous newspaper and periodical press coincided with the spread of popular education which created an increased mass of readers. The participation of peoples in government and the increased administrative responsibilities assumed and reported upon by governments have helped to give rise to a demand for paper that the old materials and methods could not possibly have supplied.

Meanwhile, on the level of purely intellectual life, the sciences have been dividing and subdividing, replacing the encyclopedic natural philosophies (of which Spencer's was perhaps the last) with highly specialized disciplines, each of which makes use of its professional journals to coördinate the work done in its own field. There were not many specialized scientific periodicals in the days of the old paper, but in the days of the new paper they have come to be numbered by thousands. Contemporary civilization is implemented on the intellectual side with wood pulp paper, as surely as it is implemented on the mechanical side with metal.

This wood-pulp paper serves well enough for carrying on the practical affairs of the day, but if we depend upon these publications to serve also as permanent records we will be disappointed. This most decisive epoch in the development of our civilization has been recorded upon paper that will not last. Our own generation of librarians is the first to feel the poignancy of this fact. Each generation of librarians since the fifteenth century has accumulated the records of its own time, added them to the heritage it received and passed them on to the new generation. Now comes the break in this great tradition. We are unable to do what they have done, for the records of our time are written in dust.

The change from the old paper to the new came about mid-century. In the fifties and sixties esparto grass was used; in the seventies and eighties wood pulp became common. The consequence of the change in the diminished quality of library books was noticed almost at once. In 1887 A. Martens of the Prussian *Materialpruefungsamt* tested the paper upon which one hundred periodicals of permanent value were published, and found that only six of them were printed on paper which was likely to last for many years. This warning had little effect upon publication practices. About ten years later, 1898, the conference of Italian librarians voted to ask the government to control the standard of paper for government publications and for a given number of books, reviews, and newspapers for government libraries. In the same year the Royal Society of Arts in London appointed a committee to inquire into paper deterioration. And at the International Library Congress at Paris in 1900 it was recommended in an excellent paper by Pierre Dauze that governments and libraries should refuse to purchase books printed on impermanent paper.

In 1907 the Prussian *Materialpruefungsamt* undertook a second investigation. Twenty years had passed since the first warning was issued by A. Martens. A survey by W. Herzberg for the *Pruefungsamt* demonstrated that the use of the very poorest paper in important periodicals had diminished, but nevertheless it remained true that the great bulk of the books which should be permanent were printed upon impermanent paper. Herzberg recommended that resort should be had to legislation requiring that all copies of printed matter deposited in, or purchased by public libraries, should be printed on durable papers. If necessary, special library copies would have to be printed. In 1912 the American Library Association appointed a committee to study the problem of newspaper deterioration. The committee made efforts to induce newspaper publishers to print special library editions on rag paper. Then came the years of the war, which not only withdrew attention from the problems of perishable paper, but even brought about the introduction of papers far worse than those which had previously been used. It is only in the last few years that the scholars of the world have taken up again the serious consideration of this problem to which Martens called their attention more than forty years ago. The International Institute of Intellectual Coöperation has appointed a subcommittee to study the matter, and the opinion of this distinguished body seems to turn in favor of the policy of special library editions on permanent paper.

In laying the question before this section of the Library Congress I am, of course, preaching to the converted. It is in the acquisition policy of libraries that the problem of the impermanent paper stock is most immediately felt. In choosing from among the almost unlimited output of the publishing trade those items which we will undertake to add to the permanent resources of scholarship, we must take into account not only the intellectual value of the printed word, but the physical quality of the material substance upon which it happens to be printed. Therefore this perishable paper has a doubly harmful effect: it gradually destroys that which has been carefully accumulated, and it warps the policy of the library in making its accumulation. If I may cite a single instance of this, let me refer to the problem of preserving newspaper files.

Certainly the newspaper of our day is a social agency of the first importance. It is not merely a record of our life; it is a part of our life. And it is a part of our life which is only too inadequately understood. Every question relating to the problems of the public mind becomes for research purposes fundamentally a problem of the newspaper. We are in a world in which men must learn to think together, and we do not yet understand fully the mechanics of the process whereby they are brought to think together. There is no one who is not impressed by the power of the press as exhibited in the course of the war. And perhaps I may add that there is no one who adequately understands that power. For the press itself, in its modern dimensions, is new—as new, in fact, as the perishable paper of which it makes such copious use.

But if we should seek to apply the tools of scholarship to the analysis of this great social fact of our day, we would find ourselves thwarted at once by the fact that libraries cannot afford to keep newspaper files which will not last, and that the newspaper files which have been stored by libraries are crumbling away. There are newspapers of the Russian revolution of 1917 which are today completely gone. They have never been read by the scholar's eye, and they never will be read. It is already too late for them. Those who know how great was the value of the study of press and pamphlet material in the understanding of the French Revolution will regard this as a tragedy of the first importance.

There is the problem. It will be expected that we draft a program to meet it. It is a world problem, to which this Congress can appropriately apply its accumulation of experience and counsel.

If I may venture to suggest some of the things that seem to me to be the outlines of a plan of solution, I will say that our task divides itself into two parts. We will wish

First: to bring it about that, in future, publications intended for permanent record use shall be printed upon paper that will permit them to fulfill their purpose.

Second: that the fifty years' legacy of decaying paper that lies on our hands shall be rescued if rescue is possible, or otherwise, that the records committed to that paper shall be copied.

In practice these two problems begin with a single problem of chemical research. We do not know the chemistry of the decomposition of cellulose. We do not know how to manufacture a paper that will be at once cheap and durable.

To illustrate: When the Royal Society of Arts reported upon perishable paper in 1898, it recommended a specification which, it was then thought, would insure permanence. It was thought that the raw material which entered into the papermaking was the all-important factor in its longevity, and that the higher the percentage of rag and the lower the percentage of wood pulp, the greater was the life expectancy of the product. A book entitled "Cellulose" relating to this matter was then printed, which stated in the preface that it was printed on paper conforming to the specification of the Royal Society of Arts. Curiously, however, the paper in this book showed early signs of rapid deterioration, probably because it was not free from acid and bleach residue.

The United States Bureau of Standards undertook in 1928 a research to determine the permanence qualities of papers. The program adopted was (1) tests of the current commercial rag and wood fiber products including the fibrous raw materials, (2) tests of similar papers made in the bureau paper mill and therefore having a definitely known history, (3) inspection and testing of papers of known age, (4) study of means of overcoming influences found to be harmful to the life of papers, (5) research to find the nature of the reaction of paper celluloses to deteriorating influences. This work is still in progress, and when completed should result in reliable specifications for durable paper, taking as a standard the fine old papers of the fifteenth and sixteenth centuries.

We do not know, of course, what these specifications will be, nor do we know how great will be the cost of durable paper over perishable paper, but it is to be expected, certainly, that the durable papers will be more costly, and therefore it will not be easy to bring about a change in the practices of publishers, so that editions will be available on the permanent stock.

However, it is absolutely necessary that such a change in the practice of publishers be introduced, and the librarians are precisely the ones who have laid upon them, by virtue of the traditions of their calling, the duty of bringing about this change. It will not be an easy change to introduce, and it will involve, at least, these two lines of activity:

First: To act upon the governments in order to bring it about that government publications are printed, at least in limited numbers, upon durable stock. This project is now being considered by the Committee on Printing of the American Government at Washington. Recently the legislature of the State of Indiana adopted an amendment to its Printing Bill to authorize the printing of a special edition of some of its important state documents upon durable paper. I have no information upon the progress of this movement, and would be very glad if anyone who is more familiar with the European situation would report upon it.

Second: To act upon the publishing trade in general in a way that will help to make it profitable for publishers to issue special editions upon durable stock, or to publish entire editions of works of permanent worth upon durable stock. At the present time the trade in books printed upon durable paper has the character of a luxury trade, carried on for those who specialize upon the possession of fine books rather than their use. We must try to bring about a more rational relationship between the permanent value of a book and the durability of its paper stock. And to effect this end, we have three possible ways of working: (1) By propaganda among book purchasers which will create a demand for a durability guarantee as part of the commercial value of the book, without at the same time placing the books that are printed on good paper in the class of luxuries. (2) We can as librarians, who ourselves control no inconsiderable part of the funds which go to the support of the publishing trade, go out of our way to purchase volumes which are printed upon good paper, so that the publishers can count upon an enhanced library sale as an inducement to the use of good paper, whether the paper is used for an entire edition, or for a part of it only. Several newspapers in America, and at least one magazine publish special rag paper editions for libraries. (3) Finally there is the device, available as a last resort, of making use of copyright registration laws to secure the use of good paper. There are very grave objections to such an interference with rights to intellectual property; such legislation must not be drawn without taking all interests into account; but among the interests must be included the right of the future generations to receive from us an adequate record of our history as we have received the records of the past.

Whatever success may attend our efforts to improve the publishing customs of the world, there remain the stacks of perishing books and journals in libraries everywhere, and we have the problem of trying to save some at least of this material.

This will require an enormous effort of research and organization. It is first necessary to discover the best way of saving this material. Then it will be necessary to organize the work of salvaging. Two fundamentally different devices suggest themselves as means of rescuing decaying documents: to try to preserve the paper stock itself, or to make copies of that which is printed upon it. For the first we turn to chemistry, for the second to photography and optics. And it is requisite of either method that its cost must be brought down to such a point that its use on a colossal scale will be possible.

As devices for prolonging the life of existing paper stocks, those which at present find use are of two kinds. On the one hand, attempts are made to add to the paper by spraying or dipping in some substance such as a cellulose acetate, which will permeate the paper, giving it a new body. On the other hand the method is used of pasting sheets of Japanese tissue on both sides of the paper, thus giving it a new surface. The former is the cheaper, the latter probably the more effective, but the absolute preservative effect of both methods is still unknown.

The photographic reproduction of printed matter has long been a library tool of great convenience, but the usual method, by taking a full-size photostatic copy, is too expensive for large-scale operations. The cost can be cut down enormously by reducing the reproduction to microscopic proportions and reading it by projection or by some other optical device. This method is being used at present by the Library of Congress in copying European archives. The image of the printed matter is reduced ten or twenty diameters in the photographing, which means that the area of photographic surface used is anywhere from one one-hundredth to one four-hundredth of the surface of the page which is being copied.

In reading reduced-scale photographic copies, the two instruments being developed are projectors and improved reading glasses. Some time ago a binocular reading glass was patented by Admiral Fiske, a retired officer of the American Navy. This glass could be used in reading copies of printed matter after a reduction of six diameters.

When we know finally the best possible ways of preserving perishing materials, a vast task of organization will lie before us. It will then be necessary to prevent the wasting of effort by unnecessary duplication of the work of preservation. A wise coördination of the salvaging efforts of the libraries of the world, counseled by the scientists as to the technique of preservation, and by the representatives of all scholarly and intellectual interests as to the selection of what is worth preserving, may then recover for civilization what a generation of thoughtless publishing practices have threatened to lose.

V

New Tools for Men of Letters *

There is taking place in the techniques of record and communication a series of changes more revolutionary in their possible impact upon culture than the invention of printing. With some of these techniques, notably those that depend upon electricity and include the telegraph, telephone, radio, teletype, and television, the world is already familiar, though what their total result will be we do not yet know. Others coming up in the graphic arts, based on the typewriter and photography and including "near-print," micro-photography, and photo-offset, are less widely understood.

These two series of innovations operate, or promise to operate, in contrary directions in their effects upon culture. The electrical devices, together with the moving picture and the modern developments in commercial publishing, tend to concentrate the control of culture and to professionalize cultural activities. Telegraph and teletype serve in this way for news, radio for music, and the "talkies" for dramatic entertainment. Meanwhile, printing has keyed literature to mass production, technologically by means of fast presses and machine papermaking, commercially by means of a union with advertising, both in the promotion of book sales and the sale of magazine space. The new graphic arts devices are, I believe, capable of working the other way—as implements for a more

* Reprinted from *The Yale Review*, Spring 1935, by permission of the Editors. Copyright Yale University Press.

decentralized and less professionalized culture, a culture of local literature and amateur scholarship.

This possibility is especially important today, when electric power promises to develop the village at the expense of the metropolis, and when shorter working hours offer a prospect of leisure to a population of which an increasing proportion is being exposed to college education.

The activities reorganized in the fifteenth century by the invention of printing, and now offered another reorganization by innovations in the graphic arts, affected bookmakers, authors, and readers. The technical processes of photo-offset and photogelatin printing disclose new prospects in bookmaking. Near-print frees the author from some present restraints upon him. And micro-copying opens a new world to readers.

When the printers drove out the copyists in the fifteenth century, there was some loss as well as gain. Typography has never captured the sheer beauty of some of the medieval manuscripts, although the early printers often produced admirable effects by drawing for their type forms directly upon the rich tradition of the calligraphers' craft. Today in certain ways artistic typography is again trying to draw closer to the art of calligraphy. In some of the finest type fonts, there are cast several slightly different forms of a single letter, used at random, so that the too faultless regularity of print may be in some measure offset. The modern typographic expert also tries to choose a type face that will seem to harmonize with the subject or style of a book. Yet it is evident that calligraphy can convey the author's individuality in a manner beyond the reach of typography. Now the way has been cleared for the return of the manuscript book.

This has been done by the photo-offset process, which transfers a text with black and white illustrations photographically to a sheet of zinc or aluminum in such a fashion that the metal sheet becomes a printing surface, laying down an image on a rubber roller, which transfers it to paper. This process has received its widest application in advertising work, because it is adapted to the handling of combinations of pictorial and textual material without added expense. It costs no more to photograph a drawing than to photograph the same area of print. The process is also used extensively in reprinting old books, but it can equally well multiply copies of a manuscript, old or new. Photo-offset renders sharp black and white; the related photogelatin or collotype process, which renders gradations of tones from light to dark, is also used in reproducing old manuscripts. In Germany a newly founded "guild" has made a number of beautiful manuscript books and multiplied them by the photo-offset method. Since the necessary press and equipment are now available as a kind of office machine, and the handcraft of book binding is widely practiced, the whole sequence of processes involved in manufacturing manuscript books might be organized without using the equipment or sharing the overhead costs of the present publishing industry.

The reader as well as the bookmaker found his world changed by the invention of printing. Books became more accessible. The first effect, in China in the Sung era as in the West in the fifteenth century, was to spread more widely the source books by which all intellectual activities were fed— the Chinese classics in the one case, and the basic Christian and Greco-Roman works in the other. So it became possible for the moderately wealthy man to possess what previously only princes or great religious establishments could afford—a fairly complete collection of the materials he desired.

This happy position was destroyed in the nineteenth century by the flood of books and journals that accompanied specialization in all fields of learning. By their cost readers and scholars were for the most part forced to give up the attempt to make complete collections and turn, as in the days before printing, to the libraries of institutions. When this happened, the institutional library developed an administrative system of great efficiency, and by its detailed catalogue made its possessions available to scholars and other readers within each. Research libraries in the country are spending about six millions of dollars a year for new acquisitions. The reader who now has all this material at his disposal is still profiting immensely from the increased accessibility given to reading matter by the invention of printing.

Meanwhile the relation of the scholar-reader to the books on the library shelves has been changing. The body of documentation that was once the common ground of all learning and culture has lost its cohesion. And it has become a relatively unimportant element in the total bulk of publication. Today the Western scholar's problem is not to get hold of the books that everyone else has read or is reading but rather to procure materials that hardly anyone else would think of looking at. This is, of course, the natural consequence of the highly specialized organization of our intellectual activity. As a result, so far as Western culture is concerned, the qualities of the printing process that began in the fifteenth century to make things accessible have now begun in our different circumstances to make them inaccessible. When many if not all scholars wanted the same things, the printing press served them. In the twentieth century, when the number of those who want the same things has fallen in some cases below the practical publishing point (American Indian language specialists are an illustration), the printing press leaves them in the lurch. Printing technique, scholarly activities, and library funds have increased the amount of available material at a tremendous rate, but widening interests and the three centuries' accumulation of out-of-print titles have increased the number of desired but inaccessible books at an even greater rate. Scholarship is now ready to utilize a method of book production that would return to the cost system of the old copyist, by which a unique copy could be made to order and a very few reproductions supplied without special expense.

Precisely this prospect is now presented by micro-copying.

The process promises to reproduce reading matter not only at a cost level well below that prevailing in the book trade but also under a cost system that will operate like that of the medieval copyists. This system is being tried out in recording the hearings of the National Recovery and the Agricultural Adjustment Administrations. The reports of these hearings constitute a very comprehensive body of useful information on contemporary business interests and practices. The non-confidential parts of the record run to 286,000 pages. It would cost more than half a million dollars to publish them in a printed edition. Since printing was found too expensive, the A.A.A. and the N.R.A. turned to hectograph and mimeograph, the so-called "near-print" processes. Purple-ink hectographed copies of the hearings were offered to libraries at two cents a page. At this rate the cost to a library of the full file of the hearings would have been more than $5,000. No library purchased a set at that price, though Trade Associations and Code authorities with money and special interests to serve provided themselves with copies of parts that particularly concerned them, paying in the case of the N.R.A. records a higher rate—ten cents a page. Nowhere save in the government offices in Washington could a complete file be seen.

Then micro-copying was tried. This is a process by which a page of print or typescript is photographically reduced twenty-three diameters in size, being copies on a strip of film ½ inch wide and one or two hundred feet long. The micro-copies are rendered legible by projection. A machine throws an enlarged image downward on a table, where the reader finds it just as legible as the original page. The cost of materials and operation is so low that the half million pages can be distributed for about $421.00 instead of $5,000 a set—and this rate will apply even if only ten libraries should purchase copies. The cost of making a unique micro-copy of a document is roughly twenty cents per hundred pages, and the cost of making additional copies drops to about twelve cents per hundred pages. These costs are well below normal production costs of printed volumes, in ordinary editions of over two thousand. Micro-copying thus offers the reader a book production system more elastic than anything he has had since the fifteenth century; it will respond to the demand for a unique copy, regardless of other market prospects. So the scholar in a small town can have resources of great metropolitan libraries at his disposal.

The organization of service that will bring about this result is already taking form. Any scholar who wants to procure the text of a few hundred pages of some rare book or inaccessible periodical from Yale University Library, New York Public Library, or the Library of Congress can send for it by mail and get a micro-copy for $1.50 per hundred pages. By using a more efficient copying camera invented by Dr. R. H. Draeger, U.S. Navy, the Department of Agriculture Library is able to offer micro-copies at 10 cents for any one article of 10 pages or less, and 5 cents for each additional 10 pages. The Library of Congress is now about to install the Draeger machine. There is some prospect of even more efficient devices for copying. Some scholars will do their own copying with portable equipment. Micro-copying is a technique that will serve in the twentieth century to do what printing and publishing cannot always accomplish: give the reader exactly what he wants, and bring it to him wherever he wants to use it.

The effect of the printing press upon writers was not so quickly felt as its effects upon readers. The first printed books were mainly not "new books" by new authors; they were editions of the Bible and the classics, educational and religious texts. Writers were able to increase their influence greatly by using the press, as Luther and Erasmus discovered, but a good copyright law and administration were necessary before they could make a good living from writing. In the eighteenth century, however, the writers were able to shift their sources of income from patrons to publishers. Writing became a profession, and then writers found themselves subjected to the mechanics and accountancy of the printing press, which restrained their freedom perhaps even more than their previous masters, the patrons, had done. For authors discovered that it was useless to take pains to write anything that would not interest and attract the number of readers or buyers that the printer required in order to absorb and distribute his costs of composition and make-up. This minimum, in commercial publishing today, at average selling prices of $1.20 per hundred pages, is some two thousand copies. In this country when editions of less than that are printed, there is generally some form of subsidy, either from the publisher, using for them profits from other books, or from the author, or from some endowment, or from the purchaser in the form of an abnormally high price. The publishing industry, technologically and in its business organization, is keyed to the prospects of profits from sales in the hundreds of thousands.

The effects of this system have long been operative in literature. The decline of letter writing (despite improved postal service) was doubtless connected with the tendency to regard "literature" as essentially printed matter addressed to a numerous anonymous and passive public. The effort made today by the Committee of International Intellectual Coöperation to revive letter writing by promoting exchanges of letters among literary notables is stultified by the avowed purpose of publication, which means, in effect, that the letter writers are not so much communicating with each other as collaborating in the production of another book. Poetry writing as a leisured accomplishment was an ornament to the social intercourse of the classical world and Renaissance Italy; it survived into the baroque era, and, in alliance with calligraphy (not printing), it continues to be a social grace in China and Japan; but Western civilization now expects even poetry to fit the Procrustean bed of the publishing industry.

The art of conversation, with its counterpart the dialogue

as a literary form for presenting ideas, has also declined since the days of Galileo, while the art of advertising has advanced. Advertising is easily recognized as the literary form that most completely responds to the technique of the printing press, because it demands, above all else, a numerous and receptive "public" of readers. A great number of improvements in the graphic arts have been adaptations to the needs of advertisers. Yet, in its development of "direct mail" methods and circular letters, advertising seems to be more emancipated than literature from the printing press. One of the most curious recent developments in the graphic arts is the effort of the advertisers to make printed matter look like typescript, while the authors of books that are not in sufficient demand to warrant publication are seeking a typescript that will look like print.

The effect of printing upon literary form has been indirect. Upon literary or scholarly activities it has been direct and decisive. An author can lay his book before reviewers and critics only by persuading some editor that it is marketable; a scholar can make only such contributions to knowledge as can be passed through the publishing process to enter the body of scientific truth. What, then, of the literary creations that do not promise to command a wide audience, or the specialized contributions to knowledge that can be utilized by only a few experts? Both these classes of intellectual products suffer one of two fates. Either they remain uncommunicated, and are as if they had never been, or they are carried to their "public" by means of a subsidy. It is true that a host of small magazines supported by special professional groups, and a number of direct or indirect subsidies to scholarly books amounting to over a million dollars a year help to relax, but cannot eliminate, the tension between the demands of culture and the exigencies of the publishing industry. If local literature lags behind local activities in music and the arts, and amateur scholarship continues to suffer from the paralysis that overtook it in the last century, these conditions can be traced in no small measure

to the functioning of our system of book and magazine publishing, with its resistance to issuing anything that will not
attract a large number of buyers.

When printing leaves the writer of a work of limited circulation in the lurch, the typewriter comes to his rescue. The
typewriter first made its way as a letter-writing machine, especially for business letters. If letter writing as a literary art
had survived into the typewriter era, it might have blossomed
to the touch of the new technique. The business culture of
the nineteenth century took another road. Even the business
letter in the year 1800 was more "literary," less "business-like,"
than in the year 1900. The typewriter saw business writing
stripped of everything but the bare bones of communication.
More recently, in connection with direct mail advertising, it
implemented a return to the letter form. Meanwhile, the
scholars and novelists learned to use the typewriter, but only as
a step in the preparation of a manuscript for publication. The
time arrived when editors refused to read anything but "typescript." Unconsciously, writers came to associate the typescript form with the failure of a manuscript to please an
editor, the printed form with success.

The typewriter soon exhibited an ability to multiply copies
by means of carbon paper, of which scholars and business men
were quick to take advantage. This limited multiplying power
was further extended by two devices: the mimeograph, which
squeezes ink through a wax stencil that has been prepared on
a typewriter, and the hectograph, which lays typescript letters
formed of thick purple dye on a gelatin bed, from which
copies can be made as long as the deposit of dye lasts—usually
until about a hundred copies are taken off. The cost of the
mimeograph process can be expected to fall sharply as soon
as the patents on the wax stencil run out. Lately the hectograph
process has been improved by a device which eliminates the
need for a gelatin bed. The operating cost of the hectographing
process is so low that it does not greatly exceed the cost of

making carbon copies, except as the paper costs mount with increasing size of edition.

Mimeographing and hectographing, together with photo-offset from typescript copy, are the processes which we have come to call "near-print." They have been widely applied to the internal documents of business, government, and education. Manuals and price lists in business, instruction material for classes in high school and college, and any number of letters of information, reports, and memoranda for groups of consultants in government and business are being multiplied by the near-print processes. At present thirty-five per cent of the documents issued by the federal government to the public are in near-print form. Some small literary magazines are using the process. Publishers have noticed a curious consequence of this use of near-print for the internal documents of business. If a book is written on some specialized business subject, it can sometimes be sold for twenty dollars a copy in mimeographed form, though it would be unsalable at three dollars a copy in print. The reason, of course, is that the near-print methods are now associated with internal, "confidential" uses, just as printing is associated with a public use.

Owing doubtless to the system of endowment of institutions and institutional presses under which they work, scholars have been slow to explore the use of these near-print methods and products, even though they might well consider that much of their specialized research publishing corresponds in character to the "internal documents" of business rather than to the stock-in-trade of the commercial publishing industry. The system by which professional research workers draw their livelihood from institutions of learning has had a curious repercussion upon their system of communication, resulting in a kind of fetishism in the attitude of the professional scholar towards the printed page. Since contributions to knowledge become effective as contributions only when they are communicated, the amount of research labor is measured by employers at the communicating point. A research scholar must "publish" or be regarded by his university as a drone. Just as tradition protected the use of parchment long after paper had become accessible, so it has protected the status of the printed book or article as the only vehicle for scholarly communication even when processes other than printing would be more appropriate. But the pressure of financial necessity is gradually forcing the scholars to accept near-print as the only means of taking up the slack between the requirements of their intellectual organization and those of the book trade. A more general use by them of near-print should relieve not only their financial situation but also that of the institutional presses, upon whose endowments too great a strain is now being placed.

These three processes, photo-offset, micro-copying, and near-print, each important when considered by itself, offer an imposing prospect when they are considered together. The production of beautiful books, as physical objects, may be turned over more and more to calligraphers, the manuscripts to be multiplied by off-set. The duty of making reading matter accessible to the scholar may be assumed increasingly by the micro-copying process, and near-print may become the normal channel by which the creative worker, whether in literature or in scholarship, can be guaranteed communication with a limited group that shares his interests, leaving publication in printed form as the channel of communication with a larger public.

It is evident that these three processes taken together offer also to the small town a better chance to escape the cultural monopoly of the metropolis, to the amateur in scholarship a more favorable opportunity to coöperate with the professional scholar, than either could expect under the regime of the printing press and publishing industry. It is not necessary to argue the case for protecting a local culture against metropolitan encroachment, or for vitalizing the cultural environment of the small town. Sinclair Lewis has shown how bare is the ground, how difficult to build upon. And yet young people in towns of five thousand do learn to play the piano. There is some music, some art, some amateur theatrical enterprise, and a public library. When the C.W.A. Public Works of Art project was set up throughout the country, the result was a surprising revelation of the vigor of local art movements everywhere. There are great potential forces in our local culture. But a rounding out of the small community as an active cell in a living culture requires, in addition to art and music, a theatre and a library, something of creative literature and something of productive scholarship. These are precisely the activities which can be implemented by the recent innovations in the graphic arts.

Creative literature and research scholarship can be expected to make somewhat different contributions to local culture. The reorganization of literary activities that might accompany the full use of near-print devices would involve, first of all, the extinction of the idea that a "writer" is a strange creature apart from the world, or that it is only with a view to becoming one of these creatures that an otherwise normal human being would write stories after leaving college. One reason why the public associates amateur literature with immature literature is that so many of the non-professional literary publications are high-school and college magazines, financed by means of browbeating local merchants into buying advertising space. If the principle should come to be accepted that literature of small circulation ought not to be printed, but ought rather to be distributed in near-print form, students who have developed a flair for writing will be more likely to develop it further after graduation. They will not feel that the only alternative before them is to become full-time professional writers or to put away their writing as a man puts away childish things.

In research scholarship, a different situation now exists. The distribution of labor among professional scholars has not been arranged in a way that will easily make room for the contributions of amateur scholars. Our intellectual world witnessed in

the last century the passing of the amateur scholar. He had
been on the scene since the time of the invention of printing,
when the church was losing its monopoly of learning. He was
usually, though not always, a man of leisure. He collected
a library in which he worked diligently. He published a volume
on the antiquities of Cornwall or the customs of the Parthians.
He engaged in bitter pamphlet wars with his adversaries. At
his worst, he was Mr. Casaubon of *Middlemarch;* at his best,
he was Benjamin Franklin. His research was his hobby.

The century of progress thrust this figure into the background and vested in the universities the monopoly that
had once lain in the church. Classical scholarship was carried
forward by the professors in tremendous strides, but the layman no longer wrote about the classics and ceased even to
quote Latin authors. Natural science moved from triumph to
triumph, but the public became a passive spectator, taking on
faith conclusions the exact meaning of which it could not follow, just as in literature people might read the popular poets
but never try their hand at a sonnet. Research ceased to be an
honored sport and became an exclusive profession.

Why did the amateur scholar drop out? It was not because
of the development of specialization in scholarship, for the
more intensive division of labor should have made it easier
rather than harder for the leisure-time amateur and the full-
time professional worker to aid each other. The reason for his
decline was partly material, partly psychological. From the
material standpoint, the professionals soon monopolized all the
available means of communication. The mushroom growth of
specialized learned journals in the later nineteenth century was
barely able to keep up with the professional scholars, and in
the twentieth century it fell behind their needs. The scholarly
publishing industry in the United States does annually a six-mil-
lion-dollar business. Naturally, the professionals get the first
chance at this fund, and it does not suffice even for them. The
non-professional scholar who cannot afford to pay for printing

his own works can enter the charmed circle only by participating in the use of this publication fund. To participate in its use, he must do about the same things the professionals are doing, and in about the same way. This is the material obstacle to the development of amateur scholarship. Near-print devices offer a way around it.

The psychological obstacle to the development of amateur scholarship is found partly in the encroachment upon quiet leisure of many modern activities and partly in the attitude of the professionals towards their craft. They have taken little trouble to divide the labor in their fields in such a way as to assign tasks to the amateurs and train them for their work. They teach creative scholarship only to aspirants for the academic career. They do not, as a rule, train "laymen" for part-time, avocational, amateur research. They have come habitually to envisage the army of research as a body organized like a Central American Army, with almost all its members above the rank of colonel, and they make no arrangements for recruiting, training, and utilizing a rank and file.

The professional scholars cannot indefinitely continue indifference to the prospects of amateur scholarship, for they are facing a crisis themselves. The strain that is appearing in their system of recruiting and maintaining financially a professional personnel will force them to consider the redistribution of scholarly labor and the reorganization of scholarly communications.

For two generations in America, the recruits brought into the academic profession have been trained in the graduate school to work in the environment of a great university centre. In the smaller colleges such recruits work at a disadvantage, and outside the college and university environment they are generally too heavily handicapped to work at all. Little serious effort has been made to inspire productive scholarship on the part of the high-school teachers.

The new hordes of college students throughout the country

in the decade following the World War created a demand for more college instructors. In response to this demand, the graduate schools expanded like a machine-tool industry, turning out every year more Ph.D.'s. When the curve of college attendance began to level off in the depression, it was discovered that the production of apprentice scholars, keyed to an expanding market, went far beyond replacement needs. A turnover of about twenty per cent a year in the university teaching faculties would be necessary to give the new Ph.D.'s the kind of places they were prepared to fill. These young people trained for research could remain in the academic world only by going into the smaller colleges and academies, whose meager libraries give them little chance of continuing to do the kind of work they had been fitted to do. It seems inevitable that they will be lost to research scholarship unless the labor of this kind is redivided so that some of it can be performed away from the university setting, by people who are not university teachers.

If that could be done, this supply of trained scholars need not be wasted; they could be fed into the secondary-school system, and then enabled and encouraged to continue, in the secondary-school environment, their scholarly interests. Of course, the heavier teaching schedules of these schools leave less time for reading and study than the university teacher has at his disposal. And yet the long vacations are common to both careers. Moreover, the internal conditions of secondary education are such that the development of research in local history, social and economic life, and even local botany and geology, is among the great needs of the present. If such local research could be reported into the present stream of culture and scientific information, the results would enrich scholarship. And the teaching career in the secondary schools would thereby be made more attractive than it now is to persons of vigorous mind and more productive for the community.

To speak of an unemployment crisis among scholars is not

to speak merely of a probability that certain individuals, trained to do research, may be without jobs. The Ph.D.'s must take their chances with the rest so far as keeping away from the bread line is concerned. But the problem of the unemployed scholar, from the standpoint of the national culture, has another grave side. There is also the sad prospect that individuals trained to do research, and willing and able to do it, may be placed in situations in which their capacities are wasted. This kind of crisis now exists. Along with it there exists an unexplored opportunity in popular education; and at the same time the innovations in the graphic arts already mentioned are offering a way out. For micro-copying can bring the resources of the Library of Congress to the small-town high-school teacher, just as the radio brings the symphony orchestra. Near-print offers the scholar-teacher a means of communication not only with his pupils and their parents but also with his colleagues through the country; and the kind of interest and ability that it might help to develop in him would serve to stimulate the whole community.

What are the fields of scholarship that lie most open to the schoolteacher trained for research in his own community, or to the amateur? Where is this intellectual vineyard in which the harvest is so great, and the laborers so few? To give it a comprehensive name, including many different things, it could be called the field of local studies. The development and significance of local historical societies have been well described in an article on this subject by Dr. Julian P. Boyd. The object of such studies is to turn the methods of specialized research upon the immediate environment—its linguistic characteristics, for example, with the word usages, slang and colloquial; the annals or the soil or the flora and fauna of a neighborhood. All such local studies, whether in natural science or history or social organization or cultural background, require long, close, and patient observation. Many of them, like the observation of variable stars, of meteors, and of insect life cycles, are scientific tasks that call for an unlimited number of helpers coöperating by exchange and contribution of detailed facts.

Throughout all local studies there runs a double thread. First, there should result from this activity a vitalizing of education and an increase of critical self-consciousness in the community, which should bring about a wholesome attachment to it, a sense of participation in it, offsetting the overshadowing attraction of the big city. Second, there should result from these studies a record of some kind, duly entered in the records of learning, duly made available to all who may wish to use it, and safely preserved for the future.

That opportunities for studies of this kind have been neglected in America even in the larger units is evidenced by the condition of our local archives, described in a recent article by Dr. A. R. Newsome. In many states, they have been barbarously neglected. Only one state, Connecticut, has reached in its administration of local archives a standard of which the country can be proud. In most states, the country records have never been inventoried, and the preservation of the archives of towns or semi-public bodies has been left to the play of accident. Towards this end, valuable work was done last winter by persons on the unemployment relief rolls. This winter the historical division of the National Park Service has been making an effort to bring about inventories of public records throughout the country as a relief project under the F.E.R.A. Pennsylvania has been exceptionally successful in organizing work of this kind, and the survey of historical materials in Virginia has been ably conducted. Similar undertakings designed to develop the care of local records and to stimulate public interest in them are being launched elsewhere.

The development of valuable local studies will call for new methods of work and their application to old fields. Such a field, for example, is family history. Here an enormous amount of time has been spent by genealogists, and a good deal of it wasted through too narrow a conception of its possibilities and through lack of trained skill in organizing the materials unearthed. Left to itself, the pursuit of family history will follow the bare tracks of genealogy; guided by an enlightened scholarship, it may lead to discoveries of value to government and social science.

It is not easy to foresee how far projects of local studies must depend for successful execution upon scholars with that degree of ability and training which has previously led to university positions, and how far they can be worked out in leisure time by intelligent and college-bred men and women, who, because they make no money from their intellectual pursuits, may be deemed amateurs. There is always much shaking of heads in the universities over any suggestion of "serious" work from the amateur. Yet even if he cannot be counted on to produce a great deal of good work, the amateur can be taught at the very least to refrain from doing harm to local studies. He can learn not to disperse a collection of Mazzini letters into a dozen autograph collections, not to burn up old family papers without considering their possible value as historical documents, and not to hold himself indifferent to the preservation of other records—those of his business or of a public body— over which he may exercise control. He can certainly learn that when he finds an Indian relic, it is a good idea to take note of the place in which he found it, and keep that notation with it. Beyond this, he can doubtless learn how to arrange and calendar his own family papers, or old business records and report his holdings to an appropriate group or society. The care of the records of contemporary civilization is a task so vast that neither the personnel nor the funds of our institutions of research can shoulder the burden. Many records will be preserved by amateurs or they will not be preserved at all.

From the moment when the social sciences undertake to help pilot a democracy, it becomes increasingly important that the people shall have towards science and scholarship and the intellectual ideal not a doctrinaire respect but a participant's interest. From Germany today comes the lesson of what things may be possible when cultural centralization is too great and its apparatus is ruthlessly used. When the program for America is laid down and the high strategy of American policies defined, let there be included among our objectives not only a bathroom in every home and a car in every garage but a scholar in every schoolhouse and a man of letters in every town. Towards this end technology offers new devices and points the way.

VI

History for a Democracy *

I shall open my remarks by paraphrasing a well-known saying: "I care not who makes the laws for a country if I can write its history." For history nourishes the spirit of any institution. Without a conception of relationship with its past, any group will lack a living sense of its unity and value. A feeling that our present activity has some meaning in the scheme of time gives a sense of continuity to our participation or membership in any society. To lead a people into the future, teach them about their past, and they will know—or think they know—whither you are leading them and whither they are going.

This can be illustrated in the life of Christendom during those ages in which its thought was dominated by the church. The Christian religion was emphatically a religion which placed man in a historic setting that reached back to Adam and forward to the millennium. It gave to every moment of the Christian life a meaning within the terms of this stupendous sequence. The history that the church taught was a history of mankind, and the future that it set before man was a future for the whole race.

The next great institution to be nourished by history was the nation. Every nationality in Europe was brought to a consciousness of its own inner unity by learning of its past. When Palacky undertook to revive the national spirit of the

* Reprinted by permission from *Minnesota History*, March 1937.

Bohemians, he began by writing the history of Bohemia. The national histories differed from that which the church had taught in that each of them applied to a particular people and gave to that people a sense of its own separateness from all other peoples. The history that accompanied the culture of Christendom was a history of mankind; the history that accompanied the rise of nations was, in fact, a number of separate histories, one for each nation.

More recently there has arisen another international history to nourish the spirit of another culture. This is Communist history, which recasts the story of mankind in terms of the conflict of classes. A friend of mine in Russia heard this anecdote of a university entrance examination. A girl taking the examination was asked in what respect the reign of terror in the French Revolution differed from the reign of terror in the Russian Revolution. She replied that she could see no difference. She was then told she could not enter the university. She managed to get another chance at the examination, and again she was asked what the difference was between the French and Russian reigns of terror. This time she replied that the French reign of terror was enacted on behalf of the bourgeoisie; the Russian, on behalf of the proletariat. She passed the examination. The Communist political system includes as an essential part an orthodox interpretation of history.

Now the world is confronted with a further development of the national type of history in the form of the new fascist and nazi mythologies. The officially approved versions of history within these national cults reach back to the most remote periods of time and down to the most recent past with a rigidly orthodox interpretation of every part of the sequence. In the fascist conception of history there is complete continuity between the Roman Empire and modern Italy; the Mediterranean is still *mare nostrum*. There is a special fascist interpretation of the World War—it was won for all the Allies by Italy in Venetia. So also the authentic nazi history includes an interpretation of the role of the Germanic element in European culture, of the causes of the World War and of Germany's defeat, and of the burning of the *Reichstag* building. The historian is not permitted to doubt, to question, or to criticize any of these official interpretations. The fascist cultures, however rugged they may be in some aspects, are delicate in respect to their historical digestions. Only the most carefully prepared history, put together according to prescription, will nourish them.

Having noted that there are different histories for different political and social situations, we may now ask, "What is the history for us?" What should be the history for a federal democracy such as ours; what is the history that nourishes the spirit of our own institutions? Can we also set up our history on the basis of myths appropriate to ourselves? I think there has been a tendency to make heroes out of democrats and democrats out of heroes, and to select for special emphasis and praise in history those states that were democracies—to seek to find in history democracy as a common denominator of value.

More specifically, it was Plutarch with his stories of Greek democracies who furnished historical material for the great democrats of the French Revolution. Throughout the nineteenth century a Whig interpretation of English history inspired the popular movement in Europe, and such historians as Freeman and Stubbs tried to carry the conception of freedom, equality, and popular rule into the remote background of early German tribal life.

Now it is the weakness of this kind of history—whether it be written for the church, the nation, the communist society, the fascist state, or even the federal democracy itself— that it stands at the mercy of objective criticism. The faithful following of the technique of historical investigation may at any time overturn elements of the story that stand as essentials in the use that is being made of it. Objective investigation may prove that the world was not created in 4004 B.C.; that the most important developments on the European scene were not the special experience of any one nation, but were shared in common by many peoples; and that the continuity alleged to be found in the life of a nation from the remote past to the present day is illusory or incidental. The communist interpretation of social evolution and political events may not be sustainable in the light of an objective criticism of the evidence, and the fascist or nazi interpretations may also go to pieces under criticism. Nor is the historical interpretation which has nourished the spirit of democracy immune. The bold conceptions of Freeman and Stubbs on early German democracy have already been relegated to the junk heap of discarded historical syntheses.

If we undertake deliberately to nourish our own institutions on a history of this kind, made to order for this purpose, we may find ourselves confronted with the tragic dilemma that the mission of our history cannot be served without abandoning the scientific historical method itself. And this would be particularly fatal to democracy, because democracy more than any other kind of government needs to sustain free investigation and criticism of everything. A myth that will not stand criticism must ultimately be protected by force. And an interpretation of history that one is not permitted to doubt and criticize becomes *ipso facto* an interpretation that one cannot sustain and prove. A history that will nourish the spirit of democracy must be one that leaves its investigators free to follow wherever the evidence leads them, whatever may be their conclusions regarding men, events, and institutions. Even if it should be discovered that the heroes of democracy were villains, and that the institutions of democracy did not function as the well-wishers of democracy would have preferred—even then, the historian must be free to reach and publish his conclusions. I think that if we are willing to analyze somewhat comprehensively the essential values of our democracy, we can mark out a field of history that will sustain those values, even while it conserves the essentials of historical method.

I shall take three elements of our own national culture and treat them as essentials which it should be the purpose of history to nourish and sustain. First, I shall place the element of respect for the value of the individual personality and the protection for him of a maximum zone of freedom. This conception is opposed to dictatorships of all kinds. Carried to an extreme this may become a kind of anarchy; kept within limits, it preserves in a society a richness and a variety that no other system can develop. This valuing of individual freedom must be tempered and balanced by recognition of social needs.

The second element of our system is its federative structure. Not the individual person alone but groups of all kinds, organized in all ways, are recognized by our society and given their zone of creative activity. This conception is directly opposed to the ideal of the totalitarian state. Here also it is necessary to think in terms of a balance to be maintained between the larger societies and the smaller; between the nation, the state, and the locality. But I think it is inevitable that the protection of the individual in his own freedom is inseparable from this federative organization of society, for in a great centralized state, democracy may become indistinguishable from dictatorship.

This brings me to the third of our fundamental conceptions —the ideal of government by the people. I think that this implies not only a federative organization which leaves local affairs to localities, even as it places national affairs in the hands of the whole nation; it means also that the people in ruling themselves must act with a keen respect for facts, for knowledge, for enlightenment. They must be willing to get together on the common platform of discovered truth, wherever that platform may be.

Let us then raise the question of what kind of history will preserve these three values of democracy as I have defined them, and my answer falls into three parts. The kind of history that will preserve our respect for individual freedom is a history of ourselves, a history of individuals—it is family history. The kind of history that will preserve the federative structure of our society is the history of our homes, of our communities—it is local history. The kind of history that will preserve the basis of government by ourselves is history written by ourselves. It is history in the study and writing of which we all participate. Those who write the laws should also write the history. Participation in government on the basis of respect for truth and understanding of the methods by which it is investigated implies participation in scholarship. Family history to nourish individualism; local history to nourish federalism; and participation of all the people in the investigation of their past to nourish the sense of their participation in determining their future—this is the triple program I wish to present.

First let me speak of the history of the self. Each of us comes into existence as a unique organism; none of us is exactly like any other. And unless we appreciate the value of that uniqueness which is in each of us, we have not caught the meaning of individual freedom. It is precisely because none of us are exactly alike that each of us must be permitted to develop himself in his own way. Just as the history of a nation stimulates the sense of nationality, so the history of a person should stimulate the sense of personality.

At the most specific level this kind of history is the diary. With what pleasure and profit any of us will read a diary of one of our grandparents! Are we leaving similar documents for our grandchildren? It is an interesting fact that the Puritans, with their keen sense of personal responsibility toward God, were great keepers of diaries.

As a projection or expansion of this history of the self, the next step is the history of the family. A program of history writing which would fulfill completely the task that is here implied is something that staggers the imagination. It is no less than the demand that every family in the country possess its own history. This kind of history is not to be conceived as mere genealogy. We have seen much of that kind of research which labors only to discover among our ancestors persons of distinction, or which tries only to trace back lists of names. I am not thinking of mere lists of names and dates, but of a history that will give each individual a knowledge of the whole complex of biological, cultural, and economic events that have made him what he is, and set him in his relation to the universe. For there is, in truth, a history of the world that stems out from each of us, and for no two of us is this history of the world precisely the same.

Through what family ties is each of us brought into relation with the great past of our whole race? In the family history of my seven-year-old son there is, to begin with, the last phase of the westward movement: pioneering in Idaho, Washington, and Oregon; migration into California. Back of that is a Pennsylvania ironmaster of the pre-Carnegie days; slaveowners in Virginia and Georgia; and a Pennsylvania Dutch peasantry with its hard religion and tight-fisted prosperity. The Civil War, in my son's family history, stands as a family affair in that a southern girl had married a Yankee. The world of European imperialism enters his picture through relatives who were missionaries. Religious conflict in the Rhineland and in Ulster is a part of the more remote background. My son has practically no distinguished ancestors, so far as I know, but his family in the last two centuries has touched scores of major moving forces in the modern world, and they have in a sense become a part of him. This is true of everyone living today.

If nations can build up a national consciousness by selecting from the stream of history those events in which the continuity of a national life is manifested and the place of a nation in its relation to the world is illustrated, does not the same rule apply to the individual?

It may be objected that such personal and family histories, making of each of us a separate focal point of world history, would constitute in each case an arbitrary melange. But this is no more true of individual than of national histories. They too are highly arbitrary. In times past, histories of nations were written as the histories of wars and kings; the histories of kings were indeed family histories, and wars were state enterprises, easily identified with the states that made them. But social, economic, and intellectual histories must be forced and mangled in order to compress them into national compartments. Paris has more in common with Berlin than with any village in Provence or Normandy. Technology, transportation, and science, and even the major movements of social policy, develop in areas that overlap frontiers of national states. National history as it is written today is just as arbitrary in its selection of facts as the personal and family history I have outlined. Moreover, a family history possesses a continuity so basic, so biological, that it might properly be taken for granted as the surest and most secure pattern in which to state the relations of the past to the present. Historians may dispute endlessly about the periodization of history; they may ask, "When did the Middle Ages end?" "When did the nineteenth century begin?" But the units of family history present no such difficulty. They begin each with a birth and end with a death, and taken together they strike a rhythm of periodization that is the same throughout history—the rhythm of the generations of man.

I believe, moreover, that the development of family history has certain practical aspects which cannot be ignored. It is in a sense the spiritual correlate of the institute of the family and the material system of private property. Private property at the material level gives to the individual a sense of significance and a range of action; and, through the institution of inheritance within a family, a contact with the past and with the future. In our day this material institution has perhaps lacked in spiritual nourishment. In an age of science we have no household gods, and a Christian culture cannot sustain an ancestral cult. Perhaps family history will nourish for us the values and the traditions that the household gods or the ancestral cult nourished in other cultures.

Now I come to the second branch of history which I conceive to be a cultural necessity in a federal democracy, and this is the history of the community. Just as the history of the self has as its primitive document the diary, so the history of the home has as its principal document the abstract of title of the house we happen to live in. And just as the history of the self expands to become the history of the family, so the history of the home expands to become the history of the locality.

What is the locality? It can mean various areas enclosed within widening circles outward from our homes. Perhaps it is the area within the normal range of the family car; perhaps it is the area from which children go to the same schools, or from which housewives trade at the same stores; perhaps it is the area in which people read the same newspapers, or the area affected by the opening and closing of the same industrial plants; perhaps it is the area governed by the same local government. A locality is in fact each or any one of these areas, each in its relation to the others and to areas yet more extensive.

Each of these areas has qualities of individuality. Like a person, it is in some respects unique. And yet it also resembles other localities and is in some respects typical. The city of St. Paul is the elder sister of Vladivostok and the younger sister of Melbourne, Australia. Like its sister cities throughout the world, it has felt the impact of the great social and economic forces of the nineteenth and twentieth centuries. But it has felt them also in a way peculiar to itself. A fifth of the people who make up the population of St. Paul have come from abroad. From the same villages out of which they migrated, other individuals migrated to Stockholm, to Oslo, and to Salt Lake City. If you would know the life of this community in its relation to the widening circle with which it is in contact, you would find that it touches ultimately the most remote margins of the world. But from no other point will the world have exactly the same aspect as it has from the city of St. Paul. Just as there is a world history that stems out from the family background of every individual, so there is a world history that stems out from the special situation of every community.

We are well aware that just as genealogy has in some cases offered a superficial travesty of family history, so a type of promotional literature in our communities has in a superficial way called attention to the special excellencies and peculiarities of our various localities, and an antiquarian interest has resulted in the accumulation of diverse and unrelated items of information. This is not the kind of local history of which I speak.

Before our task as historians in a democracy is completed, we should have not only histories of every community, but histories of everything from the standpoint of every community. I think it would almost be safe to say that in no two schools, were they only one mile apart, should the social studies be taught from the same book. This, of course, is a counsel of perfection, but it serves to emphasize an unquestionable fact which should enter into our thinking constantly, and that is that the important things that the study of history should present to the mind can in a great number of cases be illustrated either directly or by contrast from material close at hand. I doubt whether anyone is fully competent to teach social studies even in an elementary school until he has learned the possibilities of finding illustrative material within the area known to the students that he teaches. In the century of the life of this community is there any significant world movement that does not in some way find illustration? Here was a point on the great frontier of European culture that extended in an enormous sweep from the Ural Mountains and the Caucasus, along the South African rivers, along the coasts of Australia, and into the inland areas of Latin America. Here, as on the plains of Central Asia, plowmen fought with nomads for the plains. Here was felt the change from fur trading to grain farming, the coming of the factory age. Here came the shift from river to railroad transportation, and thence to automobiles and trucks. Here came the cultural development of popular education, the contact of religion and science. Go down the table of contents of any good book on western civilization and, item by item, it will be discovered that if the thing was important in one way or another, it happened in St. Paul.

Now it is not easy to discover exactly how it happened in St. Paul. If I were asked, for instance, to make a study of the influence of French culture, or Chinese art, or Darwinism upon the world generally, I would find the task very much simpler than if I were asked to identify these influences in this city. And the history I would write would be easier to write precisely because it would be farther from the ground and more remote from reality.

Consider for a moment some of the great synthetic conceptions with which historians have sought to unify their vision of many events over a long period of time. Consider such an idea as economic determinism, or the frontier thesis in American history, or even the elaborate creations of Oswald Spengler in his interpretation of western civilization. These things also, to the extent that they are true, should be capable of demonstration from materials in this historical society about events that have taken place within one mile of this platform.

I have suggested that family history is related as a spiritual adjunct to a material aspect of our culture. Let me say the same thing of local history. In everything that relates to the planning of a community and to regional development, to the work of such bodies as state planning commissions, this localized information is of the highest practical importance. And a true conception not only of the character of a locality, but also of its relation to the state and the nation, is the essential spiritual food of an enlightened federalism. It is only in the presence of a historical vision in which the local community and all the more comprehensive communities are seen, each with its appropriate values, that we can order the relations of these bodies to each other in a stable and wholesome way.

Let me go beyond this: from the problem of federalism in America to the problem of world relations and world peace. For twenty years there have been ringing in the ears of historians the words of that great president of the American Historical Association, Henry Morse Stephens, uttered during the World War: "Woe unto you teachers of history and writers of history if you cannot see written in blood the result of your writing and teaching." The Carnegie Endowment for International Peace has studied and compared the school books in which the children of the various nations of the world are respectively introduced to the history of the great world society in which we live. They have found, as Stephens found, that these histories as they are taught build a wall stronger than steel at the national frontier. The development of the nation state in modern times and the destruction of the international community were accompanied by a concentration of all the attention of each people upon the unity and distinctness of their own state to the exclusion of any other.

The kind of history of which I speak does not concentrate all attention on the national border. Rather it exhibits to the mind of a student a series of borders with the lines drawn within the national frontier as well as beyond it. If I am able to see that my own community can have its own values, its own traditions, preserved intact from the past and projected into the future, and at the same time participate securely in the life of a larger community, such as the state or nation, then I shall also be able to envisage the life of my nation as a thing having secure values, both past and future, but yet cradled within the larger compass of the world. World history alone will not make of us world citizens. We must see the whole relationship—local, state, regional, national, and international—all the way from the top to the bottom. Each community has its own membership certificate in the Great Society. And until history can teach us this, the symbols of world peace will be empty symbols.

Let me call attention to the special quality of the argument I am advancing for family and local history. It has long been recognized that a better national history can be written when biography and local history have been more fully explored. That is important, but I would hold that even if a chapter of local history should prove to be a stone unused by the builder of national history, it is worth the effort for the sake of its intrinsic value in the community to which it relates. Family and local history need not sustain any particular family or local myth. They can be investigated ruthlessly and relentlessly without any effort to reach a preconceived conclusion, and still, by their very nature, they will enrich and nourish a democratic culture. Their values are primary values. They can stand on their own feet.

I hope that I have established the importance both spiritual and material of the development of family and local history as essential historical contributions to a federative democracy. Now I turn to the third item of the program—to the participation of people generally in the labor of conducting historical investigation and writing history. This participation is indeed an essential element of the program I have just outlined. For clearly there are not enough professional historical scholars in the country to begin to touch the immeasurable task of putting together the histories that lie back of each of us and of every locality, to write histories of millions of families, and thousands of communities. We do not have at the moment the personnel; we do not have the apparatus. But I think we can see whence both the personnel and the apparatus will come. It took us several generations to build up the corpus of published material, to make the critical studies, to collect the bibliographies, to organize the knowledge from which our present historical writing is documented. Our Ph.D.'s move sure-footed through this material. If I want to work on the Clayton-Bulwer treaty, I know where to look for the material, and I can begin where the last scholar left off. But if I want to write the history of my family, or of the school district in which my son is going to school, I find nothing prepared for me. It will take us several generations to adapt and complete the documentary equipment for the writing of family and local history. It took us several generations also to train the army of scholars in the tradition of the craft. It may well take us several generations to train every man to be his own historian.

Our library shelves are already loaded with the printed product of historical research according to existing standards. The new history may perhaps develop an entirely new library technique. We have crowded the publishing industry to the limit of its financial endurance in multiplying and distributing works of historical scholars in their present vein. We may have to depart entirely from the printing technique in reproducing the written word and distributing it to readers. Profound educational and technological changes lie ahead of us in the development of this program. Let me describe these prospects.

Let me speak first of the body of research material and then of the research personnel. What is the documentation that must be accumulated and rendered accessible if the kind of history I have been discussing is to be written? There are three classes of documents in which the bulk of the record is to be found. These are the public archives, the newspapers, and the manuscript materials, such as family papers and business records that survive. Yet it is in them that all of us and all our ancestors have left the legible traces of our lives. A person who would undertake to utilize these materials under present conditions would be in the position of someone undertaking to write national history in the absence of bibliographies, guides, learned journals, and sets of published documents. The Historical Records Survey, organized as a unit of the WPA, has been working for a year, with workers in every state in the Union, to make an inventory of this material.

To put this material in order is a task so vast that it staggers the imagination. The inventory of county archives alone will be a monster set of volumes of three hundred thousand pages. The inventory of town, city, and village records will be equally extensive. The inventory of church records may be even larger. The workers who are making this inventory are giving us for the first time an accurate statement of what records are available throughout the country, where they are to be found, and what general type of information is contained within each of them. It is in these records—the records of wills probated, of court proceedings, of land transactions, of business licenses—that the common man leaves his traces. In such noble volumes as the *Documentary History of the Constitution,* only the few and the great have left mementoes of their lives; but in these millions and millions of obscure documents, standing on the shelves of thousands of public buildings throughout the country, all our names are written down. The inventory is only the beginning. When the inventory is completed, there must follow progressive analyses of these records, so that it will become progressively a more simple task to glean from them the specific information that may be desired.

For the last few years the American Library Association has undertaken for the first time to bring together a list of the newspaper files that are accessible in public libraries and university libraries throughout the country. Its work is now being supplemented by that of the Historical Records Survey, which is uncovering additional files in more obscure depositories. Relief workers in a number of cities are compiling lists of available newspaper files. Chicago's is completed. Within a short time we shall be able to know what newspaper files have been preserved, where they are to be found, what areas and what periods they cover. And again that is only a beginning, for a human life is not long enough to plow through newspaper files to glean information on topics so specific as those involved in the writing of all family history and much local history. When we know where the newspaper files are, we will require indexes, calendars, and digests to make reference to them, or to the information contained in them, as simple and convenient as reference to a topic in the *Encyclopædia Britannica*. In dozens of centers throughout the country, in half a dozen in Minnesota alone, and again in connection with the work relief program, different kinds of controls to this newspaper information are being elaborated. Here it is an index to proper names, there it is a subject index, or again it is a digest of local news. When we have found the right ways of preparing subject guides to newspaper information and to the information contained in local archives, there will be laid out for us a task that will require an army of workers over a generation of time before it is completed. But when it is completed we will have at our finger tips access to the documentation upon which an infinite number of local and family histories may be written.

As this material comes under control, we shall also look forward to increasing the control we shall have over manuscript records of various kinds—family papers and business records. The technique of rendering such material easily accessible and easily used is intricate. The Minnesota Historical Society is a leading pioneer in standardizing and developing this technique. We should not rest until we have contrived so adequate a means of making inventories, calendars, indexes, and lists of manuscript holdings that we can expect the possessors of manuscripts to render their own reports upon their own holdings in such a way as to make them the common property of the world of scholarship. When these things are accomplished—and it will take a generation to do them—then we shall have in hand for the writing of family and local history equipment comparable to that which scholars possess today for the writing of national history.

The task seems vast—but this is a vast country. And the accident of the WPA white-collar relief program has already gone far enough to show that it can be done. The material foundations for a historical renaissance are being laid.

When the materials of our vast historical workshop are assembled in the way I have outlined—archives, newspapers, and manuscripts—we must take thought of the installation of the working equipment, the conveyor belt, that will carry the product while it is being worked upon. The system that has been operated hitherto in scholarship for this purpose has been the system of publication.

In the writing of history from the sixteenth century to the present, as in all scholarly activity, scholars have keyed their activity, to a degree that they hardly realize, to the rhythm and technique of the printing press. Printing and publication stand in our culture as the means by which hitherto scholars communicated their findings to one another and to the public. These are the devices by which scholars have supplied themselves in great measure with the documentary material from which they have drawn their conclusions. So deeply has this technique worked its way into our intellectual life that we hardly think of scholarship apart from publication. It often has seemed to us that the product of the creative mind, whatever its pure intellectual value may be, must remain socially valueless and ineffective until it is published, either as a book or as an article in a journal.

This system has had great efficiency in permitting scholars to distribute the labor of scholarship, so that a task, when once well done, need not be done over again. It has been indispensable in so far as scholars have had thoughts which it was appropriate they should communicate to a wide public. But there are some situations to which it is not adapted, and those are especially the situations in which it is desirable to distribute the product of intellectual labor to a few people only, rather than to a great number. For the printing press loses its economies and ceases to be an appropriate technique for the multiplying and distributing of writings unless one or two thousand copies at the least are to be manufactured and distributed.

In a program in which we would look forward to the compiling and writing of a history of every family and of every locality with an interpretation in each case that is special for the particular family or locality treated, we cannot envisage a large-scale multiplying of any of these works in the way in which we have been accustomed to envisage the publication of historical writings. A few copies only of a family history, perhaps one copy for each near relative and a few left over to be preserved in certain depositories, are all that would be required. The smaller the locality to be favored with a special historical interpretation of its own life, the smaller the number of copies that ought to be produced.

Technology now offers the prospect that substitutes for printing may be at hand which will permit the production of books in editions small enough for the very specialized demand with which we are here concerned. There are many of these new techniques—mimeograph, hectograph, photo-offset, processes known by a number of trade names such as multilith—which are appropriate to the production of books in editions very much smaller than can be economically manufactured by the printing process. But I shall speak of one of these techniques only, and that is one that has long been familiar to us in another setting—the simple technique of blue-printing, which is used in reproducing the working drawings of architects and mechanical engineers.

Ordinarily if you go into the market to purchase a scholarly book, you will pay for it at the rate of one and two-tenths cents a page, or three dollars for a hundred thousand words. Ordinarily this hundred thousand words will be spread on two hundred and fifty or more pages, six by nine inches in dimension, each of which therefore covers a surface of fifty-four square inches. The entire book is laid out on approximately a hundred square feet of paper surface. Now you can go into any blueprinting office with a hundred square feet of the right kind of typescript, properly mounted in large sheets, and have a blueprint copy made for three dollars. More than this, by using the right kind of typewriter in the right way, you can put a typescript text on paper with such economy of paper surface that it will not take any more than a hundred square feet for a hundred thousand words. This means that a blueprint reproduction of a typescript text could actually be made to order for anyone who wanted it, and distributed to him at approximately the cost that he is accustomed to paying for a book. It might be that this text would come to him in a sheet like a newspaper page, but it would be legible and it would introduce an entirely new situation into our system of distributing the product of intellectual work.

Let us suppose that each of you is an author and that each of you, using your leisure time over a period of years, has compiled the history of your own family. You might then wish to consider whether your work should be published. If you took it to Macmillan, that publisher would tell you, quite properly, that there was no prospect that a large enough number of people would wish to buy it to make it commercially feasible to set up your manuscript on the linotype machines and print off the normal publishing edition of two thousand copies. The same might very well be true if you should write the history of your street or of your town, and then you would be in possession of your manuscript and you would realize that just because there was no prospect of two thousand potential purchasers, there was no way of laying it before the more limited number of people who would really be interested in having it. Some people, under these conditions, have been able to finance private printing, but that cannot be a general solution. The blueprint method of reproduction would make it possible for you to prepare in the ordinary way, but with certain precautions as to format, a typescript copy; and then, whether the number of persons who wanted copies should prove to be great or small, the copies could be made to order for them at a cost per thousand words no greater than they are accustomed to paying.

This blueprint method of distributing writing would resemble, from the standpoint of financing, the old manuscript method. The medieval monasteries copied books for themselves and for one another. If someone wanted a copy of a particular volume, he arranged to have it made. There was no real difference between published and unpublished material, between books in print and books out of print. If Macmillan were able to offer the same kind of service that the medieval monasteries offered, the editors would never question whether there was a probable demand for ten or a hundred or two thousands copies of the manuscript the author carried to the editorial office. It is only because the printing technique demands a very expensive first cost which must be absorbed by running a large number of copies that our publishers are unable to handle works of small probable circulation. Techniques that will permit us to manufacture a book to order, as was done in the old manuscript days, at a cost to the purchaser no greater than that which he is accustomed to paying for printed books, will completely change the whole situation in regard to the distribution of writings of all kinds, and particularly writings in the field of family and local history. Again it would be possible to say, as it was in the Middle Ages, that a book once written and deposited in the right place is in effect published, in that anybody who wants a copy of it can get it.

Now there are other new techniques which introduce other elements into the picture. There is, for example, micro-copying, a process by which documents are photographed in miniature on tiny strips of film, and then read by projecting them somewhat as one projects a lantern slide, except that the image is made to fall before the reader as if it were the page of a book. The special quality of this technique is that it permits large bodies of material to be copied very cheaply, and mailed at low transportation costs. For example, if a worker in St. Paul should discover by consulting the inventory of public archives that there are several thousand pages in Washington or in Boston of archival material that he needed to study, this technique would permit him to procure micro-copies of these pages for his own use for a few dollars. The apparatus that makes these results possible is only now being perfected; its utilization is only beginning; but the potential effect of it can clearly be foreseen. For it makes the entire documentary resources of the country available in a way that would not otherwise be possible, without travel and without great expense, to workers anywhere in the country who may wish to use any part of them.

Aside from these uses of the blueprinting and photography methods, there are many processes, intermediate between these and publication by printing, adaptable to any situation that may arise in the gathering of material for research or in the distribution of its product. Just as the complete control of our archives,—local and national,—our newspapers, and our manuscripts promises to supply us with the materials for the new history writing, so these technical processes promise to make these materials accessible to us and to enable us to distribute the results of our work as widely as their character makes necessary.

We have set up the high objective of historical enterprise in a democracy, outlined the labor that is necessary in preparing the raw materials, and sketched the description of the technical equipment that will be the substitute for publication as we have hitherto known it. Now what of the workers who are to delve into this material? When we have produced the material conditions which will make it possible for every man to be his own historian, how are we to create the intellectual conditions? This problem carries us into a review of certain of the objectives of our educational system and of certain potential lines for its development.

Our people are justly proud of the tremendous investment that they have made and are making in education. The investment is not alone in our vast plant, in the great staff of teachers and administrators, but also in the years of time which our youth spends in going to school—years which the youth in other countries may be spending on the farm, in the workshop, in the army, or in the bread line. Somewhere in that great system there are to be found the human resources, the personnel, that could carry out a program of the democratization of historical scholarship, and indeed of all scholarship.

In dealing with the personnel problem in scholarship, our learned world has looked for its recruits to the graduate schools. We have felt the need of more and better Ph.D.'s, who will find their careers in our universities or in research institutions. Our personnel program has been one of giving supertraining to potential superscholars. This personnel is only a fraction of what is potentially available to do work of scholarship. The potential resources which we have hitherto neglected, but which we might just as well develop, will be found in two large groups, which I shall define as professional and amateur.

This distinction between professional and amateur has only a financial significance. By a professional scholar I mean someone who is paid for doing a job that includes some scholarly activity; by amateur, I mean someone who engages in scholarly activity for the fun of it or for the glory of it. I do not mean to imply that there is necessarily any higher quality in the one than in the other, nor that the best minds of the country are necessarily those which inevitably will be drawn to the professional rather than to the amateur interest.

It seems evident that there are two great bases upon which research scholarship can be extended. If the teaching staff of the high schools could become in the next generation, as the teaching staff of the colleges has become in our own time, a group that would regard productive scholarship as a part of its profession, the ranks of professional scholarship would be opened and the number of professional scholars multiplied manyfold. If enough of the technique of productive scholarly research could be taught as a part of the ordinary liberal arts curriculum leading to the B.A. degree, the time would come when the upper group of our college graduates would have among it great numbers of individuals who, in their leisure time, would proceed with competence and enthusiasm in the hobby of research. This would enlarge the army of amateurs.

Certainly we cannot make great and distinguished contributors to science out of everyone. We must perhaps consider some new subdivision of the labor of scholarship, devise some simplified research techniques, and lay out the fields along the frontier of knowledge in a new way, before we can utilize fully the labors of such an army of investigators as that which I foresee. But the frontier is unlimited; there is room for everyone to stake his claim, and time for him to cultivate his garden. I believe this program would fit naturally as the next step in the development of teacher training, and in the development of the liberal arts curriculum of the ordinary American college, and even in the advancing program of our graduate schools.

In the training of high-school teachers, our educators have been aware of a growing tension in the last decades between emphasis on methods of teaching on the one hand and on content of subject matter on the other. This tension has in some cases reached almost the dimensions of a schism in our culture.

The leaders who have emphasized method in the past generation had a great task to accomplish and in the main they have
accomplished it. They led the country from the setting of the
little red school house and the teaching technique of the birch
rod to the setting of the union high school and the teaching
technique of the project method and the Binet-Simon test.

But that job is done, and leaders in the field have come
to realize that the next step will involve increasing in some
way the teacher's knowledge of the full significance of what
she is teaching along with her knowledge of how to teach
it. This should draw the teachers' colleges nearer to the liberal
arts colleges.

The synthesis of liberal arts training with teacher training,
in a combination that will deepen the values of both, stands
today as a major unsolved educational program. One way of
solving it would be to develop the ability of high-school
teachers to make scholarly investigations of their own localities
from the historical, economic, social, or cultural standpoints.
Such studies would at once provide them with significant
teaching materials and yield their data as new findings in the
inductive structure of the social sciences and history. The very
same development that would enrich and dignify the intellectual standing of the high-school teaching profession would
at the same time serve the bachelor of arts by offering him a
creative channel into which to direct his intellectual enthusiasm. The beginnings of this are already at hand, and not in the
field of history alone. In my own university, for instance, the
department of political science has consistently stood for the
training of its undergraduate students in the understanding of
politics by beginning with the city of Cleveland and ending
with Plato and Aristotle. Bachelors of arts with that training
can become contributors to scholarship in local government;
they need not aspire to be commentators on the Greek classics.
Yet I have the feeling that the students who have received that
training come to realize that Aristotle knew a great deal about

Cleveland, Ohio. We do not narrow our intellectual program when we keep one end of it rooted in the ground at home.

I do not underestimate the difficulty of the task of intellectual engineering that lies before us; but neither, I believe, do I underestimate the magnitude of possible results. By some critics it has been regarded as a tragedy that the mass development of higher education, while making us a nation of college graduates, did not succeed in making us a nation of scholars. We can go very much farther toward becoming a nation of scholars if we will mark out for ourselves this whole array of new and interesting research problems in family and local history; define the technique by which the work can be done with the new material that is being made available; organize the system by which the results may be distributed by means of these substitutes for printing; and train for the future a generation of professional and amateur scholars who will take pride in their membership in the great republic of scholarship, even as they derive value from the work they are doing. There are in the country today just enough effective scholars in our high schools, just enough amateurs who are using for scholarship their leisure time from business or family occupations, to prove that the thing can be done.

Let me now emphasize again the importance in a democracy of a widespread understanding of the scientific method and the value of research. There is no other common ground upon which all citizens of a democracy can meet than that afforded by a common respect for truth and confidence in the procedures of investigation by which the truth is discovered. Science, even social science, has built up a great prestige value in the public mind. But beware! If the public is merely looking on from the outside at the quaint and interesting labors of our research men, then, even though it may defer to the conclusions reached by research, its deference will be unsubstantial. It will set up the professor against the business man, believing in the business man one day and in the professor the next. Such things as academic freedom will be for the public catch words, the real meaning and significance of which it does not understand. To protect democracy, we must protect the spirit of free inquiry for truth; and to protect the spirit of free inquiry for truth, we must broaden the number of people who participate in the inquest.

The situation suggests a parallel from the early days of the automobile. When automobiles were owned by the few, the public attitude toward them was a mixture. In some ways there was great respect for the automobilist, but on the other hand there was any amount of hampering legislation, and the goggled automobilist drove in the dust on a road with a speed limit of eight miles an hour. But when the bulk of the people became automobilists, then public roads were built, the speed laws changed, and in general the automobile came to fit itself into our culture as a thing commonly understood by all. So also with the method of the scholar. If it be confined in its practice to the few, it may indeed be respected; but the respect given it will not be rooted to withstand the shock of interest, prejudice, and passion. For Plato the great republic was one in which philosophers were kings; if our people are to be our kings, let them also be philosophers.

Let me recapitulate: The formula of history for a democracy is exactly what is implied if we accept the dictum that the writing of history and the making of laws are things that go together. It must be a history of the people as a democracy wants them to be—each with his own individuality held sacred, each with his freedom self-restrained by his own understanding of the values of all the concentric communities in which he is a citizen. Let us therefore have history of the people, by the people, and for the people. This is a long-range program in cultural strategy.

VII

The Reproduction of Materials for Research *

I should like to begin my observations with a perfectly self-evident truth: that the library as we know it is a custodian and administrator of printed books. The implications of this fact should be analyzed, for we may face the time where some of the essential elements of this situation may be changed.

By way of contrast let us compare libraries with archives. If we look upon every volume of archives in the country as a separate title, every series as a separate series, we are forced to the conclusion that there are more titles in our public archives, local, state, and national, than there are titles in our libraries. But each archive volume is unique. It is not duplicated in any other archive. If library holdings should be so distributed that each title were held in one library and nowhere else, the libraries would in that respect resemble archives. In respect of certain rare books, of many local newspaper files, and of all manuscript collections our libraries approach this situation. But ordinarily we expect the holdings of one library to duplicate those of another. This is largely owing to the primacy of printing as a technique.

Before the days of printing libraries collected books. They sought to duplicate on their own shelves the holdings of other libraries. In general, they built up their collections by making manuscript copies of the books they desired. In other words,

* Reprinted from *Library Trends,* 1937, by permission of The University of Chicago Press.

the two functions that we now distinguish as "publishing" and "collecting" were merged. This practice was changed, of course, by the introduction of printing.

If we should now develop the use of a technique of text reproduction that avoids the cost accountancy of printing, and goes back to the cost accountancy of manuscript writing, we might expect libraries to develop more of the characteristics of archives, and we might also expect the functions of collecting and publishing to merge. Such a technique now stands definitely on our horizon. For micro-copying costs behave more like manuscript costs than like printing costs.

Another of the results of our concentration on the book as a vehicle for the recording of thought has been the standardization of a certain normal ratio between the bulk of a catalogue and the bulk of the material catalogued. Ordinarily, three or four 3×5 cards will control three or four hundred pages of reading matter. Of course there are manuscript collections which are so catalogued that the ratio is almost a card to a page. And then there are serial files in which many thousands of pages are controlled by a single card. But as a general average, we can say that three or four cards will take care of a book.

Let us now consider how this ratio might be changed by certain uses of micro-copying. It might be moved in either direction. Librarians have been studying a plan to micro-copy all the books listed in Pollard's *Short-title catalogue* of books printed before 1640, and arrange the film in the order in which the titles appear in the bibliography. If this plan is put into operation, it would be superfluous to clog the card catalogue with a card for every title. It would be far more convenient for everyone concerned simply to use Pollard as the control for the film—perhaps to regard the film copies of the books themselves as a kind of addendum to the bibliography. Thus it is conceivable that a few cards in the card catalogue would control what is, in effect, an active library.

But the ratio might also be changed in the other direction. The Bibliofilm Service of the Library of the Department of Agriculture is now making micro-copies of any article in a scientific periodical at a charge of one cent a page. At present the person who orders an article copied receives the negative, and the whole transaction is wiped out. But suppose the Bibliofilm Service should undertake to preserve the negatives of the articles it has copied and to send positive copies only to the purchasers? Or suppose libraries should order film copies of separate articles and undertake to preserve and administer them? The result would be that the article in a periodical would tend to take the place of the periodical itself as a cataloguing unit. For instance, a library might seek to build up a comprehensive collection on child health. It would subscribe, of course, to the journals that bear directly on this subject. But it would also try to acquire in micro-copy form all articles that appear in any journal, in any language, upon this subject. The logic of the case would call for the separate cataloguing of each of these articles. The case just described is one in which, because of large-scale micro-copying, a bibliography may take the place of a card catalogue. Let us now look at the contrary possibility, that the card catalogue may take the place of a bibliography. We know that this is already true in some measure, because the subject-heading system is contrived to bring about precisely this result. If the section of a card catalogue relating to a given subject is not adequate as a bibliography, it can be for one of two reasons. First, the entries in the card catalogues are limited to the actual holdings of a library, and no special collection is ever complete. Second, the section of the card catalogue is a unique holding. It is not easily duplicated.

Now micro-copying changes both of these conditions. It permits a library to make its holdings on a subject logically complete, regardless of the accident of the market, for whatever cannot be bought in original form can be procured on film. And second, the section of the card catalogue relating to the subject can itself be duplicated on film, with copies made to order at about $0.50 per thousand titles.

Can we not imagine how profoundly this fact may alter the routine of the accessions department and the practice of the cataloguing department? For the accessions department will always have two strings to its bow. It can either purchase or micro-copy. And the catalogue department may develop its subject headings to give special unity and coherence to the special collections which the library is striving to make complete.

And here we can see appearing in library science with far greater precision than it has ever possessed before the "special collection," built to logical completeness, analyzed in the card catalogue, and standing on its own feet as a new library unit. Indeed, we can imagine situations in which there would be a demand for micro-copies, not of the catalogues alone, but of the special collection in its entirety. At this point it becomes evident that the library is indeed approaching the situation of the archives and that the functions of collecting and publishing are in fact fading into one another. For libraries can select, each for itself, a field of special collecting, great or small. One field in particular is indicated for every library—the field of the life and history of its own community. Though many of the items of such a collection will be books that are widely held throughout the country, the collection itself will be unique, like an archive, and subject to complete reproduction upon demand, like a copy of the *Confessions of St. Augustine* in the twelfth century.

My discussion has pointed so far to a new unit, which is other than the book, namely, the special collection. It may be made up of units smaller than the book—manuscripts, ephemera, and articles from periodicals. It has pointed also to certain borderline functions for libraries, one of which lies intermediate between collecting and publishing; the other, intermediate between cataloguing and bibliography. And so far we have considered only the impact of one technique upon library science—the technique of micro-copying.

There is another series of techniques for the reproduction of texts which is equally weighted with a great potential influence on library practice. This is the group of techniques which the libraries are beginning to call "near-print"—hectograph, mimeograph, multigraph, and photo-offset from typescript. The essential quality of these processes is that they will produce small editions at low costs per copy and per word.

To give accurate expression to this feature of the near-print processes, let us define a new concept, in terms of which the edition size at which a process will function can be measured. We will call this the "efficiency point of the process." In multiplying text by near-print, as in printing, there is a "first cost" and a "running cost." The first cost sets up the printing surface, and is always a function of the area of pages or the number of words or both. The running cost is the cost of making copies, and increases with the size of the edition. The first cost is the same regardless of the size of edition.

In any process there will always be a point in edition size at which running cost equals first cost. Until the edition reaches this point, the first cost is the major fraction of the cost of each copy. After the edition passes this point, first cost is a minor fraction.

The efficiency point for the hectograph is eighty copies. In an edition of less than eighty we are paying mostly for typing and hectograph carbon; in an edition of more than eighty we are paying principally for liquid (in the liquid process), paper, and machine labor. The efficiency point of the mimeograph in a 300-word-page format is 440 copies. In an edition smaller than 440 we are paying principally for stencils and typing. In a larger edition we are paying principally for ink and paper and labor of running the machine. The essential difference between near-print and printing, from the cost standpoint, is not a cheaper cost per word at the efficiency point, but a lower efficiency point. Printing does not reach its efficiency point until the edition climbs to 2,000 copies, but when it does reach that point it is cheaper per word than mimeographing at 440 copies.

The low efficiency points of the near-print processes mark them as the substitutes for printing in a tremendous number of situations—in all situations, in fact, where the number of copies desired is less than five hundred, and in many where the number is less than two thousand. Business and government have seized upon these techniques for most of their documents of internal circulation. Libraries have been forced to take account of an increasing quantity of near-print material emanating from these agencies. A substantial proportion of the items that enter our vertical-file systems are of this type. But we have hardly begun to use near-print in the internal documentation of scholarship, or to apply it in the field of letters or reference work.

The failure to use near-print in scholarship and letters is remarkable because there are three distinct situations in which the logical edition size falls far below the efficiency point of printing. These three situations are those of the great research libraries, of the local library systems, and of specialized research scholarship.

The number of great research libraries in the country is somewhere between fifty and a hundred; it depends on where one draws the line. There are many types of material for research which belong in a great research library and nowhere else. To place them elsewhere would be to sterilize them because the supporting material necessary to implement their use would be lacking.

Experience in publication under subsidy by the learned societies indicates that there are many fields of scholarship in which specialization has advanced so far that two hundred copies of a monograph or document will reach everyone who can use it, either through a library or otherwise.

And in the great unworked field of local studies, it is clear that the libraries and individuals of a locality could be served by a documentation, whether of the research, reference, or literary type, that could not have a national interest and should not demand a national circulation. A book written for the use of the citizens or the libraries of a city, a region, or a state, might have as its logical edition size anything from fifty to five hundred copies. The more localized the interest, the smaller will be the appropriate edition. The smaller the edition that we learn to distribute, the more highly can we expect to develop localized reading matter.

Let me offer three illustrations of the appropriate use of near-print techniques in the distribution of texts. The first is the story of a doctoral dissertation, a three-hundred-word book of the usual type, submitted by Stanton Ling Davis to the Graduate School of Western Reserve University. Under the regular rules of the Graduate School, Dr. Davis was required to deposit a typescript and carbon copy of his dissertation. The rules were waived in his case to permit him to use the hectograph. By substituting hectograph carbon for ordinary carbons in his typing he prepared a printing surface for the liquid-process hectograph machine. He then ran off fifty copies of his dissertation. The cost to him, over and above the cost of the ordinary typing he would have had to do anyway, was less than fifty dollars. He sent twenty copies to the principal libraries of the country, gave some away, sent some out for review, and, when the reviews were published, sold enough to pay his expenses. When the first fifty copies were gone, he took the same hectograph master-sheets and ran off an additional thirty copies. The hectograph volumes are not permanent. They will last about as long as newsprint paper. But by the time they fade out the results of his research will have been absorbed into the literature of the subject. When this process is used it is wise to make a permanent black carbon copy at the same typing with the hectograph carbon. Thus there will be one permanent copy, and enough hectograph copies to serve scholarship efficiently.

Another case is that of a man who wrote a history of American entomology. A commercial publisher would not take it. He mimeographed it and sold enough copies to pay his costs.

The third case involves other features than those of the near-print reproduction process, though near-print reproduction is an essential part of the scheme. There is a W.P.A. project now under way in Cleveland, employing 425 people to digest and index 120 years of Cleveland newspaper files. We expect to publish this by multigraph. It will be a set of 200 volumes. There is a curious fact about the multigraph technique which adapts it to W.P.A. work. The labor cost is high in proportion to the materials and equipment cost. We expect to manufacture 250 sets, or 50,000 books in all. The cost of writing and editing are less than a half cent a word, and of multiplying only a little more than a dollar a page.

These examples of the use of micro-copying and near-print suggest the possibility that the library may be the institution destined to take over the function of reproducing materials in that zone, from one to a few hundred copies, which commercial publishing and printing can never occupy. Almost any day we may find a new near-print process available which will permit us to multiply materials even more cheaply than is now possible in the zone from ten to one hundred copies. The development may come through the appearance of a cheaper sensitized paper or a simplifying of the photo-offset or multilith process. Suppose, for instance, we were able to take a photostat copy of a book or document, treat the photostat pages, clamp them on a drum, and run off as many copies as we desire for the price of paper and ink! When that time comes, librarians will find themselves making and exchanging reprints at cost levels not dreamed of heretofore, stocking their libraries with copies of their rarest possessions, and making the "rare book" or the "book-out-of-print" an almost extinct species when the demand runs up to twenty-five copies. We can expect to see the libraries expanding their functions by manufacturing books as well as servicing them.

I have suggested that micro-copying and near-print processes, when their implications are fully worked out, will expand the function and services of libraries. Now let me allude to a field of expansion which is in some measure independent of the impact of these processes, and yet fully within the scope of the library of the future. I have suggested that the primacy of book publishing need no longer set the pace for all library activities, that the library may come to merge the functions of collecting and multiplying, and that the units of collecting, cataloguing, and servicing may be different in the future from what they have been in the past. Now let me place the library of the future more completely in its setting by stating in the most general terms the problem of documentation in modern culture.

Our civilization is built of steel and paper: steel in technology where man controls things, paper in activities where man acts upon man. The paper is all potential record. Every day it flows in by the trainload, is covered with symbols of thought, and moves on to the pulp mill or the incinerator. From this tremendous stream a small trickle is diverted for preservation. Book and periodical publication has been one of the channels of diversion. But there are others. And to prove it, look at the vast tonnage of archives of business and of government—local, state, and national.

Four thousand men and women are at work today making an inventory of our local archives. Already they have filled four million inventory sheets, and the work is only half-done. Within the next year, if W.P.A. continues, every library will possess a near-print inventory of the public archives of its locality. From the public archives they are pushing on to an inventory of church records and, in some cases, manuscript collections. They are finding in our local archives, in many cases, a kind of disorder that is almost unbelievable, and instance after instance of tragic destruction. The willful destruction of seventeenth- and eighteenth-century customs records of an American port is a case in point. Such things have happened and will continue to happen until intelligence is applied to the selection of that part of our record which is to be preserved. The public archives can be brought under control. We will in time cease to leave it to the janitor or to some official with no more knowledge than the janitor to decide on preservation and destruction of records. But what of the archives of business?

Business is no less important than government, and its records no less significant. Business is just beginning to be archive-conscious. It may ultimately protect its records as the old European aristocracy has protected its documents in its muniments rooms. But for the present the leadership in the preservation of business records must come from the libraries. They alone are in a position now to think in terms of the higher strategy of culture. If the libraries can become, in a sense, the normal custodians of the old business records of their communities, they will take on some of the aspects and some of the functions of an archive. And this will be wholly consistent with the other developments in library functions. The collection of business records will be a normal type of special collection, a unit that is not the traditional printed book. It will require a new technique of accessioning and cataloguing for its control and possibly, in some cases, will warrant reproduction of some of its items.

So we are back again at the concept of the library as a place for collecting, preserving, controlling, and, in some cases, multiplying holdings not duplicated elsewhere. This conception stands in marked contrast to that implied in such a work as Shaw's list of 10,000 titles for a college library. Of course this does not mean that libraries will cease to maintain these collections in which their holdings duplicate in a standard way the holdings of other libraries. But every library, from the greatest to the smallest, can also develop holdings that are unique, either because they consist of unique items, or because the items are collected and organized with unique thoroughness.

As this aspect of library function develops, all libraries will become functionally branches of each other. The task of caring for the records of culture will be farmed out among them all. And this step should logically be accompanied by the development of interlibrary cataloguing or listing systems, which may call for new routines of accessioning and cataloguing. Perhaps libraries will distinguish in their catalogue control technique between those parts of their holdings that constitute their registered portion of the great interlibrary resources of the country and those which are standard and everywhere available.

Micro-copying and near-print will force us to think through anew the whole procedure of library work, from selection of acquisitions to lending. The mass of material that is "accessible" is increased in astronomic proportions. This will mean that our traditional catalogues will no longer control the material that is accessible. They will control only a part of it. The greater the amount of material to be controlled, the greater is the need for inventions of all kinds. The Historical Records Survey will ultimately provide us with a master inventory of millions of items. The libraries can go on from there. But the "identification inventory" is only the beginning. Beyond that we can use an unlimited amount of index, calendar, and guide material. The scope of this problem leads me to refer again to the Cleveland newspaper digest. There are 60,000,000 column inches in one file of a Cleveland newspaper since 1819. The total number of column inches to be digested is close to 200,000,000. That vast record is to be reduced to 100,000,000 words. It would take a man a lifetime to scan these newspaper files. When the digesting is done, the newspaper record of events and opinion will be available in easy alphabetical reference form.

The great generation of librarians now passing away saw the problem of internal library administration solved. We will have to think of library systems rather than separate libraries. That generation dealt chiefly with two classes of material passing through our hands. They knew only one way of acquiring a book—to purchase it, and only one way to service it—to lend it. We may now use copying in both cases. Our problems will be far more intricate than theirs, and also, I believe, far more interesting.

VIII

The Cultural Program of the W.P.A. *

The National Council for the Social Studies has recently appointed a committee to coöperate with representatives of the American Council of Learned Societies and the Social Science Research Council in an effort to get maximum results for American scholarship and education from the use of relief labor under the Works Progress Administration. One of the first tasks of these joint committees is to summarize and interpret our experience in the use of white-collar labor as an agency of research.

There is sufficient probability of a continuation of work relief as a more or less intermittent part of our social economy to make it a part of the public duty of scholars and teachers to help in thinking out a foundation program of maximum utility. Such a program ought to be not merely defensible as a means of keeping people employed, but positively desirable for its intrinsic value to American culture. The amount of money devoted to the cultural part of the relief program is so substantial that it should, if properly used, date an epoch in American development.

Pick and shovel work relief is as old as the pyramids. What is new in the W.P.A. is the white-collar program. This is a specifically American experiment. The fundamental need for a white-collar work relief program arises from a new vocational

* Reprinted by permission from the *Harvard Educational Review*, March 1939.

distribution of our people. Marx in the nineteenth century thought that the proletariat would be the expanding class of modern economy. He was wrong. This class has shrunk relative to total population in all industrialized countries. The class that has grown, numerically, at the expense of all others is the class of white-collar workers.

Who are the white-collar workers? They are the people who work with paper rather than with machinery, who deal with the public rather than with raw materials. They are the clerks. The word *clerk* must be understood in its historic sense. The clerks or clerics or clergy of Medieval Europe were the men and women who worked not with tools, but with records and with people. So also the clerks of today. Modern industry recruits them in vast numbers to work with records and people. Instead of copying manuscripts in monasteries, they copy invoices in offices; instead of hearing confessions they contact the public and sell refrigerators. They are nonetheless the lineal descendants of those clerks whom Alcuin trained for Charlemagne in the schools of Aix. Private industry uses them for its purposes when it needs them, and shunts them to the streets when the need passes. There is no social advantage to be gained in trying to recondition many of these people for another kind of labor. The real problem is to define ways in which society can use their services when they have no private employment. If society is to feed them, how shall they pay for their supper? What can they do?

They can work with people and with records. The ones who have been working with people have been those employed in recreation and adult education and on various service projects. About seven hundred million dollars have been invested in this kind of work since the work relief program began. The others work with records. About nine hundred and fifty million dollars have been invested in their kind of work.

Work with records is the heart of the white-collar program because the most important common denominator of clerical skill is not the ability to teach and lead, but the ability to work with records: to make records and to interpret them, to put information on them and to get information from them. This means such things as copying and consolidating figures, adding and subtracting, filing and indexing, and in general making it possible to answer questions. The virtue of clerical work is accuracy, not genius. Its rhythm is routine. It is not intrinsically "interesting" work, and those who perform it are not even expected to know all the steps below them out of which their task arises, or the steps above them by which their work is utilized. The ones who know the whole machine are the executives; the clerks are the cogs in the machine.

The white-collar class came to its present magnitude because those who were making decisions in private industry found that they needed organized control of records; they could not carry everything in their heads. American business management has become outstanding in the world for its ability to keep essential information—cost data, sales data, accounts and so forth—constantly on tap. The age of charts came to America through American business management. But our local governments have remained far behind business in their record systems. The citizens of our communities carry on and vote on policies with far less information on local public business than would be deemed necessary by the policy-makers in a well-organized private business. This comparison suggests the basic principle of a white-collar work relief program: *the clerks who are working for society must make information that is of public value publicly accessible,* just as the clerks who work for private industry make information that is of private value privately accessible.

There are, however, four limitations that impose themselves on any clerical work relief program: (1) The work should not be of the normal type, for in that case a relief worker might merely replace a regular worker, with no net change in the employment situation. The program should make a real and visible difference in American society. (2) The task should not be an essentially continuous operation, but must allow of expansion and contraction. It must be capable of employing large quantities of labor at one time, and permit of tapering off to complete cessation, without loss of value through discontinuity. (3) It must be work that persons actually on relief are capable of doing. (4) It must be work that can be done where the needy clerical people actually live. Hence the amount of work laid out in each community must bear some relation to the number and type of white-collar workers actually on relief in that place. This means a high concentration in the great cities.

I

For purposes of analysis, the whole array of tasks confronting clerks who are to work for society can be divided into two main classes: local jobs and national jobs. Local jobs are tasks that should be done in each community, and primarily for that community. Such tasks, once defined, become a foundation program for white-collar labor everywhere. National jobs are tasks that may be done in any appropriate place, but need be done only once, the one job serving the nation as a whole.

This distinction does not prejudge any question of administrative organization. In fact, the basic local job—the inventory of local public archives—is organized nationally, and properly so for technical reasons. Many tasks of national value have been done in one or another of our cities as a part of a local program. Thus, for instance, the population census of 1890 was indexed for national purposes, especially for checking eligibility for old-age pensions, in the city of St. Louis. The national population census schedules of other years were indexed in New York City.

It is a paradox that in the United States, where local self-government is very highly developed, local statistics are most poorly kept. The *Annuaire statistique des villes* is a publication in which are brought together the statistical facts about urban communities of the whole world. The cities are listed alphabetically—Boston and Buenos Aires, Calcutta and Cleveland, and opposite them in columns, page after page, are figures that give the measure of urban life. And in column after column— on marriages and divorces, for instance—there are blank spaces that follow the names of American cities, whereas the names of other cities of the world are filled in. When the National Resources Board surveyed our knowledge about ourselves it found that our municipal statistics today are worse kept and less published than they were in 1880.

The low level of urban government in the United States is perhaps both a cause and an effect of this lack of interest in comprehensive localized information. But there are other reasons. If a citizen of Cleveland, Ohio, picks up one or another of the widely used statistical handbooks, such as the *World Almanac*, he can find how many goats there are in Egypt, but not how many automobiles there are in Cleveland. It is much easier, in the reference room of the Cleveland Public Library, to discover who was Emperor of China in 1840 than to find out who was mayor of Cleveland in 1840. Figures and estimates on levels of business activity, on employment, on distribution of income, on price levels, are far more easily accessible for the nation than for the city. Indeed, for the most part they have not been compiled in localized form. This situation results naturally from the fact that scholars and publishers can reach a much wider public if they select for study and presentation information that will interest everybody in the country equally, rather than information that will appeal principally to the people of only one locality.

This situation is found not only in statistical literature, but in literature of the social sciences generally. Local history, local geography, local economic studies do not come to a focus. Local history has been developed, in the main, with an antiquarian spirit and technique from which other fields of history

departed generations ago. Much of what passes for local economic research is literature of the promotional type, lying
nearer to the literature of advertising than of social science.
The sociologists have been, of all the social scientists, the ones
most clearly aware of the existence and importance of the local
community, but even with them a work of such significance
as the Lynds' *Middletown* is conceived of as a study applicable
to all communities of which Muncie, Indiana, stands as a
sample. Yet it is self-evident that the citizens of Des Moines,
Iowa, will not vote a bond issue on the strength of arguments
advanced from a study of Muncie.

We do not know how far a democracy will prove able to
make the decisions that the twentieth century demands in
politics. We do not know to what extent the factual information upon which decisions must be made can be made available
to the citizens who do the voting. But it is evident that each
citizen has a larger proportionate share in decisions of local
policy than in decisions of national policy, and that in matters
of local concern he is in a better position than in matters of
national concern to weigh the conclusions based on his own
observation. The foundation of the democratic hope in Jeffer-
son's time was the experience that people could run their local
affairs with wisdom; the complexity of the problems requiring
solution has increased far beyond anything imaginable at that
time, but meanwhile the social sciences developed their tools
for rendering these more complex problems manageable. These
tools, however, have been much more turned to account in
the field of national policy than in the field of local policy. If
we had information organized in a fashion that would correspond to the interests and needs of our citizens, the shelves of
every public library would be as well stocked with books
about its own community as with books about the United
States.

These reflections would have no practical value were it not
for an accident that has brought it about that in this one coun-

try, where there is so much to do to bring scientific understanding of self to our communities, there has appeared the problem and the opportunity of using an army of clerks to catch up with the back work and prepare the supply of information from which a community can answer its questions. We have been one of the backward peoples of the world in the organization of localized information. New York is not only behind London, Paris, and Berlin—it is behind Prague and Budapest. We can become one of the leading peoples in this field if we will but take the thought necessary to define the tasks for the clerks for whom a relief program is necessary in our society.

For any community, the answers to big and important questions are made up of countless answers to little questions. The solvency of the community is a big question and every little fact on payment and delinquency of taxes is a part of the answer. The vocational prospects of each child constitute a question of paramount importance to the community as a whole. Every fact about the economic life of the community in which he is to live, and about the relation of education to vocational opportunity, is a part of the answer. The attitude that the citizen will take toward his community is perhaps the biggest question of all, and it is doubtful if this attitude can meet the requirements of public interest unless the citizen sees his community as more than an aggregation of streets and houses, unless he sees it as a living thing with a many-sided past and heavy commitments to the future.

The answers to the little questions, out of which are compounded the answers to the big ones, are found, in the main, in records. The knowledge of whence we have come, from which alone we can guess whither we are going, is knowledge that must be gathered with great toil from records. What are the records that contain the information about a community to which its citizens should have access? The great bulk of them consists of the public archives and the newspaper files of that community. The printed book material is, in the main, scattered and incidental, as every reference librarian in every public library knows. The state of these basic local records has been deplorable. Local public archives have been piled like rats' nests in basements and attics, and lucky to be saved from the incinerator at that! All newspaper files of papers printed since the 1880's are doomed, for they are printed on wood-pulp paper that is disintegrating so rapidly that someone who consults a newspaper of the Spanish War era today may be the last man able to consult it; the paper falls apart when the page is turned.

The first and basic task of clerks who are to work for society is to rescue physically the records in which alone the account of the life of the community is contained. This can be done. The Historical Records Survey, with a national organization in every state, has been making of local records the most comprehensive inventory in the history of archival science, and as the records are inventoried they are arranged. The inventory is, moreover, a check list against capricious destruction, and the work itself is making local custodians of records more archive-conscious. The newspapers can be saved. They need only be micro-photographed on film. The process has been worked out, and the film is known to be permanent. While they are being filmed for preservation, they can also be indexed by clerical labor, so that the information in them can be readily accessible to the public. This work is now under way in a number of cities.

Not only past records, but current ones, may need attention. We know that the relief workers cannot assume a normal current routine function of record keeping in the office of a county auditor or police department; but wherever the public officers who are in charge of current records wish to improve their system of current record keeping, but are inhibited by the difficulty of installing a new system, the W.P.A. clerks can reorganize their records to fit an improved routine. When work of this kind is done, it can be so planned that the records become not only more adapted to efficient current administration, but also more useful for research purposes.

Finally, the relief workers can make up for the failure of the publishing industry to care for local needs. This failure results from the technique and accountancy of the publishing industry, which has operated for generations against the development of readily accessible information for local purposes, because publishing requires a wide market—a minimum sale of two thousand copies—and therefore prefers to issue books of national interest. Near-print techniques of book production in editions of one or two hundred can be used by relief labor to make available to the citizens of the community, on the shelves of their public libraries and in their schools, the kind of information that the national publishing industry serves to the nation as a whole. And relief workers can do everything from compiling the information to binding the books.

The three institutions to which the work of the relief clerks must be keyed are the public administrative and policy-making records and information for government and voters, more adequate local reference material for libraries, and more satisfactory local teaching material for schools.

II

Most public libraries try more or less systematically to maintain a file of local information that becomes available to their readers in the library's holdings of books, journals, and ephemeral publications and reports of all kinds. But no public library is able, as a part of its normal routine, to comb thoroughly all its materials to bring to light all the information in print that they contain on local matters. The periodical indexes such as the *Readers' Guide* cover only a fraction of the intake of American periodicals in a public library of a great city, and bring out only a fraction of the local reference information in these periodical files. A check of some magazines indicates that there is six times as much material on Cleveland,

Ohio, in a magazine covered by the *Readers' Guide* as can be found by looking up the topic "Cleveland" in the *Guide*. The relief workers should give the local library a guide to printed information about the community, available in the community, that is complete. The task would be a large one, but it would have the effect of increasing tremendously the usefulness of resources which have already been paid for. The hundreds of millions of library dollars expended over the past fifty years will go further in service today if there is adequate bibliographical control of the contents of the materials that have been acquired and stored.

The cities of America, in general, have not merely one public library, but a number of special and institutional libraries. It may happen that a book that is needed may be somewhere in the city, but the man who wants it cannot find it without a costly and difficult inquiry. Libraries can mobilize their holdings by establishing union catalogues locally. This has been done with relief labor in a number of centers, notably in Cleveland and Philadelphia. It is possible that union cataloguing operations would be carried on most effectively within the framework of a national union catalogue, printed in book form, with adequate listing of holdings for each locality.

A third matter of interest to a locality is a list of the books and other items printed locally, especially in the earlier period of its history. Under the leadership of Douglas McMurtrie a comprehensive combing of American libraries for a complete list of early American imprints, to be arranged by locality and date, is under way as a W.P.A. project that is technically coordinated with the Historical Records Survey.

The foundation program for libraries, viewed as a local program, includes union cataloguing, guides to printed items of local reference, and check lists of items printed in the locality, wherever they may be held at present. It may be wise in all three elements of this foundation program to organize the work nationally, but the results of the work will nonetheless come to a focus locally, and will meet on the shelves or in the files of the library the products of strictly local work, such as newspaper indexes or compilations of statistical information.

Let us look at the shelves of a public library, in that section of the reference room devoted to local matters, as they stand today, and as they will look when the W.P.A. program has got well under way. At present there are four or five local histories, one of them written by an early nineteenth-century antiquarian, another by a real historical scholar of the last generation, the rest subscription books praising the families that bought space in the publication. Then there is an array of incidental pamphlet and report material, the files of two local magazines, and of the *Journal* of the Pioneers' Society, which had an active life fifty years ago, and has since died down.

In the future there will be first the fundamental guides to records—the inventory of public archives, the bibliographies of printed items of local reference, and the list of items printed in the locality. Then will come the many volumes of a newspaper index. Following this index, which controls information in the newspaper file, will be a set of abstracts of court cases, abstracted for facts rather than points of law, which constitute almost a second running account of the life and social history of the community. Then (since the city includes a number of immigrant groups which have maintained their own foreign-language press), there will be a set of volumes of translations or abstracts from the foreign-language press in which the opinions there expressed, and the activities of the foreign-language group there recorded, will become part of the body of accessible information. Next will come the statistical series. It begins with a bibliography of statistical information available in print, and then tabulates with encyclopedic thoroughness the statistical record of the city as completely as Finland's or Budapest's statistics are presented in the statistical publications of those governments. There will also be the biographical series— the body of information collected under the names of people who have lived in the city. The population census schedules from 1790 to 1870 will have been brought from Washington in film form, copied off, rearranged alphabetically, and bound in book form, and will stand on the shelves for easy reference. Beside them, also in the form of bound typescript books, will be found an alphabetical list of interments. If the guide to public records shows that vital statistics are adequately kept in one of the public offices, the library need not duplicate the public records locally available, but somewhere at least the gaps in the record should be filled as far as possible. Then will come a more selective series—a list of all public office holders from the earliest times with that minimum of information about each which comes to light when newspaper index, indexed public records, alphabetized census schedules, etc., are systematically checked. Following this will be a list of all veterans, with information drawn from these fundamental sources, and also from pension records filmed in Washington and used by local workers. Then teachers, clergymen, physicians, journalists, printers, lawyers—with no selective search for great and distinguished names but rather a comprehensive combing of the field. Of course, these biographical indexes do not pry into the privacy of living men, or seek to flatter pride by circulating questionnaires of the *Who's Who* type. The work is solid, controlled, routine, and historical. Then will come information on the history of business. The newspaper advertisements will tell something; and there is additional material in the public records. Moreover, the records of schools as well as the factors locally conditioning educational progress will be found.

Such are the contributions which the relief workers can make to library resources. The catalogue is not exhaustive, but illustrates the principle that the locality, by the careful and disciplined use of relief labor, can provide itself with resources of checked and accessible information about itself comparable to that which scholarly enterprise, public appropriations, and the work of the publishing industry have provided for the nation as a whole in the course of generations of work.

Beyond this, the relief workers can discover in library records some things that communities ought to know. For instance, what is the effect of the teaching program in the schools upon adult reading habits? In a city of several hundred thousand population there will be a large number of people who happen to have gone through the schools of the city and become its permanent residents. The schools may have their school records, and the library records tell the story of their reading habits. Is it true, in general, that those who took the courses in literature in high school are readers of literature? Or will the library records show only a chance distribution between reading interest and educational experience?

III

This suggestion leads to an analysis of what can be done in the schools. In improving the work of the schools, as in enriching the libraries, relief workers can provide from records two things: materials to be used in teaching, and information to be used in policy-making.

First, as to teaching materials. When the writer of this memorandum went to school in California, the school books, written and printed in the East, took for granted the climate and flora of the East. I read stories about foxes, not coyotes, and the wild flowers that appeared in my reading were not those that I saw in the fields. I suppose it did no harm, but as a teacher I now realize how much better it would have been if the world presented in those books had more nearly resembled the world I saw about me. The idea of tying the teaching of the social studies to the scene of the local community has become one of the objectives of the teaching profession. But for this purpose the foundation of teaching materials is lacking. Consider, for instance, how much could be taught to a grade-school child if the schoolroom possessed not only the relief map of the

United States but a miniature model of the school district area itself as it was when the white man came, as it was in the 1850's, or at such successive periods as would indicate the main changes in culture! To prepare such materials for visual education would not be mechanically difficult. Relief labor could do it. But underlying the work there would have to be a control of information from the records of the county engineer with respect to roads and streets, from the file of building permits or from other sources with respect to construction, and from land title records and other sources with respect to the use of land. The foundation program in public records and newspapers makes possible the foundation program in the preparation of teaching material.

It is in the upper grades of instruction, however, that the availability of adequate teaching material would be most definitely felt, and this not only in the possible provision of reading material for pupils, but perhaps even more in the supplying of classroom illustration material to the teacher. In every American city there was a particular time when the railroad came to town. The textbooks, published for national circulation, tell of the Baltimore and Ohio. The teacher should be able, quickly and easily, to find the information that would point up the lesson with facts of local pertinence. The textbooks tell of a log cabin, hard-cider campaign of 1840. The teacher should not meet the class without knowing how their own town voted in that election. The provision of this teaching material merges, as a practical matter, with the provision of library reference material outlined above.

Beyond the high-school level, in the colleges and universities, there is place for a new dispensation. In general, for the last few generations scholarship has become professionalized and keyed to the resources of great libraries. The amateur scholar has not kept the place in the world of culture which our great investment in higher education, and our resources of wealth and leisure time, would indicate as appropriate. Here, right at our feet, in every community, are mountains of the raw materials of research, never touched, or edited, or used for scholarly purposes. Our Bachelors of Arts are not now expected to be graduated as professional scholars, but if we provide for our adult population great resources of controlled materials for research, we can expect greater participation of the public in the creative work of our culture. And one of these fields will be that of local studies.

Second, as to policy-forming in our schools. Here a curious situation has arisen. The graduate students in schools of education are turning out tons of dissertations, and still our ignorance of the productivity of our school investment is appalling. In general, we do not know what is being offered in the curriculum of our high schools. Latin fell out of the curriculum, and was practically gone before we knew it. Mathematics may be going the same way. Given the curriculum of our schools, as it would be revealed in a study of course offerings, we do not know what courses of study the students are actually following, what selections they make, in what combinations, and with what success as revealed in the school's own methods of measurement. Beyond that we do not know what goes on in the classrooms. We do not know how individual choice of courses and individual school experience are related to later vocational career or cultural achievement. Does vocational training in the high school result in a probability that the pupil will actually work in the vocation for which he and the community have made the investment of time and money? We do not know, and many people think that the answer is negative. Do the courses in current events have the effect that the pupils exposed to them are more alive than other pupils to current problems after they leave school? We do not know. How accurate are school judgments on the character of children? Do the records of juvenile and later delinquency indicate that the teachers who made out report cards with appraisals of moral or social qualities were good judges?

Not all of these matters could be investigated from records, but some of them could be investigated. If the present output of research work in the field of education has failed to exhaust matters of such basic importance, the reason lies not in any lack of importance in the problem, but in the fact that the investigation of such things is a factory job, not a craftsman's job. It requires large-scale and coördinated clerical work with records.

IV

The public records are a part of the process of government. Where there is no will to efficiency, a change in the record system may have little effect; but where there is a will to efficiency, the whole process of administration will respond to an improvement of administrative records. But there are two principles that could well be worked out. The first has to do with bringing all records of widely kept classes—such as tax records—up at least to the minimum level required by law, and perhaps above that level. The second is so to manage the improvement of records that the various record series, though administered independently by different offices, nevertheless key in with each other.

For instance, in New York City there are 815,000 parcels of land. If the records of the tax department, the land title and mortgage records, the building construction and inspection records, and records of occupancy are all trued up for current administration and reference by being keyed or indexed under the heads of these same 815,000 land units, the information in each of these different series will be readily available to help in interpreting the information in the other. When the records of one department of public administration are improved, some thought should be given to the importance of making the information they yield more easily comparable with the information yielded by the records of other departments.

As housing comes more and more to be seen as an area in

which the public interest is involved, the inadequacy of our knowledge of the basic factors affecting a housing problem comes more clearly to light. For housing as a social problem touches all aspects of urban life—taxation, public services, education, income distribution, transportation, health, and business and financial structure. How rapidly do style changes in housing become effective? The brownstone front and the brick apartment, the urban imitation of a farm house with its front porch, and the Tudor residence of the suburbs with its garage, are points in a sequence in which no locality has exactly the same history, and of which we know very little because our historians of architecture have been more interested in historic houses than ordinary houses, in public buildings than in ordinary residential construction. Yet the facts on style obsolescence will give us vital information on the rate at which new materials and styles will become accepted, and current ones outmoded. Just as in biographical information we can afford to pay more attention to the ordinary man, so in housing information we can afford to learn much more about the ordinary house.

With the study of the house comes the study of land. The equity of a tax system on land and housing turns in part on the rapidity with which real estate changes hands, reflecting in purchase price the tax situation. In the general formation of capital, and in the credit structure of a community, the real-estate mortgage situation is a factor of prime importance. Yet on these matters our records are pitifully defective. The Secretary of the State of Ohio publishes reports on recordings of mortgages and deeds, but the reports for certain years on Cuyahoga County do not check with account of instruments made in the County Recorder's Office. Why? Because the report was made out and sent to the Secretary of State by some underling in the department who did not take the trouble to count. When questions involving the ability of local communities to sustain a certain share of the relief load were up for decision, and as questions involving differentials under the

Wages and Hours Act come up, the records are found to fail us because they are inadequately kept and inadequately summarized.

An example of the type of work that can be done to learn more about city land is furnished by the real property inventories, made by W.P.A. labor in a number of cities. These inventories, like the Domesday Book of William the Conqueror, summarized the situation on land occupancy and rental. But they fell short, technically, of the work of the great English king because he recorded not only the current data, but also the situation as it was in the time of Edward the Confessor. We could make our real property inventories as complete as the Domesday Book; the work could be done by clerks from records, with some help from the decennial population census records. Bear in mind that there are more people in the Boston metropolitan area, or in Brooklyn and Queens, than there were in all England in the time of William the Conqueror.

The local program ought to control and preserve public records and newspapers, mobilize local library resources, serve the schools. In each community as much or as little can be done as the relief labor situation and the interest of the community require. This part of the program serves national needs in so far as the situation in any one community is typical, or comparable with the situation of another.

v

The national jobs are the jobs that need to be done only once for the whole country. Some of them are big, some little. An understanding of the national organization of our world of research and information is necessary to a planning of this part of the program. The institutions involved are the Federal Government with its various departments, the library system of the country as a whole, and the whole system of organized research.

Some assistance may be given to national government agencies—witness the indexing of the census schedules. Some national government agencies may choose to organize large-scale research projects, such as the survey of health. These are things that the relief program can take in its stride.

The library system of the country ought to have a union catalogue in book form, like the *Gesamtkatalog* of the German libraries, so that no one who wants to consult a certain book that happens to be in any American library need go without it for lack of knowledge of its location. The potential usefulness of such a catalogue has been greatly increased in recent years by the development of the technique and practice of microcopying as a feature of library service. Except for limitations in the case of recent books still under copyright, any book in the country will soon be available anywhere in the country in microfilm form, the film being made to order on demand. It is particularly important that this mobilization of American library resources should take place soon, because European libraries are standing at a turning point in service policy. There is a chance that they may adopt the practice of placing heavy burdens upon microfilm service. Our national answer can only be to show them the wealth of our own resources, so that mutual exchange by micro-copy will seem equitable and profitable to them.

When we have a comprehensive list of titles in American libraries, the time will come for various comprehensive bibliographies, for the bibliography is useful in proportion as the works referred to in it are available. The comprehensive bibliography on aviation compiled in New York City is an example of what can be done. Even more important as a model is the bibliography and guide to geological literature on Foraminifera. In all bibliographic and control work organized on factory production basis by the W.P.A., the technical problem is always to find objective units of classification. The binomial system of the biological sciences offers such a system of units.

Beyond this lies the possibility that the purchasing power of

American libraries may be used more effectively in the acquisition of foreign material. As Europe falls, state by state, under the control of regimes that deny free inquiry to scholars, America becomes more and more the last place in which free scholarship can live. Hence the importance of avoiding wasteful duplication in increasing our library resources of foreign books and periodicals. After the union catalogue will come the union want list—the list of books that ought to be in the country—to be used by libraries in executing their purchasing policies.

Moreover, the usefulness of foreign works in this country can be greatly increased if they are translated. This is especially true of books in the Central and Eastern European languages. We have thousands of potential translators on our relief rolls. A single typescript copy of a translation, serviced by interlibrary loans, would be sufficient, and is it not appropriate that those who come from abroad should help to make the product of their native culture more useful to America?

While the library system of the country can be looked upon as a unit, and the big job defined, the whole field of cultural research presents so varied a character that only a few general principles can be applied to it. It is, in the main, a university world, and while it is not wholly enclosed in the universities, at least it is principally organized there. Its conventional techniques are not those which involve the mass use of clerical labor. But on the relief rolls there are always a number of people with genuine technical research training, able to work according to the ordinary methods of scholarship. The policy of allowing a university to assume responsibility for the value of research projects undertaken by its own faculty members with the aid of W.P.A. personnel of this exceptional quality is a sound policy, and should relieve the central administration of much costly and burdensome detail.

Beyond this, it is necessary to establish contact between the W.P.A. and the national scholarly bodies, to the end that within each field there may be adequate study of the best uses of

W.P.A. labor. Committees appointed for this purpose by the National Council for the Social Studies, the Social Science Research Council, and the American Council of Learned Societies, will work with such bodies as the Committee on Historical Source Materials of the American Historical Association, and the Joint Committee on Materials for Research, to clear the channels of consultation and action.

VI

A few general principles should be stated. The edges of each project should be clean cut; the material to be covered should be definite; the factory system rather than the craft system must prevail generally. That which W.P.A. workers can guarantee is, in the main, that they have accurately performed certain definite operations upon certain specific materials. They cannot, in the main, guarantee that they have done the kind of selecting and subjective evaluating that is intrinsic to the craftsmanship of the scholar. Since a task undertaken should be done thoroughly, it should usually be carried back as far as the records go. A study of taxation from records of the past ten years will be most woefully out of date ten years from now. But a study of taxation that runs as far back as the record system permits will always stand as a foundation for later work.

The administrative unit for work is the project. The unit which scholars are able to help in defining will, in many cases, be a larger unit than a project. The unit that the public will understand ought to be something that is cumulative through many projects. The program will succeed best if the technical men, the scholars and administration, understand it, and the public understands it, but it is not necessary that all should emphasize exactly the same thing in the program.

Yet the program can mean much more than is shown by its concrete documentary product in improved files and in books on the library shelves if it is so conducted that the public generally comes more and more to share in it. The beginning was made when the Historical Records Survey succeeded in making custodians of public records more conscious of the value of archives. Another great forward step will be made when schools concern themselves with the materials and aid in focusing them on educational practices and policies. Ultimately, then, the American people will be more conscious of the possibilities of the democratization and enrichment of our culture.

IX

World Intellectual Organization *

There is an issue that confronts all teachers, all serious men of letters, all scientists, who take seriously their share as human beings, infinitesimal though it be, in determining the fate and future of the world. The issue has confronted the American National Committee on Intellectual Coöperation and the Social Science Research Council for years. As the Phi Beta Kappa Society launches its drive for the defense of the humanities and of academic freedom, it comes forward again. The issue has to do with the relation of the world's intellectual organization to its organization of wealth and power.

Shall those who are within the world's intellectual organization seek to use it to influence power policies—as in passing resolutions at meetings of learned societies against acts of foreign states—and risk thereby the weakening of the international fabric of intellectual organization? Shall the students of economic phenomena become sponsors of a practical program for which they would have such responsibility that their science itself may be turned out of office? Recently a renowned physicist made public his decision to bar from his laboratory all visitors from the totalitarian states and to refrain from discussing his experiments with citizens of those states.

To make this issue clear, let us assume that there is in the world a body of specific institutions within which intellectual

* Reprinted from the *Educational Record*, April 1939, by permission of The American Council on Education.

coöperation takes place. These institutions include everything from education and research to entertainment and publishing. They constitute, in a sense, a world of their own. It is with these institutions that the League of Nations' Institute of International Intellectual Coöperation, the Social Science Research Council, and the Phi Beta Kappa Society are concerned. As a world of intellectual institutions, they are at once distinguished from and related to two other worlds—the worlds of power, and of debts and markets.

The world of power—the political world—has been studied as a whole. Its processes have been examined; its history and its physiology are analyzed in whole libraries of books, descriptive and analytical. The same can be said of the economic world. However, most of our descriptive and analytical study of the intellectual world has been devoted to the product rather than the process. Our scholarly literature, critical and historical, is in the main a travel literature. We have indeed collected much information about the functioning of different parts of intellectual organization. In the field of education, for instance, and perhaps in the functioning of the press, a great amount of information has been collected. But we do not have, even in outline, a conspectus of the organization as a whole.

We have at hand the cumulated results of the thinking of many generations in analyzing the economic and political worlds. We know something of the quantities that are involved; we can estimate resources and armaments; we have statistics on credits and business activity. We do not all agree in the analysis of the dynamics of these worlds, but at least we are accustomed to looking at them as wholes. But we have no corresponding vision of the world of intellectual coöperation.

Yet intellectual organization is the house in which we live. We have lived in it so long that we think we can take it for granted. We have looked from its windows and described the other houses; we know that some alterations have recently been made. But we lack even a floor plan of the building as a whole.

We are aware of great and recent changes in this world of intellectual coöperation: radio, movies, literacy, censorship, propaganda, the multiplying of culture languages and of culture centers, business formations, as in radio and movies; power formations, as in the totalitarian states, have brought new situations into existence. Our primary practical concern is with the functioning of this world of intellectual organization, with its growth or decay, its survival, and with the use we make of our place in it. It is a world divided not territorially, like the states, but into disciplines and arts, most of which are essentially international.

Let us take note of two characteristics of the intellectual world which exhibit its peculiarly international character. First, there is still in existence a world-wide acceptance of the results of experiment in the natural sciences. A scientific experiment, properly recorded in our highly institutionalized system of learned journals, has not only world currency but world authority. Its credit is better than bank credit; its authority is more definitive and universal than the authority of any judgment of a court of law. The assumption of good faith that obtains in the field of scientific work is the kind of assumption that exists only among insiders in a going concern. The power world has restricted the jurisdiction of the high courts of science, it is true. Nothing on race and anthropology can pass in Germany without the *nihil obstat* or the *praemunire*. But in general the authority of the jurisdictions of science is a world authority.

In the field of intellectual property there is a peculiar relation of public property to international organization. For the public domain in intellectual property is international domain. In publicly owned tangibles—bridges and roads, buildings and battleships—public domain concentrates in the object the qualities of sovereignty and of property. But intellectual property that is public domain becomes something from which no one is excluded. Only the open sea shares with intellectual property the character of international domain. International *action* (as in international copyright) may have the effect of diminishing international *domain*. Only in the presence of a clear picture of the functioning of this world of intellectual coöperation can its citizens make sound policy. We should have a picture of the present situation, a definition of the directions in which we would wish to see the situation change, and then a selection of the acts best calculated to accomplish the change.

Let us first consider how far this world of intellectual organization permits of measurement. It may be that the objects we seek to attain are not measurable, but they are at least related to measurable features of the intellectual world.

We must assume that there is in some way a possible distinction between American intellectual organization on the one hand, and international intellectual organization on the other. The simplest distinction, which may be taken as a first approximation, is the distinction between events occurring here and abroad. A more refined analysis may then show that some events occurring here belong rather to international than to national intellectual organization, and that some events occurring abroad belong to our own intellectual organization.

In what units can intellectual organization be measured? The simplest are men, money, product, and time. In the publishing industry we should inquire, for instance, how many people are employed in each of the kinds of writing, how much money is involved in publishing and how it is distributed, how many items are published, by how many people they are bought, by how many people they are read, and how much time is involved in the reading. We should inquire how the writers are motivated to write, and the readers to read. So far as possible we should break down these quantities into appropriate classifications.

The same units of measurement can be applied to the educational system, to the research system, to entertainment, to music, radio, moving pictures, lectures, perhaps even to travel and to mail communication, if that be adjudged a part of intellectual organization. Perhaps even commercial advertising should be accorded some gross measurement, and certainly the work of propaganda agencies should be given at least a quantitative estimate.

In so far as dollar estimates of quantity can be made, and the particular channels of the flow of money described, the relation with the economic world is clarified. In so far as the positive action of government (as in education) and its negative action (as in censorship) are defined, the relation of the intellectual world with the world of power is also defined.

With these gross measurements in hand, and they might be tabulated in huge cross-section charts, it will be possible to begin the analysis of international intellectual organization in so far as the intellectual organization of this country shares in it.

It is at this point that we could bring together the answers to such questions as these: What proportion of newspaper space is given over to foreign news; what proportion of teaching time is given over to the teaching of foreign matters, including such things as foreign literatures and international relations; what proportion of research energy is committed to these fields; in what degree are our library resources committed to foreign as against domestic materials? What proportion of our consumption of intellectual goods comes from abroad, what proportion goes abroad, etc.? These are broad categories, but in the course of measurement they would be refined.

If it is possible, even as a crude estimate, to measure world intellectual activity, and set against its quantities the quantities for America, and the amount of overlap, the quantitative framework for the making of policy will be established.

A very important issue will have to be faced at this time: Is it the object to *use* the existing intellectual organization of the world to accomplish certain effects in the world of power, or to *protect* the organization and develop it as a value in itself? These two objectives may prove inconsistent with each other. Efforts to use intellectual organization as a means of influencing power policies may recoil against the organization itself, either directly, as when an effort to bring pressure to bear in Germany results in the withdrawal of Germans from international association, or indirectly, as in the case of an invitation to governments to restrain international name-calling by police power (moral disarmament), which may prove a boomerang against full freedom of the press. (Note the restraints on Dutch and Swiss press in respect to Hitler.) If we are to function as an unofficial propaganda agency for America, our actions may be received in some quarters with the same attitude that greets communist and fascist propaganda here. Any of these policies are open to us, but we must think them through clearly.

I can only compare our situation to that of the Church when it faced the difficult problems of adjustment with the world of secular power. Intellectual organization has quietly accomplished in the course of the past century for the world as a whole an intellectual unification such as Christianity once accomplished for Western Europe. Communism and fascism may reject part, but they do not reject all, of the bases of world collaboration.

With our objective defined, and our measurements established, it will be possible to find the critical points for action. We may discover, for instance, that the study of international relations in our schools is moving forward without the need of extra pressure, but that the study of modern languages is declining and needs help. If our figures show this situation, we should concentrate on the point where help is needed. And so on throughout the whole field.

In the presence of the magnitudes that our survey would disclose, the resources of our committee must appear very small indeed. We will not spend over many years what it costs to produce one movie. If we undertake to propagate a particular idea by direct action, we must do it with resources that would not suffice to put on the market a new brand of tomato sauce, let alone a brand of cigarettes. But this consideration should not discourage us; rather it should impress us all the more with the unique importance of the situation we occupy, as the only body in America with terms of reference that fit it for general staff work in the world of intellectual organization. Of all the countries from which delegates go to Paris, is there any which is really so well situated to assume freedom from political constraint and financial limitations in intellectual activities?

At the same time, a consideration of the meagerness of our resources should counsel us against drop-in-the-bucket activities, and against action and effort in matters where we do not see clearly the exact character of the interest we are serving. None of us really knows whether one or another of many possible new systems of international intellectual property will serve or obstruct the functioning of the system of world intellectual coöperation. Neither are we sure what operations in promoting abroad the *idée américaine* will fulfill our desires, and what ones will kick back, like dollar diplomacy.

X

Strategic Objectives in Archival Policy *

Those unacquainted with the problems of archival science often think of archivists as people of extraordinarily narrow interests, whose eyes are trained on the most remote past. The insiders realize that the archivist is a man of the future, and not of the past; he is professionally preoccupied with a more distant future than that of any profession save that of astronomy; and he cannot lay down sound policies in the preservation and destruction of documents without taking into account interests broad enough to make up the composite fields of the faculty of a liberal arts college.

I think we understand this among ourselves, but the people at large do not as yet share our vision of the role of archival policy in American culture. We have among ourselves our little technical problems, such as the question of the distinguishing between archives and manuscripts: we cannot expect the public to be very much interested in technical minutiae; but we can expect the public to become conscious of an archival problem generally, to assist in laying down a broad archival policy, and to share our vision of the place that the preservation of records has in the whole culture of our country.

In our conception of the place of archives in American culture, we might well keep before our eyes the role of the public library system. There have been public libraries for many cen-

* Reprinted by permission from the *American Archivist*, July 1939.

turies. The American public library system made a phenomenal growth a generation ago with the impetus of the Carnegie fortune behind it. The archival system of this country is now entering a similar period with the launching of the National Archives, the work of the Historical Records Survey, and the organization of the Society of American Archivists fostering it. The public libraries had as their primary problem the procurement of books, with cataloguing and organization secondary; the archival materials are already on the ground, and the essential problem is organization and preparation for use. The libraries could count on the public school system to provide a literate population which could take advantage of their resources; in the development of the use of our public archives, we will find that people will need not only to have the materials preserved and organized for them, but must also be taught to use them. True, libraries often offer reading counselling services; fully developed archives may have to go much further than the library in teaching people to use them.

Of course it would be possible to dodge all these problems if we should adopt as a foundation of archival policy the idea that only the professional scholar would be welcomed, or possibly that only the professional scholar would be served. But to take such a view would be to miss our great opportunity. I hold that even the most amateur genealogist ought to be welcomed in our archives, and the people should be allowed to browse through old legal records. The public should learn to expect in the archives of its own community the same kind of reference service that its public library gives. A check of the questions asked at the reference desk of the Cleveland Public Library indicates that a substantial proportion of them is the type of question that can be and should be answered from archival records. If we develop such a policy in the utilization of our public archives, we will not only find the voters willing to provide the buildings and to employ the technicians needed to give these services, but we will also find our people increasingly interested in private as well as public archives. I am told that the late Harvey Firestone was planning to establish just such an institution for the history of his firm and of the rubber industry as McCormick has set up in Chicago and placed in the competent charge of Herbert A. Kellar. The more archive-conscious our people become, the more such establishments there will be.

A public interested in public archives will extend its interest to private archives. Have not many of us been consulted at one time or another on the disposition of the papers of some person deceased? We could imagine it might become a matter of routine, that just as one consults the funeral director on the disposition of a body, so one would consult an archivist on the disposition of the papers. This kind of consultation is now given in innumerable cases by secretaries of historical societies and by librarians.

Parallel to the development of a consciousness of the importance of family papers, we should hope for an increased consciousness of the importance of business archives. Here also technical advice will be needed and should be available. No one should apply in vain to the archivists of this country if he wants to know what to preserve, what to destroy, how to deposit, and how to organize the documentation of family or business firm.

When I link the profession of archivist with that of the librarian, of the business counsellor, and of the funeral director, I see the outlines of a profession which must build up not only a high level of technical competence and a high standard of service, but a clear-cut ethic which can deal suitably with problems that arise in the protection of the privacy or secrecy of what ought to be private and secret, and the servicing of information that ought to be publicly available. There are many fine points of practice to be defined. In some cases the archivist with his feeling for values to be realized in the very remote future may advise the sealing of the documents for very long periods; in other cases he may advise their destruction. His responsibility toward American culture on the one hand, toward the families or organizations whose records are involved on the other, should in time come to be defined in a kind of a code, so that a duly certified archivist can claim the confidence of a client just as members of the medical or legal professions claim the confidence of their patients and clients, and just as journalists protect confidences as a part of the code of their profession.

For instance, there is the case of a scholar working in the field of literary history. Among the private papers of an American author, he discovered coded letters. He cracked the code and found that these letters contained a record of a personal scandal which incidentally completely explained the origin of one of the most important literary works of this author. The scholar had been allowed to consult these papers through the courtesy of the author's family. When he made this discovery he was, of course, under an ethical obligation to suppress the truth that he had discovered so far as present publication was concerned; was he also under an obligation to inform the family of the compromising character of the documents he had discovered, knowing that these documents would then be destroyed by the family and a certain significant fact lost forever to American cultural history; or should he have returned the documents without explaining his discovery to the family, confident that the papers would then be preserved because of the ignorance of their contents; or should he have explained the documents to the family and endeavored to persuade them to preserve them under long-term seal?

In developing archival policy in the field of business records, the archivist meets a professional enemy in the office manager. With office management he must reach a working agreement. According to a president of the Office Managers Association, one of the first things that an expert does when he comes into an old-fashioned office and begins to modernize it is to segregate and destroy records not currently in use. In one case a roomful of files was found in a business firm. "What are these dead files doing here? Why don't you throw them out?" asked the expert. "Our legal department advises us that we must keep them," was the reply. "Well, get another opinion from your legal department and throw them out," said the office manager.

It may be that microphotography will facilitate the archivist's work in that it will make possible the preservation of more records in less space, but certainly that will not be the whole answer. The archivist must interpret to a business client the value of business history in the formation of business policy, and compromise with the needs of office management by careful distinction between the destroyable and the preservable records.

The archivist ought to be qualified and ought to be trusted to handle matters of this kind, and to function as a public relations counsel for the relations of the people of today with the historians of future centuries.

The archival interest as the public comes to understand it must be broad enough to include family and business papers no less than public archives, but leadership lies in the public archives field. At this particular moment we have come to a turning point in policy. Hitherto we have been principally worried becaues we knew so little about the state of our public records; now they are all being inventoried. The inventories, made with unprecedented thoroughness and accuracy by the thousands of workers in the Historical Records Survey, are describing a body of documentation equal in amount to the contents of our public libraries, and just as widely distributed through the country. With our knowledge of what we have, we can begin to study the question of how it is to be used. It would be a mistake to think that the use of our archives is merely to provide documentation which scholars can work into books. We must think of it also as a place in which teachers in our schools will read for interesting information to be used in their classes; we must think of it as a reference room in which whole classes of questions—such as the date of this, the cost of that—will normally come for answer. The Social Security Act has given rise to many very practical reference questions in connection with the claims of people who do not possess birth certificates.

The public archives of a community can become a kind of local encyclopedia, and the public can be taught to use it. The people generally will then come to be shocked by the destruction of records that ought to be preserved just as they are shocked by cruelty to animals and as they are coming to be shocked by cruelty to automobiles. Have we not seen a generation growing up so sensitive to machinery that bearings burned out for lack of oil, or gears stripped through senseless handling, offend their sensibilities even though the car is not their own, just as their sensibilities were once offended by the teamster flogging his horse? Certainly there are many of us who already feel deeply concerning the destruction of unique and irreplaccable records, but that feeling is not yet sufficiently widespread to guarantee the adequate support of public archival activities, let alone the adequate preservation of business and family records.

We must hasten that time, and to hasten it we must expand the public use of archives; and to expand the public use of archives we must do more than make inventories. We must classify, develop, and define archives for purposes of general use. What is the next step? I have already suggested it in setting the parallel between the archival system and the library system. The libraries are already collaborating with the schools; let them now enter into a three-cornered combination with the local public archives. Let us take the inventory of the public archives of some community which already enjoys good library facilities; get a group of librarians who know the kind of question that the public brings to the library to help us in defining and analyzing the kind of questions that the public might bring to the archives if the archives are ready to answer them. We will find that certain of our archival series are not adequately indexed for reference purposes; we may be able to get them indexed. We find that others to which the public might wish to refer are housed in inaccessible cellars and attics; we may get them properly housed. When we have found by conferring with librarians what kinds of questions people would be interested in answering from archives, let us secure the coöperation of the libraries and the schools in informing the public of what they can find in their local public records.

We might perhaps assume that our scholars who are engaged in research in the social studies and other fields are already familiar with the wealth of archival material in this country, but I doubt that this is true at present, for the archival establishment, national and local, is a little too new to have had its effect on professional research. It is possible that the study of our archival resources in each of our research fields would lead to a diversion of much research energy from working with books to working with unpublished public records. At least this inquiry should be made and we should recognize the fact that American scholars generally have been far more extensively trained in the use of libraries than in the use of archives. It is quite possible that a whole new set of problems will come to the fore as research problems when the availability of archival resources is better understood. We might think that this matter could be left to the sociologists, the economists, or the historians, and that theirs might be the initiative; but I think it would be wise to take the lead and to present the problem of the use of archives to the scholars of this country in the form of the very practical question: Which of these classes of archival materials, which of these specific series which our inventories exhibit, ought to be preserved for you and your purposes; and which would you be willing to see destroyed? It may be that only the experts in the different fields of research can answer these questions; on the other hand, only the archivists can ask them.

I noted a case in Cleveland in which a graduate student was about to undertake a little research work on a problem of relief policy. The task was organized just as the inventory of county records was completed. Of the fifteen hundred series of county records exhibited in the inventory, fifty series that he had not previously known about or planned to consult were found to have a bearing on his problem.

I believe that a study of our problem from this standpoint may show that the traditions of the archival craft were defined in connection with the control of bodies of record so much slighter than those that now confront us that a new approach to the science may be necessary. The bulk of the records of the Hundred Years' War between France and England was probably equalled every day in the conduct of the World War.

The new archival rules ought quite properly to evolve after clearing the questions of value, destruction, preservation, and control, with all interests. These interests include the public, whose needs can best be interpreted by the public library; the research scholars, who can interpret their own needs; and of course, the administrative users of the records, with whom there is already adequate consultation.

Just as the public archives are the immediate center of attention, so of the public archives those that are found throughout the country are the most important, for it is only through them that the whole public can be reached and taught.

This means that above all else, the strategic objective of archival policy at this time must be to work with the relief labor program to develop and improve local archives. The Historical Records Survey has amazed the scholars of America by the competence and thoroughness of its work. The kind of thing it is doing can be carried further.

I do not regard the use of relief labor as an emergency, as an occasion of the moment, but as a probable permanent feature of American cultural economy, intermittent, of course, but recurrent in times of depression. And the natural and normal occupation of the white-collar worker on work relief is with the archives, with the public records.

For who is the white-collar worker? He is essentially the clerk. I mean by this the clerk in the historic sense, the descendant of those clerics whom Alcuin trained for Charlemagne in the free schools of Aix. He is the worker who works not with tools but with people and records. The old economy of medieval Europe used him for this purpose, and modern business economy uses him in the same way. Instead of copying manuscripts he copies invoices; instead of preaching sermons and hearing confession he sells refrigerators. But he is and will continue to be an essential part of our population, and there is no advantage in trying to retrain him for nonclerical labor during a depression, for when employment rises, clerks are needed by private industry just as much as hand laborers are needed.

The archivists are in a position now to plan for the recurrent use of quantities of labor that will help to make the archives useful to a wide public. This is one of the most important duties that faces archival science at the moment. It is a problem never posed before.

Just as librarians promote the use of books, and as teachers defend before the public the value of education, so archivists have as a part of their duty to give stimulus and guidance to the use of archives, and to their use not by the few but by the many.

The objective of archival policy in a democratic country cannot be the mere saving of paper; it must be nothing less than the enriching of the complete historical consciousness of the people as a whole. If we, as archivists, accept this as our problem and our duty, our profession will grow to be comparable in cultural signficance with librarianship, teaching, and the professional research of scholarship. That time is a long way in the future, but, as I have suggested, the archivist is and ought to be concerned with the most distant futures, and less than any other professional man in the country can he afford to be hesitant in defining long-term objectives.

Part III

IDEAS AND INSTITUTIONS

XI

Europe Faces the Customs Union *

I

The Austro-German customs union project has two meanings which tend to become confused with each other. On the one hand it is an episode in the long-drawn-out duel between France and Germany; on the other hand it offers a pattern to which Europe may or may not wish to conform in developing its economic system.

Both French and German nationalists are chiefly interested in the political aspect of the proposal. The French see in it the threat of the Anschluss, the incorporation of Austria with Germany, or of its extension into the whole Danube territory to reconstruct a Mittel-europa. The German nationalists see it as a gesture of independence toward the victor states, which may lead to revision of the treaties.

Europe has before it three other proposals of economic reorganization: the Economic Committee of the League is trying to secure a stabilization of tariffs, the Financial Committee is working on the problem of agricultural credits for eastern Europe, and the proposal for an economic Pan-Europe is being worked up on the principle that each state will regulate imports or exports under some kind of a quota system. Along with the proposals relating to tariffs, credits, and quotas, it is now necessary to take into account the idea of the customs

* Reprinted by permission from *The Virginia Quarterly Review*, July 1931.

union. The economic significance of the Austro-German scheme must be measured by its relation to the other proposals which it offers to supplement or replace. What is there latent in the idea of a customs union, and how does it fit into the pattern of Europe's unfolding institutional development?

II

In appraising the customs union of today the mind reaches back naturally to examine the customs union of a hundred years ago, created between 1829 and 1834 by Prussian statesmanship. It was the harbinger of a free-trade movement which captured England in the forties and France in the sixties, and of which the greatest triumph was the Cobden treaty between England and France in 1860. It was in this period that the unconditional most-favored-nation clause became a customary addition to commercial treaties. It was in this period that the Declaration of Paris marked the high point of renunciation of belligerent rights against commerce in time of war. Free trade in Victorian politics became more than a commercial policy; it became an ethical system. As an ethical system it opposed itself to the idea of nationalist politics and war.

The historians have never been quite clear in their interpretation of the free-trade movement of the mid-nineteenth century. On the one hand they have recognized its international implications, and on the other hand they have taught that it was an agency of national unification. They have taught that Prussian leadership in the Zollverein prepared the way for Prussian leadership in the reconstruction of Germany, forgetting that in the critical war of 1866 Prussia's Zollverein colleagues fought against her. They have taught that the railway age imposed upon the petty states of Germany and Italy a need for union, when the railway was, in fact, an indifferent instrument which could serve just as well to unite an Italian province to Austria as to join it to Piedmont. By looking at the tariff policies and doctrines of the mid-century through the glasses of the nationalist historians, we have become accustomed to think of customs union as the corollary or precursor of political union, when, in fact, it could more accurately be interpreted as the expression of the opposite principle.

The customs unions did not create unified national states; Germany and Italy were created by war, not by trade. The customs union, by satisfying the requirements of trade without going the length of political union, made political union less needful than it would otherwise have been. The antagonism between the principles of nationalism and war on the one hand, and free trade on the other, was confirmed when the new nationalist states adopted protective tariff policies within a few years of their establishment.

The period of the protective tariffs began in the seventies and has continued down to the present time. In the first two decades of protectionism, tariff schedules were generally adopted in direct response to the pressure of agricultural or industrial interests, without much regard to the tariffs of other countries. Then came the era of bargaining tariffs. Schedules were boosted beyond the point which national interest demanded in order to have a trading margin to be used in securing concessions. The tariff treaties that became standard after this period were like inverted Cobden treaties; they were international agreements to maintain protective rates rather than to get away from protection. Two kinds of bargaining policies were followed. Some powers adopted double schedules, a maximum rate for imports from states which would make no concessions, and a minimum rate for imports from states which would contract favorable commercial treaties. France uses this method. It leaves in the hands of the government complete control over all rates at all times. The alternative method is to establish a conventional tariff schedule, which binds a government not to change a particular rate during the life of an agreement. European tariff systems were constructed on this basis prior to the war.

Wilson struck at this system in the third of his Fourteen Points, in which he made it an American war aim to demand "the removal, so far as possible, of all economic barriers and the establishment of an equality of trade conditions among all the nations consenting to the peace and associating themselves for its maintenance." The idea in Wilson's mind was not alone his democratic predilection for free trade but also his opposition to the schemes for a postwar boycott of Germany, which had been developing in Allied circles.

This point was elaborated in the memorandum which Lippmann and Cobb prepared for Colonel House at the time of the Armistice negotiations:

The proposal applies only to those nations which accept the responsibilities of membership in the League of Nations. It means the destruction of all special commercial agreements, each nation putting the trade of every other nation in the League on the same basis, the most favored nation clause applying automatically to all members of the League of Nations.

Thus a nation . . . could not discriminate as between its partners in the League.

The only concrete result which emerged in the Peace Treaties from this point was the unilateral obligation imposed on the defeated powers to give most-favored-nation treatment to victors. In 1920 an Economic and Financial Commission of the League of Nations was created as the heir of the Supreme Economic Council which had administered such things as blockade and famine relief during the transition from war to peace. In 1927 the Economic Committee took up the thread of the free trade movement in the World Economic Conference of that year.

In the meantime the tariff practices of the European states had gone from bad to worse. Europe with its twenty-four states and its fifty thousand miles of customs frontiers was repeatedly advised to look across the Atlantic to admire the great republic whose vast area of unrestricted trade gave it a guarantee of perpetual prosperity. But the states of Europe obdurately continued their tariff policies, using the bargaining methods inherited from prewar days, but proceeding under far greater difficulties because of the narrowness of their economic bases and the general uncertainty which overhung them. All the new states had to pass through their currency inflation troubles, and only in 1927 were they sufficiently stabilized economically to begin to plan in more than hand-to-mouth terms. Under the leadership of the Economic Committee of the League they recognized that their prosperity required that they should imitate the United States by having a broad and unrestricted market. While they found it impracticable to consider reducing their tariffs, they at least entertained the suggestion that they should stop raising them. This proposal resulted in the Tariff Truce Conference of 1929, which began its sessions at the very time when the American Congress was beginning its wholesale upward revision of the American schedules, and ended in November, 1930, when it had been demonstrated to an incredulous world that the American economic colossus had feet of clay, and that even its continental trading area could not save it from industrial depression and misery.

In the meantime, it had appeared that none of the European countries were willing to freeze their schedules at the level then existing. Some of their rates were bargaining rates not intended to be permanent, others were experimental and intended to be transitory. As a substitute measure it was then suggested that the powers should refrain for a time from denouncing existing treaties. Only those tariffs already fixed by treaty would be frozen in place. This could be the starting point of stabilization, and the first step toward a truce and a general policy of reduction. An agreement in this sense was drafted in November, 1930, to go into effect in April, 1931, but failed of sufficient ratification. Upon the announcement of this failure, the German-Austrian customs union project was notified to the world.

III

Under the terms of this proposed treaty Germany and Austria undertake to adopt a common tariff and to abolish the customs line on their common frontier, and to share the revenue produced by the tariff levied on all goods entering the union from outside. It is exactly the same arrangement as that established in the 1830's, and in exactly the same way it is far from implying the assimilation of Austria by Germany. If it does result in annexation to Germany, this result will follow, not from the customs union itself, but from the nationalist sentiment which favors equally both customs union and Anschluss. To the extent that it tends toward political assimilation, the idea of customs union loses its significance as a general remedy for European ills. It leaves European economy exactly as it finds it except for the few million people of Austria who are directly affected.

The economic program for Europe which is inherent in the customs union idea is contained in that article of the project which invites the adherence of other states to the convention which Germany and Austria have signed. This article points toward the formation of a Danubian customs union. The Austro-German area is principally industrial, the lower Danubian countries chiefly agrarian. The farmers of Rumania, Bulgaria, Hungary, and Yugoslavia are in need of privileged markets where they will not have to compete against Russian, American, and Argentine wheat growers. They have more to gain than Austria herself from a customs union with Germany, for Austria is uniting with a competitor, while all the lower Danube countries would be uniting with a customer. While economic interest would draw them toward such a union, political interest would restrain them, for they have organized their international relations on the basis of French hegemony. And the creation of such a Mittel-europa would not only deal a death blow to French leadership, but would also put an end to any more general plans for European economic coöperation. France, for instance, could never enter it, not only for reasons of national sentiment, but also because such action would destroy the marvelous equilibrium of her economic system.

IV

The chief alternative to the idea of customs union is the principle of controlled importation and exportation. Tariffs are only one of the ways in which countries can control the flow of goods. A method of limiting and controlling export and import of goods was worked out before the war in thirty or forty industries which organized international cartels. These cartels worked without government coöperation, or even against government opposition. Their object was to stabilize industry by restricting competition and preventing overproduction. They would farm out export markets among a number of producing nations, and sometimes centralize all orders in a central sales agency.

The stress of war administration forced the governments into a similar effort to control production and to distribute quotas of goods among the different nations which required them. The Allies built up huge purchasing agencies which handled the interests of the consuming countries as the prewar cartels had handled the interests of the producing firms. In postwar days the principle of the cartel and of government control of export was made the subject of several experiments, notably the Coffee Valorization Plan in Brazil and the Stephenson Plan for controlling the rubber market. Both these schemes were piratical in nature, because they aimed at stabilization of profiteering prices. Another application of the principle occurred in the French and Luxemburg steel industry. The Treaty of Versailles provided that a certain quota of steel from these regions should be allowed free exportation into Germany for five years, to give the industry a chance to accommodate itself to the separation from the German customs system. At the expiration of these five years the steel men of the three countries worked out among themselves a rationing agreement which virtually continued the right of the French and Luxemburg steel to enjoy a share of the German market. This private arrangement was then confirmed in a Franco-German commercial treaty. The most recent and the most extensive arrangement of this nature is the Chadbourne sugar control plan, under which seven sugar-exporting countries will aid in stabilizing market conditions by controlling the volume of exports on a quota basis. The United States and Canada have both been pressed by their farming population into efforts to stabilize agricultural prices by undertaking the role of an exalted middleman, with the result that the decision to give or withhold wheat from the world market has become a matter of government policy. So far as present dispatches indicate, Briand's economic program for Pan-Europe will be in line with this economic trend. The industrial countries of Europe will offer to the agricultural countries a privileged market for a certain quota of food, in exchange for which the agricultural countries will receive a proportionate quota of manufactured goods. The quotas will be set at such a level that the new industries in eastern Europe will be able to survive the competition of the west, and the western farmer to hold his own against the eastern peasantry. This will involve a continuous intervention by the state in all economic affairs. It is a step that goes further from the doctrine of liberalism and laissez faire than the protective tariff at its worst. Therefore the issue of Mittel-europa versus Pan-Europe is not merely the issue of French versus German leadership, but also the issue of old-fashioned liberalism in economics as against modern state control.

v

From this standpoint the most significant quality of the Mittel-europa customs union as a pattern for general European adoption is the element of political abdication which it con-

tains. To create a great area of free trade over the territories of
a number of independent states would be to leave the governments helpless in the presence of the great international corporations. A European customs union at its best would still
differ from the American union in that there would be no general government to control the great corporations operating in
the area. The great modern super-corporation did not exist in
the days when free trade was the pinnacle of enlightened statecraft. The free-trade age did not have the problem of "ration-
alization" and control which the modern corporation and cartel
seek to solve. In the fifties and sixties the limited liability company as a form of ownership had just begun to enter the industrial field; its potentialities were unknown. The sufficient object of all industrial enterprise was then production rather than
discipline, progress rather than stabilization. The principle of
the customs union is in contradiction with the modern trend
because it is a step toward greater anarchy in production. It is
based upon an analogy doubly false—an analogy with the productive conditions of Europe in the middle of the nineteenth
century and with the political conditions of the United States
today. Since the depression came to America, it ceased to be
possible to regard the principle of the customs union as a
panacea for Europe's economic ills. The need is rather for more
enlightened coöperation of government and business in the
field of planning. This is the road along which Briand seeks
to go, while the Germans and Austrians are moving in the
opposite direction.

XII

The Twentieth Century Looks at Human Nature *

I

To the ancient riddle, "What is man?" each age returns its own reply. Could we but determine, in all its rich implications, the answer that this age will give to the eternal riddle, we would have in our hands a thread to guide us through the labyrinth of contemporary culture. Perhaps we may find that no small part of the apparent incoherence of things is the result of our effort to believe and apply certain great secular dogmas—those of democracy, capitalism, or socialism, for instance—when we no longer accept the views of human nature that go with them.

What is the western world's conception of human nature? Dig down deep enough and at bottom it is Christian. There will not be found in it, for instance, the Hindu species of soul which flits from life to life toward an extinction of personality. The Christian individual human life is a unique thing with eternal values attaching to it. Upon this deep Christian foundation two swirling torrents of thought, of the age of Rousseau and of the age of Darwin, have laid down their successive strata. The human nature of the age of Rousseau operated under laws of absolute morality and reason between the poles of good and evil, truth and falsehood. The human nature of

* Reprinted by permission from *The Virginia Quarterly Review,* July 1934.

* Reprinted by permission from *The Virginia Quarterly Review,* July 1934.

the age of Darwin was only a special kind of cause in a universe of change and movement whereof each moment was linked to the next in an iron chain of cause and effect, so that man operated between the poles of success and failure as an economic automaton in the world of production or as a mammal in the world of nature. Down in those cultural strata, in the writings of the eighteenth-century *philosophes* or the nineteenth-century economists, these views of human nature are to be found worked into designs of marvelous beauty and intricacy. In the age of Rousseau there was the dogma of democracy and the cult of humanity, in the age of Darwin the dogma of socialism and the cult of nationalism. These were indeed great creations. To know them is to admire them. But are they living beings in the contemporary world, or only fossil forms?

If, after making due allowance for the fact that cultural eras are not sharply cut off from each other, and that they are always much greater and more complex than any name we can give them, it is permissible to speak of an Age of Rousseau in the eighteenth century and an Age of Darwin in the nineteenth, then with somewhat less assurance we can perceive in the twentieth century an Age of Freud. It could not be claimed that Freud's personal contribution to learning is so great that it towers over all else, but it is certain that he has been both typical and influential, like Rousseau. He typifies the widespread effort to look more deeply into the inner processes of human behavior. This effort is a cultural fact as far-reaching and conclusive for this generation as the political philosophy that preceded the French Revolution or the Victorian constellation of economic and scientific ideas were for their respective times. The vogue of Freud and of the intelligence test has been an illustrative episode in a great adventure in the understanding of human nature. The other episodes are taking place on a wide front that stretches from the economics of advertising to the politics of the Nazis, from the new prose to the New Deal.

The effective thought of the day is now willing to proceed on the hypothesis that reason is not the master of human conduct but a petty valet coming afterward to tidy up, explain, and justify. Our generation is willing to admit that the distinction between "good" and "bad" in people may be a superficial distinction, if in the depths of the psyche these qualities are ambivalent: the vice crusader and the libertine are drawing their energies from the same deep spring. Whereas the economists taught that man is a being who buys in the cheapest market and sells in the dearest, we have come to realize that in the presence of choices that most profoundly determine his fate—the choice, for instance, between war and peace—he will sell in the cheapest market, and buy in the dearest. We insist that all the biographies be rewritten in new terms, and all the old human situations be described anew, not because of a mere passing fad for psychological novelties, but because the older expositions are no longer convincing.

II

How does a particular conception of human nature, be it the eighteenth-century moral-rational, the nineteenth-century mechanical-causal, or the twentieth-century psychological, permeate the intellectual and practical problems of its time? The process can be illustrated from eighteenth-century experience. There was then no universal agreement that mankind was good, or that reason was the key to truth. These were the questions upon which disputants took sides. The agreement was only the implied and unexpressed consensus that the important thing about humanity was its goodness or badness, its ability or inability to know truth through reason. The debate over these issues formed the intellectual lines behind which the great vested interests of the day entrenched themselves for the battle of the French Revolution. The Church held that man was naturally bad, and in need of the sacraments for his salvation. The theologians argued that reason could not know the truth without the aid of revelation. The *philosophes* replied that man was naturally virtuous unless corrupted by society, that his mind was open to the persuasions of reason, and that reason would light him all the way to eternal truth.

The prevailing conceptions of human nature determined many of the speculative preoccupations of the most exalted intellects. The theologians, believing in God and sin and distrusting unaided reason, faced certain characteristic metaphysical entanglements: how could a good and omnipotent God permit the existence of evil in the world? This was the Problem of Evil. It was sometimes solved by the assertion that the world was as good as possible, "the best of all possible worlds." Another question: how could mere man force the hand of God and by his own efforts compel God to accord him salvation? This was called the Problem of Free Will and Grace. The philosophers had other difficulties, chief among which was the one they called the Problem of Knowledge. How could man know the truth through the agency of reason if the objects of knowledge lay in the realm of things while reason itself dealt only in ideas? These problems fed the minds of thinkers from John Locke to Immanuel Kant, and from the Jansenists of Port Royal to Voltaire.

In practical application the philosophers' view of human nature became the dogma of democracy. Man's competence to govern himself was a corollary of his natural virtue and endowment of reason. The law of nature therefore indicated the people as their own natural sovereign; any other authority over them was either unnecessary or evil. Since the people were both good and wise, to thwart them would be wickedness and folly. Rousseau's "citizen" was a romantic idealization of man, whose actions accorded always with reason, whose desires were directed constantly toward the general good. For such citizens the device of an election was a means of discovering the general good, of pooling the total intelligence of the community; it was not intended to be a war of hostile interests waged with paper weapons. The leaders of that day dared to write freedom of speech and press boldly in the program of democracy because they were confident that truth would conquer error in a free contest before the tribunal of reason. Even those who opposed the democratic dogma merely reversed the postulates, arguing that virtue and reason were a monopoly of the few rather than the heritage of all.

The prestige of reason contributed to the practice of formulating all political attitudes in terms of jurisprudence. Political controversialists concerned themselves more with the principles of government than with its mechanics, more with legislation than with administration. When Napoleon set up his operations in terms of administrative mechanics, the transition to nineteenth-century practical politics began. Soon afterwards the Continent learned with some surprise the mechanical secret of British "liberty," namely, the neat device by which a ministry would automatically go out of office when it ceased to command a majority of votes in Parliament. The objective of the revolutions of 1830 was not so much democracy or popular sovereignty as the introduction on the Continent of the English cabinet system. Jeremy Bentham began to write constitutions for young Latin-American states, convinced that if the political machine were correctly set up it would run perfectly. Then came the Second Empire in France, making a mockery of the democratic dogma by setting up a popular dictatorship, a tyranny with the consent of the people. Those who still clung to the eighteenth-century conceptions were compelled to explain away the Second Empire by closing their eyes to the fact that Napoleon III was endorsed by the overwhelming majority of his nation. In the same way the twentieth-century dictatorships are sometimes explained away by people who try to believe that the great masses of Germans do not "really" approve of Hitler, and that the overwhelming majority of Italians do not "willingly" follow Mussolini.

III

In the nineteenth century, even while democratic institutions were making great conquests, the intellectual atmosphere became inhospitable to those assumptions regarding human nature in which the dogma of democracy had been born. The reaction against the eighteenth century took place on a wide front. Experimental science captured the prestige that had once belonged to philosophy, mechanical invention changed man's material environment, and the idea of evolution came to govern thinking as the conception of reason had once dominated it. The great social dogmas established in this age were those of capitalism, socialism, and nationalism. These dogmas still carry with them the odor of the nineteenth century wherever they go.

Science, invention, evolution appeared at the threshold of the century as isolated elements of culture, but by the middle of the century they had been synthesized. Hegel, the great philosopher of the eighteen-twenties, developed a universal metaphysic of evolution, but he was not a scientist. The first inventions that had such a profound effect upon economic life were the products not of the scientific laboratory but of the artisan's workshop. And science itself, in the year 1800, was not drawn together in a great system, but consisted rather of a number of almost unrelated studies of natural phenomena.

But in the middle of the century the physical sciences drew together their fifty years' cumulation of experimental data in a great mechanical synthesis, and Darwin came forward with a scientific rather than metaphysical application of the principle of evolution, offering a mechanical explanation of the development and course of life itself. At the same time the scientists began to be useful; in chemistry and electricity they contributed to the world of mechanical invention. The prestige of facts increased at the expense of ideas and principles; the patterns of mechanics overshadowed those of pure logic. Social thinkers shared the prevailing prejudice in favor of tangible realities. John Stuart Mill wrote an inductive logic; Karl Marx presented a materialistic interpretation of history. The beautiful mechanics of the free market and the gold standard charmed every observer of economic life. Society seemed to be a machine equipped with automatic controls. The high objectives of eighteenth-century philosophy were dismissed by Herbert Spencer, philosopher of evolution, into the limbo of the unknowable. The "natural law" of the nineteenth century (unlike its predecessor of the eighteenth century) became something purely mechanical, quite unrelated to human jurisprudence.

What kind of humanity inhabited this mechanical cosmos? Instead of the citizen of Rousseau's politics there appeared the "individual" of economic doctrine; in the place of the sovereign people of the French Revolution, the proletarian masses of Marx. It was a new human race, occupying a new universe.

Virtue in nineteenth-century man appeared as an incidental or accidental quality. Success and survival were the essentials. The economic individual was primarily productive or unproductive, and only incidentally good or bad. Self-interest rather than virtue furnished the motive force of the economic machine. This was a view accepted alike by capitalists and socialist theorists. Capitalist economics looked upon the individual entrepreneur, socialist economics upon the embattled class, as the decisive agency in economic action. Both doctrines agreed in their vision of an underlying compulsion, either by the pressure of the immutable laws of competition upon the individual businessman, or by the opposition of irreconcilable classes in unavoidable conflict. The Darwinian theory of struggle for existence confirmed what the pre-Darwinian economists had already outlined.

When the pattern of Darwinism was applied to the situation of international relations an even more complete repudiation of moral principle took place. Survival of the fittest was a doctrine of anarchy which made stable international life impossible. Neither Thrasymachus nor Machiavelli had possessed such potent doctrinal weapons for the defense of political immorality. And morality itself was worn down by the sociologists and anthropologists until it appeared as a mere cultural accident, valid for its time and place but for no more. Not hypocrisy, but a stupendous power of intellectual digestion, made it possible for the age to accept all this and still believe in God.

Symptomatic of the nineteenth-century view of human nature was the metaphysical problem of Free Will and Mechanical Determinism, which began to compel attention when the problem of Free Will and Grace had dropped out of sight. This metaphysical dilemma has left deep traces in contemporary socialist dogma. In the dialectics of Marxism it has always been difficult to hold the balance between the two sides of a theory that proclaims at once the inevitable coming of the revolution and the duty of leadership and agitation. It was precisely upon this issue that Lenin took his stand in the decisive programmatic document "What Is to be Done?" which marked the beginning of his leadership. It is in terms of this dilemma that Trotsky has just analyzed the November Revolution. Economic issues in the capitalist thought-world clothe themselves in similar guise, for they take form as assertions and denials of the possibility of effective intervention to control the economic machine.

The nineteenth century did not succeed in reconciling the experience of individual freedom with the dogmas of mechanistic science. How could man exercise freedom in a universe knit through and through by complete relationships of cause and effect? Was the criminal to be blamed for his crime if the crime is the product of heredity and environment? How could leadership intervene to deflect, retard, or accelerate a process moving inevitably by its own momentum?

As the tantalizing dilemma of Free Will and Natural Causation, in all its personal and social implications, worked its way through popular thought until it found a place even in the armory of the village atheist, it became apparent that the century that had tried to make its whole political and economic system a tabernacle of freedom had ended by doubting whether freedom was possible at all.

IV

The twentieth century turned to psychology from the pressure of necessity. The Order of Nature so copiously illustrated and exhibited in nineteenth-century thought was no longer offering adequately comprehensive and significant certainties. Cumulative specialization among the scientists broke into fragments that marvelous mid-Victorian synthesis, and ended the real popularization of authentic science. Not since the days of Herbert Spencer, Clerk-Maxwell, Lord Kelvin, and the ninth edition of the *Encyclopædia Britannica* has it seemed feasible for scientists to take the cultivated layman fully into their confidence. Fewer and fewer have become the proclaimed truths of science that can be made evident to the ordinary intelligent man by demonstrations that touch his sense of fact. And among the scientists themselves the sector of the horizon of knowledge that lies within the field of vision of any one of them becomes pitifully smaller with the passing of each decade. As the science of the nineteenth century took on more and more the aspect of a fragmentary and inconclusive faith, the time came to seek elsewhere for unity and synthesis. Perhaps it could be found in the depths and mystery of human personality!

The psychologists participated in this change of front, although they had not brought it about. In general they kept step with their time. In the eighteenth century they had been philosophical; in the nineteenth century they tried to be scientific. They began the century with phrenology and association of ideas, and ended it with laboratory measurement of sensations. The urge to go more deeply into the study of personality was felt in literature before it touched the professors of psychology. And when Freud and James stepped with Henri Bergson across the threshold of the nineteen-hundreds they were accompanied by two strange guests from other centuries, St. Thomas Aquinas and Immanuel Kant. These champions of thought undertook, each in his own way, to restore a man-centered, rather than to enlarge a thing-centered, universe. The revolt against materialistic science was under way. It was under these circumstances that the vogue of the new psychology began.

Before long it became apparent that the world of the nineteenth century was dead. Its monstrous tangibilities had been dissolved. A new physics and a modern art redefined space to suit a new fancy. The additive simplicities of inductive logic were superseded by the logic of probability. The crudities of historical materialism yielded to more mystical creations such as those of Spengler. In the economic world the corporations replaced the individual as owner; functions replaced commodities as the principal objects of value; paper securities succeeded tangible property as the most common form of wealth; bank credit assumed the duties once performed by hard coin and visible paper currency; and of the arts of the market place those which, like market analysis and advertising, lay in the field of applied psychology became preëminent. In politics the propaganda of the World War era revealed the range and importance of political techniques that were not nineteenth-century blood and iron, nor yet eighteenth-century jurisprudence. To these techniques postwar nationalism and communism have given further development, sound film and radio further equipment. In the new politics myths supersede facts; they become a necessity. Symbol and ritual, black shirt and red flag, song and color—these and not the ballot are the vehicles of political activity. The historians are scurrying to study public opinion in past politics, the social scientists are undertaking research in pressure groups and propaganda, and it becomes increasingly evident that contemporary culture demands of the educated man some familiarity with the postulates of psychology.

How can such a thing as the nazi movement be understood without psychiatric knowledge? To appraise the movement by judging that Hitler or his followers are good or bad people, or even by estimating how far they succeed or fail in obtaining a German national interest, is to misstate the whole problem. To subject their race doctrine to objective analysis for truth or falsity is like calling in an interior decorator to decide whether red, white, and blue are the colors that go together in the national flag. The evidence on the *Reichstag* fire may be ambiguous, but what of it? The nazi account of the fire has been elevated to a state myth and is no longer subject to the canons of historical evidence as a mere historical event. The nazi movement must be understood in terms of psychology or not at all.

Not only in understanding the great social movements of the day do we resort to these forms of thought. We require them and make use of them in understanding our fellow men. We can no longer make much use of the assumption that these creatures are created equal in the eighteenth-century sense, endowed with a common heritage of reason, and engaged equally in the pursuit of happiness. This was good enough as a canon of jurisprudence, but it is useless as a principle of vocational guidance. Differences rather than equalities in endowment and sensitivity, in aptitude and character, now seem to be a better starting point for social policies. The fiction of equality is useless when the concrete problem is that of adjustment of individuals to society. Moreover, we are dissatisfied with the nineteenth-century generalization that man sinks all his qualities in a dominating urge to acquire and survive. Time was when we expected nothing else of our neighbors and demanded nothing more of ourselves. According to our fortunes in this common activity we became rich or poor, bourgeois or proletarian. But when the authors of *Middletown* made a first-hand analysis of the stratification of the people, they drew the line not between rich and poor but between the business class and the working class, even though some of the working class were better off than some of the business class. The difference they found was one of outlook—in other words, it was psychological. And there are many more of these significant classifications with which we become familiar. We classify ourselves as introverts or extroverts. We belong to the "sensual," "heroic," or "contemplative" types. In the learned tomes of Kretschmer, Spranger, Adler, and Jung, in the practice of personnel departments and vocational guidance bureaus, in the revised attitudes toward marriage situations that are taught in the colleges, it is evident that the twentieth century hypothesizes in human nature complexities that the nineteenth century ignored.

In the nineteen-twenties psychology aroused great public interest as a new popular science. Freud and Watson reigned over a million tea tables. The liberation of women from the restraints of certain conventions took place in an atmosphere that reeked with the language of psychology, as the atmosphere of the French Revolution reeked with the language of Reason and Natural Laws. This interest has in some measure abated, but the steady encroachment of the psychological techniques in practical life goes on. The magazines carry few articles on Freud—but look at their advertising columns. Compare the soap advertisement of the eighteen-eighties—a child and a Newfoundland dog on a rocky shore with a bar of soap and a life buoy—with the provocative theme of the contemporary appeal. There is now less popular writing on psychology than there was in the twenties but there is more fundamental research. The women's clubs turn from Freud to politics, but the institutes of human relations, of child guidance, of euthenics go right on.

V

As the psychological conception of human nature develops before our eyes we can see rising over the horizon the great issues that will define themselves in its terms. These oncoming problems arise in the marriage and family system, in the control of culture by society, and in the relation of different cultures to each other.

The family, as the sociologists have been preaching, is now shorn of so many of its older functions—religious, economic, protective, educational—that its chief remaining service is to the human need for affection and personal response. This is a psychological need. The spread of contraception has increased the incidence of the psychological element in marriage at the expense of the biological. The modern state cannot avoid the issues raised by the social control of culture. The fascists, communists, and nazis undertake to monopolize the entire life and soul of the people. Capitalist society seeks to bring its production and distribution fully into mesh and then has before it the problem of leisure. When there is bread enough to feed all of man that Darwin could explain, the time comes to nourish the much more complex man that psychology depicts. The state that abandons liberal principles of government sets up a ministry of propaganda. The state that tries to retain liberal institutions in the presence of modern propaganda techniques faces the difficult problem of preventing the irresponsible manipulation of public opinion without sacrificing freedom of thought. These are some of the internal aspects of the problem of culture control. Externally there are the questions involved in the contact and interpenetration of the great old civilizations, Indian and Chinese, with the Western, and in the relations of communist, nationalist, and liberal societies among themselves.

The contact of Western with Eastern cultures has hitherto been confined to superficial borrowings. Now it is going deeper. Nineteenth-century Europe with its naïve sense of superiority was no nearer than Marco Polo to an understanding of China and India. Missionary and trader went out; traveler's tale and *objet d'art* came back. This was the level of cultural contact so far as the West was concerned. The impact upon the East was greater. India received a ruling class; China obtained in the course of foreign trade opium, Asiatic cholera, manufactured goods, and finally railways and factories. The disturbance created by this contact is now propagating itself as a great cultural crisis throughout the East. The twentieth century must decide whether a syncretism of these cultures with Occidental civilization is to take place, and if so, upon what terms.

It is not impossible that the tables may be turned upon the West. The technological preëminence of the Western nations may be lost in the next half century, as that of the British Isles was lost in the last, through the mere dispersion of machinery throughout the world. The differences of culture will then stand out nakedly at the level of social psychology; they will be differences in what men are, not in what they have. If it should happen that passive resistance should succeed as a tactic in India, and Bismarckian methods fail in Manchuria, the postulates of Occidental politics will stand discredited by Asiatic experience. If there should then come about a crumbling of Western self-confidence, a loss of morale in the presence of a culture exhibiting superiorities at the psychological level, the time will have arrived to balance the books of civilization by subjecting the West in its turn to revolutionary internal pressures arising out of contacts with the East. That will be a crisis to challenge our understanding of human personality!

If the century should keep free from tensions arising out of the contact of East and West, it will still be confronted with the more recent nationalist and communist-capitalist schisms in the West itself. The divisions cut through Western culture by the nationalisms that culminated in the nineteenth century were trivial compared with those of today. Those differences were largely matters of language, literature and history; these are of world-outlook. A communist can easily surmount the language barrier separating him from a fellow communist, but his mind cannot meet in any language the mind of the fascist or liberal. The theme of the last free editorial of the doomed *Frankfurter Zeitung*, organ of German liberalism, before it was crushed by the nazis, was not the brown-shirt atrocities or the rape of the constitution, but the greater tragedy: "It has come at last to this, that Germans no longer understand one another."

The twentieth century faces the possibility that this may become true of the world in general. The improvement in means of communication (and hence of propaganda) may result, not in closing the cultural chasms between groups of men, but in digging them deeper, till the age meets the ironic fate that its ability to communicate has resulted in an inability to understand. This is on the plane of social psychology. In individual psychology there may be equivalent ironies in store for us. The knowledge of human nature that psychology brings into the relationship of marriage and family life may introduce there more difficulties than it disposes of. But it is now too late to draw back; we are rehearsing once more the fable of the Garden of Eden, and have bitten into the apple from the fatal tree.

XIII

An Anatomy of Revolution *

I

When friends and enemies of the Roosevelt administration
united in calling it revolutionary, the word revolution entered
the vocabulary of American politics in a new way, for which
no adequate preparation has yet been made. However hard
the political campaign speeches may strain at parallels, they
cannot successfully portray contemporary America as a mirror
of Soviet Russia or Fascist Italy. The epithet "Tory" fails to
establish a resemblance of present events to those of 1776. If the
New Deal is a revolution, it belongs to a species hitherto un-
noted by the American political observer, who might profitably
extend his catalogue of types to include some specimens of the
less familiar varieties.

The idea of revolution comes to us as a political conception
from the Greek experience in city government, where it was
associated with the turning of the wheel of fortune, which
brought one party up and sent another down. The nineteenth
century, with the example of the French Revolution so mani-
festly before it, used the word to describe great institutional
changes. Moreover, in connection with a Darwinian thought-
pattern we have come to use the word to designate a certain
tempo of change: revolution is rapid, evolution is slow.

* Reprinted by permission from *The Virginia Quarterly Review*,
October 1934.

We expect to find all three of these elements in a revolution: displacement of power, important institutional changes, and a tempo of crisis. How far does the Roosevelt administration show these characteristics? How great is the real displacement of power in America, and how profound the institutional change? Has the change been as sudden as it seems, or have we merely come to see that gradual and continuous developments are now approaching a configuration that we had not previously happened to notice?

We are still willing to call a change a revolution though it lack some of these elements, and the Roosevelt revolution may be of such a class. The industrial revolution, for instance, involved a displacement of power, but took place gradually; the average Latin-American revolution is a sudden and violent displacement, but is not accompanied by important institutional changes. That it is also possible to have a revolution without any displacement of power is illustrated in the history of the Frankish kingdom of the eighth century.

The school books used to tell the story of the long-haired Merovingian kings of the Franks who in some way became "weak," and ceased to rule actively. They were the "do-nothing" kings. The mayors of the palace, on the contrary, exhibited strong masculine characteristics, and revelled in activity. So it came about that Pepin the Short, mayor of the palace and father of Charlemagne, with the approval of the Pope, displaced the Merovingian line and set himself up as king of the Franks. It used to be implied that there was nothing in this interesting episode that could not have been prevented by feeding the Merovingian kings more spinach and cod liver oil.

There is another way of understanding the story. The Frankish kingdom of that day was a backwoods area in which the principal form of property was land; there were few cities and very little money economy. In this area a Germanic tribal king had fallen heir to the relics of a Roman administrative apparatus which he did not understand, and made an alliance with the Church, which served him as a broker in his relations with God, demons, and people.

Whether because of the absence of an adequate political training, or because the decline of the cities rendered government of the Roman type impossible, it came about that the Frankish kings could no longer protect life and property in their realm. Then there developed, partly out of the old Frankish institution of *mainbour*, or sworn companionship, and partly out of the relics of Roman landholding institutions, a system that came to constitute a secondary government parallel to the Frankish state. This extensive *mainbour* system bore a certain resemblance to the structures of modern racketeering or machine politics. The little man who needed protection would get it by becoming the pledged follower of a magnate who would accept him. He might surrender his land to the leader, receiving it back on dependent terms corresponding to his pledged allegiance. The protector could procure from the king a royal letter of immunity exempting him from royal jurisdiction.

The system lent itself like the corporate organization of modern business to the creation of widely ramified mergers. The family that succeeded in becoming the head of the most extensive combination of all—a kind of consolidated land trust incorporating all the chief magnates of the kingdom with their followings—was the family of Pepin of Heristal, whose family fortune had been built up by marriage and by graft in the service of the king. His place was analogous to that which might have come to the House of Morgan if the elder Morgan had been able to carry out the plans of trust formation attributed to him, while adding the resources of a political boss and gangster chief to his repertory.

From such a strong position, the mayor of the palace was naturally tempted to strike for the crown. One of them tried it, but failed because the superstitious reverence of the Franks for the Merovingian line made it seem to them impossible that a member of another family could occupy the throne. Seven hundred years before this time the keen Roman observer, Tacitus, had noted that the Germanic tribal kings were always chosen from the blood royal. A king of the authentic blood seemed a necessity, if for no other reason than for the sake of the calendar, in order that the year might be dated correctly from his reign. This reverence for past traditions was good enough in ordinary times, but in 732 came a crisis in the kingdom—the Moorish invasion.

In the presence of this crisis the Frankish king was unable to raise an army, but Charles Martel, mayor of the palace, called upon all his sworn followers, then seized the church lands and gave them out to bring still more followers to his standard. With this army he beat off the Moors in the Battle of Tours. Thereafter it was evident that the sworn following of the mayor of the palace was a more effective organization than the traditional government of the king. But it was still necessary to overcome the resistance of tradition to a formal change. This was accomplished by using the authority of the Church against the vestiges of tribal legitimacy. The Pope authorized Pepin the Short, son of Charles Martel, to assume the tribal crown.

There was no shifting of power. The same men, the same families, continued to do the same things in the same way, but the two kinds of government were combined as one. Charlemagne ruled not only as King of the Franks but also as the head of a great body of sworn followers who had taken his pledge.

Modern man also lives under two regimes, to one of which he renders patriotism and loyalty, while to the other he looks for his livelihood. It has often been suggested that the business organization of modern society is becoming more important than its political organization, and that the leaders of business are more powerful than political leaders. Such suggestions encounter resistance in the tradition of popular sovereignty, which rejects big business dictatorship in government as an evil. Perhaps this traditional attitude, like the feeling of the Franks for their royal family, might have weakened in time of crisis, and the public might even have allowed itself to be sacrificed to business leadership as the Frankish churches and monasteries were sacrificed when Charles Martel seized their lands. But the American magnates did not go out to meet the crisis, or win their Battle of Tours.

American business, therefore, is not in a position to have the merging of business and government legitimated under its own control. It is still possible that the future may bring a development resembling that of the Frankish kingdom, if the N.R.A., as a legalized continuation of the trust movement, should leave the same people doing the same thing that they did before, in the same way, excepting that they will be metamorphosed into code authorities with legal powers, just as the mayors of the palace were changed into kings.

II

Another kind of revolution was engineered by the young Emperor Meiji of Japan in the year 1867. This revolution took place in the presence of a crisis arising out of contact with foreign powers. It put an end simultaneously to the three peculiarities of the Japanese political system: dual government, feudalism, and isolation.

Dual government was the name given to that system by which the emperor, descendant of the prehistoric tribal leader of the race, continued to be titular ruler while the shogun governed the country. The powers of the shogun dated from the medieval era, when his office of military commander eclipsed in practical importance the office of the emperor. It was as if the Frankish mayors of the palace had continued as governors acting in the name of the Merovingian kings. When Perry visited Japan he thought the shogun was the emperor. He heard that somewhere in the back country there was some kind of a pope who was highly venerated and who lived in august poverty, but the man with whom he made his treaty was the shogun.

The shogun's government was feudal; he had his sworn followers, the daimyo or heads of the great families, who were committed to hereditary loyalty to his rule. They held the strategic points throughout the Empire. There were also some great clans who were, traditionally and by hereditary transmission, legally hostile to the shogun. From them he exacted a strict obedience. He made them come up once a year to his capital in Yedo (now Tokyo), and leave hostages with him when they went back to their estates.

The third peculiarity of the Japanese system, the policy of isolation, dated from the seventeenth century. Western missionaries entering Japan at that time had exercised bad judgment by getting on the wrong side in one of the civil wars. As a result all foreigners were excluded, and Japanese were forbidden to travel abroad. Only one tiny door was left open at Nagasaki, where Dutch traders were permitted to bring in one ship a year. That was the Japanese regime that lasted from the seventeenth to the nineteenth century: shogunate, feudal system, and isolation.

In the first half of the nineteenth century there developed in Japan internal pressure against this system. A cultural renaissance was taking place, a revolt against Chinese culture and a new interest in the antiquities of Japan. There was a revival of the native Shinto cult as against the imported Buddhist religion. The historians, responding to this interest, propagated the knowledge that the legitimate ruler of Japan was not the great shogun at Yedo but the emperor in his obscurity at Kyoto. This historical school received support from the younger branches of the shogun's own family, just as the French revolutionary philosophy had an adherent in the Duke of Orléans, of the younger branch of the royal family of France.

There was another cultural movement that seemed to threaten the established order. It was a philosophical school that followed the teachings of the Chinese philosopher, Wang

Yang Ming—a pragmatist. Whereas the official doctrine of the Japanese state insisted upon the implicit obedience of the retainer to his lord, the pragmatists taught that action should be governed by circumstances. The gesture that illustrated the meaning of the teaching of the new school was the act of an official who opened the granaries without proper authority on the ground that the people were hungry. The doctrine seemed as dangerous to a feudal Japan as communism seems to modern Japan. These ferments were at work, wholly unconnected with outside influences.

When Commodore Perry arrived, he completed the destruction of the equilibrium of the regime, for his treaty, signed by the shogun, ended the three-centuries policy of isolation. This gave the hereditary hostile clans an issue to be used against the shogunate. They contended that the treaty was invalid because a decision of such importance would require the ratification of the emperor. The doctrine of the historical school provided ammunition for these imperial legitimists. Their samurai, rallying to the slogan "Honor the emperor, expel the barbarian," attacked foreigners in the streets.

European states in the nineteenth century did not tolerate such treatment of their nationals; the British government sent a fleet to punish the clan of Satsuma whose samurai had attacked an Englishman, Richardson, on the highway. Thus internal dissension threatened to cause foreign conquest.

The emperor saved the situation by ratifying the treaties that the shogun had signed, and then a new shogun, coming into office in 1866, resigned his powers into the emperor's hands. That was a year of marvels; for when the shogun resigned his powers he was followed by all the great daimyo, who surrendered their powers as well. In a great burst of generosity and patriotism the whole people rallied around the imperial throne.

The young emperor, ably advised by a brain trust of samurai, reorganized Japan as a modern state with a centralized administration. Many of those who had surrendered feudal powers received back new authority as officials of the imperial bureaucracy. Those of the samurai who had been administrators in feudal Japan became the prefects and subprefects of the new regime; the others were "liquidated" as a class.

It seemed in the spring of 1933 that the shogunate of American business was almost ready to end dual government, and the daimyo of finance and industry were prepared to surrender their powers into the hands of an emperor—especially if they were pretty sure to receive them back and become prefects of their economic provinces. But that period of generous gestures seems to be ending, so that another possibility opens. It may come about that business and government may come into chronic opposition to each other, like Empire and Papacy, State and Church, in medieval Europe.

III

The conflict of Empire and Papacy grew out of that eleventh-century revolution known as the struggle over investiture. The situation of that time was one that might have been described as "too much Church in feudalism" by one party, and by the other as "too much feudalism in the Church." In fact, Church and feudal society were interlocked like business and government today.

The bishops in some places, especially in the German kingdom, had worked with the kings, and the kings had helped to build up the bishops as a counterweight to the great dukes and margraves. The oath of fealty and the ceremony of investiture were the cement of the whole system—like credit and contract in our modern society.

Church office under these circumstances, so closely tied up with feudal government, tended to become a kind of property, just as the management and directorship of a modern corporation tend to become a kind of property. The Church had its recognized functions in the society of the time, as business has its recognized functions today. It appeared that this feudalizing of the Church interfered with the function of the Church as the religious organ of society. The Archbishop of Narbonne, for instance, simply bought his office and then exploited it for all he could make, selling bishoprics right and left and even seizing the church plate. He cleaned out his Archdiocese as a crooked management cleans out a corporation. Then he was ready to buy another church office and start again.

Such scandals as this constituted the grievance that led to a reform movement. The reform program was drawn from the traditions of the Church, nourished in the monasteries, and propagated with evangelical zeal throughout Christendom at the time of the crisis. The propagandists of reform, knowing the psychological value of simplicity in a program, had three main points and stuck to them: there must be no more buying and selling of church office, no more marriage of the clergy (so that office would not be inherited), and no more investiture in church office by other than churchmen. These articles of the reform program led to elaborations of the doctrine of papal supremacy over Christendom. This was the doctrinal ferment in the midst of which Pope Gregory VII railroaded the reform program through a Church Council.

The reform decrees were a challenge to vested interests everywhere. They meant that the Church would pull itself out from its feudal connections, taking its property with it. It was as if the American Congress should pass a law providing that the managers of business corporations should no longer be designated by the stockholders through a board of directors, but should be appointed by the government, or as if the magnates of business should be given the right to appoint all public officeholders.

Henry IV, German King and Emperor-elect, whose predecessors had made such heavy grants of property in building up the German bishoprics, resisted the step that seemed to be depriving him of his control over his own possessions. To break his resistance the Pope made use of a weapon more powerful in the eleventh century than the control of credit or currency is in the twentieth—he absolved all German subjects from their oath of fealty, thus dissolving the cement of German political society.

The conflict that followed was never brought to a clear-cut decision. It lasted until both these great all-embracing authorities in Europe, Papacy and Empire, had dragged each other down, depriving Europe of that unitary political structure which the League of Nations has not been able to restore, and leaving Christendom a prey to the tragic consequence of unrestrained nationalism.

If business and government should come to be set against each other in chronic conflict, each using its ultimate weapons, such as sabotage and expropriation, which of the two institutions would prevail, or would they destroy each other?

IV

The French and Russian revolutions of 1789 and 1917 exhibit the standard revolutionary characteristics of class displacement, rapid tempo, and comprehensive institutional change. They illustrate also the physiology of the revolutionary process. As a starting point in the process there were certain concrete grievances of French and Russian peasant and middle class, comparable to the grievances of unemployment and low farm income in America.

The grievances were discussed in an atmosphere full of conflicting doctrines. The teaching of the historical and pragmatic schools in Japan, the writings on papal and imperial power at the time of the investiture dispute, the philosophy of popular sovereignty and laissez faire on the eve of the French Revolution, the various hybrids of socialism and democracy prior to the Russian revolution, and the babel of technocrats and economic planners in early 1933, stand as comparable symptoms of impending change.

Then comes the crisis. It may be a danger from outside the society or a growing strain within it. French public credit collapsed in 1788; the food shortage hit Petrograd in February, 1917; and the bank crisis ushered in the New Deal.

Along with the crisis, it is to be expected that the most generous gestures will be made on all sides, in an atmosphere of highest optimism. The good will that marked the first few months of Roosevelt's administration was more than the normal honeymoon period of an incoming president; it was more like the spirit in which the representatives of the French nobility renounced the feudal rights of their class on the night of August 4th, 1789; it was more nearly comparable to the fervor with which the Japanese feudality surrendered their powers to the emperor, or the joyous coöperation of classes in Petrograd in the hopeful spring of 1917. This spirit seems to be a psychological opiate that anesthetizes a social parturition. When the effects have passed away, it will be seen that some new doctrines or catchwords from among those that were in the air before the crisis have assumed the character of obvious truths, while some of the older truths appear hopelessly discredited and out of date. A grievance, a ferment of doctrines, a crisis, and a moment of generous coöperation—and after that—what next?

In observing the course of a revolution the next thing to watch for is the vesting of new interests. In France the peasants get their land, the speculators and other middle-class owners buy into the sequestered estates of nobility and church. It will not be easy to displace them. In Russia the peasant seizes the adjacent lands of the proprietor; the proprietor can never come back. The subordinate group leaders of the modern fascist type of party install themselves in their bailiwicks as little dictators, maintaining their dictatorships by fostering the cult of the dictator. It will not be easy to squeeze them from their places. What new interests are becoming vested under the New Deal?

Throughout the country union labor is demanding seniority

rights, which have the effect of transforming a job into a kind of personal property, like the French peasant's farm. On one railroad an employee even now is granted the right to trade jobs with an employee of the same class in another city, provided each takes the other's seniority rating. Since there is nothing to prevent money payments in connection with such an exchange, seniority becomes a kind of property, convertible like other property into money.

Business under the N.R.A. is acquiring a valuable right to exclude or limit competition. Let there be no doubt of the property value of this right. It was sought by many kinds of business before the N.R.A. at the risk of costly violations of law—either of anti-trust laws, in the case of big business, or of the common criminal law, in the case of racketeered small business. Another illustration of the property character of these rights to limit competition comes from the history of the decline of the guilds. In some countries, such as Prussia, the possessors of guild rights were compensated with a money payment when their businesses were opened to free competition. Such is the quality of the vested interest that the business man may secure under the New Deal.

The third and most conspicuous type of vested interest is that of the unemployed relief client in a system of relief or made work. When the Civil Works Administration was rapidly demobilized in the spring it was evident that a property conception of the right of an unemployed man to a C.W.A. job was rapidly forming. If the right to a job, as a vested interest of the working class, is guaranteed by the government, much of the ensuing course of development of the New Deal is thereby determined.

The extent of these new vested interests, of employees, employers, and unemployed, is the measure of the revolutionary quality of the New Deal. If the class that has the most valuable of these new rights turns out to be the same class that had the best position under the old deal, it will mean that the Roosevelt revolution, like the Carolingian revolution of the eighth century, is not displacing one class with another, but only changing the forms by which power is exercised.

If no new vested interests appear, then it is certain that there is no comprehensive and permanent institutional change. The great upheaval of the spirit that accompanied America's entry into the World War could collapse like a bubble and leave nothing behind it, because there were no vested interests tied up with it. No one was committed by a situation into which he had been placed by Wilsonian idealism to fight tooth and nail for the Wilsonian program. The prohibition system was transitory for the same reason. It created no vested interest of any social importance or decisive political power. The forces maintaining prohibition at the end were of the same kind as those which had brought in the system in the beginning, namely, a group of people who entertained prohibitionist senti- ments. The bootleggers and snoopers were the only groups whose living depended on the continuance of prohibition, and it proved easy to push them aside.

The New Deal cannot live permanently on favorable senti- ments and opinions. Unless it creates powerful vested interests committed to its maintenance, or legitimates the powers of some existing interests, it will be in 1937 what the Wilsonian crusade was in 1920; it will prove that it was not a revolution at all.

XIV

Versailles to Stresa—The Conference Era *

I

In the nineteen-twenties, it was generally accepted that the objectives of world politics were comprehended within the term "reconstruction"; the nineteen-thirties are accepting the status and psyche of a prewar rather than a postwar period. In the nineteen-twenties, it was taken for granted that the normal agency of reconstruction was the international conference; the nineteen-thirties turn their attention from the conference technique to alliances. The change is sufficiently clear to suggest that the period from the establishment of the League of Nations through the Washington Disarmament Conference, Locarno, and the Kellogg Pact, to the Japanese and German withdrawal from the League, is a distinct historical epoch. Already it seems to belong to a very remote past; already it invites that kind of calm dissection and analysis that can be given to a thing that is dead.

In analyzing the character of this decade of conferences, the temptation is very great to use the idea system that developed during the World War as a part of war propaganda. Within the terms of that system of ideas, the "Conference Era" was a period during which Europe labored to make good the promises of allied war propaganda, and to realize a certain ideal of world order. It would appear that progress in

---

* Reprinted by permission from *The Virginia Quarterly Review*, July 1935.

this direction was halting and uncertain; there were missteps and backslidings, but on the whole the record showed constructive achievement. In 1933 it might have been said, with some reason, that though Woodrow Wilson was dead, his soul had gone marching on.

Yet it was evident, even during the Conference Era, that the Wilsonian conception of the nature of international politics was inadequate, and perhaps misleading. What made it excellent as war propaganda made it irrelevant as a basis of peace-time politics, because it emphasized moral rather than structural elements in interstate relations. The critics of Wilson who called him an impractical idealist shared this error with him, for they merely reversed his postulates. Wilson thought that states, especially democratic states, could be expected to display morality in their behavior, and that therefore world peace could be realized; his critics asserted that states would not act according to the dictates of morality, and therefore world peace was an impractical dream. From these premises, the Conference Era seems to have been a period of relatively high political morality, followed by a collapse. For a while the Good People were in control, and then the Bad People began to get the upper hand. This analysis will be very useful in another war to end war, but it does not help to make international politics intelligible.

This kind of thinking is the same as that which is encountered in histories when the historian personifies states as the actors in the historical drama. We read in history that Russia "feared," Germany "hoped," Japan "felt," the United States "understood," France "suspected." The cartoonists give their help in popularizing these fictions. International law developed in the modern world as the law of personal obligations of monarchs to each other, and has now become a body of rules applying to the conduct of peoples personified as states. The so-called "war-guilt question" was intelligible so long as it was stated as the question whether or not a certain individual, the

Emperor William II, conceived and executed a plan to have a world war, but when it became an analysis of the operation of the whole interstate system of Europe during fourteen days of the year 1914, it became a tissue of inconclusive fictions.

It ought to be possible to examine and appraise the Conference Era without resorting to these concepts of political morality based on the personification of the modern state.

II

What is the essential characteristic of the political process? Whether it be examined from the standpoint of world politics or of the internal politics of a state, two alternative aspects present themselves. On the one hand, political relationships appear to be relationships of power or authority; on the other hand, they have to do with the conciliation of variant group interests.

For reasons that can be explained historically, modern thought has been greatly preoccupied with the relationship of authority or power. It has accepted the centralized state, with a "sovereign" at the top, and subjects underneath, as the norm. With perfect logic, it has concluded that an exceptional, inexplicable, or confusing situation arises when a number of supreme powers are to be "forced" to agree on something. The only institution that can assure their agreement is an authority superior to them. This superior authority may be God, the Pope, the Moral Law, or the League of Nations. If God or the Moral Law or the League of Nations exhibits weakness in asserting its own supremacy, the unchecked supremacy of each of the various states gives the world over to anarchy.

This is a logical, self-consistent way of looking at world politics, if politics is regarded as a phenomenon of power. Yet it leads to two paradoxes: the one in connection with the policies of a sovereign state, the other in connection with the behavior of a world organized to preserve peace.

The sovereign state is presumed to pursue its own interests. This is its natural duty to itself. It will pursue these interests regardless of others; it will not sacrifice itself for interests not its own. As soon as a state embarks upon such a policy as this, it discovers the paradox that it cannot pursue its interests safely without getting some assurance that it will not be isolated and overwhelmed by a superior combination. To get this protection for itself, it must seek allies; to get allies it must offer to protect other interests than its own. Germany, in 1914, illustrated fully the tragedy of this predicament. It was Bismarckian *Realpolitik* that made the Austrian alliance necessary as a means of holding what Germany had won in 1871; it was the Austrian alliance that dragged Germany into the war that cost her more than she had won in 1871. The state policy of serving exclusively one's own state interest contradicts itself. This is the first paradox.

If international society steps into the picture as an authority that is to preserve order and prevent war, it is led straight to the task of "enforcing" peace. The means of enforcing peace may be other than war, but war lies in the background as the final means of enforcing peace when all other means fail. Thus international society, if it is conceived as an agency of power and authority, is effective to the degree that it is organized to fight for peace. French policy during the drafting of the Covenant, and in the ten years of the Conference Era, insisted upon this conclusion, which was after all quite logical as a deduction from the premises as to the nature of the political process. In practice, it meant that organized international society would take on the character of an alliance group against a violator of peace. Organization to fight for peace is as much a paradox as a state-interest in the interests of another state. In practice, the alliance based on state-interest and the alliance deduced from the need of enforcing peace showed more similarities than differences.

To hope that common deference to morality on the part of

all states would escape the consequences of these paradoxes was natural to men of exalted mind. But it was out of line, not only with the actual situation in ethics, but also with the actual mechanics of modern government. Imperialism puts the question: Are all cultures equally to be cherished in the world, or does one "higher" culture rightly subdue a "lower" and barbarous culture? The Pan-Serb movement asked: Is not the right of a nationality to national statehood superior to the right of an ancient empire to continued existence? Other questions arise: Does a crowded people, straining against the limits of subsistence, have any rights in a sparsely settled territory to which another people has staked out an incompletely exploited claim? Does a state controlling some essential natural resource have a duty to make it available to people living in another state? These are still open questions in the field of ethics.

Moreover, modern government is a "soulless corporation," not subject directly to the controls of personal morality and individual conscience, as were the monarchs of the absolutist state. In 1914 no foreign minister had any right to retain his seals of office if he really believed in peace at any price. It is not inconceivable that the contemporary dictatorships may increase the hold of morality upon government. For the mechanism by which a public forms its attitudes on public policy is so keyed that one people can develop the highest moral enthusiasm for one set of symbols, while another people reaches an equal degree of moral enthusiasm for the opposed symbolism.

These are the conclusions that seem to flow naturally from the postulate that political relationships are essentially relationships of power. But the alternative postulate may equally well serve as the basis for an analysis of world politics. If political experience is fundamentally an experience of compromising interests rather than asserting authority, then the so-called sovereign state is an abnormal, exceptional, or inexplicable entity to the degree that it approaches the ideal of deciding everything without compromising on anything. The norms of political life then appear to be federative situations; an international order of some kind or other is one of the fundamental political facts, the pretensions of a sovereign state are an anomaly.

This does not mean that the structure of international society is always the same; it means only that there is always something structural about international society, that the world, the alliance group, the state, the province, the city, the political party are all specimens of species of the genus "political group," each a field in which subsidiary group interests are in balance or in conflict, each engaged in the enterprise of adjusting its own group interest to that of other groups. The "world" differs from these subordinate groups only in the absence of any need to make adjustments with other "worlds." It does not differ from them in its lack of absolute and supreme power over everything that takes place within it. Nowhere in any group are such powers to be found. There are limits beyond which the most totalitarian dictatorship cannot go in asserting its authority, even within its own frontier. There has never been international anarchy; there will never be an omnipotent world authority. These are the natural and logical deductions that follow in any analysis of politics that emphasizes relations of adjustment rather than relations of superiority and inferiority of power.

III

The history of international relations in the past century suggests the conclusion that there are four types of commitment in which states have formulated adjustments of their interests. These are the guarantee type, the conference type, the division-of-spoil type, and the promise of action in a hypothetical war. The Quadruple Alliance that followed the Napoleonic wars was a guarantee treaty with a provision for conferences to meet new situations. The treaty proved strong enough to maintain the territorial settlement of 1815 intact for more than forty years, except for changes made by conference. After the breakdown of the 1815 settlement in the 1860's, a new type of treaty became standardized in the Bismarck alliance system; it was duplicated in the Franco-Russian alliance of 1894. The basic commitment of all the treaties of this system was a promise to do some definite thing in the event of certain hypothetical wars. The wars were sometimes described by naming the possible enemy powers, sometimes without mentioning names. The pledge of action might require either aid or neutrality.

Another treaty system that developed in the decade preceding the World War, and which received the name of "entente," was made up neither of guarantees nor of pledges of action in future wars. The formula was set by the Anglo-French agreement of 1904, in which England received a free hand in Egypt, France a free hand in Morocco. It was a type of treaty commitment in which two or more powers would pledge their friendship by dividing between them what belonged to neither. This pattern was followed in the Anglo-Russian agreement of 1907 and the Russo-Japanese agreements of the years following the Russo-Japanese wars. England and Germany were about to conclude one at the expense of Portugal in 1914. Lichnowsky and Grey, on the eve of the World War, initialed a compact under which Germany would have been permitted to take African territory from Portugal.

In the framing of the Covenant, three ideas met. The English plans for a League of Nations started with the precedent of the Quadruple Alliance, and worked toward a guaranteed conference procedure for settling international disputes, but not a guarantee of the treaty settlements. The American plan, on the contrary, was built around a proposed guarantee of the treaty settlement—Article X, which Wilson called the heart of the Covenant. The French ideas were in line with the precedent of commitments for action in hypothetical wars. The Covenant, as finally adopted, included only one clear-cut obligation imposed on League members in the event of war—a neutrality obligation. Members of the League bound themselves not to go to war with a state that would fulfill its duties by submitting its disputes to the procedure of adjustment outlined in the Covenant, and accept the results.

French policy, and the policy of European states of the victor group throughout the Conference Era, was directed toward the extension of the fabric of commitments regarding action in future wars. This was the so-called "search for security." It was the theme of the Draft Treaty of Mutual Assistance; it was the achievement of Locarno. Even the Kellogg Pact originated in a French move to bring the United States to agree on neutrality in the event that France should be engaged in a war.

These commitments for action in future wars were deemed necessary by European states as a pre-condition to the limitation of armaments. The delay in securing an adequate network of these treaties lasted so long that limitation of armaments itself became impossible. What made it seem necessary to weave this treaty network was the progress of military science, especially the highly developed importance of the time factor in mobilization. The same technological development made these agreements difficult to negotiate because they made it hard to distinguish between a defensive and an aggressive war.

The distinction between a defensive and an aggressive war had been consistently an important element in the description of the hypothetical wars to which alliance treaties apply. The reason for this is not derived from any abstract value set upon peace or non-aggression as such. It is rather the result of the fact that any power which undertakes to aid another's aggression is giving up more of its own security in return for less reward than would be involved in a promise to aid another power in a hypothetical defensive war. Bismarck saw this as clearly as Briand and Beneš, and wrote it just as clearly into his alliance documents.

When two powers try to agree on their future conduct in the event that one of them is attacked, a means of defining acts of aggression becomes an essential part of the treaty engagement, for otherwise the treaty lacks certainty in application.

The Foreign Office staffs of the European states were not fully instructed in the whole significance of modern mobilization techniques until after the crisis of 1914. Every Foreign Office was caught unprepared. The diplomats of the Conference Era had learned fully the truth that mobilization may constitute an aggressive act even before a single soldier crosses a frontier. They were willing to accept the conclusion that sending soldiers across the frontier in response to mobilization might be, in fact, an act of defense. The distinction between aggression and defense that turns upon the presence of soldiers on foreign soil did not satisfy them.

This left them with an alternative approach to the definition of aggression. The distinction between aggression and defense might be made procedural, not territorial. A state that refused to follow a certain procedure in a dispute with another state would then designate itself as an aggressor. Thus there could be some certainty in interpreting alliances drawn to apply to defensive wars against aggressor states. This consideration led straight to the political articles of the Covenant that define procedures for adjusting disputes.

As the treaty network grew in complexity, and the freedom of action of every state became increasingly limited thereby, there arose increasingly doubts as to whether the treaties would be honored on the occasions for which they had been drawn. A cartoonist pointed the moral with the picture of a group of diplomats around a table. One of them was saying: "We want you to guarantee the guaranty that you will guarantee the guaranty." Publicists declared that the currency of international obligation had been depreciated by over-issue. The same kind of doubt was present in the minds of those who worked in the prewar treaty system. The doctrine *rebus sic stantibus,* under which changed circumstances render treaties inapplicable, operates constantly to undermine the certainty of any treaty system. Bismarck's treaty system suffered from this corrosion. It was not peculiar to the treaties of the Conference Era, except as their greater number and complexity increased the number of points at which treaties were exposed to it.

IV

The present-day pacts of mutual assistance and non-aggression are both forms of that type of treaty commitment that provides for action in the event of a hypothetical war: one provides for aid, the other for neutrality. They incorporate a specific procedure for distinguishing between aggressive and defensive war. If the European treaty system be examined from this standpoint, it seems that present-day Europe is extending the treaty network and carrying it further than it was carried in the Conference Era. The Conference Era wrote more of these treaties than were written in the age of Bismarckian alliances; the foreign ministers of today are writing even more of them.

The drafting and signing of these treaties is hurried by the development in military science that makes the use of air forces in attacks upon the civilian population and industrial plant of an enemy a part of the normal war plan of a modern state. Railway and mobilization techniques of the prewar era, as they were understood and interpreted in the Conference Era, made use of the *day* as the time-limit for planned action on the outbreak of a war: military science now uses the *hour* as the time-unit.

What part in this evolution of the treaty network is played by the collapse of arms-limitation prospects and the rearming of Germany? The principal result so far established seems to be that Russia and Great Britain are drawn more fully into it. The type of engagement undertaken by the contracting powers has not changed, except in relation to Austria, where the guaranty type of engagement appears. It has been rumored that the friendship of Poland with Germany was an arrangement of the entente type, providing for a sharing of prospective conquests, but this rumor has not been verified. Preparation for the Italian conquest of Abyssinia, and for the Japanese conquest of Manchuria, does not seem to have conformed to the entente pattern. These imperialist efforts have not been used to cement friendships by division of spoil.

But the structure of international relations, as it reveals itself in devices for adjusting interests on the European continent, does not exhibit the discontinuity that seems to be present if the observer looks for evidence that during the Conference Era, states were disposed to subject themselves to international authority, and that in the new era they have lost this disposition. The understanding of present-day diplomacy is not aided by the assumption that there has been a change in the level of morality among states.

The Wilsonian element of the Covenant, the guarantee commitment of Article X, had a strange history. More than any other article it led to the refusal of the United States to enter the League. Then, having accomplished this negative service, it gradually faded out of its central position in the Covenant. Finally a committee of the League interpreted it in a way that deprived it of specific force. It was interpreted as a mere general objective, the actual attainment of which was provided for in Articles XI to XVI, which set forth procedures of adjudication.

While the Wilsonian guarantee element in the treaty system was disappearing, the spread of treaties of mutual assistance and non-aggression (defensive alliance and neutrality) tended to realize the objectives that had once been Clemenceau's without losing touch with the British objective of standard diplomatic procedure in time of crisis. There is no significant difference from the standpoint of political morality between these types of commitments. Neither is it evident that the Wilsonian type has more pacific implications than the Clemenceau type. They are alternative ways in which states can compromise their interests. The treaty system that evolved during the Conference Era happened to be more in line with the state of military science than a Wilsonian guarantee treaty system would have been. For that reason the rearmament of Germany has speeded and extended the development, the outlines of which were already defined in the Conference Era.

XV

Myths of the Twentieth Century *

I

The story of the Tower of Babel has for the twentieth century a profound and desolating relevance. It is told in the Book of Genesis that there was a time when "all the world was of one language and one speech." The fortunate denizens of Shinar thereupon said, "Come, let us build us a city and a tower that will reach to heaven." Then an act of inscrutable malevolence intervened "to confound their language so that they could not understand one another's speech . . . *and they left off building the city.*"

The world of the nineteenth century also had its common language, with science for its grammar and progress for its syntax. And the men of the nineteenth century were no less bold than those of the plain of Shinar in their scheme for the building of a great city. The time has now come when they no longer understand one another; the plans for the great world-community are abandoned, the citizens of the world are dispersed.

The confusion of tongues came so quickly upon the twentieth century that the consequences were upon us almost before the fact itself was known. As Germany entered the Third Reich, Germans ceased to understand each other. The ordinary medium of speech and writing ceased to function as a means

* Reprinted by permission from *The Virginia Quarterly Review,* Summer 1937.

of communication. Then the censorship clamped down, and it became impossible even to seek for understanding. Yet the Nazi dictatorship was only one of a series of acts that sent the world reeling into its cultural crisis.

Those who prepared the way for this debacle were supremely innocent in their intentions. They were men like Bergson, James, Vaihinger, Pareto, Sorel, Spengler, and even Sir James Frazer with his *Golden Bough*. Some were merely seeking a new highway to truth—by intuition rather than by reason; some asked only for a new test of truth—the test of practicality; some were bravely seeking to give a more profound interpretation to other cultures by accepting for purposes of the discourse the beliefs that prevailed in those cultures. They ended by betraying truth itself. For truth became a variable, determined by a personal equation, a problem, or a culture. As the prestige of truth fell, the prestige of myth rose. The word "myth" to the nineteenth century meant a naïve and fanciful tale; to the twentieth century it came to mean a primordial substance from which the stuff of all ideas may be drawn. Men began to talk of the myth of science, the Christian myth, the myth of the nation, the myth of socialism, the myth of the general strike.

These developments in the field of metaphysics are not, as they might seem, removed from importance in everyday life. Upon them have fed the Luthers, the Calvins, the Rousseaus of the contemporary world. The Russian university student today takes a required course in "dialectical materialism," just as the American high school student takes his required course in civics. The Fascists and the Nazis have official philosophers, Gentile and Rosenberg, whose metaphysical conceptions are incorporated in the imposed culture of the state. The great leaders who set the world on its new course at the close of the World War were, most of them, philosophers. Lenin had hammered out his thought on "empirio-criticism," Balfour on the foundations of belief. Smuts wrote on metaphysics,

Masaryk taught it, and Clemenceau left as his legacy a rear-guard defense of positivism. Woodrow Wilson, whatever his reputation for interest in pure theory, was less preoccupied than his distinguished confrères with the specifically metaphysical problems that the nineteenth century left to the twentieth, yet he was in a measure a philosopher too. Only Venizelos and Lloyd George, among the most influential men of the year 1919, were not in some sense active practitioners in the field of philosophy.

The World War not only brought to the top statesmen who were philosophers; it also brought the professional philosophers down from their intellectual pedestals. In every country these men used their high talents to give to the "issues" of the war a cosmic significance. They proved that the iniquities of the adversary had been present all along as implications of a national philosophy and culture, and that the triumph of their own party was necessary in the ethical scheme of the universe. Immediately upon the outbreak of hostilities, Bergson discovered that the war was a conflict between "life" and "matter," with the Entente Powers ranged on the side of life and the Central Powers defending matter. Scheler proclaimed that English philosophy and character were alike manifestations of cant; Santayana wrote of "egotism in German philosophy"; and the gentle Josiah Royce, himself deeply in debt to Hegel, reached the conclusion that "Germany is the willful and deliberate enemy of the human race; it is open to any man to be a pro-German who shares this enmity." The philosophers were making a Great Schism out of a mere political conflict. Then, as if to make a permanent record of the prostitution of the philosophic art, the victorious governments issued to each soldier in their armies a bronze medal with the inscription, "Great War for Civilization."

Philosophy never recovered from its war experience. The international journal literature was reëstablished, the professors resumed their exchanges, the old problems were still mooted in the old way in classroom and seminar, and among the scholars themselves it appeared that the old international society of the intellect would take a new lease on life. But a new relationship with the public had been created. The masses had been induced to taste of the fruit of the tree. Wartime vulgarizations were followed by postwar vulgarizations, and ideologies took the place of ideas. The confusion of tongues did not begin at the bottom, among the unlettered, the ignorant, and the naïve. It began at the top, among the cultured and sophisticated. It spread downward among populations who were taught to accept philosophies as they were taught to buy war bonds. And there it did not end when the war was over.

The postwar world fell heir to a highly developed apparatus for the propagation of ideologies among the masses. Universal literacy had combined with the linotype, the rotary press, and wood-pulp paper to create modern journalism. The use of color in the graphic arts culminated in a poster art that could in the space of a few months set up an iconography as elaborate as that which the medieval church created through generations. Advertising, as an adjunct to competitive business, had played with these media; war propaganda made them its own. Then, in the postwar era, radio was added to the equipment. Public education, organized sports, and entertainment were brought into line. The apparatus for the control of opinion can now be tuned like a great organ and made to play whatever music is written in the score. And the modern political police, superior to the police of Joseph Fouché as a Ford factory exceeds in efficiency the establishment of James Watt, can prevent all dissonances and discords.

If this vast apparatus for the propagation of thought had been available at a time when a common ground for thinking was still universally accepted, the world-city of which the nineteenth century dreamed might have risen to its music, like Camelot to the music of the fairy harps.

II

It is not certain that a twentieth-century mind can really know more than one of the great myths that are in conflict with each other, for a myth is something that is believed, not something that is merely understood. A language can be *learned;* when a German learns the French language he can understand a Frenchman in so far as language is concerned. But the process by which a Nazi becomes acquainted with the full meaning of liberalism, or a liberal with the full significance of Fascism, is the process not of *learning,* but of *conversion.* The Christian tradition has prepared the Western world for this peculiar relation of mythology to mind. For Western civilization has tended to define its religion in terms of its myths. In most cultures the religious person is one who is in the possession of powers that he has acquired by religious practices; in modern Christianity he is one who believes a particular cosmology and mythology. "Religion" in contemporary Europe and America comes to be defined as a state of mind alternative to skepticism regarding Christian myths.

There are four great myths in the contemporary Western world, all of them grown from one root. These four are: the original Christian myth, from which the others are descended; its secularized version of the world order or great society; the materialistic version with its eschatology of the proletarian paradise; and the antithetic or reactionary myth of the nation, with its mystery of blood and soil.

The Christian myth presents a narrative of a past, a prediction of a future, and an appraisal of man's place and problem in the world. This structure is common to all the competing mythologies. The discoveries of science could be harmonized with the Christian myth so long as they merely illustrated the qualities of a universe which was fundamentally God-made and God-directed. The ultimate unit of value in the Christian myth was the human soul; it was for its salvation that the great drama of the universe was enacted. The myth carried with it a profound ethical content in which peace was valued above strife, and love above hatred. The great Schoolmen of the Middle Ages were able to take all the elements of this myth and all their far-reaching implications and weld them together in a coherent system.

The myth of the world order or the great society was almost identical in pattern with the Christian myth, except that it left out God. It saw the vision of "the fields of peace." Woodrow Wilson was profoundly right when he linked up the ideal of political democracy with the ideal of the orderly world, for political democracy merely secularized the tradition of the Church. That every soul was equally valuable was taken intact from the ethos of Christianity and became the democratic ideal that every citizen has equal rights. For a few weeks at the close of the World War the body of ideas organized in this myth and known as "Wilsonian idealism" was accepted on a world scale and with an enthusiasm that made it the credo of the greatest politico-religious revival of modern times.

But even in 1918, during the brief apotheosis of Woodrow Wilson, the competing myth of the proletarian paradise revealed its strength and comprehensiveness. Like the myth of democracy and the world order, it was universal in its application. It was a system for all mankind. It had its narrative of the past, its prediction of an inevitable future. It drew its special character from its preoccupation with the problem of property, and because the problem of property was so deeply imbedded in it, it was highly materialistic in its metaphysics, highly realistic in its style. Where the Christian myth gave attention to the distribution of salvation, and the myth of the world order and democracy to the distribution of rights, the myth of the proletarian paradise dealt with the distribution of commodities.

Modern nationalism, the fourth great myth, differs from the three others in that it is not, and does not pretend to be, universal. It is a system of thought posited upon the differences between men rather than their resemblances. In the nineteenth century, nationalism was not indeed inconsistent with democracy and the world order, but was an appropriate deduction therefrom. The differences among men which it emphasized were primarily linguistic, and since it appeared that peoples speaking the same language would usually have a preference for living under the same government, it could deduce a political geography from the principles of democracy. But the nationalist mythology that arose after the World War and defined itself first in Italy and then in Germany became an entirely independent body of thought, antithetic to the myth of democracy and the world order, in which the primary elements were not grace and salvation, nor political rights and peace, nor yet labor and commodity, but blood and soil.

Francis Delaisi has observed that the myth of the national state is essentially an agrarian myth. The state is likened to a farm with fixed boundary lines. As such, it may take and lose land. The strength of this way of thinking can be noted in the Irredentist propaganda coming out of Hungary. There it is asserted that Hungary lost two-thirds of her forests, one-half of her mines, one-third of her railroads, etc. Were it not for the underlying agrarian metaphor present in the minds of all those who interpret such statements as these, they would seem unimportant or confusing. The same forests are still growing on the same slopes, the same people are cultivating the same fields, yet because the people have shifted their allegiance to a new state, and another public law prevails in the area, Hungary has "lost" territory. Clearly the only interpretation that can be given to the word "Hungary" in such a sentence is that Hungary is, like a farm, an acreage of soil. The material unit of the nationalist myth is real estate rather than commodity. The human element is equally distinct. Man, in the Nazi myth, is identified neither by his soul (as in the Christian myth), nor by his political will (as in the democratic myth), nor by his capacity for productive labor (as in the proletarian myth), but by his racial character, that is to say, his biogenetic relation to ancestors and descendents. The relation of race to soil is ecological from the standpoint of science; from the standpoint of institutions it is one of inheritance.

All three of the secular myths—democratic, proletarian, and nationalist—which now have the Western world as their field of conflict, appear self-evident when viewed from within themselves and by their own believers. All three of them are riven by deep self-contradictions when viewed from the outside by their critics. The internal contradictions inhering in the myth of democracy and the world order are two: first, in relation to peace; second, in relation to democracy. The object of world order is peace, but if peace is sought without taking action against peace breakers it will be broken; if action is taken against peace breakers, the action can be none other than war. "Wars to end wars" can become as normal and recurrent as war for any other purpose. The contradiction in the democratic element of the myth lies in the nature of the process by which a consensus is sought and obtained, for consensus or agreement is the product of persuasion. The successful persuader is none other than a ruler, and the processes of persuasion are so varied that democracies may be indistinguishable from dictatorships.

The contradiction in the proletarian myth has to do with the conception of property. Property was defined originally as a relationship between an individual and a thing. The extension of ownership from the one to the many in a given item of property changes the meaning of property. When an entire class (whether it be of laborers or not) owns collectively all the means of production, ownership loses its character. A long step in this direction is already taken in the development of the modern corporation with its large body of stockholder owners. The communist economy moves in exactly the same direction and somewhat further. In both cases the powers of management come to transcend in importance the rights of ownership, so that property as traditionally conceived disappears in that measure that its general distribution is effected. But management, which replaces it, can be as arbitrary in respect of social justice as ownership. It is the *management* of Soviet economy that shoots down the leaders of the Trotsky faction.

The antinomies of the nationalist myth of blood and soil are found, like those of the myth of democracy and world order, both in the field of world affairs and in internal matters. First, in respect of the relation of the nation to the world, the myth lays down only one rule of action—the rule of self-interest. But in a world made up of many nations, one which pursues its own interests exclusively will be isolated and weak unless it has allies. In order to secure its interests it must find allies, and in order to find allies it must sacrifice itself for interests not its own. Second, in respect of its internal arrangements, the myth requires that each nation have its own comprehensive culture, its own art, letters, science, and conscience. These are conceived as the products of blood and are found localized on the national soil. This is a more extended application of the sixteenth-century principle *cuius regio eius religio* which made the demarcation between Protestantism and Catholicism. It is the necessary foundation of the cultural policy of the totalitarian state.

The guarantee of authenticity in such a culture cannot be intellectual. The symphony composed by a German must be adjudged superior to a symphony composed by a Jew, not by any intellectual critique but because the one composer is German, the other Jewish. It is necessary that such a culture should depart from the whole tradition of Europe and "think with the blood" instead of the mind. But this involves a repudiation not only of European culture generally, but of some of the contributions to it made by the sacred race itself. How can Kant live where Einstein is rejected?

No one of these great myths can find common ground with

any of the others at the present time. Men who are now fifty years old learned the *lingua franca* of nineteenth-century thought, and to them the present situation in world culture is nothing but chaos. The younger men, the myth makers, and those who have been schooled in one or another of these myths, are still inspired by that special evangelical fanaticism that a new cult or a cult in conflict with others can generate. The time will come for a reaction against the contemporary myth makers. A generation will doubtless arise to whom all the idols will have feet of clay. It will be so profoundly skeptical of everything that it will be ready for cultural suicide. Even if it should learn again to speak a common tongue, it will speak a language of negation. It will build no city.

III

Beyond the age of skepticism which lies in the nearer future there is the possibility of a stupendous syncretism which will draw together common elements not only from the West but from the two great cultures of the East, which are also passing through their period of crisis. All these mythologies have very deep roots. The three secular myths of the West have their respective antecedents in the later Roman Empire. Democracy is rationalist like Stoicism; Marxian materialism is Epicurean. It was not for nothing that Karl Marx wrote his doctoral dissertation on the philosophy of Epicurus. And the nationalist cult is deeply mystic, like the Eastern religions of the later Roman Empire.

It is ironical, indeed, that this mystical element in the Nazi philosophy should show a resemblance to the specifically Semitic element in the religions of the early Christian era. But one who reads Alfred Rosenberg's statement of the Nazi creed is constantly reminded of the tradition of mysticism in Western religion. Rosenberg has more in common with Bernard of Clairvaux than with Immanuel Kant. Professor Orton has suggested in an explanation of this turn in German culture that

National Socialism is a revival of the romantic South Germans against the intellectual hardness of the Prussian north. Geographically, Munich is not so far from Clairvaux, and a long way from Königsberg. And the Monastery of St. Adolf is the Brown House in Munich. Rosenberg is true to a tradition that is not only South German, but also Christian, when he writes of "the new faith, the myth of the blood, that the divine essence of man survives in the blood." When his extreme straining of historical evidence in defense of the thesis of the primacy of the Nordics has reached the limits of credibility, he resorts to mysticism directly. "Nordic blood is itself a mystery that supplants the mystery of the Christian sacrament of blood." Against liberal democratic rationalism and dialectical materialism Rosenberg asserts that "the life of a people, of a race, is not a philosophy that develops logically, nor yet a chain of events taking place by natural law, but the *building up of a mystical synthesis.*"

Rosenberg buttresses his faith against rational criticism by using the legacy left by those well-meaning metaphysical rebels of the first decade of the twentieth century—James, Vaihinger, and the others: "There is no pure science without presumption," he says; "ideas, theories, hypotheses, are at the bottom. One soul, one race, puts a question that for another is a problem or a puzzle that has been solved. Democratic councils talk of international science and art, but art is also a creation of the blood . . . Science also comes from the blood."

This suggestion, while presented primarily as a rebuttal against Western critics, is not without value in interpreting the complex problem of mythologies throughout the world. In the cultural crises of the East there is contact no less vital than in the West with the most ancient philosophic roots of culture. Dr. Sun Yat-sen, in his *Three Peoples' Principles,* rings the changes on an old Chinese theme: "To know is easy; to do is difficult." Gandhi's tactics of non-resistance draw meaning from a metaphysical analysis of the distinction between action and non-action that was already old in the Bhagavad-Gita. "Knowledge and deed," "action and non-action"—these are not the basic dichotomies of Western metaphysics. The West begins rather with "matter and spirit," with the "city of the world and the city of God," or more recently, materialism and idealism. If there is ever to be a language really common to the world, perhaps it can be invented only after each culture has gone back to its own roots and prepared to build up anew from the ground.

Meanwhile, in everything material the different parts of the world come to resemble each other more closely. Manufacturing, transport, electric power, spread everywhere. That which is called Taylorism or scientific management in America is the Stakhanov movement in Russia. When things are alike, but called by different names, the struggle over names can be no less intense than the struggle over things. But when the time ultimately comes to find again a common denominator in thought as in action, the material conditions will be ready.

There may have been a certain effrontery in the effort of nineteenth-century Europe to build a world city, as if its language were a world language and its thought a world thought. Was its language rich enough, was its thought deep enough, did it have real catholicity, or was it merely provinciality overgrown? A new syncretism great enough to draw together the mythologies of Europe can also be great enough to bring in the mythologies of Asia. Without them there can be no world myth, and until that synthesis comes we can only wait. When the world again has one language and one speech, it can resume the task of building the city.

XVI

The Holy Roman Empire versus the United States: Patterns for Constitution-Making in Central Europe *

For sixteen years, from 1790 to 1806, while the United States was beginning its one hundred and fifty years under its Constitution, the Holy Roman Empire was ending the one hundred and fifty years of its political life as organized in the Peace of Westphalia. While the United States was living under its Constitution, the area that had lived under the shadow of the Holy Roman Empire experienced eight different political systems, proposed or operative. In this area, as in the area of the United States, there was a fundamental problem of maintaining a federative society, balancing unity with diversity, and protecting security. But this area was unlike the United States and more like the world in its variety of languages and historical particularisms. In fact, sixteen of the thirty-two political languages of the world are spoken in the Central European area.

These eight Central European systems were: sixteen years of the old Empire, eight years of Napoleon, thirty-three years of the Metternich system, two years of revolution in 1848–49, the reform movement of the early 1860s, the Bismarck system, the Mittel-Europa projects of Friedrich Naumann during the World War, and the triumph of Wilsonian principles at the Paris Peace Conference.

* Reprinted from *The Constitution Reconsidered*, 1938, by permission of the Columbia University Press.

Throughout this sequence of eight political structures, the elements of two contrasting patterns can be traced: that of the native tradition and constitution of the Holy Roman Empire on the one hand, and that of the imported pattern of the United States of America on the other. In the setting up of the Metternich system the influence of America was nil; in 1848 it was very high; in 1863, because of the Civil War, it was low again; and in 1918 with Wilson it was again high. It was characteristic of the pattern of the Holy Roman Empire that it always tended to hold Central Europe together; of the American pattern, that it tended to break it to pieces.

What were the essential characteristics of these two great political formations? Commentators disagreed over both of them. Some held that the Holy Roman Empire was a very much limited monarchy; others, that it was a peculiar republic of princes. Some held that the United States Constitution was the supreme law of the land; others, that it was a compact between states. But whichever theory of structure was adopted, for the analysis either of the Empire or of the United States, the differences between the two systems were comprehensive and systematic.

These differences are summarized in three particulars: the Empire was based on hierarchy, the United States on equality; the Empire, on an unbroken fabric of law from top to bottom, the United States, on concurrent or superimposed systems of law; the Empire operated upon states, the United States operated upon individuals. These contrasting features of the two constitutions are systematically interrelated.

The American principle of equality, as contrasted with the Empire principle of hierarchy, is shown in three distinctive ways. First, American citizens were equal. No titles of nobility were permitted them; they were directly active as citizens of the federal government, and the federal government operated directly upon them. The subjects of the Holy Roman Empire, on the other hand, were ranked not only in orders of nobility, but were divided into two main classes: the few hundreds who were immediately members of the Empire, and the remaining millions whose membership in the Empire was only indirect, through their own princes or the lords of their lands. Second, the American states as such were equal. In the Empire, on the contrary, nine of the two hundred immediate princes were designated as electors, with special rights and duties. Not only did they elect the Emperor, but they constituted a separate house in the imperial diet. They were the "Great Powers" of the Empire system. In each of the circles into which the Empire was divided, certain princes were ranked as leading princes with special rights and duties. Some of these exercised a kind of regional hegemony. Finally, the constitutional principle of America was republican, that of the Empire monarchic.

These three differences, taken together, led into another significant distinction. Every American citizen had a dual capacity, as a citizen of his own state on the one hand, of the United States on the other. The subject of the Empire, whose membership was through his prince, did not have such a dual capacity. But every prince of the Empire, as a monarch, was a member not only of the Empire, but also of the community of European monarchs. By the Treaty of Westphalia he had a right to transact in international politics, to make treaties and alliances, to declare war and to make peace, provided only that he did not direct his diplomacy against the Empire. The American states, on the contrary, were excluded from foreign policy activity. The politics of the Empire were consequently inextricably interwoven with European international politics; in America there developed a tradition of isolation—a tradition that could not have been sustained if each American state had possessed and utilized a right of diplomatic negotiation abroad. Moreover, among the princes of the Empire most of the more important ones possessed lands outside the Empire. Their dual capacity as members of the Empire and as rulers of other lands tended further to merge Empire politics with international politics. In the United States, the lands not organized in the states were held by the federal government, and their defense against foreign encroachment was a federal function.

This political situation is related to the juristic distinction that was the second principal difference between the two patterns: namely, that the system of law in the Empire was an unbroken continuity from international law through public constitutional law to private law; while the system of law in the United States was divided into separate spheres and levels of law.

The constitution of the Empire was unwritten, and was compounded of usages, traditions, charters, laws, and international treaties. The Constitution of the United States was a written document, in a class by itself. It was so far from being fitted into the framework of international law that the federal government, though it screened the states in international relations, lacked the power to compel them to make reparation for international wrongs. The princely or inheritance settlements in the Empire were carried through all the levels of jurisprudence; they were private law contracts between great families, enacted as law in the diets of their lands and carried up for imperial ratification. Some succession provisions were even made the subject of international treaties, notably the Pragmatic Sanction of 1723. As in all Old Regime systems, private property rights and political rights were indistinguishable. America had the simple private-law institution of chattel slavery, while the varied and complex relations to which we give the name "serfdom" were found in the Empire. Finally, the American system set the legal sphere of the states apart from that of the federal government in such a way that very little connection between them existed until 1868. But the Holy Roman Empire offered to every subject of every prince protection of his right to due process of law at the hands of his prince. This was the most signal evidence of the continuity of the fabric of law in the system of the Holy Roman Empire.

Although the greater princes of the Empire all obtained before the end of the eighteenth century the privilege of *non appellando*, that is, the right to keep their own subjects from appealing to imperial courts, there was one class of complaint to which the privilege of *non appellando* never extended, and that was "denial of justice." Any German subject who had been denied due process of law by his own prince could appeal to the Empire. Thus, in 1737, the Elector of Cologne was called to order by the Imperial Court when he failed to respect the privileges of Münster in a homicide trial; in 1738 a subject of the Elector of Brandenburg successfully appealed to the Imperial Court for an order asking the Elector, who was king in Prussia, to give the case a new trial. In the same year the court issued a writ against the Duke of Holstein, who was king in Denmark, on behalf of a man who was imprisoned without trial. In none of these cases would an American federal court have heard an appeal against action of a state until after the adoption of the Fourteenth Amendment.

What protection did the American Constitution give the private law rights of its citizens against the states? When Chisholm sued the state of Georgia and the Supreme Court took jurisdiction, the immediate reaction was the Eleventh Amendment, closing the federal courts to suits brought against a state government. The American Constitution did indeed forbid states the right to pass *ex post facto* laws, bills of attainder, or acts impairing the obligations of contract; but it was not until 1868, when the Fourteenth Amendment was adopted, that the American citizen had the right to due process of law protected against the states by federal law.

When it came to executing the laws or the decisions of courts, with perfect consistency the Empire operated through the princes or immediate members; the American government operated on the individual citizens. This was the third major distinction between the two systems.

What if a princely government should refuse to execute the

law of the Empire? In such a case, another prince would get an imperial mandate to invade his domains and compel obedience by armed force. With perfect consistency the Empire acted not only through but upon its member princes and their states.

In the American system, on the contrary, there was absolutely no provision for the use of federal armed force against a member state, or for giving to one state a commission to invade another state in order to punish its government.

It is often said that the Empire in its last 150 years was ineffective, as if all this fabric of law was on paper only. But here was a community that maintained the separate existence of two or three hundred small principalities settled in the midst of greater states, and maintained them intact for 150 years. It could not have been force and arbitrary violence that secured this amazing result; it must have been law. The very success of the system in maintaining collective security for a century and a half became later a theme of disparaging criticism.

The structure of the Empire, its hierarchy of powers, held together in a comprehensive fabric of law, and operating upon individuals only indirectly, may have possessed values that historians have forgotten. And among those values was its supreme symbol—the emperor. Along the Danube, far beyond the territorial limits of the Empire, the influence of the dignity of the imperial office made itself felt through the person of the monarch who wore the holy crown. In the north there lived the legend of the emperor sleeping in his cave in the *Kyffhauser*, symbol of ultimate law in a Christian world. What the emperor as symbol and legend was to Central Europe, the written constitution became in the United States.

The emperor abdicated in 1806, but did the Empire die? To answer that question I turn to the analysis of the Metternich system. The Metternich system, which stabilized Central Europe after the Napoleonic wars, was operated in Germany by men whose student training had versed them in the law and tradition of the Empire. At the Congress of Vienna it was an open question whether or not the Empire itself would be restored. The system established at Vienna must be seen both in its Central European and general European aspect. In both it continued some features of the Empire.

In Central Europe was established the complex of the German Confederation and the Hapsburg monarchy; over Europe as a whole, the Concert of the Five Great Powers. The German Confederation was simply a modified adaptation to nineteenth-century conditions of the constitution of the Holy Roman Empire. The essential feature of hierarchy was there; the princes were the only members of the Confederation; their subjects entered it indirectly through the princes. The federal diet consisted of the delegates of the princes, not the representatives of the people. The princes retained their dual capacity as members both of the German Confederation and of the family of European sovereigns. They exercised their right to foreign intercourse under the limitation that they must make no treaties directed against the Confederation or any of its members. The continuous fabric of law was also retained. The Act of the Confederation was a part of the public law of Europe through its incorporation in the final act of Vienna. The constitutions of a number of German states were in turn guaranteed by the Confederation, and the content of all the state constitutions was controlled by the Confederation in that they dared not allow the powers of state diets to impinge on final sovereignty of the princes. This limitation was justified by the final doctrine that the princes must be free to fulfill their obligations to the Confederation. Whereas Woodrow Wilson held that faithfulness to external obligation could be expected only of popular governments, Metternich assumed that it could be expected only of absolute governments.

The Carlsbad decrees exhibited the continuous fabric of legality of the Metternich system. They were drafted by a diplomatic conference, adopted by a federal assembly, and promulgated in each state as state law. They reached the

German subject as Bavarian, Prussian, Hessian law, not as federal law. Compare this procedure with that of international labor legislation. An international conference drafts a text of a labor law; the member states are then obligated to submit this draft to their parliaments for a vote. But the American government, unlike the International Labor Organization, lacks not only the power to compel a state to pass a labor law, but even the power to compel a state legislature to vote yes or no on a specific text. The American legal system is one of concurrent separate systems of law, whereas the tradition of the Empire interwove them. This specific method of enacting uniform laws in a confederation I shall refer to henceforth as the Carlsbad system.

It must be added that the German Confederation assumed the same responsibility that the Empire had once held, to enforce against the princes the right of each of their subjects to due process of law. There was no specific provision for such a guarantee of due process of law in the text of the Federal Act of 1815, but the federal assembly strained the letter of the act to fix this principle as part of the constitution of the Confederation. Article XII of the act permitted small states to combine to establish a common court of third instance. The federal diet deduced from that article the conclusion that every German subject had a right to three instances of appeal. The members of the diet argued that the Confederation must "compel a state to do its duty," for "otherwise there would be a general state of lawlessness which would be contrary to the aim of the Confederation, and defeat the establishment of a general legal order which it is the object of the Confederation to bring about."

What if one of the German princes should prove recalcitrant? The means of executing the will of the Confederation on a prince or his state were those of the Empire—the Confederation would give a mandate to one German state to enforce federal decrees upon another state.

Where were the electors? In many of the drafts for a proposed German constitution that were introduced in the Congress of Vienna there was provision for a directory of the greater German princes, who would function in the Confederation as the electors had functioned in the Empire. The resistance of the small states prevented the adoption of the directory plan; but from that time to the final destruction of the Confederation it was characteristic of all the reform plans that sought to strengthen the Confederation without separating the Austrian Germans from the rest of Germany that they involved the setting up of a directory of the most powerful states.

Even in the Metternich era, the principle which the Empire had legalized in the position of the electors survived as a principle of European politics. The great powers of Europe became, in a sense, a collegium, with claims to special political rights and responsibilities. They were the heirs of the electors. Moreover, the practices of international government in the days of the Pentarchy were not far from those of the Confederation; the Confederation had its Carlsbad Conference, Europe had its Troppau, Laibach, and Verona. The Confederation adopted the principle of intervention by mandate in an unruly state; Europe put the principle into execution against Italy and Spain. Good precedent existed in the role of the leading princes of the Circle in the Holy Roman Empire.

The revolutionists of 1848 intended to substitute popular for monarchic sovereignty; they wanted to destroy the Metternich system root and branch. Their attitude toward the later Holy Roman Empire was one of grief and shame; toward the United States, one of open admiration. They learned their political science from Rotteck and Welker's *Staatslexicon*, whose fifteen volumes stood beside the complete edition of Schiller in thousands of German homes. Rotteck's estimate of the relative importance of the United States and the idea of the Empire in Europe may be measured by the fact that he gave almost as many pages in the *Lexicon* to Benjamin Franklin as to Joseph II and Napoleon put together.

The men of the Frankfurt Assembly were constantly alluding to the American example. They borrowed from the American Constitution both in broad matters of principle and in matters of drafting and detail. They defended an article by saying that it resembled the American model, and attacked it by saying it resembled the Confederation or the Empire. America seemed to prove that a great federal state could be based on the sovereignty, and hence the citizenship, of the whole people.

Two key articles of the Frankfurt Constitution that were drawn almost textually from the American model were those which provided for the monopoly of foreign relations in the hands of the new German union, and for the direct elections to the *Reichstag*. On the other hand, there remained in the Frankfurt Constitution equally significant elements that were in the pattern of the old Empire. One of these was a comprehensive list of fundamental rights that the new German union would guarantee to its citizens against acts of the governments of the member states. The members of the Frankfurt Assembly thought that they were imitating the American Constitution in this feature of their draft, for they did not note that the American Bill of Rights, as it existed at that time, limited only the powers of the federal government and not of the states. So a feature of the pattern of the old Empire came into the Frankfurt Assembly of 1848 disguised with the stars and stripes.

In the organization of the army and in leaving the execution of federal law to administration by the states, the Frankfurt Constitution also followed the old pattern.

It is significant that those elements of the Constitution of 1848 which were within the pattern of the Holy Roman Empire were consistent with the maintenance of Austria in the new Germany; but the elements drawn directly from the American Constitution forced the exclusion of Austria from the new Germany. The American elements of the Frankfurt Constitution led to the conclusion that no state could be partly in and partly out of the new Germany, for in such a state the "German people" would not be sovereign and the ruler would not be subject in his foreign relations to the policy of the new Germany. Georg Waitz, in the constitutional committee, concluded that the Austro-Germans could not enter the new Germany unless they formed a state separate from the other Hapsburg lands. Any other solution, said Waitz, "would resemble the unhappy features of the Holy Roman Empire." But this decision meant that the Frankfurt Assembly could neither organize Central Europe nor unite Germany, for neither the Austro-Germans nor the Austrian government were willing to split the monarchy into German and non-German segments.

The principle of sovereignty and citizenship that worked in America could not apply to Central Europe as a whole because the people did not want to be citizens of a Central Europe, but rather of a Hungary, an Austria, or a Germany. The states that the people wanted could only be made by breaking up Central Europe, and the people were not agreed as to how they wanted Central Europe broken up. The Magyars and the Slavs were at war; the Bohemians were disputing with the Germans; the northern Germans could not agree with the Austro-Germans; and therefore the men of 1848 could neither divide Central Europe nor hold it together, and all their labor of constitution-making fell apart in their hands.

After the Frankfurt Constitution of 1848 had been fumbled by Prussia, Schwarzenberg came on the scene with a strong Austrian program of reorganization for Central Europe. No longer, as in 1815, was the Holy Roman Empire a matter of living memory; its jurisprudence was forgotten and its name despised. But the plan that Schwarzenberg backed in 1850, and the plan that Francis Joseph submitted to the Congress of Princes of 1863, were in the pattern of the old Empire, not of the United States. The members of the reformed German Confederation were to be the princes and their states; the larger states were to constitute a directory; though there were to be representatives of the people in a central parliament, they were to be chosen by the diets of the German and Austrian states, not by direct vote; there would be a supreme court which would protect subjects against their own states; the federal government was not to have a monopoly of foreign relations; the princes were to retain their dual capacity as members both of a German union and of the European state system. A constitution along these lines could hold Central Europe together, whereas the Constitution of 1848–49 divided it.

Meanwhile there was a return to the Carlsbad method of uniform legislation, though not in the Carlsbad spirit of conservatism. A uniform commercial code for all Germany was drafted by a commission set up by the Federal Assembly, communicated by the Assembly to the separate states, and adopted by all of them save Luxemburg in 1861.

The Congress of Princes in 1863 failed. Bismarck opposed it on the very ground that the proposed parliament of the reformed Confederation was to consist of delegates of diets, rather than representatives directly elected by the people.

Then came the Bismarck system for Germany, which was essentially the territorial program of 1848, and it brought with it the penalty that it divided the German nation instead of uniting it.

But while Bismarck did not organize Central Europe at the level of constitutional law, he proceeded in the seventies and eighties to build for it a marvelous organization at the level of international law. He not only reunited as allies the Germans whom he had separated from each other, but he held all the surrounding nationalities in his alliance system—Serbia from 1881, Italy from 1882, Rumania from 1883. Russia, which governed part of the Polish nationality, was held in the orbit of Bismarckian diplomacy. The Bismarck system stabilized the relations of the nationalities of Central Europe, though it operated only at the level of international law.

In the World War, while there was a prospect of a German victory, Friedrich Naumann popularized a plan for the reorganization of Mittel-Europa. In a sense his plan was a return to the working principles of 1850 and 1863, of Schwarzenberg and Francis Joseph. He would establish a constitutional law fabric under the international law framework of the Dual Alliance. His technique was to be the development of agreements on specific problems, the setting up of coöperative administrative agencies for railways, customs, banking, and so forth, and the preparation and adoption of identical laws by the states. His method was the method of Carlsbad, and his proposed institutions for common action on banking, transportation, and so forth had as their remote and forgotten ancestor the Central Investigating Commission at Mainz, established under the Carlsbad decrees to investigate revolutionary plots. Despite the German defeat, this method was used after the war to prepare for the adoption of a common criminal code by Austria and Germany.

The principles actually realized in Central Europe were not those of Naumann, but of Woodrow Wilson. They were a return, pure and simple, to the ideals of 1848. They succeeded this time in breaking up Central Europe, but not in organizing it. The model of the American Constitution was influential in the constitution-making of some of the individual states— notably Germany and Czechoslovakia; but it was not useful in maintaining organization in Central Europe as a whole.

The principal recognition given to the problem of Central Europe as a whole was in the minorities treaties. What were those treaties? They remind one of those articles of the Peace of Westphalia which guaranteed the religious *status quo* of the subjects of the princes of the Holy Roman Empire. The treaties operated against states by giving to injured individuals the protection of super-state authority. They were not in the pattern of the pre-Civil War American Constitution, but rather in the pattern of the constitution of the old Empire. There was no place in Central Europe for the American principle of dual citizenship, for the people of Central Europe did not want to be citizens of Central Europe; the conditions for the application of the American pattern were lacking.

The area of Central Europe, the Holy Roman Empire and its overlapping monarchies, is the principal seat of the modern European nationality problem. To the nineteenth century, Central European nationalism was a domestic problem of three great monarchies; today it is a problem for Europe as a whole.

Reviewing the experience of the monarchies and Europe, we can say that Metternich held Central Europe together with a political system on the pattern of the Holy Roman Empire; that the men of 1848, using the pattern of the United States in their constitution-making, could neither divide it nor organize it; that the reform plan of 1863 attempted reorganization at the constitutional level and failed; that Bismarck divided Central Europe at the constitutional level, but united it at the level of international law; and that the Wilsonian principles left it with neither kind of organization.

The contrast between the two types of federal structure has world meaning. The Wilsonian system of 1918 required for its success a sense of world citizenship in the moral and political sphere, fortified by individualist interests in world commerce. His system was to give to all peoples control of their own states, and he expected them to exercise this control in a double capacity—as citizens of their own state and as citizens of the world—and to hold in their hearts a dual loyalty—to their own country on the one hand, and to world order on the other. It is only on this hypothesis that it can be deduced that democratic governments are specially qualified to maintain the regime of peace.

But the new state and world society is developing in another direction. The individual is increasingly removed from world relations by the interposition of his state. Morally and politically his ideas come from information filtered through the machinery of a propaganda office; his trade relations with business men in other states go through a national control. It took centuries for the German princes to establish themselves as the sole operative link between the Empire and their subjects; this new process of mediatization, this new *Landeshoheit*, is establishing itself with incredibly greater rapidity.

Meanwhile the American system has drawn nearer to the rival pattern, not only in the development of the application of the Fourteenth Amendment as a federal control over the states, but also in the method of bringing state laws to conform to a model established by Congress. Witness the little N.R.A.'s, the little Wagner Acts, and especially the social security laws. Likewise, the British Empire, in developing the right of the dominions to independent foreign policy and giving to each a dual capacity as a member both of the Commonwealth and of the international family of nations, approaches the pattern of the Holy Roman Empire.

What of the League of Nations? It was also somewhat in the Empire pattern. It operated directly upon states; its enforcement scheme was a feeble imitation of the ban of the Empire or of federal execution in the German Confederation, and had nothing in common with the American pattern. But on a crucial point the drafters of the Covenant yielded to small-state pressure and departed from the Empire pattern: this was in the make-up of the Council. Cecil proposed that the Council should consist of the great powers, purely and simply. It would then have been heir to the whole tradition of international political organization since Metternich, and through Metternich it would have been the true heir to the Empire. But small-state pressure in 1919, like the pressure of the small German states in 1815, forced a compromise. The Golden Bull of Woodrow Wilson put into the College of Electors powers whose potential role in the high politics of Europe did not justify their presence in that body. Instead of building on the tradition of the old diplomacy, there was an effort to create a new diplomacy and to establish a sacred symbol—sacred like the United States Constitution—in the written Covenant. Today we have the benefit neither of the old order nor of the new.

It is not inconceivable that, if an era of law establishes itself again in the world, it may exhibit more elements of the Holy Roman Empire pattern than of the American pattern: for instance, no attempt at world citizenship; a hierarchic arrangement of states under a directory of a few great world powers; a fabric of law, in which the distinction between international, constitutional and private law has faded, in a society that makes no clear distinction between property rights and political functions. The juridical doctrine to implement such a system is already evolving in the works of Hans Kelsen and Alfred Verdross. We may discover that we will not have world order save by recognizing hierarchies of privilege that are offensive to our present sense of justice. Still, if we weary of our present symbols, find our going political mythology inadequate, and seek another dispensation, let us not forget the old man sleeping in the cave of the *Kyffhauser*.

XVII

Mill's Liberty Today *

Eighty years ago the European continent was passing through the last moments of conservative reaction that had followed the Revolutions of 1848. Serfdom had three more years to run in Russia, as slavery had six more years to live in the United States. Napoleon III, dictator of France, was clearing the ground for the war in Italy that was destined to shake the foundations of his dictatorship. The Hapsburg Monarchy was in the last year of its bureaucratic strait jacket under the Bach regime. Prussia, still among the autocratic states, stood on the eve of the "New Course" that was to lead to an era, first of conflict between Parliament and king, and then of compromise. More than half of the Balkan area was still under Turkish rule; and in most of Italy, harsh police measures filled the prisons with men who called themselves "liberals." Acre for acre, man for man, the political Europe of 1858 seemed not less hostile to the spirit that called itself liberalism than seems the Europe of 1938. But there was this difference: that the liberals of that day were confident that they were pulling with the tide. They faced the dawn with hope. They knew their day would come.

It was in that year that John Stuart Mill wrote his essay "On Liberty." It is a statement of principles so fundamental and so comprehensive that it takes rank with Rousseau's "Social Con-

* Reprinted, by special permission, from *Foreign Affairs*, July 1938.

tract," Marx's "Communist Manifesto," and Leo XIII's "Encyclical on the Conditions of Labor" as a basic programmatic document of modern times.

In the decades that have supervened, there has been no end of writing and speaking about liberty. Some of it has been frothy and sweet, like a meringue; some has been stimulating, like a cocktail; some has been soothing and pleasant for political children, like an all-day sucker. Mill's essay is of another sort. It is the good hard bread of thought, such as the Victorians were wont to consume—leavened by the philosophy of the eighteenth century, kneaded in the turmoil of the English Reform, and baked in the furnace of the Industrial Revolution. It may be dry, but it is nourishing. Take it and bite into it:

 . . . the only purpose for which power can be rightfully exercised over any member of a civilized community, against his will, is to prevent harm to others. His own good, either physical or moral, is not a sufficient warrant.
 . . . the appropriate region of human liberty . . . comprises, first, the inward domain of consciousness . . . absolute freedom of opinion and sentiment on all subjects. . . . The liberty of expressing and publishing opinions . . . is practically inseparable from it. Secondly . . . liberty of tastes and pursuits; of framing the plan of our life to suit our own character; of doing as we like, subject to such consequences as may follow; without impediment from our fellow-creatures, so long as what we do does not harm them. . . . Thirdly, from this liberty of each individual, follows the liberty, within the same limits, of combination among individuals; freedom to unite, for any purpose not involving harm to others: the persons combining being supposed to be of full age, and not forced or deceived.
 A person may cause evil to others not only by his actions but by his inaction, and in either case he is justly accountable to them for the injury.
 There are also many positive acts for the benefit of others, which he may rightfully be compelled to perform; such as to give evidence in a court of justice; to bear his fair share in the common defense, or in any other joint work necessary to the interest of the society of which he enjoys the protection.
 . . . opinions lose their immunity when the circumstances in

which they are expressed are such as to constitute their expression a positive instigation to some mischievous act.

. . . trade is a social act. Whoever undertakes to sell any description of goods to the public, does what affects the interest of other persons, and of society in general . . . the principle of individual liberty is not involved in the doctrine of Free Trade. . . .

If society lets any considerable number of its members grow up mere children, incapable of being acted on by rational consideration of distant motives, society has itself to blame for the consequences.

The State, while it respects the liberty of each in what specially regards himself, is bound to maintain a vigilant control over his exercise of any power which it allows him to possess over others.

I regard utility as the ultimate appeal on all ethical questions; but it must be utility in the largest sense, grounded on the permanent interests of a man as a progressive being.

The worth of a State, in the long run, is the worth of the individuals composing it . . . a State which dwarfs its men, in order that they may be more docile instruments in its hands even for beneficial purposes—will find that with small men no great thing can really be accomplished.

Has anything happened since 1858 to make this closely reasoned argument less applicable to human affairs? We have become more dependent upon each other as our economy has become more highly geared, but Mill acknowledges that to compel men to do their share of what is necessary for society is not a violation of their liberty. Economic organization has given to some men a stature of power beside which other men, be they laborers or stockholders, are as pygmies; but Mill declares that the state must exercise vigilant control over any power it allows one man to hold over another. We have seen the "freedom to unite" used to build up parties that have made it their first enterprise to destroy the conditions of freedom in which they grew; but Mill limits the freedom to unite to purposes not involving harm to others. Radio and all the arts of propaganda have made "the liberty of publishing and expressing an opinion" more potent in inducing action than Mill would have thought possible; but Mill was willing to permit restraints on the expression of opinion if the circumstance should be such as to lead directly from the expression of opinion to wrongful acts. Forms of competition may have become more destructive since Mill's day, and the human damage suffered in the competitive struggle may have increased; but Mill concedes that society can make the rules of the competitive game in accordance with the general interest. Mill's statement that "trade is a social act" is broader than the commerce clause in the Constitution in its justification of all needful regulation of business. And Mill sees very clearly that liberty defeats itself if it is interpreted to exclude compulsory education. If collectivists argue their case with a promise of high productivity, Mill will meet them by accepting utility "broadly conceived" as the supreme ethical criterion. There is much that has happened which Mill did not foresee, and not a little of what he discussed has become a dead issue (his defense of the Mormons, for instance). Yet the main structure of his argument still holds against all the material and political developments of the last two generations.

In the year that Mill wrote the essay "On Liberty" he ended his life career in the India Office. For the next fifteen years, until his death in 1873, he saw the doctrines of political liberalism sweep everything before them. France, Germany, Austria-Hungary, Italy, Sweden—all fell fully into line with new or renovated parliamentary institutions. Even Russia passed through its liberal phase under Alexander II. Everything liberal was dubbed desirable, and everything desirable was dubbed liberal. But while the world became liberal, what was happening to liberty—to liberty as Mill defined it and championed it?

The liberty that Mill championed was not realized automatically by the introduction of parliamentary government or popular rule. It might indeed be threatened thereby. He sought to erect a bulwark of principles not only against the power of despots, but against the power of majorities, and not only against the tyranny of magistrates, but against "the tyranny of

the prevailing opinion and feeling; against the tendency of
society to impose, by other means than civil penalties, its own
ideas and practices as rules of conduct upon those who dissent
from them." In this sphere Mill felt, even as he wrote, that
the tide was running against him. He saw that "the tendency
of all the changes taking place in the world is to strengthen society, and diminish the power of the individual," and that "this
encroachment is not one of the evils which tend spontaneously
to disappear, but, on the contrary, to grow more and more
formidable." On the eve of the triumph of liberalism, he already feared for liberty.

The fears he felt were not unlike those that came to the mind
of Henry Adams as he meditated on the degradation of the
democratic dogma—the fear that mediocrity would triumph
over originality, and servility over independence of character.
"He who lets the world, or his own portion of it, choose his
plan of life for him, has no need of any other faculty than the
ape-like one of imitation. . . . It really is of importance, not
only what men do, but also what manner of men they are that
do it." "Formerly, different ranks, different neighborhoods,
different trades and professions, lived in what might be called
different worlds; at present to a great degree the same. Comparatively speaking, they now read the same things, listen to the
same things, see the same things . . . have their hopes and fears
directed toward the same objects, have the same rights and
liberties, and the same means of asserting them."

The twentieth century continued this process of clamping
down on individuality, and of imposing conformities on ways
of living. The catalogue of imposed conformities is extended
by such things as movies, radio, national advertising, and chain
stores in democratic countries, by police measures and positive
propaganda in totalitarian states. The technological requirements of mass production call not only for regimented workers,
but also for regimented consumers.

But the change of material conditions, and even of social

attitudes, has opened some new zones to individuality in life. The shortening of working hours has extended the possibilities of leisure-time pursuits. The spread of knowledge of contraception has increased the power of individuals over their life plans. The growth of the metropolis has granted the shelter of anonymity to millions. And, in America at least, the automobile has supplemented the metropolis in curbing the power of the neighborhood. The encroachment upon individuality does not come today from society so much as from the state. The enemy of liberty today, as in the early nineteenth century, is the state.

Free living, as Mill saw it, and as we must see it today, is not separable from free thinking. And with this step, the argument reaches the very heart of Mill's idea and of the world's present uneasiness. What is the place of liberty in the sphere of consciousness? Here Mill's stand was absolute and intransigent. Man must be just as free to hold and defend wrong opinions as to hold and defend right ones. "If all mankind minus one were of one opinion," he writes, "and only one person were of the contrary opinion, mankind would be no more justified in silencing that one person, than he, if he had the power, would be justified in silencing mankind." There can be no distinction made on the basis of the utility of an opinion, for "the usefulness of an opinion is itself matter of opinion: as disputable, as open to discussion, and requiring discussion as much as the opinion itself."

In arguing for freedom of opinion from political control, he was preaching, as he thought, to the converted. He thought the time had gone by when a defense was needed of freedom of the press. It was social pressure against heterodox opinion that he most feared. He saw the danger of mass rule by public opinion, unleavened by new ideas, and feared that the wearing down of heterodoxy would make England another China. Against this prospect he argued with irrefutable syllogism that only by confronting opinions with their contraries could the road to truth be lighted, that truths unquestioned must remain truths unproved.

Point for point his argument is unassailable: if an opinion is right, its suppression deprives people of a chance to exchange error for truth; if it is wrong, people lose by its suppression the livelier impression of truth produced by its collision with error. The ordeal of persecution is no test of truth. "It is a piece of idle sentimentality that truth, merely as truth, has any inherent power denied to error of prevailing against the dungeon and the stake." But the ordeal of reason is always a test of truth. Man rectifies his errors by discussion and experience; "as mankind improve, the number of doctrines that are no longer disputed or doubted will be constantly on the increase." Action, whether individual or social, flows from the correct apprehension of truth as demonstrated in discussion. It is this principle that justifies faith in progress for men sufficiently civilized to use discussion as a control of action, that justifies the use of force against backward peoples not capable of using the same instrument, and that forces a society that wishes to move on this path to compel the education of its children to the point where they can participate in the symposium.

This demonstration of the value of free discussion is monolithic. Around it all the rest of the argument is built, and yet it is here that twentieth-century thinking has moved farthest from John Stuart Mill. In its political practice, a substantial part of the world is still with him in defending freedom of opinion. In its social manners, it has relaxed controls, and has come to regard the word "Victorian" as describing a stuffy repression of parlor conversation. The material world has not registered a decision against liberty of thought; at least half of the political and social world continues, in the main, to respect it. But the metaphysical foundations are no longer what they were.

For two generations since Mill we have studied, talked and discussed together—hundreds of thousands of us in laboratory and library, hundreds of millions of us in sweatshop and barber shop, in hotel lobby and in homes. And do we still think, as Mill said eighty years ago, that "the number of doctrines which are no longer disputed or doubted will be constantly on the increase"? If we accept Mill's dictum that "the number and gravity of the truths which have reached the point of being uncontested" are a measure of the well-being of mankind, must we conclude that "well-being" thus measured has increased or diminished since his day?

It was a magnificent feast of reason for which Mill planned the menu and laid the table. He had, it is true, some misgivings that guests at the universal banquet might lack the fine sense to appreciate all that was offered; he did not foresee that they would come to the banquet, share in it, and then go hungry away.

The drift away from the metaphysical foundation of Mill's argument is a drift away from his assumption that truth is divisible for purposes of discussion and verification. Now it is evident that a Nazi, a Communist, and a Catholic hold each to a vast body of interlocking opinions, so integrated that they cannot be broken down into separate parts and subjected to separate analysis; and at the same time so comprehensive that they cannot be carried as a whole to the point of verification or disproof by evidence and information that any man, in his lifetime, can accumulate. Free discussion, under such conditions, does not lead to conclusions.

There is a profound harmony uniting Mill's *A System of Logic* with his essay "On Liberty." Both point the same road to the apprehension of truth. It is the road that Francis Bacon surveyed in the seventeenth century; it is the road by which learning in the nineteenth and twentieth centuries organized its stupendous achievements. The road is paved with monographs and learned journals. But now we ask, what if every word is true separately, what if each item of truth has been polished with verifications, what if we know the syntax of Bantu and the effect of ultraviolet rays on the chromosomes of a sea-urchin's egg—are these separate truths, the truths that men can live by? Taken all together, do they constitute a truth that men can understand? The technique of verification which Mill deemed universal is applicable to fragments; but the very unity of personality for which Mill pleaded is not satisfied with fragments of truth.

Consider, for instance, one method of investigation which would seem to be the unassailable stronghold of objectivity, the method by which contrary assertions can be led to confront each other with perfect intellectual decorum, with error always yielding to truth. This is the method of statistical analysis. It has grown by leaps and bounds since Mill's day. Our supply of statistics is beyond his dreams; our use of them permeates government, business, and education, as well as the fields of scholarship. Hitler's speeches are full of them; Soviet reports bristle with them; they chart themselves in the offices of the sales managers; they send shivers down the spines of bankers. They may be abused at times, but the liars who figure can ultimately be confronted with the figures that do not lie. The free discussion of the interpretation of statistics should furnish an ideal vehicle for the application of reason to human affairs.

But there is lurking in the development of the statistical controls of social policy a potential danger to the principle of individuality itself. Already in large classes in the schools, individual students and individual teachers are fighting a losing battle against the normal curve of distribution. Every refinement of statistical method is an exquisite device for making men look like atoms. Universal suffrage, unable to take into account subtle differences among individuals in the degree of their interest in a subject or the extent of their capacity to understand it, is but a special case of the application of the adding-machine technique to the determination of social policy. Proportional representation is a statistical refinement. Taxation policies are already made on calculating machines, and standards of living are measured by the method of least squares. When mankind becomes an equation of N variables and the horizon of his life is plotted on a Y axis, when individuality is a parameter of variation and personality an exponential function, will not the disciples of Mill quail before the monstrosities of statistical abstraction? Statistics do indeed render truth divisible for purposes of verification, but the great truths escape while the small ones are verified.

Perhaps there is another method by which free discussion of opinion can be relied upon to sift errors from truths in terms of the vast units of truth which are necessary for significance. Mill thought that the interpretation of experience would be such a method. But what does this mean? It means that we regard the League of Nations as an experiment, the Soviet union as a laboratory enterprise, and problems of policy as subject to the method of trial and error. In small matters the method is full of merit. On great affairs the laboratory fees are paid in blood, and when the reports of the experiment are written they are found to have contributed to the world an embellishment of mythologies rather than a bundle of verified truths.

Little as Mill foresaw that western Europe would reach this state, yet the framework of his thought was vast enough to take it into account: "Liberty, as a principle, has no application to any state of things anterior to the time when mankind have become capable of being improved by free and equal discussion." Fundamentally, Mill's faith in progress was so unconditional that he did not imagine that a people which had learned to improve itself by free and equal discussion could lose the art. But the conclusion would have to be drawn from his argument that if the time should ever come when the thought structure of the world should lose its anchorage in induction, the day of improvement by free discussion would have passed, and with it the day of liberty.

It has now come to pass that the whole system of liberty has been reduced to one among a number of competing ideologies; it no longer furnishes the universal framework within which ideologies compete. Half the world still holds to this ideology, preferring it to others; the other half has undertaken to carry the police regulation of thought to a point of efficiency unprecedented in history. Propaganda and counter-propaganda are organized state activities, into which even the democratic countries are drawn. Just as the early modern state squeezed out the private administration of justice, so the totalitarian states squeeze out the private administration of thought. The democratic states at least engage in competition with non-state agencies in propaganda. Within the states that are still loyal to the ideal of liberty, two questions arise: To what extent shall the state undertake to propagate opinions? Can the state impose some restrictions on the propagation of opinions without destroying liberty in its entirety? Mill's principles would seem to rule that, just as thought is *divisible* for purposes of discussion and verification, so liberty of thought and expression is *indivisible*. One cannot lose any of it without losing it all. The sole limitation that Mill was willing to concede was restraint upon the expression of thought that would lead directly to mischievous acts. He would not allow a man to shout, "Hang the baker" during a bread riot, but he would permit anyone to shout "Down with capitalism" on Union Square.

This concession made by Mill may be like the thin end of a wedge which, driven by twentieth-century conditions, will render liberty divisible. Fraudulent advertising claims would seem to be subject to state police measures, since "trade is a social act." And perhaps fraudulent political claims might be included by stretching the doctrine that "freedom to unite" is defensible only on condition that the persons uniting are "undeceived." A law requiring the registration of lobbyists and public relations counsellors would not seem to be contrary to Mill's principle of liberty.

In the propagation of opinions by the state, the state-con-

trolled schools are first in importance. Mill saw that state education would tend to become state propaganda. He hoped to
avoid the evils of this by leaving the schools so far as possible
under private control and by restricting the role of the state to
that of an examiner. The examination, he thought, would be
exclusively on questions of fact. Here again his confidence that
great and significant truths were merely the sum of a great
number of facts gave him a solution which modern educators
must regard as all too simple.

These problems would exist in a regime of liberty even if it
had no contact with foreign states or with totalitarian regimes.
But the propaganda activity and the threats of force that arise
in the totalitarian states render these problems more pressing.
It happened that while Mill was writing his essay, Orsini attempted to assassinate Napoleon III, and the British government complied with a French request that the British press
should be restrained from attacking the heads of foreign states.
Napoleon demanded, though on a modest scale, what Hitler
demands today. Mill was shocked by the violation done the
freedom of the press. He evidently did not regard English press
campaigns against Napoleon as coming within his definition
of expressions of opinion leading directly to mischievous acts.

But the issue involved is not simple, for the regime of liberty
cannot survive during modern warfare. A regime of liberty
implies a policy of peace, and peace between nations may in
fact be threatened by press campaigns that arouse international
hatred. This situation has led many partisans of collective
security under the League of Nations to advocate "moral disarmament," a program which means the restraining of international hate-mongers by their own governments. The famous
Carlsbad Decrees of 1819 that were enforced against the
freedom of the press in the German states were based on precisely this principle. They did not compel the state of Baden,
for instance, to suppress journalistic attacks upon the government of Baden; they applied only to pamphleteering in one state

against another state, or against the German Confederation as a whole. Radio, which leaps across political parties, has sharpened this dilemma for the adherents of the principles of liberty. Italy can blackmail England with a pro-Islamic radio campaign, and totalitarian radio propaganda in Latin America can drive the American Government to counter measures.

Finally, the adherents of the system of liberty face the more serious dilemma of whether to aid each other in defending their system by armed force. John Stuart Mill wrote down the rules of a game in which people write letters to *The Times*. Do circumstances now indicate that it is not enough to write letters to *The Times*, that we must rather go overseas and string barbed wire in Spain? If paid agents of a totalitarian state are building up a party in a free country, must the free country give freedom even to them?

These problems confronting the adherents of liberty today are not insoluble. Already our thinkers are working to shore up the crumbling places in the metaphysical foundations of liberty by turning their attention from the verification of small truths to the analyses of great ones. The Encyclopedia of the eighteenth century was a philosophy; the Encyclopedia of the nineteenth century was a disorderly museum of facts; the Encyclopedia of the twentieth century is only in the making. It need not and cannot contain the answers to all questions, but it may turn out to be an intellectual achievement that will inspire confidence that even the most comprehensive and meaningful opinions are ultimately capable of objective verification or disproof. The dilemmas encountered in applying the principles of liberty to human affairs are by no means so serious as those encountered in applying the alternative ideologies. The totalitarian states have yet to show that they can produce great characters. It takes forty years to make a man. The great names in these states are the names of men who were made by liberty, whether under a regime of liberty or despite a regime of repression.

John Stuart Mill ruled a great empire of thought and ruled it well; his satraps were principles and his army was an army of facts. The law of that empire was the law of liberty, progress, and utility. The empire still stands, though there are barbarians swarming on the frontiers, and the satraps have set themselves up as semi-independent rulers of petty domains. But the good law that he laid down is still good law, and the empire will stand wherever men believe with him that "the worth of a State, in the long run, is the worth of the individuals composing it."

XVIII

Peace in Our Time *

I

The wars of modern nations are not wagers of battle, but crusades. The wars that threaten on the so-called ideological front between Communists and Fascists, or dictatorships and democracies, will be crusades. The first secular crusade of modern times was the War of Propaganda of the French Revolution. Since then there have been some wars of the other kind —wars fought without great fervor for ideals not unduly high. But the war danger of today does not arise from a prospect of such conflicts. Great population masses cannot be set in motion for anything less than an issue between eternal right and satanic evil. None but the highest ideals will sustain war morale in the modern world. This will be found equally true on both sides of the next war's no man's land.

A peculiar feature of the crusade is that it combines in itself extremes of barbarism and culture. As a war for an ideal— for Jerusalem the Golden, for Democracy, for the Rights of Small Nations—it brings man to a high level of heroic and poetic existence. In the attitude which it induces toward the enemy it repudiates even the commonest decencies of humanity. And of all possible crusades, no doubt the most fervid will be the next war to end war.

The generation that saw the rise and fall of the League of

* Reprinted by permission from *The Virginia Quarterly Review*, Autumn 1938.

Nations has learned to classify attitudes toward world politics as idealistic on the one hand, realistic on the other. The idealists are those to whom that symbol of peace, the Covenant, means much; the realists are those to whom it means little. But the highly articulated character of the nationalist ideologies that have repudiated the League, the romantic tissue of which these ideologies are composed, and the colossal sacrifices of material interests to which they have led the peoples who have followed them, are enough to indicate that idealism is not monopolized by any camp. The idealists are all potential crusaders, whether they are ready to crusade for the nation, for the proletariat, for freedom, or for peace. In the setting of contemporary world politics, "realist" and "idealist" have become interchangeable terms.

The Middle Ages had another doctrine by which to classify the attitudes and principles of political action: the doctrine of the two swords. There was the sword spiritual and the sword temporal, the sword of Holy Church and the sword of the Holy Roman Empire. According to the great popes from Gregory to Boniface, the sword spiritual was above the sword temporal; according to the letter of Holy Writ, these two swords were enough.

Can we, taking into account the complex institutional metamorphoses of the past five centuries, identify today these two swords? What is the legacy of the medieval Church to modern politics, and what the legacy of the Empire? Unless we can distinguish today the things that are God's from the things that are Caesar's, we cannot render unto each his own.

II

Despite all that is happening in China and Spain, and all that has happened in Ethiopia and Central Europe, it is evident that there is still some universality in human organization. The world is not wholly anarchic. Even the networks of alignment for future wars that are woven daily and unraveled nightly like Penelope's web, even the neutrality policies fashioned and refashioned, are evidence that the medium of world politics is a continuum.

The family of nations is older and far more deeply rooted than the League of Nations; the League was never more than an organ of the world commonwealth. The period of maximum growth of the family of nations preceded the organization of the League. Metternich dealt with a political world of two hundred million people; the World War closed on a world of nearly two billion. This tenfold increase is partly the result of a net population increase; it is also a result of the expansion of European politics to the dimensions of world politics. Non-European political systems have been successively incorporated into the European, some by colonization and conquest, some by initiation and reception. In 1856 the Ottoman Empire was admitted to the circle of the European powers. Japan and China adapted their practices of international intercourse to those of Western Europe in the last half of the nineteenth century. And every political society accepted into the family of nations is assumed to have consented without reservation to follow all the rules and practices of international law and custom. There has been no reciprocity; neither the Caliph nor the Son of Heaven contributed in practice or doctrine to the rules of the political world order. The order into which the novitiate states were initiated was purely and simply that which had grown in Western Europe.

From what roots in Europe did international political order grow? Not from feudalism, not from kingship, for these were essentially centrifugal institutions in respect of Europe. The two historic institutions that expressed the idea of universality were the Church and the Empire. Which of these is the parent of the family of nations?

Both Church and Empire were Holy and Roman. Both of them, in medieval times, laid claims to universal jurisdictions. Both claimed the right to sever a man from his social ties—by the ban of the Empire or the penalty of excommunication. And both could reward as well as punish—the Empire by granting dignities to the living, the Church by canonizing the dead. Each had its sword, the sword spiritual and the sword temporal. Both used war as an instrument of policy. Yet neither of them was, essentially, a war organization. The crusade was incidental to the life of the Church; and the Empire, though it gave Europe, especially Eastern Europe, a political framework within which armed resistance to the infidel and expansion among pagans could be organized, was not primarily a war-making machine, nor was it, like the Ottoman Empire, an army of occupation in permanent possession. Both were for Europe primarily symbols of law, not of armed force.

Today there are three universal jurisdictions: that of law in the family of nations, that of credit in the structure of capitalist economy, and that of experiment in the method of science. The universality of the family of nations is probably an expanded and diluted derivative of that which infused the Holy Roman Empire; the universality of the method of science is a secularized and dehumanized survivor of that which lived in the faith of the Church.

Universality does not survive in either of the bodies that are commonly regarded today as the institutional continuations of medieval Empire and Church. The Third Reich, though it covers much of the territory once the home of the Empire, is dedicated to a nationalism that is the very antithesis of the universalism of the Empire. The Roman Catholic Church, though its teaching is still keyed to a statement of universal human values, speaks today for only one-sixth of the people of the world, and for less than half of the world's Christian population. And national patriotism, enemy of all universal jurisdictions, owes far more to the Church than to the Empire.

III

The distinction between spiritual and temporal was funda-mental in Christian dogmatics. It did not exactly correspond to the metaphysical distinction between ideal and material. In a

Selected Papers of Robert C. Binkley

context removed from Christian dogma, it can best be translated as the distinction between short-term and long-term expectancies. Spiritual values exceeded temporal values because they would be realized through an infinity of time; temporal ills were endurable when measured against spiritual goods because the latter were eternal. The potency of Christian dogma as a determinant of rational conduct turned upon its ability to sell long-term investments in eternity by inducing men to make present sacrifices for the sake of benefits to be enjoyed, or pains to be avoided, after death. The spiritual sword symbolized the force of this feature of Christianity as an instrument of social control; the temporal sword symbolized those instruments of control which operate by granting day-to-day rewards, or by inflicting immediate pains.

Neither contemporary nationalism nor Communism could survive on a merely day-to-day conception of the objectives of human existence. Both direct the eyes of their devotees to a blessed future, the preparation for which justifies present inconveniences. Both make use of the spiritual sword.

The medieval popes asserted that the sword spiritual must be served by the sword temporal. This claim may have been bad jurisprudence, but it was undoubtedly good social psychology. The monarchs of the rising states rejected the papal claim to supremacy over them; rather they seized the sword spiritual into their own hands. They claimed divine rights to rule; they made themselves heads of state churches, openly in Protestant countries, covertly in those which were still in the Roman fold; they forced religious conformity upon their peoples, and laid down long-term state policies. "Austria ultimate in the world" was the mystic formula in Vienna. As divine-right monarchy died out, democracy claimed rights no less divine, and the religion of nationalism took over the forms even as it perverted the substance of the Christian cult. Carlton Hayes has described in his profound critique of nationalism the result of the metamorphosis:

To the modern national state, as to the medieval church, is attributable an *ideal*, a *mission*. It is the mission of salvation and the ideal of immortality. The nation is conceived of as eternal, and the deaths of her loyal sons do but add to her undying fame and glory. She protects her children and saves them from foreign devils; she assures them life, liberty, and the pursuit of happiness; she fosters for them the arts and the sciences; and she gives them nourishment. Nor may the rôle of the modern national state, any more than that of the medieval church, be thought of as economic or mercenary; it is primarily spiritual, even other-worldly, and its driving force is its collective *faith*, a faith in its mission and destiny, a faith in things unseen, a faith that would move mountains. Nationalism is sentimental, emotional, and inspirational.

Must we not conclude that the supremacy of nationalism is in effect the supremacy of the sword of the spirit? What an ironic realization of the dreams of the great popes! Can we not recognize even in the extreme Nazi development of this cult—the idea of the mystic synthesis of blood and soil—a formula, the elements of which are present in the Old Testament? It is there that the idea of a race of chosen people bound by blood, and of a supremely symbolic territory, the Promised Land, is most clearly recognizable in the canon of medieval thought.

It was not in the form of Christianity, but in the form of nationalism, that the religion of the Western peoples became world-wide. China and India became nationalist; they did not become Christian. And nationalism is of all evangelical cults the one least fitted to be a world religion, for it creates over the area through which it spreads, not ties that bind, but walls that separate.

Communism, as Henri de Man has shown, is another derivative of the Christian heritage, with a mythology and liturgy no less imitative of those of the Church. Though it claims, like the Roman Church itself, a universal outlook, it speaks for only a fraction of the human race. Nationalism and Communism renounce their parent, and their parent disavows them; they are none the less true heirs, who have been wasting and spoiling the heritage.

IV

It is the nation, not the family of nations, that is derived from the Holy Roman Church. The family of nations, on the other hand, is derived more closely from the Holy Roman Empire. The road from the Holy Roman Empire to the family of nations was traveled quietly. That we have often failed to take note of it is due to our tendency to accept national statehood as the measure of all political values. Since the Empire of the eighteenth century was clearly not a state, the German nationalists of the nineteenth century thought it must be a monstrosity. Napoleon's dissolution of the Empire in 1806 seemed to destroy the last vestiges of its life and relegate it to history. The fall of Vienna in 1938 seemed to kill even the shadow. But meanwhile, through three centuries in which historians saw only a process of decline and death, the life-force of the Empire was passing into another body, which still survives as the basic element of universal order in the political world.

The Holy Roman Empire, from the days of the Great Interregnum in the thirteenth century, lived in Europe as a system of law without a centralized administration. This one feature is sufficient to suggest comparison with the modern family of nations. In the fourteenth century it took on a second feature, duplicated in our contemporary political world, by giving special duties and privileges to seven of its more important princes as Electors, or as one might say, as "Great Powers" within the Empire. The Concert of Europe, which assumed its clear-cut status only after the abdication of the Holy Roman Emperor in 1806, is the institutional successor to the College of Electors.

At the end of the fifteenth century came the next step in the development of the Empire: the proclamation of the "Peace of the Land." The statute of the peace of the land outlawed war among the princes of the Empire and set up a court for the settlement of their disputes. Within the general system there was a regional arrangement of circles, each with its leading princes designated, as the Electors were designated, for the Empire as a whole. Throughout the whole fabric there was hierarchy, but not of the close-knit bureaucratic or administrative kind. It was rather a hierarchy of law. It left room for the most vigorous local spirit, and for all manner of leagues and organized communities of family interest or confession. Political consciousness spread up from the localism of city or land to a kind of universalism in the Imperial Diet and the Emperor. There was no end of pettiness in the dealings of the lesser princes with each other, and there were wars in the relations of the greater princes. But despite the disturbance of the Protestant Revolution and the Thirty Years' War, the structure remained intact until 1806, and survived until 1866 in a modified form as the German Confederation. Its system of collective security did not prevent war between the greater princes, but it protected the separate existences of over two hundred small political units, the "immediate" members of the Empire, to the last. Its very success in maintaining collective security was turned against it by the later publicists of German nationalism, who deplored the survival of principalities that could never have protected themselves by force of arms.

The organization of collective security within the Empire served as a model upon which projects for collective security in Europe were later based. In the eighteenth century, the Abbé de St. Pierre's project for rendering peace perpetual in Europe was a frank appeal for the adoption of the institution of the Empire by Europe as a whole. And St. Pierre's plan was substantially realized in the Metternich system that followed the defeat of Napoleon. The political complex of the early nineteenth century—Holy Alliance and Concert of the Five Great Powers—was managed from the ancient seat of the Empire by men who had been schooled in its jurisprudence, ac-

cording to principles—including the principle of intervention—
which were wholly in accord with its precedents. The Concert
of Europe and the German Confederation divided between
themselves in 1815 the heritage of the Holy Roman Empire.

The traditional line of development influenced the Paris
Peace Conference. The underlying draft of the Covenant of
the League of Nations, the Phillimore Plan, was a document
based upon an interpretation of the role of the Concert as it
had functioned in the days of Metternich and Castlereagh. In
a feature now seen as crucial, it followed the tradition by re-
serving all authority in the League to the Great Powers. The
pressure of the smaller states, and Wilson's confidence in the
power of humanitarian world opinion, had the effect of shifting the basis of the Covenant away from this institutional tradition, to which Chamberlain now seeks to restore it.

The Peace of Westphalia in 1648, at the end of the Thirty
Years' War, stands as a landmark in the absorption of the
Empire into the European states system. At Westphalia all the
immediate princes of the Empire received the right to make
treaties and alliances with princes outside the Empire. Their
status in the Empire was thus converted into status in Europe.
The role of the Emperor followed that of the princes in that
his dignity came increasingly to be merely that of one among
a number of great European monarchs, and when the dignity
was abolished in 1806 the repercussions were slight because
the office had long ceased to be associated with power. (The
monarchs of national states came in the course of time to find
their offices no less superfluous in the political societies that
had once been organized around them.)

The Europeanizing of the Empire was marked, moreover, by
a growing interpenetration of territories. Dynasties whose
seats were within the system spread outward; dynasties whose
seats were outside the Empire came in. The Hapsburgs spread
down the Danube, the Hohenzollerns along the Baltic; the
Wettins struggled for the Polish crown; the Brunswicks ob-

tained the crown of England; the Bavarian Wittelsbachs sought a crown in the Belgian Netherlands; and the royal houses of Denmark and Sweden gained lands within the Empire. It was therefore inevitable that the relations that had once been held within the net of the Empire should require a wider net to contain them. The Treaties of Westphalia were made law of the Empire, not by the procedure of legislation in the *Reichstag* but by the procedure of negotiation in the first modern diplomatic Congress. The medieval Empire had been actively European; the modern, passively. Only in this way could the heritage of universality have been preserved.

While the status of princes and of the Emperor was shifting to a European base, the law of the Empire was fertilizing the soil out of which international law was developing. The peace of the land had not only established courts to judge disputes between princes, but had recognized the validity of Roman law. In France the reception of Roman law contributed to the development of royal power by virtue of its application to the relations of a prince to his subjects. In the courts of the Empire it had a different currency in providing the basis of the relations of princes with each other. The Roman law elements of substantive international law, the form of international law as a net of personal duties of personal sovereigns to each other, and even such procedural features of international practice as arbitration, were richly developed in the Empire and came diluted into application in the family of nations while the principalities of the Empire were becoming the sovereignties of Europe.

v

It may be that the resemblance between the Holy Roman Empire and the family of nations is a result not so much of imitation as of similarity of situation. In both cases a residual fabric of legality subsists in the relations of a group of political units of different degrees of power. But even at that, the

Empire's history is a treasure-house of experience calling for interpretation and application to contemporary problems.

Let us consider the kind of world organization that is suggested by the example of the Empire. It is first of all a world dominated by a few Great Powers. It is divided into circles of influence, with leading powers in each. The hierarchies of law and loyalty run all the way from the top to the bottom of the political pyramid. The extravagances of national patriotism are overcome not by supernational patriotism, but by quiet disintegration into provincial and local loyalties. Wars there may be, but on the fringes; wagers of battle, not crusades; fought by technicians in warfare, not by peoples; as wars of adjustment, not of annihilation. There is for every area of power a relation intermediate between isolation and solidarity with every other area of power, and the object of political technique should be to find the appropriate relationship. As such relationships are stabilized they become part of the living law. Statements of law do not create, but record what is already created. (Witness the abortiveness of the effort to outlaw war.) Such a system might bring with it collective security, but on a day-to-day basis, as practice, not as religion.

It was in Central Europe, where the Empire left its deepest mark on the political world, that the conflict between the religion of nationalism and the pure political tradition of the Empire was sharpest. The revolutionists of 1848, devotees of the religion of nationalism, could neither organize Central Europe nor divide it. Their work and their problem have been misunderstood. The German National Assembly in Frankfurt that resulted from the uprisings of 1848 began its constitution-making, as is well known, by elaborating a comprehensive bill of rights. These were rights which the new Germany would have guaranteed to every German citizen. German historians have scoffed mercilessly at the Frankfurt Assembly for its preoccupation with a bill of rights when it should have been organizing the framework of a national administration. And yet the Assembly was more practical than was realized. Both the Empire that vanished in 1806 and the German Confederation that succeeded it in 1815 had been guarantors of due process of law. The Frankfurt Assembly was adding to living tissue when it wrote the bill of rights; but when, in order, as it thought, to make a more purely national Germany, it went further and ordered the Hapsburg Monarchy to choose between dissolution (into a German and non-German state) and exclusion from the new Germany, it was destroying living tissue. This program meant the exclusion of the Austro-Germans from Germany; it would have forced the partitioning of the Germany the Assembly had intended to unite. It failed.

Then Schwarzenberg, the great Austrian minister, offered his alternative plan. He would have reconstituted a College of Electors—a Directory of the larger states in Germany—leaving the German princes each in full charge of the administration of his government. Schwarzenberg would have held all Central Europe together, but in a framework resembling that of the Empire. A similar plan was promoted by the Great-Germany party in the 1860's, and adopted by a Congress of Princes in 1863. But Bismarck opposed Prussian state patriotism to the tradition of the Empire, went the full length of a war of secession from the German Confederation, and accomplished the partitioning of Germany by separating the North Germans from the Austrians. Then, having partitioned Germany and divided Central Europe at the level of constitutional law, he reunited it at the level of international law by means of the permanent Dual Alliance between the new German Empire and the Austro-Hungarian Empire.

With the defeat of the Central Powers in the World War, the religion of nationalism proved strong enough to break Central Europe into fragments, and the sentiment of international solidarity was inadequate to offer a corresponding guarantee of order at the level of international law. That region is

now one of the most troubled in the world, and no crusade
will end its trouble. It may in the future find stability in so
far as it works its way back toward the pattern of the Holy
Roman Empire and develops from that base.

VI

What is true of Central Europe in the little may apply also
to the world at large.

The doctrine of the two swords, applied to modern international problems, distinguishes two techniques for the improvement of the world's political order. The first is the promotion of a religion of internationalism and international solidarity
by which the religions of nationalism are to be confounded
and overcome. As a possible foundation for such a religion we
have the world community of ideas in the field of science. The
validity of a laboratory experiment in chemistry is acknowl-
edged everywhere in the world on equal terms. It remains to
bring about a situation in which the same accord will be given
by men's minds throughout the world to a statement that such
and such an act constitutes unjustified aggression. The religion must further so motivate men that this statement, thus
believed, will arouse a sufficient response to stir them everywhere to action against the aggressor. From an effective world
religion to an effective world state would be only a step.

Auguste Comte proposed in the nineteenth century to establish on the basis of positive science a religion of humanity;
but since the world of positive science was thing-centered,
not man-centered, the religion of humanity gave rise only to
pale and subordinate loyalties that shriveled at the first contact with national patriotism. Yet it was upon that foundation
that the statesmen of 1919 undertook to establish what they
thought would be a new world order. The characteristically
spiritual quality of this outlook on politics is attested by its
characteristic promise of permanent blessings to be obtained

in a future for which no present sacrifice is too great—even the sacrifice of a new crusade.

The second technique takes international law and the family of nations as it finds them. It works from day to day with engagements of relatively short term. It measures distances and limits commitments. Though we may not try to guarantee that nobody will ever be at war, we can reasonably anticipate that somebody will always be at peace. Even during the World War there were in Europe fifty million people whose governments were at peace. This figure—fifty million—was the approximate total population of Western Europe in the fifteenth century. American policy and opinion are learning this second technique, in which there is neither a world mission nor splendid isolation, but something safer and sounder than either. Our almost scholastic evaluation of legality, which causes us to refuse recognition to acts of conquest, and our practical regional hegemony in the New World are expressions of a statecraft that would have been at home in the Holy Roman Empire. It does not promise us eternal peace—that is for the next world. But it may bring us peace in our time.

APPENDIX

Excerpts from Reviews and Review Articles

Hitherto, we have played with various theories to account for the discrepancy between that which the war was fought to secure and that which it actually brought into being. We have, on the one hand, the tardy recognition theory, still sponsored by Clemenceau and a few Americans, according to which the Entente was all along engaged in a war for human liberty, while the United States, at first unaware of the issue, came to the aid of the Allies as soon as its real character was made plain to her. On the other hand, we have the tit-for-tat theory, of which Ambassador Houghton made himself the spokesman. According to this theory the United States had a private quarrel with Germany over the submarine question. It was merely by way of convenience in fighting this German-American war that we coöperated with the Entente. And our statements of war aims were nothing more or less than propaganda operations designed to weaken enemy morale.

As against these two theories of American participation in the war, it is now established that Wilson knowingly led the nation to associate itself with belligerents whose war aims were contrary to his own. Those high purposes which he ascribed to the Allies were really the purposes which he wished them to pursue, not those which he knew them to be pursuing. The attempts to substitute American for Entente war aims was a Herculean task in which even so strong a will as Wilson's could hardly have prevailed. (37)

No mass of documentary evidence, however mountainous, no scholarly labor, however patient, can result in a sound judgment on war responsibility except as a corollary of this or that ethical postulate. . . . Impartiality and industry alone will not guide a historian to a conclusion on responsibility. . . . Having made no ethical assumption, the writer can reach no ethical conclusion. (40)

The patterns used in the discussion of war guilt have derived not from the facts revealed in historical research but from some pressure of practical interest. Thus the war-plot pattern was needed to keep up fighting spirit, the "responsibility" pattern to justify collection of reparations, the "powder-barrel analogy" to clarify thought on non-aggression pacts and the "inevitable cataclysm" pattern to enlighten far-reaching reform projects. (Abstract of 40)

Any textbook of history, however dull and factual its style may be, contains an implicit philosophy. If history is indeed a fable agreed upon, it is chiefly the process of manualization which decides between competing fables. A manual such as this history of Europe since 1914[1] is therefore valuable not only as a reference book, but also as an index to the interpretation which is given at the textbook level to the fifteen turbulent years from the outbreak of the World War to the calling of the London Naval Conference.

It may surprise some of the veterans who once thought that the fate of the universe hung upon the issue of their battles that in a book of six hundred pages only fifty-one can be spared to give an account of the campaigns of the World War. H. G. Wells gave these campaigns two percent of the total space in a history of mankind from paleolithic times to the present; what then is the meaning of a style of textbook writing which can afford to this topic only eight and a half percent of a narrative covering fifteen years?

---

[1] F. Lee Benns, *Europe Since 1914* (New York, F. S. Crofts & Co., 1930). This review, written for the *Saturday Review of Literature* but never published, is here printed in full.

Not only in the restriction upon space given to the campaigns, but also in the style used in describing them, the war forfeits its traditional place in the historical narrative. The adjective "heroic" occurs but once, and the word "bravery" not at all. Only five phrases recall the ancient bardic practice of glorifying the psychic qualities of the fighter. It appears that the Belgians conducted a "stubborn defense" at Namur, the British offered "determined resistance" at Ypres, the Germans "fought doggedly on" with "determination little less than the French" at Verdun, there was "stubborn resistance" by the Austrians on the Izonzo, and the American first division "proved its mettle" at Cantigny. A battle is allowed to "rage" for seven weeks on page 109. Beyond that, the war is conducted on a cold business basis, and with a tremendous deficit.

Moreover, it appears, as the political and economic history of the period unfolds, that the war decided very little, that it accelerated tendencies already present in world civilization, and that its accelerating effect was felt indifferently among victor and vanquished powers. The rise of nationalities profited Ireland at England's expense, just as it profited Czechoslovakia at Austria's expense. The agrarian and economic revolutions ignored the difference between victorious and defeated powers. No selfishness at Versailles restrained the general sharing-out of misery among all the peoples of Europe.

The verdict which Benns arrives at, that "the war and its aftermath merely hastened the natural course of historical development," bringing to the world at enormous cost what it might have had for nothing by a little patience, is what corresponds in historiography to the Kellogg Pact in diplomacy. It denies to war the role of arbiter in civilization, and renounces war as an instrument of historical causation. (63)

The origin of the war has been for years a theme of historical, political, and juridical writing; in Ludwig's work it enters *belles lettres.* . . . The author has been more than fertile in the use of dramatic apparatus. The oldest and the youngest devices meet together in his pages. The scenes shift rapidly from one colorful location to another, as in a five-reel movie; the masses are paraded at intervals, like the chorus of a Greek drama. . . . There is a theory once propounded by Hebbel that in great tragedy all the characters are right, and the essence of the tragic situation is just that fact—that being right, they are carried onward to disaster. Ludwig's drama does not rise to the height of tragedy so conceived; there is too much irritation at the follies of men, too much indignation at their crimes. Had Ludwig set forth more clearly that the statesmen no less than the military men were enslaved by their creations, that the War Counts were doing their duty, that the peoples who were to suffer were co-makers of the system which demanded suffering of them, he would have written not only better history, but better tragedy. For the events of July, 1914, were even more truly tragic than Ludwig makes them out to be. (52)

The zeal of the historians who have labored to take the bitterness out of the war guilt question will not be misplaced if it is now directed to clearing up the confusion surrounding American foreign policy, thus preparing an era of enlightenment in which Americans will no longer insist on formulating every international question as an issue between isolation more or less splendid and alliances more or less entangling. (56)

[Poincaré] has given up his old habit of citing Article 231 of the Treaty of Versailles as a source of prewar history. (67)

Those who contended against French policy at the Peace Conference were wont to ascribe to it a certain completeness and consistency which it did not possess. When the history of the discord within the French government came to be known, Clemenceau was still portrayed as the man who knew exactly what he wanted and had his plan worked out. These books in which his mind is laid open for inspection suggest that there were implicit contradictions and inconsistencies in the very thoughts and ideals to which he clung with such Vendean stubbornness. He thinks that to detach the Rhineland from Germany would have been to violate the idea of "a Europe founded on right"; but to occupy the Rhineland, perpetually if necessary, under Article 429 of the Treaty, should be France's defense against Germany's congenital wickedness. His faith in right conflicts with his belief in a cosmic law of struggle. His ideal of a Europe freely organized by its peoples is cancelled by his picture of the Germans as a sub-human species. His philosophy and his politics mark him as a man who learned nothing since 1918, and forgot nothing since 1871. It was just such a leader that France needed in the dark days of the war when he took his premiership. The peace negotiations found him with no crafty schemes, but only with his confused ideals and a character "obstinate, limited and savage" to defend them. (69)

"Wilson made many mistakes," writes Dumba, "owing to his utter ignorance of European conditions." How much of this ignorance was itself the result of Dumba's mistakes, owing to his utter ignorance of American conditions? (89)

George D. Herron, an Iowa doctor of divinity and professor of "applied Christianity," residing in Geneva during the World War, became a leading interpreter to Europe of the policies and opinions of the country from which he had been self-exiled for fifteen years. This role came to him by accident. Carried away by a profound emotional commitment to the Allied cause, he persisted in prophesying, during the period of American neutrality, that Wilson was planning with "divine cunning" to bring America to the side of the Allies. When Wilson campaigned for reëlection with the slogan "he kept us out of war," Herron wrote an article explaining that this was mere subterfuge. When Wilson's note on war aims in December, 1916, and his "Peace without Victory" speech in January, seemed to show "an unemotional and reprehensible impartiality," as if all belligerents were put on the same moral footing, Herron declared that this was only a mask, that the hidden meaning of the speech was an ultimatum to Germany to be followed by war. The turn of events gave to these extravagances, untrue at the time they were written, the aspect of officially inspired pronouncements. (90)

The American college student with his metered reading capacity has imposed upon the writers of his weekly assignments a rigid form no less compelling than that which the Athenian audience imposed upon Aeschylus. Instead of the three unities there are the three chapters of thirty pages each. The historian and artist who fits his subject matter beautifully and completely to this form has performed for his colleagues a creative service of great value. (93)

The rich thought of the early nineteenth-century authoritarian writers is neither explained nor alluded to. De Maistre and Bonald are left out; Burke's name does not appear; and Chateaubriand is remembered only for his interest in the Greek revolt, not for his part in the revival of conservatism and Catholicism. Even the giant Hegel receives only the passing mention that he influenced Marx and Proudhon. In the opinion of the reviewer, early nineteenth-century reactionary thought was original in its whole design, while nineteenth-century liberal thought merely elaborated patterns established in the eighteenth century. Contemporary politics is borrowing far more from these authoritarian writers than from liberal doctrinaires. It is unfortunate, therefore, to find them so much neglected. (110)

In this book there is nothing bad and nothing new. . . . It covers the ground that the planners of the series intended it should cover. . . . Historical scholarship hardly needs this book, but stands in great need of another . . . that could be put into the possession of an intelligent novice to furnish him with the guidance he would need in writing the history of his home town. Such a manual would fill a real need. This volume fills none except the need of completing a series. (113)

The editor of *The Living Age* has made a scrapbook of month-by-month news stories and comments covering the last five years. He has made his selections principally from the writings of foreign journalists, and has shown a special preference for those which portray a business reality behind a political façade. . . . Mr. Howe's book . . . tells us neither whence we have come nor whither we are going. It makes no effort to draw together the threads of a story; there is no order or system or conclusion. As the meaningless sequence of political revolutions, business intrigues, financial and economic crises proceeds through the five years, the narrative takes on an unhealthy glamour. Where have we read such things before? Was it not in the tales of Merovingian times, when those Frankish princes, with names like Chlodomir and Gundobad, spent their time in waylaying and assassinating their brothers of the royal blood? And in the faithful chronicler, Quincy Howe, diligently transcribing the anecdotes and tales of wonder that come to his ear, and slipping into the pages from time to time a little of his own mild prejudice, do we not recognize the counterpart of Gregory of Tours? (115)

Here are seven men—one economist, three political scientists, one journalist who is a distinguished expert on foreign affairs, and two historians. Like the fabled blind men who made a study of the elephant, they interpret to their readers this strange monster, the contemporary world. . . . These books are sound books; they are well worth reading, each is adequate in its own way. And yet, taken together, they make no symphony, they point to no conclusion; they suggest rather the fatal inadequacies of our system of division of labor in the intellectual world. (128)

A question that brings to light the character of a book in this field can always be put: "How much of the historical material selected for presentation is broken down into national history compartments?" Professor Slosson's book meets this test with a score of thirteen chapters out of thirty. More than half of its material deals with Europe as a whole; and of the chapters devoted to national histories, there are several—like that on Italian Fascism—which are really analyses of a problem of general import in terms of the experience of one nation. (130)

The English political biography is almost part of the British constitution, and these two biographies conform to the quasi-constitutional practice. They are apologetic in spirit, they touch enough on family life to tie the men in with their traditions, and they publish some state papers that would not otherwise have seen the light of day. . . . With Grey and Balfour, heirs and epigones of Gladstone and Disraeli, the last Victorians left the stage. And they left the Victorian contradictions—political, aesthetic, and intellectual—unresolved. (141)

I warn you, Thomas Mann! I warn you, Reuben Osborn! You have given the devil your little finger and he will take your whole arm! You, Thomas Mann, have acted knowingly, walking into intellectual inferno like Giordano Bruno, whose heroic passion carried him into the flame. You, Reuben Osborn, have acted in a blundering fashion, stumbling into peril. . . .

Osborn is interested in selling Freud to Marxists. He cites passages indicating that Marx and Engels were really not far from Freud. . . . The new formula specifically contributed by

Osborn is that the id and the ego, if left to themselves, without the restraint of the super-ego, would follow the party line into a collectivist society. But there is danger in his system, for the id may turn out to be something that is better satisfied by an opportunity to beat up a Jew than by a chance to have "freedom"; it may prefer war and a low standard of living to peace and a high standard of living. Once Osborn cuts loose from the firm anchorage of nineteenth-century science, in the faith of which Marx lived and wrote, he has nothing but his own super-ego to keep him from wearing a swastika and a brown shirt. . . .

After this discussion of the artist's movement from a non-Freudian world of scientific objectivity and individualism into a Freudian world of myth, Mann predicts that Freud's work will be the foundation of a "future dwelling of a wiser and freer humanity." But how is this possible if the kind of humanity that Freud teaches us we are is not wiser and freer than the kind we thought we were? . . .

When Thomas Mann wrote *Joseph and His Brothers* he was writing of a Jew and of the long influence of race experience upon an individual. There is someone in Germany who will agree with him and help fill out the scheme; his name is Julius Streicher. And Alfred Rosenberg will accept every word of Mann's Freudian metaphysic and apply it to the Nordic race. . . .

. . . Go on with your myths, Thomas Mann; proceed with your id, Mr. Osborn; you are probably right and the century is with you. But, for God's sake, look where you are going! (147)

The age-old problem of nominalism and realism still confronts us. The historian who undertakes to analyze the sequences of the past in terms of forces and interests and state policies, personifying for the purpose Germany and Russia and France, can manipulate these abstractions according to certain conventional rules, and create a fabric of statements that have the aspect of truth wherever the conventional rules of interpretation are accepted. But lines of thought and investigation that proceed from different assumptions will not reach the same truth. . . . Viereck now adapts his thought to another pattern—that of the trial in a court of law. He presents the materials of history as evidence presented by a prosecutor and public defender in a trial of the Kaiser on a whole miscellany of charges. The facts take on a new color, because the procedure of a trial is one in which the nominalist conception of the individual human being comes directly into contact with a conception of certain generalized norms of conduct. Inevitably, the historical scene, when it takes the form of testimony in a trial, comes to be peopled with persons rather than abstractions; inevitably, the individuals turn out to be very small in comparison with the world in which they operate; the conclusions rise no higher than the evidence, and we are left with an understanding of the Kaiser but not of the World War. (161)

"The economic history of the postwar period is to extend to a time when the economic consequences of the war shall reach an equilibrium." This statement was written in 1921 by Friedrich von Wieser, Austrian economist, in a circular letter to collaborators in this great history of the World War. For fifteen years thereafter scholars of world reputation and ministers of cabinet rank worked under the general guidance of Professor Shotwell in this coöperative intellectual enterprise comparable in magnitude to the *Monumenta Germaniae Historica*. Whether the equilibrium that Wieser, like all classical economists, believed must come in the long run has arrived, we cannot say. But if it has come, then, by an ironic turn, the equilibrium is the crystallization of war economy itself. That which was launched as a study of the social and economic structure of the world in an abnormal phase—the phase of war—has become an analysis of the structure of a normal so-

ciety of the nineteen-thirties. Even the two volumes of the
American series—Clark's masterful analysis of the cost of the
war in America and Hines's account of the war history of
American railways—have become strangely contemporary as
the problem of social income in the large is set before the
American people and as the American railroads reach their
financial impasse. . . .

It is an encyclopedia, but not an encyclopedia of destruction.
That which comes to mind in going through volume after
volume is not the destructiveness of war, not the conflict of
nations with each other, but the conflict within each nation
between the ideal of a free capitalist economy and the need for
organized production, transport, and distribution. Wartime
socialization, it is only too evident, was put into effect by men
who were not prepared for it and did not believe in it. We
know now that they paved the way for men who did believe
in it as an article of faith and for whom it provided the preparation. Socially and economically we are in the midst of a second
world war. The Shotwell series was completed in time to b
contemporary. (164)

With this volume of his memoirs, Lloyd George lea
testament to history. There was a time during which it mig
have been possible to say that Lloyd George was more successful than Wilson. Today even that cannot be said. . . . He was
merely a medium through which energies were conducted.
There was nothing lasting—literally nothing—for which he
stood or for which he stands. (166)

In *New York's Making*, the story of a family and the story
of a city are intertwined with rare literary art, and with scholarship as sound and graceful as a Sheraton chair, by someone
who is separated by only six lives from the Johannes de Peyster
who built a house on Manhattan Island three hundred years
ago. . . . From works such as this, and only from works such

as this, can we be recalled to the realization that our state-centered political history as learned in the schools is out of focus with life and that life values will be reflected only in historical writing that portrays the world as we see it in our own lives, from the human center of our own families, from the geographic center of our own homes. (167)

There is one great generalization which stands in the evidence that M. Weill brings together and which yet remains outside the framework of his synthesis. This is the fact that some nationality movements are associated with power-programs, and some are not. Do the German and French forms of the nationality idea, respectively irrational and rational, corporative and individualist, include, of necessity, a power-program? If we should look first at the continent and then at the idea . . . it would appear that the continent consists of a number of power-areas, constantly subjected to a process akin to gerrymandering. The idea of nationality does not everywhere, nor   it always, involved an effort to modify the structure of the   areas. When such modifications as independence, auton-   ification have been demanded, the "idea of national-   ariably summoned to furnish ethical justification for   ns that are essentially power-programs. Naturally, to   this function, the idea of nationality must be as elastic   the conscience of a Jesuit or a journalist. (176)

21. Editorials: "Patriotism in San Jose," "Upton Sinclair's Thesis," "Intellectual Honesty in Journalism," "The Old Question of Academic Freedom," *Stanford Spectator*, 1:98, April.
22. Editorial: "Can France and Germany Agree?" *Stanford Spectator*, 1:136, May.

1924

23. "The Re-establishment of the Independence of the Hanseatic Cities, 1813–1815" (MS.), M.A. thesis, Stanford University Library.
24. Graham, Malbone W., Jr., assisted by Binkley, Robert C., *New Governments of Central Europe* (New York: Henry Holt and Company).
25. "The Trend in Europe," *San Francisco Journal*, February 24, 27; March 3, 13, 20, 28; April 3, 9, 11, 14; May 5, 11, 14, 29.
26. Review of *Black Magic*, by Kenneth W. Roberts, *San Francisco Journal*, June 8.

1925

27. "The Hoover War Library," *Concerning Stanford* 1.9, June.

1926

28. "New Light on Russia's War Guilt," *Current History*, 23:531–533, January.
29. Binkley, Robert C., and Mahr, August C., "Eine Studie zur Kriegsschuldfrage," *Frankfurter Zeitung*, February 28 (70. Jahrgang, Nr. 157), 2:2–4.
30. "Russia's War Guilt," a letter to the editor, in reply to an unsigned editorial by Harry Elmer Barnes criticizing No. 28, *Nation*, 122:233, March 3.
31. Binkley, Robert C., and Mahr, August C., "Urheber or Verursacher, that is the question," *San Francisco Chronicle*, May 23.

32. Binkley, Robert C., and Mahr, August C., "A New Interpretation of the 'Responsibility' Clause in the Versailles Treaty," *Current History*, 24:398–400, June.

1927

33. "The Reaction of European Opinion to the Statesmanship of Woodrow Wilson" (MS.), Ph.D. thesis, Stanford University Library. (Abstract in *Abstracts of Dissertations*, Stanford University (1926–1927), 2:189–194.)

1928

34. "Revision of World War History," *Historical Outlook*, 19:109–113, March.
35. "The Concept of Public Opinion in the Social Sciences," *Social Forces* 6:389–396, March. (A chapter of No. 33.)
36. "The Hoover War Library," *New York Herald Tribune*, November 11.
37. Review of *The Intimate Papers of Colonel House*, edited by Charles Seymour, *New York; a four-page journal of ideas for the general reader*, 2.46, November 17. Review title: "For What Did We Fight?"

1929

38. Binkley, Robert C., and Binkley, Frances Williams, *What Is Right with Marriage; an Outline of Domestic Theory* (New York: D. Appleton-Century Company, Inc.). (See No. 51.)

    Reviewed in *New York Herald Tribune Books*, October 6, p. 2; *Nation*, 129:386–387, October 9; *Saturday Review of Literature*, 6:367, November 9; *Survey*, 63:231, November 15.
39. "Do the Records of Science Face Ruin?" *Scientific American*, 140:28–30, January. (See No. 41.)
40. "War Responsibility and World Ethics," *New Republic*, 57:208–210, January 9. *Social Science Abstracts*, 1:4118.

41. "Our Perishable Records," *Reader's Digest*, 7:591, February. (Condensed from No. 39.)

42. "Renouvin and War Guilt," a letter to the editor in reply to Harry E. Barnes, *New Republic*, 58:47, February 27.

43. "Communication," a letter to the editor regarding wood-pulp paper preservation, *Journal of Modern History*, 1:87, March.

44. "The 'Guilt' Clause in the Versailles Treaty," *Current History*, 30:294–300, May. *Social Science Abstracts*, 2:1430.

45. "The Ethics of Nullification," *New Republic*, 58:297–300, May 1. (Incorporated in No. 50. See No. 46.) *Social Science Abstracts*, 1:10635.

46. "Nullification and the Legal Process," *Massachusetts Law Quarterly*, 14:109–115, May. (Reprint of No. 45.)

47. "Note on Preservation of Research Materials," *Social Forces*, 8:74–76, September.

48. "A Nation of Realtors," *New Republic*, 60:196–198, October 9.

49. "Ten Years of Peace Conference History," *Journal of Modern History*, 1:607–629, December. (Cf. Birdsall, Paul, "The Second Decade of Peace Conference History," *ibid.*, 11:362–378, September 1939.) *Social Science Abstracts*, 2:6142.

1930

50. *Responsible Drinking; a Discreet Inquiry and a Modest Proposal* (New York: Vanguard Press). (See No. 45.) Reviewed in *New York Herald Tribune Books*, November 2, p. 14; *Saturday Review of Literature*, 7:469, December 20; *New Republic*, 65:226–227, January 7, 1931.

51. Binkley, Robert C., and Binkley, Frances Williams, "The Function of the Family," in *Twenty-Four Views of*

Marriage, edited by Clarence A. Spaulding, pp. 173–192. (Taken from No. 38, chap. xiii.)

52. Review of *July '14*, by Emil Ludwig, *Saturday Review of Literature*, 6:615, January 4. Review title: "The Tragedy Evolves."

53. Review of *The New German Republic; the Reich in Transition*, by Elmer Luehr, *New Republic*, 61:257, January 22.

54. "Should We Leave Romance Out of Marriage? A Debate between Husband and Wife," I. Binkley, Robert C., "Marriage as an Experiment," II. Binkley, Frances Williams, "Science and the New Innocents," *Forum*, 83:72–79, February.

55. "Free Speech in Fascist Italy," *New Republic*, 61:291–293, February 5.

56. Review of *The Imperial Dollar*, by Hiram Motherwell, *Saturday Review of Literature*, 6:801, March 8. Review title: "Our Imperial Task." (See No. 62.)

57. Binkley, Robert C., and Binkley, Frances Williams, "Without Benefit of Sociology," *Scribner's Magazine*, 87:374–379, April.

58. Review of *Germany's Domestic and Foreign Policies*, by O. Hoetzsch, *Current History*, 32:15, 194, April. Review title: "The German Nationalist Attitude."

59. Review of *Foch; My Conversations with the Marshal*, by Raymond Recouly, *New Republic*, 62:226–227, April 9.

60. "Franco-Italian Discord," *Current History*, 32:529–533, June. *Social Science Abstracts*, 2:16668.

61. Review of *The Rise and Fall of Germany's Colonial Empire, 1884–1918*, by M. E. Townsend, *Current History*, 32:431, 602, June.

62. Review of *Why We Fought*, by C. H. Grattan, *Saturday Review of Literature*, 7:140, September 20. Review title: "Isolation and Imperialism." (The review has at its head

under the title two books. The part concerning Motherwell's was published separately in No. 56.)

63. Review of *Europe Since 1914*, by F. Lee Benns. [Above,
pp. 386–387.]

1931

64. *Methods of Reproducing Research Materials; a Survey
Made for the Joint Committee on Materials for Research
of the Social Science Research Council and the American
Council of Learned Societies* (Ann Arbor, Mich.: Edwards Brothers). (See No. 119.)

65. "The Problem of Perishable Paper," *Atti del 1° congresso
mondiale delle biblioteche e di bibliografia*, 4:77–85,
Roma. (Paper read at First World Congress of Libraries
and Bibliography, Rome, June, 1929.)

66. Review of *The Coming of the War, 1914*, by Bernadotte E. Schmitt, *Yale Review*, n.s., 20:631–632, March.
Review title: "Responsibility for the War."

67. Review of *Les responsabilités de la guerre*, by R. Gerin
and R. Poincaré, *American Historical Review*, 36:643–
644, April.

68. "Report of the Joint Committee of the Social Science
Research Council and the American Council of Learned
Societies on Materials for Research," American Council
of Learned Societies, *Bulletin No. 15*, 73–77, May.

69. Review of *Grandeur and Misery of Victory*, by G. Clemenceau; and *Georges Clemenceau*, by J. Martet, *Journal
of Modern History*, 3:331–333, June.

70. "Europe Faces the Customs Union," *Virginia Quarterly
Review*, 7:321–329, July. *International Digest*, 1.10:24–
26, July. *Social Science Abstracts*, 4:6480.

71. "New Light on the Paris Peace Conference." Part I:
"From the Armistice to the Organization of the Peace
Conference," Part II: "The Organization of the Confer-
ence," *Political Science Quarterly*, 46:335–361, 509–547,

September, December. *Social Science Abstracts*, 4:7565.

72. Review of *Readings in European History Since 1914*, by J. F. Scott and A. Baltzly, *Mississippi Valley Historical Review*, 18:298, September.

73. Review of *Lenin, Red Dictator*, by G. Vernadsky, *Mississippi Valley Historical Review*, 18:299, September.

74. "Scapegoat Germany," *American Monthly*, 24:27–28, October. (MS. title: "The Commission on War Responsibility at the Peace Conference; How the Report Charging Germany with War Responsibility Was Drawn Up; a Study Based upon Records Here Used for the First Time in America.")

75. Review of *Berkshire Studies in European History*, edited by R. A. Newhall, L. B. Packard, and S. R. Packard, *American Historical Review*, 37:89–90, October.

76. Review of *Documentation internationale. Paix de Versailles*, vol. III, *Responsabilités des auteurs de la guerre et sanctions*, *Journal of Modern History*, 3:672–674, December.

77. "The Franco-Italian Naval Discussions," *American Year Book*, *1931*, pp. 64–66.

1932

78. Review of *Documentation internationale. Paix de Versailles*, vol. VI, *Régime des ports, voies d'eau, voies ferrées*, *Journal of Modern History*, 4:155–156, March.

79. Review of *The Little Green Shutter*, by B. Whitlock, *Mississippi Valley Historical Review*, 18:615–616, March.

80. Review of *A History of Europe from 1815 to 1923*, by Sir J. A. R. Marriott; and *Contemporary Europe and Overseas, 1898–1920*, by R. B. Mowat, *American Historical Review*, 37:550–551, April.

81. Review of *One Hundred Red Days; a Personal Chronicle of the Bolshevik Revolution*, by Edgar Sisson, *Mississippi Valley Historical Review*, 19:143–144, June.

82. Review of *The Prohibition Experiment in Finland*, by J. H. Wuorinen, *Mississippi Valley Historical Review*, 19:154–155, June.

83. Review of *The First Moroccan Crisis, 1904–1906*, by E. N. Anderson, *Mississippi Valley Historical Review*, 19:155, June.

84. Review of *L'Article 231 du traité de Versailles, sa genèse et sa signification*, by C. Bloch; and *Germany Not Guilty in 1914*, by M. H. Cockran, *Journal of Modern History*, 4:319–322, June.

85. Review of *Readings in European International Relations Since 1789*, edited by W. H. Cooke and E. P. Stickney, *American Historical Review*, 38:160–161, October.

1933

86. Binkley, Robert C., and Crobaugh, Mervyn, "The High Cost of Economy," *New Republic*, 73:285–286, January 25.

87. "Russia; a Reading List," *Alumnae Folio of Flora Stone Mather College*, 9.2:8–10, February.

88. Review of *Historical Scholarship in America: Needs and Opportunities; a Report by the Committee of the American Historical Association on the Planning of Research*, *New England Quarterly*, 6:227–229, March.

89. Review of *Memoirs of a Diplomat*, by Constantin Dumba, *Mississippi Valley Historical Review*, 20:141, June.

90. Review of *George D. Herron and the European Settlement*, by M. P. Briggs, *Political Science Quarterly*, 48:306–308, June.

91. Review of *The States of Europe, 1815–1871*, by R. B. Mowat, *American Historical Review*, 39:169–170, October.

92. Report of activities, 1931–1932, of the Joint Committee of the American Council of Learned Societies and the Social Science Research Council on Materials for Re-

search. American Council of Learned Societies, *Bulletin No. 20*, 63–72, December.

1934

93. Review of *The Age of Metternich, 1814–1848*, by A. May; *A History of Geographical Discovery, 1400–1800*, by J. E. Gillespie; and *The British Empire-Commonwealth*, by R. G. Trotter, *American Historical Review*, 39:563–564, April.

94. Review of *Un débat historique, 1914; le problème des origines de la guerre*, by J. Isaac, *Journal of Modern History*, 6:217–218, June.

95. Review of *The World Since 1914*, by W. C. Langsam; and *Beginning the Twentieth Century*, by J. W. Swain, *Mississippi Valley Historical Review*, 21:128, June.

96. "The Twentieth Century Looks at Human Nature," *Virginia Quarterly Review*, 10:336–350, July.

   Reviewed in *New York Times*, June 24. Editorial entitled: "Political Human Nature."

97. "Austria Again Made Europe's Football," *Cleveland News*, July 25.

98. "Parties in Europe; Dollfuss, the Martyr, Still Aid to Party," *Cleveland News*, July 26.

99. "Germany and Austria," *Cleveland News*, July 28.

100. "Is Hitler Guilty?" *Cleveland News*, July 31.

101. "An Anatomy of Revolution," *Virginia Quarterly Review*, 10:502–514, October.

   Reviewed in *New York Times*, September 21, 22:3. Editorial entitled: "Tests of Revolution."

102. "Report of Activities, 1933, of the Joint Committee on Materials for Research," American Council of Learned Societies, *Bulletin No. 22*, 60–68, October.

103. Review of *American Diplomacy During the World War*, by Charles Seymour, *Mississippi Valley Historical Review*, 21:441–442, December.

104. Review of *Vereinigte Staaten von Amerika, Versailler Vertrag und Völkerbund; Ein Beitrag zur Europa-Politik der U. S. A.*, by Martin Löffler, *Mississippi Valley Historical Review*, 21:442–443, December.

105. Review of *A Study of History*, by A. J. Toynbee, *Mississippi Valley Historical Review*, 21:445–447, December.

106. "The Place of Reduced Scale Copying in Library Policy," In [American Library Association, Committee on public documents], *Public Documents, 1934* (Chicago: American Library Association, 1935), pp. 219–222.

1935

107. *Realism and Nationalism, 1852–1871* (The Rise of Modern Europe, edited by W. L. Langer, vol. 16.) (New York: Harper & Brothers). (See No. 178.)

Reviewed in *American Historical Review*, 42:124–126, October, 1936; *American Review*, 6:502–506, February, 1936; *Annals of the American Academy of Political and Social Sciences*, 186:199–200, July, 1936; *Catholic World*, 144:116–117, October, 1936; *Christian Science Monitor*, February 15, 1936, p. 14; *New Republic*, 87:358, July 29, 1936; *New York Times Book Review*, March 1, 1936, p. 9; *Journal of Modern History*, 8:503–505, December, 1936.

108. "Conspectus of the 19th and 20th Centuries in Europe" (MS.). Several mimeographed copies in the Library of Flora Stone Mather College, Western Reserve University.

109. "New tools for men of letters," *Yale Review*, n.s., 24:519–537, March.

Note: This article was privately mimeographed by the Joint Committee on Materials for Research at Western Reserve University under the title "New Tools, New Recruits, for the Republic of Letters; a Memorandum," 34 pp.

110. Review of *European Civilization and Politics*, by E. Achorn, *Annals of the American Academy of Political and Social Sciences*, 178:237–238, March.

111. Review of *Some Memories of the Peace Conference*, by R. H. Beadon; *Les Dessous du traité de Versailles* (*d'après les documents inédits de la censure française*), by M. Berger and P. Allard; *Peacemaking, 1919*, by H. Nicolson; and *Versailles, Die Geschichte eines missglückten Friedens*, by W. Ziegler, *Journal of Modern History*, 7:91–93, March.

112. "Innovations in History," *Alumnae Folio of Flora Stone Mather College*, 11.3:2, April.

113. Review of *Aids to Historical Research*, by J. M. Vincent, *Annals of the American Academy of Political and Social Sciences*, 179:267, May.

114. "Versailles to Stresa," *Virginia Quarterly Review*, 11:383–393, July.

115. Review of *World Diary, 1929–1934*, by Quincy Howe, *Yale Review*, n.s., 25:208–209, September. Review title: "A Five-Year Chronicle."

116. Binkley, Robert C., and Norton, W. W., "Copyright in Photographic Reproductions," *Library Journal*, 60:763–764, October 1. (Repeated, with a few prefatory paragraphs, in No. 118.)

117. Review of *Freedom versus Organization, 1814–1914*, by Bertrand Russell, *American Historical Review*, 41:187–188, October.

118. Binkley, Robert C., and Norton, W. W., "Copyright and Photostats," *Publishers Weekly*, 128:1665–1667, November 2. (See No. 116.) (See also "The Gentlemen's Agreement and the Problem of Copyright," *Journal of Documentary Reproduction*, 2:29–36, March, 1939.)

1936

119. Binkley, Robert C., with the assistance of Schellenberg, T. R.; Hanley, Miles; McCarter, Josephine; Barry, Ade-

line; and many others, *Manual on Methods of Reproducing Research Materials; a Survey Made for the Joint Committee on Materials for Research of the Social Science Research Council and the American Council of Learned Societies* (Ann Arbor, Mich.: Edwards Brothers, Inc.). (Revision of No. 64.)

Reviewed in *Publishers Weekly*, 131:1119–1120, March 6, 1937; *Library Journal*, 62:288–289, April 1, 1937.

120. "Le Développement de l'outillage pour la microcopie des documents," Union Française des Organismes de Documentation, *La Documentation en France*, 5:14–18, March.

121. Review of *The Treaty of St. Germain*, edited by N. Almond and R. H. Lutz; *The Saar Struggle*, by M. T. Florinsky; and *The Causes of the German Collapse in 1918*, by R. H. Lutz, *Annals of the American Academy of Political and Social Sciences*, 184:237–238, March.

122. Review of *Sawdust Caesar*, by George Seldes, *Yale Review*, n.s., 25:633–634, March. Review title: "Personal History of Mussolini."

123. "New Debts for Old," *Virginia Quarterly Review*, 12:237–247, April.

124. "Blame for W. P. A. Projects, a Letter to the Editor," *Cleveland Plain Dealer*, May 3, A23:4.

125. Review of *Foreign Interest in the Independence of New Spain*, by John Rydjord, *Annals of the American Academy of Political and Social Sciences*, 185:268, May.

126. Report of activities, 1935, of the Joint Committee on Materials for Research. American Council of Learned Societies, *Bulletin No. 25*, 64–69, July.

127. Review of *The Treaty of St. Germain*, edited by N. Almond and R. H. Lutz, *American Historical Review*, 41:757–759, July.

128. Review of *Democratic Governments in Europe*, by R. Buell, E. Chase, and R. Valeur; *World Finance, 1914–1935*, by P. Einzig; *American Foreign Policy in the*

Post-War Years, by F. Simonds; *Dictatorship and Democracy*, by Sir J. Marriott; and *The Post-War World, 1918–1934*, by J. H. Jackson, *Virginia Quarterly Review*, 12:461–465, July. Review title: "Post-War Europe."

129. Review of *The Heritage of Freedom; the United States and Canada in the Community of Nations*, by J. T. Shotwell, *Mississippi Valley Historical Review*, 23:298–299, September.

130. Review of *Europe Since 1870*, by P. W. Slosson, *American Historical Review*, 42:164–165, October.

131. Review of *The Post-War World*, by J. H. Jackson, *American Historical Review*, 42:165, October.

132. "New Methods for Scholarly Publishing," *Publishers Weekly*, 130:1678–1680, October 24.

133. Review of *The Care and Cataloging of Manuscripts as Practiced by the Minnesota Historical Society*, by G. L. Nute; and *Copying Manuscripts; Rules Worked Out by the Minnesota Historical Society*, by G. L. Nute, *Minnesota History*, 17:448–450, December.

134. "The Camera," in *Microphotography for Libraries*, Chicago, American Library Association, pp. 3–9.

1937

135. "History for a Democracy," *Minnesota History*, 18:1–27, March. (Presented on January 18, 1937, as the annual address of the eighty-eighth annual meeting of the Minnesota Historical Society. Condensed versions in *Museum Echoes of the Ohio State Archaeological and Historical Society*, 10:25–27, July; and *Journal of Adult Education*, 10:377–382, October, 1938.)

136. Review of *The War in Outline*, by Liddell Hart, *Mississippi Valley Historical Review*, 23:591, March.

137. "The Microphotographic Camera," an interview with Robert C. Binkley, member of the Committee on Photographic Reproduction of Library Materials, written by

the interviewer, M. Llewellyn Raney, chairman of the Committee. *American Library Association Bulletin,* 31:211–213, April.

138. "Myths of the Twentieth Century," *Virginia Quarterly Review,* 13:339–350, Summer.

139. "Report of Activities, June, 1935–June, 1936, of the Joint Committee of the American Council of Learned Societies and the Social Science Research Council on Materials for Research," American Council of Learned Societies, *Bulletin No. 26,* 52–57, June.

140. Review of *"We or They"; Two Worlds in Conflict,* by H. F. Armstrong, *Mississippi Valley Historical Review,* 24:132–133, June.

141. Review of *Grey of Fallodon,* by G. M. Trevelyan; and *Arthur James Balfour,* by Blanche E. C. Dugdale, *Yale Review,* n.s., 26:826–829, June. Review title: "The Last Victorians."

142. "The Fascist Record in Italy," *Events,* 2:32–36, July.

143. Review of *Die Petersburger Mission Bismarcks, 1859–1862; Russland und Europa zu Beginn der Regierung Alexander II,* by Boris Nolde, translated by Bernhard Schulze; and *Russland und Frankreich vom Ausgang des Krimkrieges bis zum italienischen Krieg, 1856–1859,* by Ernst Schüle, *American Historical Review,* 42:758–759, July.

144. "The Reproduction of Materials for Research," in *Library Trends; Papers Presented Before the Library Institute at the University of Chicago, August 3–15, 1936,* edited with an introduction by Louis R. Wilson (Chicago: University of Chicago Press), pp. 225–236.

145. Review of *On the Rim of the Abyss,* by J. T. Shotwell, *Mississippi Valley Historical Review,* 24:279–280, September.

146. Review of *Policies and Opinions at Paris, 1919,* by G. B. Noble, *Journal of Modern History,* 9:403–404, September.

147. Review of *Freud and Marx*, by Reuben Osborn; and *Freud, Goethe, Wagner*, by Thomas Mann, *Virginia Quarterly Review*, 13:612–615, Autumn. Review title: "Of Freud and the Future."

148. "Memorandum on Auxiliary Publication," in *Microphotography for Libraries, 1937* (Chicago: American Library Association), pp. 67–72.

1938

149. Editor of Sanford, E. M., *The Mediterranean World in Ancient Times* (New York: Ronald Press), Ronald Series in History, edited by R. C. Binkley and R. H. Gabriel.

150. "The Holy Roman Empire versus the United States; Patterns for Constitution-Making in Central Europe," in *The Constitution Reconsidered*, edited by Conyers Read (New York: Columbia University Press), pp. 271–284.

151. "Microcopying and Library Catalogs," *American Library Association Bulletin*, 32:241–243, April.

152. "Deciding on Belligerency," a letter to the editor, *New York Times*, June 24, 18:7.

153. Studies in the Restoration Era, 1815–1820; prepared under the direction of Robert C. Binkley in a history seminar taught at Columbia University in 1937–1938. New York, Columbia University. (Hectographed copies in Columbia University and Western Reserve University libraries.)

154. "Mill's Liberty Today," *Foreign Affairs*, 16:563–573, July.

155. "Peace in Our Time," *Virginia Quarterly Review*, 14:551–564, Autumn.

156. "Report of Activities, 1937, of the Joint Committee of the Social Science Research Council and the American Council of Learned Societies on Materials for Research," American Council of Learned Societies, *Bulletin No. 27*, 44–48, November.

157. "Typescript Formats for Blueprint Reproduction," *Journal of Documentary Reproduction*, 1:75–78, Winter.

158. "The Why of the White Collar Program. Works Progress Administration" (Mimeographed MS.) Extracts from a paper prepared for joint meeting of the Society of American Archivists and the American Historical Association, Chicago, December, 1938. (Incorporated in No. 160.)

159. "Techniques and Policies of Documentary Reproduction," International Federation for Documentation, 14th Conference, Oxford-London, 1938, *Transactions I*, pp. C121–C124. (Also in International Federation for Documentation, *Quarterly Communications*, 6.1:12–15, 1939.)

1939

160. "The Cultural Program of the W.P.A.," *Harvard Educational Review*, 9:156–174, March. (See Nos. 158, 171.)

161. Review of *The Kaiser on Trial*, by G. S. Viereck, *Journal of Modern History*, 11:97–98, March.

162. "Newspaper Indexing for WPA Projects," *Journal of Documentary Reproduction*, 2:46–47, March.

163. "World Intellectual Organization," *Educational Record*, 20:256–262, April.

164. Review of *Social and Economic History of the World War*, 150 vols., 1921–1937; general editor, J. T. Shotwell, *American Historical Review*, 44:629–632, April.

165. Review of *The Struggle for Imperial Unity*, by J. E. Tyler, *Annals of the American Academy of Political and Social Sciences*, 203:242–243, May.

166. Review of *Memoirs of the Paris Peace Conference*, by David Lloyd George, *Yale Review*, n.s., 28:853–855, June. Review title: "Lloyd George's Testament."

167. Review of *New York's Making*, by Mary de Peyster Conger, *Journal of Adult Education*, 11:285, June. Review title: "A City and a Family."

168. "Strategic Objectives in Archival Policy," *American Archivist*, 2:162–168, July. (Paper read at luncheon conference of the Society of American Archivists, Chicago, December 29, 1938.)

169. "Principle Held Self-Evident," a letter to the editor, *New York Times*, July 31, 12:6.

170. "Photographic Reproduction of Library Materials" [report of the Committee on photographic reproduction of library materials], *American Library Association Bulletin 33*, 657–658, September.

171. "A Specifically American Experiment," *Journal of Adult Education*, 11:396–401, October. (Partial reprint of No. 160.)

172. Review of *The Diplomacy of the Balkan Wars, 1912–1913*, by E. C. Helmreich, *Annals of the American Academy of Political and Social Sciences*, 206:181, November.

173. "Assumptions Underlying Political History," *University Review*, 6:83–87, December.

174. Binkley, Robert C., and Robbins, Rainard B., "The Efficiency Point in Quantity Reproduction," *Journal of Documentary Reproduction*, 2:270–274, December.

175. "Citing Photographic Reproductions," *Journal of Documentary Reproduction*, 2:304–305, December.

176. Review of *L'Europe du XIXᵉ siècle et l'idée de nationalité*, by G. Weill, *Journal of Modern History*, 11:546–547, December.

177. Review of *Allied Propaganda and the Collapse of the German Empire in 1918*, by G. G. Bruntz, *Mississippi Valley Historical Review*, 26:464–465, December.

1940

178. *Realism and Nationalism, 1852–1871*, second edition (New York: Harper & Brothers). (See No. 107. p. 175 revised.)

II. SOME PUBLISHED WRITINGS ABOUT ROBERT C. BINKLEY

179. Adams, E. D., *The Hoover War Collection at Stanford University; a Report and an Analysis* (Stanford University Press, 1921). See pp. 16–19, 70.

180. "Current History Bureau Comes to Mather College; Dr. Binkley Interests National Research Body in Methods of Preserving and Indexing Records," *Cleveland Plain Dealer*, November 13, 1933, 9:2.

181. "Robert Cedric Binkley," *America's Young Men*, 1:50, 1934; 2:51, 1936–37.

182. Kirkwood, Marie, "They're Studying 'Good Queen Bess' in a New Way at W.R.U.," *Cleveland Plain Dealer*, April 22, 1934, Magazine Section 7:1.

183. " 'Get Rid of Davey' Keeps Phones Hot; Ouster Demand Generates Spontaneously Here from Relief Charges," *Cleveland Plain Dealer*, March 17, 1935, A1:6.

184. McCarter, Josephine, "Robert Cedric Binkley," *Alumnae Folio of Flora Stone Mather College*, 12.3:7, February, 1936. (See also the article on p. 6.)

185. "Robert Cedric Binkley," *Who's Who in America*, 19:310, 1936–37; 20:320, 1938–39; 21:331, 1940–41. *Who Was Who in America*, 1:96, 1942.

186. Birnbaum, Louis, "Tracing a City's History," *New York Times*, September 6, 1936, IX, 9:3.

187. "War Peril to Lore Arouses Scholars; Council of Learned Societies Moves to Make Archives of America Complete," *New York Times*, January 27, 1940, 6:2.

188. "Embalmed Archives," *Newsweek*, 15:41, February 12, 1940.

189. "Prof. Binkley, Noted Scholar, Dies at 42," *Cleveland Press*, April 11, 1940, 17:4–5.

190. "Dr. Robert Binkley, Historian, Archivist," *New York Times*, April 12, 1940, 23:2.

191. "Private Funeral for Prof. Binkley," *Cleveland Plain Dealer*, April 12, 1940, 21:4.

192. "Loss to Scholarship," editorial, *Cleveland Plain Dealer*, April 12, 1940, 10:2.

193. Mellon, De Forest, "Tribute to Dr. Binkley," *Cleveland Plain Dealer*, April 21, 1940, A21:3.

194. Barry, Adeline V., "Robert Cedric Binkley, 1898–1940," *Alumnae Folio of Flora Stone Mather College*, 16.4:6, May, 1940.

195. Clement, Mary Louise; Ice, Marjorie; White, Elise; Miller, Edith; and Robinson, Lucy, "Tributes to Robert C. Binkley," *Sun Dial* (Flora Stone Mather College), 23.3:6–9, May, 1940.

196. Baldwin, Summerfield, III, "Book-Learning and Learning Books," *College and Research Libraries*, 1:257–261, June, 1940.

197. Burnett, Philip Mason, *Reparation at the Paris Peace Conference from the Standpoint of the American Delegation*, 2 vols. (New York: Columbia University Press, 1940), esp. vol. 1, pp. 145–146, 148, 152.

198. Kellar, Herbert A., "An Appraisal of the Historical Records Survey," in *Archives and Libraries* (American Library Association, Committee on archives and libraries). (Chicago: American Library Association, 1940), esp. pp. 56, 57.

199. Lydenberg, Harry M., "Robert Cedric Binkley, 1897–1940," American Council of Learned Societies, *Bulletin No. 33*, 56–59, October, 1941.

200. Dix, William S., *The Amateur Spirit in Scholarship; the Report of the Committee on Private Research of Western Reserve University* (Cleveland: Western Reserve University Press, 1942), pp. 13–20 and *passim*.

201. Kidder, R. W., "The Historical Records Survey; Activities and Publications," *Library Quarterly*, 13:136–149, April, 1943.

202. Kellar, Herbert A., "The Historian and Life," *Mississippi Valley Historical Review*, 34:3–36, June, 1947, esp. 14–17.
203. Tate, Vernon D., "From Binkley to Bush," *American Archivist*, 10:249–257, July, 1947.

Index

This is an index primarily of personal names, omitting Robert C. Binkley. It includes also the more important conferences, commissions, committees, societies, and libraries referred to. Countries, states, and cities are excluded. The foreword, preface, chronology and bibliography are not indexed.